LEE'S ARMY DURING THE OVERLAND CAMPAIGN

LEE'S ARMY DURING THE OVERLAND CAMPAIGN

A Numerical Study

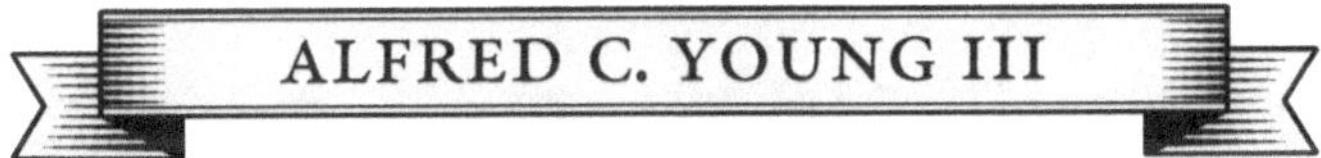

WITH A FOREWORD BY
GORDON C. RHEA

LOUISIANA STATE UNIVERSITY PRESS BATON ROUGE

Published by Louisiana State University Press
lsupress.org

Louisiana Paperback Edition, 2026

Designer: Barbara Neely Bourgoyne
Typeface: Adobe Garamond Pro

The manufacturer's authorized representative in the EU for product safety is Mare Nostrum Group B.V., Doelen 72, 4831 GR Breda, The Netherlands. Email: gpsr@mare-nostrum.co.uk

Material from the author's article "Numbers and Losses in the Army of Northern Virginia," *North & South,* vol. 3, no. 3, pp. 14–32, is reprinted here by permission of *North & South.*

Cover Image: *Battle of Spotsylvania,* by Thure de Thulstrup

Library of Congress Cataloging-in-Publication Data
Young, Alfred C., III, 1946–
Lee's army during the Overland Campaign : a numerical study / Alfred C. Young III ; with a foreword by Gordon C. Rhea.
pages cm
Includes bibliographical references and index.
ISBN 978-0-8071-5172-3 (cloth : alk. paper) — ISBN 978-0-8071-5173-0 (pdf) — ISBN 978-0-8071-5174-7 (epub) — ISBN 978-0-8071-8875-0 (paperback) 1. Overland Campaign, Va., 1864. 2. Confederate States of America. Army of Northern Virginia—Statistics. 3. United States—History—Civil War, 1861–1865—Casualties—Statistics. 4. Virginia—History—Civil War, 1861–1865—Casualties—Statistics. I. Title.
E476.52.Y68 2013
973.7'37—dc23

2012044950

Contents

Foreword

The Overland Campaign of 1864 ranks as one of the most crucial—and least studied—campaigns of the American Civil War. In the summer of 1863, the Union Army of the Potomac repulsed Gen. Robert E. Lee's foray into Pennsylvania and drove his Army of Northern Virginia back to the Old Dominion. But Union commanders frittered away their Gettysburg victory, permitting the eastern theater's premier Rebel army to repair its losses. Eighteen sixty-four was an election year, and President Abraham Lincoln was not at all confident that Northern voters would award him a second term. Unless Union armies could win victories, the presidential race might well go to a candidate willing to negotiate with the South, enabling the Rebels to achieve through political means the ends that had eluded them thus far by force of arms. The spring of 1864 stood to determine the outcome of the war.

Painfully aware of the need for military successes, Lincoln summoned his best general to Washington. Maj. Gen. Ulysses S. Grant was the architect of Federal triumphs in the West, boasting a string of victories at Fort Donelson, Shiloh, Vicksburg, and Chattanooga. Hoping that Grant might work his magic in the East, the president arranged for his promotion to lieutenant general and placed him in charge of the nation's military might.

Grant devised a campaign that capitalized on the North's advantages in manpower and materiel. No longer were Federal forces to squander their resources attempting to capture and hold enemy territory; Rebel armies were now their goal, the destruction of those armies their chief aim. Henceforth, the armies of the United States were to move in tandem, preventing the Confederates from shifting troops from one front to another. And gone were the days of short battles followed by months of leisure to refit and regroup; under Grant, Union armies were to engage their foes and hold on like bulldogs, fighting until they had destroyed the secessionists' capacity to resist.

Grant delegated his trusted subordinate Maj. Gen. William T. Sherman the prime responsibility for managing the Union war effort in the West and turned his own attention to the knotty problem of defeating Lee. Employing the same principles that governed his national strategy, Grant planned to focus irresistible force against his wily opponent. At his signal, the Army of the Potomac, commanded by Maj. Gen. George G. Meade, was to press across the Rapidan River in Central Virginia and attack the Army of Northern Virginia. Meanwhile the Army of the James, commanded by Maj. Gen. Benjamin F. Butler, was to advance up the James River, capture the Confederate capital of Richmond, and continue north into Lee's rear. A third Union body, under Maj. Gen. Franz Sigel, was to move south through the Shenandoah Valley, threatening Lee's left flank and completing the disruption of the Rebel commander's supply lines. Caught in the jaws of a three-pronged vice, Lee's army would face certain destruction.

The battles and maneuvers that followed would take Grant and Lee, the Civil War's premier generals, from the Rapidan to the James. Historians later called those forty bloody days the Overland Campaign, implying that Richmond was Grant's goal. In truth, Grant's objective was the destruction of Lee's army, not the capture of Richmond; he meant to fight Lee and beat him, not to campaign overland against the Confederate capital.

The venture got off to a rocky start. Crossing the Rapidan downriver from Lee on May 4, 1864, the Army of the Potomac became ensnared in a grueling, two-day battle in the inhospitable Wilderness of Spotsylvania. Fought to impasse by the Confederates, Grant withdrew his forces and sidled ten miles south to the crossroads hamlet of Spotsylvania Court House, expecting that Lee would follow and give battle on terrain more favorable to the Union host. Lee, however, won the race to Spotsylvania and barred Grant's progress with an imposing line of earthworks. During the ten bloody days spanning May 8–18, the Army of the Potomac unleashed a welter of assaults, but the Rebel line could not be broken. Disheartening news also reached Grant from his supporting armies: Confederate forces had defeated Sigel at New Market and Butler at Drewry's Bluff. The operation that had started two weeks before with so much promise seemed about to unravel.

Once again Grant maneuvered, shifting southward toward the North Anna River. And once again Lee deftly countered his opponent's move, winning the race to the North Anna and parrying Grant's thrust a few days later by arranging his army in an ingenious wedge-shaped defensive formation. Stalemated, Grant again maneuvered, shifting the military center of gravity across the Pamunkey River and Totopotomoy Creek to a nondescript crossroads at Old Cold Harbor, ten miles northeast of Richmond. With Lee's force backed against the Confederate capital, Grant ordered an armywide assault. On June 3, for the fourth time in as many weeks, the Confederates fought the Union juggernaut to a standstill. Sheltered behind an impregnable wall of earthworks, its flanks anchored on marshy streams, the Rebel force barred the way to Richmond. Undeterred in his strategic objective, Grant maneuvered for a final time, striking across the James River in an attempt to sever Lee's connection with his supply depot at Petersburg. That gambit failed as well, and with a new stalemate at Petersburg, the Confederacy's clock began ticking off its final hours. In the fall of 1864, Union victories at Atlanta and Winchester (in the Shenandoah) would secure Lincoln's reelection. The Army of Northern Virginia's demise, and with it the demise of the Confederacy, was but a matter of time.

The Overland Campaign was a contest of wits and guile between the American Civil War's two best generals. Grant's strength was his unwavering adherence to his strategic objective—he made mistakes, but the overall pattern of his campaign was that of an innovative general employing thoughtful combinations of maneuver and force to bring a difficult adversary to bay. Lee's strength was his resilience and the fierce devotion that he inspired in his men. He too made mistakes, often placing his smaller army in considerable peril. But each time Lee improvised a solution that turned a bad situation his way. In many respects the generals were similar. Each favored offensive operations and took fearless courses of action that left traditional generals aghast. Each labored under handicaps, although of different sorts, and each was bedeviled by subordinates who often seemed incapable of getting things right. Grant and Lee were about as evenly matched in military talent as any two opposing generals have ever been.

For the past quarter century, I have devoted considerable intellectual energy studying this fascinating campaign and trying to chronicle its every twist and turn. But until now, one important body of information remained elusive: what were the Confederate troop strengths and losses? Thanks to the detailed returns collected in the National Archives in Washington, Union casualties can be ascertained with some precision. But Confederate records are fragmentary and, for many units, nonexistent. Postwar writers have valiantly attempted to determine Confederate strengths and losses during the campaign's key battles, but estimates have varied widely, and none rest on a sound empirical foundation.

Alfred Young has bravely stepped into this historical void. A diligent and meticulous researcher, he has undertaken to reconstruct Confederate casualties during the Overland Campaign from the ground up, not only by a rigorous examination of compiled service records and other sources in the National Archives but also through painstaking analysis of casualty reports as they appeared in newspapers across the South during the war.

Young's study is an original work of profound importance to scholars of the American Civil War. For the first time ever, students of that conflict now have at their disposal reliable data on Confederate troop numbers for the Overland Campaign ranging through the regimental level. No future study of the campaign will be complete without reference to this work.

The implications that follow from Young's analysis are profound. Lee's numbers at the campaign's outset were greater than historians have formerly assumed, and his casualties by its end were considerably larger than anecdotal accounts have led us to believe. When compared against the respective sizes of the armies at the campaign's outset, Confederate losses approximate 50 percent, while Federal losses were about 45 percent, suggesting that Grant lost soldiers at a lower overall rate than did Lee. As Young convincingly demonstrates, the campaign thoroughly gutted many of the Army of Northern Virginia's veteran units.

Young's analysis of strengths and casualties at the small-unit level are especially revealing. Until now it has been difficult to ascertain with certainty which units were engaged in various actions and which ones bore the brunt of the combat. Historians have generally had to rely on surviving accounts of individual soldiers to deduce who made a charge or defended a position. Because of this fragmentary evidence, it was impossible to say with confidence what companion units were engaged and which outfits really carried the weight. Now, however, we can see which regiments and brigades lost soldiers and how many they lost, figures that offer objective evidence about who really carried the burden of the actions.

Each year witnesses an avalanche of new books about the American Civil War, most of which simply regurgitate old information in a new format. Alfred Young's study is refreshingly different: it is a detailed, accessible compilation of new information that provides fresh insights and grist for a new generation of Civil War historians. It is a work in the finest tradition of Louisiana State University Press.

GORDON C. RHEA
June 2012

Preface

People have asked about the original interest and impetus for doing this study. The seeds were apparently planted during my childhood. My late mother, Mary Wendell Young, always had an avid interest in history, and perhaps I inherited this avocation from her. I recall finding and reading books on Robert E. Lee and other Civil War generals in the local elementary-school library. Starting at age thirteen and continuing for the next three years, Mother gave me one volume of *Battles and Leaders of the Civil War* as a Christmas gift. She began with volume 4 and progressed consecutively to volume 1 three years later. I never asked or knew why she obtained the volumes in reverse order. In any event, during the first year I poured myself into the contents of volume 4. The opening articles, pertaining to the siege of Charleston in 1863 and the Battle of Olustee (Florida) in 1864, were not stimulating to me at that time, but the material addressing the Overland Campaign caught my immediate interest and became an almost daily obsession. The listings titled "The Opposing Forces at the Beginning of Grant's Campaign against Richmond" and "The Opposing Forces at Cold Harbor" (*Battles and Leaders,* 4:179–87) especially became a focus of meticulous study. I recall drawing replicas of maps of the opposing forces at the Wilderness and Spotsylvania during school when I had a few idle moments or admittedly was bored in class.

It was not, however, until I received volumes 3 and 2 of *Battles and Leaders,* which cover all of the major engagements during the years 1862 and 1863, that I realized that something was missing from most of volume 4. The respective lists of opposing forces in these books provided the casualties for every brigade at each battle, something clearly missing from volume 4, which only lists the Federal brigade casualties at Cedar Creek and Nashville. Later, as I examined the *Official Records* (as an adult), I found that Federal casualty figures were available for all the major battles. Since there were so many battles and minor engagements, the casualty figures were probably omitted from volume 4 by the editors for purposes of space.

That still left me with the problem of Confederate casualties for the battles of 1864. The first comment regarding the losses in Lee's army at Wilderness and

Spotsylvania is as follows: "The losses in the army are only partially reported" (*Battles and Leaders,* 4:184). As for the losses at the other battles of the campaign (such as North Anna and Cold Harbor), there is no mention at all. In contrast, the total losses for Grant's army at each of these battles are at least provided.

This vacuum in historical knowledge apparently bothered me more than I realized. About thirty years ago, I happened to visit the Spotsylvania battlefield and the nearby Battlefield Center in Fredericksburg, Virginia. I struck up a conversation with a tall gentlemen employed by the National Park Service (NPS) regarding the conflicts at the Wilderness and Spotsylvania. He offered a comment that Lee clearly outfought Grant at these battles and inflicted huge casualties with little loss to his own forces. I responded with words to the effect that the casualties for Lee's army at these battles should be determined. The NPS employee then replied, "You couldn't get that if you had a million—no ten million—dollars." Reeling with some degree of surprise, I asked why. His reply was something to the effect that the Confederate records were destroyed or lost after the war and thus no one will ever know.

A year or two earlier, I had purchased a copy of John Busey and David Martin's *Regimental Strengths at Gettysburg.* The authors had used pre- and postdated muster rolls along with casualty figures to estimate the strength of Lee's army at this major battle. In my limited experience, their methods were both practical and historically accurate. I mentioned this book to the NPS employee and offered the hypothesis that someone should do a similar-style study of Lee's army during the Overland Campaign. He replied: "That's a great idea. Why don't *you* do it?" My first thought and reply was that I work for a living and that he likely had more time than I did. I have since regretted these hasty thoughts and words.

On the return trip home (I was then living outside our nation's capital in northern Virginia), I thought about his comments. The statement that this information on Lee's casualties could never be obtained must have struck some chord because the following evening after work, I went to the Library of Congress in Washington. While perusing through available books there, I met a gentleman who was a graduate from the Citadel. He directed me to the Confederate service records (CSRs) at the National Archives. This started a process of many trips to this facility and compiling unit rosters from the CSRs on countless reels of microfilm. After several evenings, I started meeting fellow Civil War researchers at the archives. It was common for this group to discuss and share research goals and methods, and I often fielded questions from new acquaintances regarding the subject of my study. During one of these usual discussions, I learned of the existence of unit casualty lists published in Southern newspapers. Once I obtained these nominal lists and compared them to personnel rosters compiled from the CSRs, reasonable figures for the strength and casualties in Lee's army gradually began to take form.

After several years of work on this project, I began to receive frequent encouragement from fellow researchers to write a book on my findings. These suggestions were initially not well received, for in my limited view this study was done solely to satisfy my personal quest for knowledge. I also knew that there was one major gap in my research, information on several infantry units in Lee's army recruited from the southwestern portion of Virginia. These units sustained very heavy combat losses in May 1864. Their records in the CSRs, however, were among the most incomplete in all of Lee's army, and no newspaper was found from their home area. The leading newspapers in Richmond, the capital of the Confederacy, often made references to a newspaper in Abington, a town located in Washington County in the heart of this region. I was told by Jeffrey Weaver, a fellow researcher then living in the nearby town of Saltville, that no issues of this paper had survived into the twentieth century or were known to be in existence.

About five or six years ago, I happened to be conversing with Jeff on the telephone and he related that something amazing had recently occurred in his area. An elderly lady had died, and her children had returned to her home to tend to the necessary details and clean out her possessions. While doing this, they reportedly found copies of all of the original issues of the *Abington Virginian* during the Civil War in a cedar-style chest in the attic. Jeff said that these newspapers had been donated to Emory and Henry University, a private college located in Abington, and then inquired if I would be visiting him soon. Needless to say, I made plans to travel to southwestern Virginia, ultimately finding casualty lists for most of the companies in the previously deficient regiments. With this finding and some other smaller items from this area, I realized that I had a generally finished product and that this book should be written.

I could not have completed the extensive project presented here without assistance from many people. I am indebted to them all. My gratitude is foremost extended to Jeffrey Weaver. In addition to sharing his extensive personal collection and proofreading my manuscript, Jeff has been a constant source of guidance and encouragement. He passed away in April 2012 after a long illness. During this final period, he displayed a valiant and consistent attitude toward life and his terminal condition.

Other researchers and writers also made important contributions. I received invaluable assistance from Bryce A. Suderow, who initially informed me of the existence of Southern newspapers and thereafter freely loaned me his extensive collection. He also was very generous in finding and providing me with copies of numerous diaries, unit histories, and postwar articles—I really believe he can find something on any aspect of the Civil War. Forest Pedlar, an acquaintance of Bryce and a fellow researcher, was also helpful in finding additional sources. I received similar contributions from Keith S. Bohannon in Georgia, Chris Daw in North Carolina, Zack C. Waters in Florida, John Chapla and Robert H. Moore in Virginia, Marc and Beth Storch, and Richard J. Sommers at the U.S. Army Military History Institute in Carlisle, Pennsylvania. I recall spending an entire Saturday years ago with Robert J. Driver at his residence during an especially cold winter. He was very cordial and freely shared his personal detailed records regarding all of the Virginia infantry in Lt. Gen. Richard Ewell's Second Corps.

It was my privilege to have Gordon C. Rhea also review my manuscript. Years earlier I had supplied him with specific information regarding casualties in Lee's army for his four recently published works on the Overland Campaign. He has been urging me for years to publish this research. Rhea has also been gracious to permit me to use many of the battle maps from his books and to write a foreword for this work. These maps were prepared by George Skoch, who additionally afforded me permission to use his maps. Scott C. Patchan and Lawrence Lee Hewitt also examined my manuscript. Scott provided very beneficial feedback regarding the outline and direction of the text. Larry saved me from several potentially embarrassing historical inconsistencies and typographical errors. I should also include William L. Snyder II, a distant cousin and an American history teacher at a local high school. He was the first to proofread my manuscript and pointed out numerous errors in my text.

Finally, I would like to include my wife, Susan Riker Young. She accompanied me on several trips to Virginia and graciously assisted with research and also provided frequent expertise with computer applications.

LEE'S ARMY DURING THE OVERLAND CAMPAIGN

Introduction

On May 4, 1864, the Federal Army of the Potomac began crossing the Rapidan River in north-central Virginia and moving toward its rival, the Confederate Army of Northern Virginia. This was the inevitable meeting of the two leading commanders of the Civil War, Lt. Gen. Ulysses S. Grant and Gen. Robert E. Lee. The 1864–65 battles in Virginia between the armies of these foremost leaders have historically never received the focus of study and the degree of scrutiny afforded other notable battles and campaigns, such as Gettysburg, Antietam, Vicksburg, Chickamauga-Chattanooga, and Chancellorsville. The Lee-Grant confrontation consisted principally of two major consecutive campaigns, the Overland Campaign (the Wilderness to Cold Harbor) and the siege of Petersburg/Richmond.

The Overland Campaign was a grueling and terrible ordeal for both the officers and the common soldiers. In many ways the horror exceeded anything experienced in the first three years of the war. For example, during the Battle of the Wilderness, small fires broke out in the dense vegetation on parts of the battlefield. The fires quickly spread and reached some of the severely wounded soldiers trapped in no man's land between the opposing lines.[1] The screams of these unfortunate men could thereafter be heard throughout the battlefield. Following one desperate day of fighting over a section of breastworks at Spotsylvania, the Confederates withdrew to a new line in the rear during the hours of darkness. The following morning, Federal troops discovered the bodies of dead and severely wounded Southern soldiers piled and partially buried in the mud.[2] After a disastrous assault on the Confederate earthworks at Cold Harbor, Grant and Lee consumed four days to agree on a truce to help the wounded, mostly Union men, caught in the open between the opposing lines.[3] Until the truce was arranged, sharpshooters or snipers on both sides kept the armies pinned down and prevented medical personnel from succoring these unfortunate soldiers.

Many men on both sides spoke of the numbing exhaustion from the continuous marching and fighting. In a postwar article, Martin T. McMahon wrote of "[t]he wide and winding path through the tangled Wilderness and the pines of Spotsylvania, which that army [the Army of the Potomac] had cut from the Rapidan to the Chickahominy, had been strewn with bodies of thousands of brave men, the majority of them wearing the Union blue."[4] For the most part, the thousands of Federal wounded from Wilderness and Spotsylvania were transported to Washington in a steady stream of ambulances. To the residents of the capital, "it seemed that Grant's whole army was being carried back to the city."[5]

The hospital network for the Southern side in Virginia was similarly overstressed. For example, Lynchburg, a community with a prewar population of about 6,000 people, was overwhelmed with 10,000 wounded and sick soldiers during the period immediately following the Battle of the Wilderness.[6] The facilities in neighboring Charlottesville, Farmville, Gordonsville, Liberty (Bedford), Staunton, and especially Richmond also left similar records of admissions following the commencement of the fighting in May. The personnel sent to these hospitals came from all of the Confederate armies in the field in Virginia but, given the intensity of fighting, primarily from Lee's Army of Northern Virginia.

Historical figures on the casualties and overall strengths of the opposing armies offer a widely differing picture. Accurate figures concerning the Union army's unit strengths and casualties are well documented and are readily available for any interested researcher. According to the returns in the *Official Records,* the total loss for the Army of the Potomac during the Overland Campaign was 54,929 men. The breakdown of this total is as follows: the Wilderness—17,666; Spotsylvania—18,399; the North Anna and Totopotomoy—3,986; Bethesda Church and Cold Harbor—12,737; Sheridan's First Cavalry Raid (Richmond)—625; and Sheridan's Second Cavalry Raid (Trevilian Station)—1,516.[7] According to the last muster roll before the start of the campaign (April 30, 1864), the Army of the Potomac fielded in excess of 118,000 men.[8] Taken at face value, the total casualty figure of about 55,000 men represents a loss of almost 47 percent from the original starting strength. It should be recognized, however, that Grant was reinforced considerably during the campaign and that many of the casualties incurred at the later battles of the campaign (beginning on May 19) were absorbed by units newly assigned to the army.

The corresponding figures for the opposing Confederate forces are not well documented. The major difficulty is the lack of thorough and reliable records and information. Many unit reports apparently were never filed or filed months later, or they were lost or destroyed at the end of the conflict. The result has been speculation by historians with respect to both the strength and casualties of Lee's army. The standard figure for the strength of the Amy of Northern Virginia at the start of the campaign is 61,000–62,000 men. This is based on a return dated April 20, 1864, that does not include significant portions of the army's full composition and changes that occurred to its order of battle between April 20 and May 5 (the first day of the Battle of the Wilderness). As for a determination of the number of reinforcements it received, historians often rely upon an estimate provided by Maj. Walter H. Taylor of Lee's staff. This officer listed several units that joined the army from the Shenandoah Valley and from Beauregard's forces at Richmond, placing their combined strength at 14,400 men.[9] A more modern examination of the composition of the Army of Northern Virginia in mid-June reveals that Major Taylor neglected to include all the units that joined Lee in May and early June.

Available figures for the casualties sustained by Lee's army during the Overland Campaign vary widely. They appear to have little historical basis and appear to be primarily estimates. For example, the numbers for the Wilderness range from a low of 7,500 to a high of 11,400 men. Those for Spotsylvania similarly range from 9,000 to 13,400 men. The estimates for battle losses for the Confederate side at Cold Harbor, the last major sanguine action of this campaign, range from 1,500 to 5,000 men. The higher ranges of casualty figures are the product of more-current writers and apparent estimating. An example of this is provided by R. Ernest Dupuy and Trevor N. Dupuy in their book *The Compact History of the Civil War.* In this work the authors estimate that Lee's total loss for the Overland Campaign was at least 39,000 men and that the casualties for the Wilderness and Spotsylvania alone were in the range of 12,000 to 14,000 men each. These figures were based upon "comparable losses in other comparable but better recorded conflicts."[10]

The lower figures noted above were offered by earlier, more general studies (such as those by the National Park Service or in the *West Point Atlas*), several modern authors or traditional southern writers such as Shelby Foote, or former Confederate generals. In the opinion of some, the latter parties attempted to understate battle losses for the Confederate side (especially during the campaigns of 1864) and thereby reinterpret the history of the war. Compared to the above-stated Federal casualties (during the Overland Campaign), Lee's losses were disproportionately low, unfairly gaining Grant the reputation as a bumbling commander and the title of a "butcher." In their view the Confederates (and especially Lee) fought heroically but in the end had to yield to the prevailing if not overwhelming manpower pool and resources of the Union.

There has also been considerable disagreement between the opposing sides and subsequent historians regarding the number of prisoners taken by the Union army during the campaign. The major focus of these conflicting claims was the number captured on May 12 at Spotsylvania. As described in detail later in this book, Federal forces attacked a portion of the Confederate earthworks on this day, achieving a decisive breakthrough and capturing most of one Rebel division. The respective Confederate corps commander, Lt. Gen. Richard Ewell, claimed that this command lost over 2,000 prisoners; the Federals claimed they captured 4,000 men.[11] These conflicting numbers have never been resolved.

Regardless of one's preferences or allegiances, an assertion can be made that accurate determinations for both the casualties and strength of the Army of Northern Virginia have never been made based on specific reports or study. As addressed above, every attempt to provide this information to date has been largely speculation. Recent research, described in this work, reveals a very different picture. Most of this research is based upon a previously underused source, Southern newspapers. This study indicates that both the initial strength of and the losses incurred by Lee's army were significantly higher than previously believed. Based upon this information, it may be possible to gauge the condition of Lee's army at the start and the close of the Overland Campaign and determine the effect of this operation upon the eventual outcome of the war.

PART ONE

Lee's Army: An Overview

CHAPTER 1

The Initial Strength of the Army of Northern Virginia

The typical historical account of the campaigns of 1864 and 1865 in Virginia has the forces of Lee's Army of Northern Virginia getting the most out of limited, if not meager, manpower, armaments, commissary supplies, and other resources before finally being overcome by Grant's numerically superior and significantly better equipped and supplied Army of the Potomac. Regarding these meager manpower resources, historians have generally concluded that Lee's army entered the Wilderness on May 5, 1864, with about one-half of the numerical strength of Grant's army.

Estimates for the Confederate army at the commencement of the campaign conventionally have ranged from about 60,000 to 62,000 men. The primary source for this information is the "Abstract of Field Returns for the Army of Northern Virginia," dated April 20, 1864, found on pages 1097–1098 of volume 33, series 1 of the *Official Records*. This is the last available return or muster roll for the Confederate forces prior to May 5. The units listed as present for duty in this return are shown in Table 1, Appendix A.

Excluding the headquarters units and the Maryland Line (which on May 5 was posted in the rear along a principal line of communications with Richmond), the grand total is 52, 984 men. This return, however, does not reflect a complete listing of all the troops assigned to the Army of Northern Virginia nor all the troops that entered the Wilderness on May 5 or 6. Missing are Hoke's Brigade, two regiments of Rodes's Division, and more importantly all of the infantry and three battalions of artillery from the First Corps. Pickett's Division and Read's and Eshelman's Battalions of artillery of this command were serving temporarily within the Department of North Carolina and Southern Virginia on April 20, along with the above-noted infantry units from the Second Corps. They were all transferred in early May to the forces assembling under Gen. P. G. T. Beauregard to defend Petersburg and Richmond against the Army of the James under Maj. Gen. Benjamin F. Butler.

The other principal omissions are Kershaw's and Field's Divisions and Huger's Artillery Battalion of the First Corps. These units, along with Longstreet himself, were on April 20 rejoining the army from the previous fall and winter campaign in East Tennessee. Having reached Virginia and rejoined the main army, they were reviewed by General Lee near Gordonsville on April 29. The latest previous return available for these units in East Tennessee in the *Official Records* is dated March 31.[1] This return is reproduced as Table 2, Appendix A.

The sum total of these various organizations yields 63,888 men. But there is one significant problem with this number: it fails to take into consideration changes in the returns that occurred between April 20 and May 5 for the Second and Third Corps and the Cavalry Corps and between March 31 and May 5 for the First Corps. Unfortunately, the next available return for Lee's army in the *Official Records* is dated June 30.[2] This return is reproduced as Table 3, Appendix A.

The June 30 return does not provide clear information that could assist in determining the overall army and individual unit strengths on or about May 5. The Second Corps is missing, and there are several new units that did not start the campaign in the Army of Northern Virginia. Although not of apparent immediate benefit, this later return was subsequently found to be of considerable help in determining Confederate numbers during the Overland Campaign. For this reason, it has been included.

One approach to determining the changes in Lee's army between April 20 and May 5 is to examine the earlier returns in 1864. The available returns provided in the *Official Records* are dated January 20, February 20, March 20, April 10, and April 20.[3] These items, and especially the last three, reveal a steady increase in the strength of the various units of the Second, Third, and Cavalry Corps during the early spring. Judging by these muster rolls, it appears that a concerted effort was made, as one would expect, to build up the manpower of Lee's army in preparation for the anticipated 1864 spring campaign. Many of these soldiers were likely three-year veterans who had received a special furlough, a process that commenced early in the year and tapered off in the weeks leading up to May. The others were probably new personnel. It seems probable that that these units continued to experience an increase in their ranks during the two weeks between April 20 and May 5.

In order to explore and confirm this assumption, it became necessary to research and categorize the personnel who accounted for this increase in the army's strength. This was accomplished by an extensive examination and compilation of the individual Compiled Service Records (CSRs) for all the units comprising the Army of Northern Virginia during this period. The CSRs consist of individual carded records for every soldier found on file during the war. They were compiled principally from available company muster rolls, hospital records, clothing issues, and Federal prisoner-of-war lists and are filed alphabetically by last name by unit. The full collection is currently housed at the National Archives in Washington, D.C. The cards for any individual soldier are available upon special request. More readily, though, they are available on microfilm for quick public access and study, typically presented on one or more microfilm reels for each unit.

The major component of the CSRs are the unit muster rolls. Ideally, these were filed every two months on the last day of the even-numbered months (February 28/29, April 30, June 30, and so on). The primary purpose was to determine the status of each individual soldier for pay. The availability of these rolls and the accuracy of their information vary significantly from one unit to another. For example, some of the brigades in the First Corps, Hoke's Division (of Beauregard's command), and the artillery have all or most of the critical rolls for 1864 on record. Other units, such as the Second and Third Corps and the cavalry, are missing one or more rolls for this year. The least-documented units were two regiments from Jones's and Colquitt's Brigades (from the Second Corps and Hoke's Division, respectively). For these regiments there exists only one muster roll for the entire war, and these are from 1862. In some cases the missing rolls were lost or likely destroyed at the close of hostilities in 1865. In other cases they were clearly filed at the end of a four- or six-month period (such as May–August or May–October 1864). This is the case with most of the units in the Second Corps and Breckinridge's Division.

Quite apart from the fact that many are missing, there are other problems with the muster rolls. In most cases the date on which the record was filed is indicated. Often this date is weeks or even months later than the period to which the return ostensibly refers. In many cases it is not clear if the recorded information reflects the status of the soldier at the end of the period listed or on the date at which the roll was filed. In other instances two or more consecutive rolls were apparently filed on or near the same date. These anomalies sometimes create confusion as to the actual status of a soldier at a specific time.

There is another problem with the information in the rolls. Soldiers are often marked "Present" even though a careful study of hospital records reveals them to be clearly disabled and unfit for field service. The actual status of these personnel can ultimately be determined with a careful study of all the available records for each soldier.

Where early rolls for 1864 are missing or clearly reflect a later period in the year, it can be difficult to determine a unit's strength on or about May 5. One compensating record contained in the CSRs and found to be of benefit in filling in some of the gaps is the clothing issue. Clothes were typically issued for enlisted personnel on a quarterly basis. In the second quarter of 1864, this occurred in April. Soldiers for whom clothing was issued in April were likely present at the commencement of the campaign in May.

The CSRs for most of the personnel in four Mississippi infantry regiments (the 2nd, 11th, and 42nd of Davis's Brigade and the 21st of Humphreys's Brigade) and some of those in Law's Alabama and Hays's and Stafford's Louisiana Brigades contain, in addition to the muster rolls, record-of-events cards. These were apparently prepared from memory after the war and incorporated with the other documents. They provide the status of the soldier at each of the major engagements for his unit throughout the war. Although they appear to contain some errors, they nevertheless were found to be of considerable value in determining the percentages of men present for the various battles and those sick, detached, or otherwise temporarily absent from the ranks.

Returning to an earlier theme, the individual CSRs reveal that the Army of Northern Virginia grew in strength between the last recorded return and May 5. The personnel swelling the strength of the army fell into three categories. First, there were new recruits and conscripts. The individual muster rolls for each soldier provide the date of enlistment and, in many cases for those enlisting in early 1864, the date of the actual assignment to the unit. Men returning from sick leave, recovery from wounds, or earned furlough comprised a second group. The third category was exchanged prisoners of war. An examination of their records reveals that many soldiers captured in battles in 1863 were exchanged between March 3 and 20, 1864. These men were usually sent to a Richmond hospital for examination and then furloughed for thirty days. Depending upon their furlough date and the possibility of overstaying for several days, they then returned to their respective units during the period of mid-April to mid-May 1864.

Judging by the various categories of men joining or returning to a unit, some conclusions can be reached. Most of the new enlistees to Lee's army came from the states of Virginia, North Carolina, and South Carolina. The remaining states of the Confederacy supplied significantly fewer recruits and conscripts, their new personnel likely going to other armies in the field, such as the Army of Tennessee. Few, if any, new men joined the Army of Northern Virginia from the Trans-Mississippi states or from Federal-occupied Tennessee. In addition, the units that sustained the heaviest casualties in 1863 appear to have experienced the greatest increases in strength due to the return of many wounded and exchanged prisoners.

Despite the various shortcomings of the muster rolls and the CSRs, it has been possible to arrive at a more accurate determination of the strength of Lee's army on or about May 5 than has previously been possible. This process involved compiling and tabulating the CSRs, comparing these results to the returns of April 20, 1864, and developing a mathematical model for adjusting the totals to reflect personnel not actually in the ranks. The best results were achieved for the Third Corps and the artillery arm. Less satisfying results were obtained with the infantry units of the First and Second Corps and the Cavalry Corps. Each of these three organizations presented specific problems. The First Corps appears to have left a trail or detached/furloughed personnel in its return from East Tennessee; judging by the CSRs, most of these men eventually caught up with their commands in May or June (during the campaign). The muster rolls for the Second Corps and the Cavalry Corps are collectively among the worst on record and lack consistency. For men of the latter command, there was the additional problem of finding a horse. Some personnel, according to the rolls, were still on furlough procuring a mount from their home area on April 30.

In applying this analytical method, the goal has been to obtain consistency. This has been achieved for the most part. Occasionally, assumptions varying from the norm were unavoidable and had to be made. These were weighed on the conservative (low) side based on the overall available data. As a further check of the accuracy of this approach, the derived strength figures were compared to the June 30 returns. Incorporating the sickness and battle losses between May 5 and June 30 together with the continuing personnel additions to the units, these derived figures were found to yield numbers that corresponded to the June 30 strengths.

In examining the individual CSRs, an obvious attempt has been made to include only those personnel who would have been in the ranks and engaged in battle. This excludes personnel who served in rear positions in the field and staff (such as quartermasters, surgeons, assistant surgeons, chaplains, ordnance sergeants, quartermaster sergeants, and commissary sergeants as well as band musicians, couriers, ambulance drivers, teamsters, headquarters guards, and others). On rare occasions, these personnel drew enemy fire and became casualties. In these limited instances, they are included with their respective company or the field and staff personnel. Using this process, the estimated strength of the Army of Northern Virginia on or about May 5, 1864, was almost 66,000 men. (See Table 4, Appendix A.) For purposes of simplicity, the unit strengths have been rounded off to the nearest 5 men. The actual individual-unit strengths (if ever found) may be around 10 to 50 men higher or lower for each infantry and cavalry unit and, similarly, around 5 to 10 men for each artillery battery.

It should be remembered, though, that the total army strength shown in Table 4 is a "present for duty" compilation and not the actual or effective combat strength. John W. Busey and David G. Martin in their work *Regimental Strengths at Gettysburg* (1982) indicate that for Lee's army, the effective combat strength was about 94 percent of the "present for duty" strength for the infantry and artillery and about 88 percent for the cavalry. This reduction reflects the absence from the battlefield of stragglers and of personnel who became sick or were detached close to the start of combat. An examination of the individual records for Army of Northern Virginia personnel indicates that these assumptions are basically applicable throughout the Overland Campaign. For cavalry dismounted and employed as infantry, the effective or engaged force should be further decreased by 25 percent to account for one man in four having to hold the mounts.

There is some documented historical evidence to support this approach and to validate the mathematical model. Although it is a rather diminutive sampling, the strengths of four regiments starting out in the campaign or entering the Battle of the Wilderness are available. For example, in Louis H. Manarin and Weymouth T. Jordan Jr.'s *North Carolina Troops, 1861–1865: A Roster*, the 7th North Carolina Infantry Regiment is indicated as having twenty-seven officers and 425 enlisted men available for the campaign.[4] This appears to be an approximation of the unit's "present for duty" strength and may include some men who were detached or joined/rejoined the unit after

May 5. The report of Col. James R. Hagood of the 1st South Carolina Infantry Regiment provides a second source for this study.[5] In his report, this regimental commander states that twenty-six officers and 235 men were carried into action on May 6. The May 31 issue of the *Lancaster Ledger* printed an excerpt from a letter written by Chaplain H. N. Craig of the 5th South Carolina Infantry Regiment on May 9. In his correspondence, Chaplain Craig states that his regiment went into the last fight (May 6) with 270 men. A fourth source was obtained from the published diary of Joseph P. Fuller of Company B, 20th Georgia Infantry Regiment. In this document, Fuller similarly states that his unit numbered 265 men on May 6. These numbers are indicative of effective combat strengths. Divided by 94 percent, the resultant numbers compare very favorably with the "present for duty" figures for the latter three regiments.

CHAPTER 2

Reinforcements to the Army of Northern Virginia during the Overland Campaign

The Army of Northern Virginia was considerably reinforced with many new units during the Overland Campaign. Many of these were drawn from General Beauregard's forces facing Butler's Army of the James. Some originally belonged to Lee's army, others were drawn from the military departments and commands along the Atlantic Seaboard. Breckinridge's Division was temporarily loaned from the Department of Western Virginia. The identities and strengths of these units (as they joined the Army of Northern Virginia) are listed in Table 5, Appendix A. The total strength of these units was 25,495 men.

In addition to these new units, Lee's army continued after May 5 to receive personnel to units in the original table of organization. As discussed above, the strength of the Army of Northern Virginia was increased during the immediate period preceding the commencement of the campaign by the addition both of recruits and of personnel returning from furlough and prisoner exchange. A study of the individual personnel records reveals that this process did not simply end with the start of active hostilities but continued throughout the entire year of 1864. For the cavalry arm, most of these men consisted of returnees with a new mount. For the original six brigades comprising this corps, the increases in personnel between May 5 and mid-June (after Cold Harbor/Trevilian Station) were about 120 per brigade. For Butler's South Carolina brigade, the increase (during June only) was about 40 men. For the artillery, the increase during this period averaged about 3 to 4 men per battery. For the infantry arm, the number of new recruits and returning men varied considerably. The average increase per brigade between May 5 and mid-June (after Cold Harbor) for each infantry division is shown in Table 6, Appendix A.

Regarding the figures in Table 6, it is not surprising that the largest increases occurred in the divisions of Kershaw and Field in the First Corps. As mentioned above, these divisions left a trail of men in the wake of their movement from East Tennessee. They also had a substantial number of men returning from wounded furlough. Hoke's Division (from Beauregard's forces) similarly had men come in late from earlier assignments along the Atlantic Seaboard. The other larger figures are associated with commands that overall had large enrollments, sustained heavy casualties in 1863 (principally at Chancellorsville and Gettysburg), or, as with Wilcox's and part of Heth's Divisions, received large numbers of recruits in late May or early June 1864.

There were other minor increases to the infantry not covered above. Hays's Louisiana Brigade (of Early's Division in the Second Corps) had, for the most part, been captured at Rappahannock Station the previous fall (on November 7). Most of the captured enlisted men in this brigade were exchanged in March 1864 and represent one of the significant increases to the strength of this division between April 20 and May 5. Judging by the CSRs, it appears that about 100 more men of this description or category returned to the brigade in May after the start of the campaign.

In addition, the 1st Confederate Infantry Battalion and the 26th Mississippi Infantry Regiment had been transferred from the Department of Alabama, Mississippi, and East Louisiana to Davis's Brigade (of Heth's Division in the Third Corps) in the early spring. According to inspection reports filed for these units and held in the National Archives, the main body of these units left Demopolis, Alabama, on March 28 and joined Lee's army on April 12–13. An examination of the individual CSRs reveals that about 130 men followed later and rejoined these two commands in May and June.

Summarizing the above, the additions to Lee's army from these other various categories were about as follows: artillery, 180; cavalry, 760; and infantry, 4,845. The total of these figures is 5,785 troops, yielding an estimated grand total of 31,280 men reinforcing Lee during the campaign.

These figures represent the maximum number of men available to Lee during the Overland Campaign. During this five- to six-week period, the cavalry experienced significant losses in mounts. No specific numbers are available for the men who became dismounted, but judging by the muster rolls in the CSRs and available diaries, this figure may have been as much as one-third of original strength. In addition, there is information to indicate that many of the personnel in new units assigned to Lee's army arrived in

Richmond with broken-down horses. The best example of this occurred with Butler's Brigade. The three regiments of this new command rode the entire distance from South Carolina to Richmond during the last half of May.

Beginning with the Battle of Spotsylvania and continuing through the subsequent marches to the outskirts of Richmond, the Army of Northern Virginia experienced significant reductions in strength from sickness. Figures regarding the total number of men and periods of their absences are not readily available. Individual records for many of the rear hospitals are included in the CSRs, but no field-hospital records appear to have been compiled, or at any rate, none survived the war. Judging by available data, the sick troops in the veteran units starting the campaign appears to be in the range of at least 10–13 percent. For newly organized units or those joining the army from rear or inactive areas in April through June (such as the 61st Alabama Infantry Regiment in Battle's Brigade, Finegan's Florida Brigade, and the 20th South Carolina Infantry Regiment), the rate of sickness was considerably higher (as much as 45 percent).

CHAPTER 3

Casualties during the Overland Campaign

AN OVERVIEW

Any historian or researcher seriously studying the Civil War will quickly discover that there are few if any reliable records regarding casualties for all of the Confederate armies in the latter part of the war (after 1863). This situation equally applies to the Army of Northern Virginia during the Overland Campaign. The *Official Records* contain reports with casualties for only five brigades (Henegan's, Bryan's, Mahone's, Lane's, and McGowan's) at the Wilderness and one brigade (McGowan's) at Spotsylvania.[1] Additionally, a report for Lane's Brigade for all the battles (stating casualties) is presented in the March 1881 issue of the *Southern Historical Society Papers*.[2] Lastly, the surgeon for Field's Division provided a report detailing the casualties for four of the five brigades in the division for all of 1864. A nominal list of these men by battle and date is currently housed in the National Archives.

Because of the scarcity of official figures, all casualty numbers for Lee's army in the battles of the Overland Campaign historically have been estimates. A quick check of available sources indicates that the estimated combat losses range from about 10,000 to 14,000 for the Wilderness; 9,000 to 12,000 for Spotsylvania; 2,000 to 2,500 for North Anna and Totopotomoy; and 1,500 to 5,000 for Cold Harbor. The historic consensus is that the army overall sustained less than one-half of the casualties incurred by Union forces.

The individual CSRs provide minimal information for this study. A few of the unit CSRs contain company inspection reports, which detail the number of casualties at many of the battles during the campaign; however, they are not very comprehensive. The muster rolls are also of little benefit since (as previously mentioned) many of the critical rolls are missing. Furthermore, Confederate company officers often filed their unit reports a considerable time after the event, which caused the loss of much date-specific information. Thus, the rolls do not accurately reflect the status of personnel during the May–June 1864 period. Lastly, even the rolls that are all present and properly filed frequently do not show or report the occurrence of slight wounds. The critical May–June roll reflects the status of a soldier on June 30. Even if he was slightly wounded in an engagement in May, sent to a hospital for a short period, and returned to the ranks, this would not be shown on the June 30 report.

Clearly, a study based upon historical official records and the individual CSRs will not yield the desired results with any degree of reliability. Additional sources are needed. In some cases, published unit histories have filled some of this need, though only in rare instances. Fortunately, while compiling rosters from the CSRs at the National Archives and conversing with other Civil War researchers, the author stumbled upon another and ultimately the best source, newspapers published in the South during the conflict.

These newspapers, published in cities and large towns in the area still controlled by Confederate forces, contain lists arranged by unit of soldiers who became casualties at specific battles or within a defined period in the campaign. In most cases, they provide information regarding units raised from their local area or, at least, their state. Often they open with a statement such as, "For the friends and families of the ______ Regiment, here are the casualties in the late battle(s) at the ______." The listings are typically provided on a company basis. Current copies of the newspapers are found at federal, state, and local libraries and historical societies, often available on microfilm.

These published lists reflect the status of the men at the date of the correspondence. Casualties are typically listed as killed, wounded, and missing or captured. The wounded are usually further described as mortally, painfully, seriously, or slightly. Sometimes wounded men falling into the hands of Federal forces are indicated as wounded and missing or captured. Frequently, the names of the men are difficult to read or decipher, though a comparison of the casualty listings from the newspapers with the corresponding CSRs almost always enables the researcher to identify each individual. Often the information provided in the newspapers clears up or resolves confusing data contained in the rolls and hospital records. Sometimes a newspaper listing will contain the names of one or more soldiers who are not in the CSRs. This does not necessarily indicate an error; the man (or men) was likely assigned to the unit just before the commencement of the campaign and was quickly killed or seriously wounded and sent to the hospital before ever being officially noted in the unit's records. As might be expected, this occurs most frequently in units where many of the rolls are missing or where they were filed well after the period to which they refer.

Taken together, the CSRs, muster rolls, and newspaper listings yield surprisingly accurate and complete results. The first source usually provides a more long-term resolution to the status of a soldier, for example, whether a man who was listed as "missing" was killed or captured or whether a seriously wounded soldier subsequently died. The CSRs also provide a guide as to which ones ultimately returned to their unit. The newspapers often list men who were slightly wounded and thereby fill in one of the major weaknesses of the CSRs and rolls.

Personal diaries proved to be excellent supplemental sources of information. Usually, the individual writers are very descriptive of the action and circumstances experienced by their units in the various battles. In many instances, they provide nominal lists of casualties sustained in these actions. Postwar records, mostly held on the state level and stemming from pension applications and other unit rosters, were also checked. They can be beneficial but on their own can be unreliable. These records have been carefully analyzed and considered with information from other historical sources (such as the muster rolls and newspapers).

Using all of the above sources, the total casualties for Lee's Army of Northern Virginia during the Overland Campaign are shown in Tables 7–15 in Appendix A. The results are provided chronologically by battle and are presented for the infantry by division, for the cavalry by corps, and for the artillery by a single grouping. Further breakdowns of the casualties are provided in Part Two. The numbers in the following tables are classified as follows: number killed in action (with number mortally wounded); number wounded in action (with number subsequently died of wounds and/or complications); number wounded and captured (with number subsequently died); and missing in action or captured.

The definition of "mortally wounded" is open to some debate. Many soldiers wounded in action later died anywhere from one day to several months afterward. This study considers a soldier mortally wounded if he died within four days of being wounded or within a week if sustaining an obviously life-threatening wound (such as in the head, neck, or abdomen). The four-day period was chosen because this was the time typically needed to move a seriously wounded soldier to a rear hospital. Once there, the regimental or battalion surgeon or adjutant could not easily track the status of the man.

The category designated "wounded" is the one area where there is the most room for individual interpretation, conjecture, and debate. Where they are reasonably complete, the muster rolls in the CSRs clearly reflect the moderately to seriously wounded personnel, who are usually indicated as being on wounded furlough. If the rolls fail to divulge the date or location of the sustained wound, the accompanying hospital records usually provide some reasonable clue. The rolls, however, usually fail to list slight wounds. Given the format of these records, a soldier who was wounded early in the campaign, hospitalized for one to five weeks, and ultimately returned to the ranks in late May through June would not be reported as wounded. If the rolls for 1864 are partially missing or filed at a later date to cover more than the standard two-month interval (as is prevalent with the Second Corps), then the omission of slight wounds is even more likely.

Another reason as to why slight wounds were often not listed is that General Lee earlier in the war ordered that slightly wounded personnel who were not incapacitated and who returned quickly to the ranks should not be included among the reported casualties.[3]

It is my contention that slightly wounded soldiers should be included among the classification of wounded, for a check of subsequent records (muster rolls and hospital documents) reveals that many of these men were later sent to a hospital with symptoms of an illness, furloughed, and were absent for a period ranging from one month to the remainder of the war. For purposes of this study, then, a soldier is considered wounded if he is listed as such on the muster rolls, is admitted to a rear hospital with a wound, or is listed in a newspaper as wounded (regardless of the severity). As a general rule, a man categorized as "wounded" should miss at least one engagement of the campaign.

A number of soldiers became casualties twice during the Overland Campaign. The number is relatively small, typically amounting to about two to ten per brigade. The most prominent example of this occurrence was Capt. C. Seton Fleming of Company G, 2nd Florida Infantry Regiment, Perry's Brigade. Captain Fleming received a contusion wound to the abdomen while serving as the brigade assistant inspector general at the Wilderness on May 6. This condition was reported in a casualty list for his brigade in the issue of the

Savannah Republican dated June 2, 1864. He returned to duty sometime in the latter half of May and was killed at Cold Harbor in an ill-fated attempt to regain the skirmish line after the massive Federal assault on June 3.

The category of "missing" presents an entirely different set of problems for interpretation. Some men are listed on the individual muster rolls as missing in action, but there is no corresponding Federal prisoner-of-war record. In these cases, three explanations are possible. First, the Union clerk failed to accurately note their names or their units. Second, these men may have deserted during the heat of battle, never to be seen again. Third, they were killed but fellow soldiers failed to observe the events. In the absence of any additional information, these men have simply been referred to as missing.

THE WILDERNESS (MAY 5–7, 1864)

With the exception of one regiment in Field's Division, several regiments in Jones's and Walker's (Stonewall) Brigades of Johnson's Division, and Rosser's Brigade (cavalry), the figures for the Wilderness (Table 7) are all substantiated with individual names. In the case of the exceptions, the totals were slightly increased to reflect figures given in appropriate diaries or to compensate in cases where a less-complete newspaper listing or a diary with a partial list were the only available sources. In the latter cases, the increases were made only after a careful comparison of the killed/wounded ratios in all the units in the same brigade or regiment. The adjustment in each was minimal. Overall, the increase to the total army loss was about 2 percent.

Judging by an evaluation of the figures for the remaining units, it is possible that the total loss for the army was actually higher than indicated above. For example, some of the units in Heth's Division reported substantial numbers of slightly wounded, while other units in the same command listed very few. The inclusion of this class of wounded often depended upon the date of the published list. Slightly wounded men frequently returned to the ranks in one to several weeks. A list published later would typically fail to include these men. One may conclude that the proportion of slightly wounded in all these units would have been similar, thus producing a higher total loss.

The total number of about 11,000 casualties for this battle is close to some of the more conventional estimates of 10,000 to 12,000 for the Army of Northern Virginia. A study of the breakdown of the figures reveals much about the severity of the action. Clearly, the most desperate fighting occurred on the Confederate right flank, where the infantry of the First and Third Corps participated. Heth's and Wilcox's Divisions were on the defensive throughout most of this battle, and their low killed/wounded ratio reflects this posture. The brigades of Cooke and Davis sustained the highest proportions of casualties in these divisions. The ratio for Kershaw's, Field's, and to a lesser extent Anderson's Divisions is higher. Gregg's and Perry's (Florida) Brigades sustained the highest proportions of casualties in these three divisions. With the exception of the Wright's and Harris's Brigades, the remaining nine brigades in these commands suffered moderate losses.

For the Second Corps, the highest percentage of casualties was recorded in Jones's Brigade. Moderate losses were also sustained by Battle's, Doles's, Gordon's, Walker's, and Hays's Brigades. With the exception of Hays, these units were heavily engaged during the opening round of fighting on May 5. The remaining brigades sustained proportionally light losses, perhaps a testament to the leadership and execution of the Second Corps. With less than its full strength, this command successfully blocked and stalemated a substantial portion of the opposing Union army for two days. As for the cavalry at the Wilderness, Rosser's Brigade sustained the heaviest losses by far, engaged on the army's right flank against Federal cavalry.

SPOTSYLVANIA (MAY 7–21, 1864)

As with the Wilderness, the totals for Spotsylvania (see Table 8) were slightly increased to reflect the fact that the numbers were obtained from incomplete sources. These adjustments were deemed necessary in only elements of two brigades (Jones and Walker) in Johnson's Division of the Second Corps. The increase consisted of only 0.3 percent of the total army loss.

The above total of about 12,700 casualties is somewhat higher than many of the conventional or historical estimates. The numbers of killed and wounded are not appalling (by Civil War standards), but the number of unwounded missing is over 5,700 men. By far the majority of these troops were captured on May 12 at the "Bloody Angle." Most of the remaining missing or captured men became such on May 10 (during Upton's charge) or May 19–20 (following the action at Harris Farm). An examination of the figures for this battle reveals that the casualties were not evenly distributed. The loss in the Second Corps is in the range of 53 percent. Johnson's Division, which was overwhelmed at the Bloody Angle during the morning of May 12, was nearly annihilated. The casualties in Early's and Rodes's Divisions were also extremely high, especially in the units (Doles's and Daniel's Brigades) that were heavily engaged in the actions of both May 10 and 12.

As evidenced in Table 8, the losses in the First and Third Corps were comparatively lighter. The exceptions were the Third Corps brigades heavily engaged on May 12 (McGowan, Harris, and Lane). Most of the loss in the artillery occurred in the Second Corps on May 10 and 12 as well. As for the cavalry, Fitzhugh Lee's Division suffered the highest loss during Spotsylvania. This occurred in the preliminary actions to this battle at and south of Todd's Tavern on May 7 and 8. Although the first day of this fighting occurred while the main armies were still entrenched and skirmishing in the Wilderness, this engagement is considered to be part of Spotsylvania.

SHERIDAN'S RICHMOND RAID (MAY 9–24, 1864)

The principal casualties to the Confederate cavalry during Sheridan's raid were sustained by Fitzhugh Lee's Division at Yellow Tavern on May 12 and by Gordon's Brigade at Ground Squirrel Church and Brook Church on May 12 and 13. The infantry units engaged consisted of elements of the brigades of Hunton and Corse (of Pickett's Division), Gracie's Brigade (of Alabama troops) from Beauregard's forces, and the 25th Virginia (City) Battalion from the Richmond garrison. See Table 9, Appendix A.

In addition to the above-noted battles, there was one other engagement that, depending upon interpretation, could be included with the Overland Campaign. This occurred at Wilson's Wharf (or Kennon's Landing) on the James River on May 24. In this action, elements of the Cavalry Corps of Lee's army assaulted troops that actually belonged to the Army of the James. The loss for this engagement is shown in Table 10.

NORTH ANNA (MAY 20–26, 1864)

The Confederate Second Corps was reorganized at Spotsylvania, with changes in leadership and brigade assignments. Specifically, several brigades in Johnson's Division were combined together because of the heavy losses they had sustained in the Wilderness and, in particular, at Spotsylvania. For purposes of clarity and brevity, the new alignment and reorganization of this corps is ignored in the casualty tables.

The casualty figures for the North Anna are shown in Table 11, Appendix A. They include the actions at Guinea Station on May 20 and at Milford Station on May 21. Many of the missing personnel recorded at this battle were, in fact, stragglers picked up by the Army of the Potomac during the move from Spotsylvania. Most of the casualties sustained by Pickett's newly arriving division occurred on May 21 at Milford Station. Most of Kershaw's losses occurred at the Chesterfield Bridge on the evening of May 23. By far the heaviest casualties sustained by any unit were those of Wilcox's Division at Jericho Mill on the evening of the same day.

TOTOPOTOMOY, BETHESDA CHURCH, AND CAVALRY ACTIONS (MAY 27–31, 1864)

The principal infantry battles during the last days of May involved the Second Corps on May 30 at Bethesda Church and the Mechanicsville Road. Pegram's Brigade of Ramseur's (Early's) Division was especially punished heavily. The Cavalry Corps confronted the Federal cavalry on nearly every day during this period. The most severe engagements occurred at Hawes Shop on May 28 and at Old Church on May 30 (resulting in nearly 600 total casualties). For many of the cavalry regiments engaged in these actions, no newspaper listings were found. As a result, the total number of their casualties could be higher than shown in Table 12, Appendix A.

COLD HARBOR (MAY 31–JUNE 12, 1864)

The compiled casualties for Cold Harbor are presented in Table 13. In order to render comparisons easier, the original organization of the Second Corps has been retained in this table. The casualties for Finegan's Brigade, newly arrived from Florida, are included with Mahone's Division of the Third Corps.

Most of the losses sustained by Lee's army in this battle were incurred as follows: first, on the evening of June 1, when the Federal VI and XVIII Corps assaulted and broke the Confederate line at the junction of Kershaw's and Hoke's Divisions on the army's right; second, on the Confederate left flank, where the Second Corps and Heth's Division of the Third Corps engaged the Federal V and IX Corps over the course of several days; and third, at the breakthrough in Breckinridge's divisional front during the massive and costly

Federal assault on June 3. For the cavalry, more than half of the loss incurred was sustained in the action at Ashland on June 1.

It is possible that the casualties for the later battles of the campaign (that is, Spotsylvania to Cold Harbor) have been inflated at the expense of the earlier actions (principally the Wilderness and the first week of Spotsylvania). This particularly applies to Cold Harbor and is due primarily to difficulties in determining the dates or battles when some of the wounded became casualties. Where only hospital records are available, the dates used for these men are based upon their first recorded arrival with the wound. Many may have been sent to another facility first or have been held for some time in a field hospital, causing difficulty in accurately determining the original date of their wounding.

SHERIDAN'S SECOND, OR TREVILIAN, RAID (JUNE 7–24, 1864)

The inclusion of this raid in the Overland Campaign is open to interpretation. The primary engagement occurred at Trevilian Station on June 11 and 12. The casualties shown in Table 14 cover the period only from June 7 through 12, 1864.

THE CAMPAIGN

Table 15 in Appendix A provides the total number of casualties sustained by the Army of Northern Virginia during the Overland Campaign as revealed by this research. Exclusive of Wilson's Wharf and Trevilian Station, the grand total of casualties in all categories is 32,770 men. Including the latter two engagements brings the grand total to 33,646.

These figures should not be viewed as a complete and accurate representation of the Confederate losses during the campaign. Given the limitations in source materials that survived the war, this finite total will likely never be known. But the above data provides a relatively accurate tabulation of these numbers. With the exception of several small additional estimates where reference and source materials were limited or unavailable, the various numbers can be substantiated with individual and nominal lists by unit. The occurrences of these estimates in the casualties are described in detail in the unit discussions in Part Two. The actual figures for the Confederate casualties are probably somewhat higher.

As a further component of this study, it is also possible to gauge or approximate the infantry strength in the Army of Northern Virginia at selected points during the campaign. These figures are presented in Tables 16–19 in Appendix A. They represent the maximum possible number of men available at the commencement of the campaign, at Spotsylvania on May 8, at the close of Spotsylvania on May 21, at Cold Harbor on May 31, and at the close of the campaign on June 12. The actual number in each case was likely less due to sickness and detachments from the ranks for a myriad of short-term assignments. An examination of the figures reveals that the infantry strength of the army on May 20 was dangerously low (only about 31,500 men) before the arrival of much-needed reinforcements in the form of Breckinridge's Division from the Shenandoah Valley and Pickett's Division and Lewis's reinforced brigade (Hoke's) from Beauregard.

PART TWO

Unit Discussions, with Casualty Breakdowns

The figures for the battle casualties in Tables 7–15 were compiled from individual brigade and battalion totals. These unit totals are presented in a similar form in fifty-nine individual tables in Appendix A using the same format as described above, except for one change. A second, lesser figure is provided in parentheses for the "Campaign Total" loss of the brigade as well as for many of its component regiments. These figures represent the actual number of men in the respective commands who became casualties. As noted earlier, a small number of individuals became casualties twice during this campaign. Thus, these figures will be less than the compiled total losses.

Some historians might question the need for detailed casualty information regarding the Army of Northern Virginia during this period. The Overland Campaign consisted of five major battles and numerous smaller (mainly cavalry) actions. Although some form of hostilities occurred nearly every day, the degree of fighting varied substantially. Most of the severe fighting occurred during the first two days of the Wilderness, four or five days at Spotsylvania, one day at North Anna, and two days at Cold Harbor. The degree of involvement for the various individual units in Lee's army varied widely and, from an overall viewpoint, was complex. The figures for the casualties are beneficial in that they can help the historian sort through the complexity of the campaign and reveal what actually happened to the various Confederate commands during specific battles. They also can reveal, to a large degree, which units performed well, which performed less credibly, and which were present at the wrong place at the wrong time.

A discussion of each respective brigade or artillery command follows, providing the composition of the units, their brief histories in the preceding years of the war, and their activity during the Overland Campaign. They should be viewed in conjunction with the casualty tables in Appendix A.

CHAPTER 4

First Corps

KERSHAW'S DIVISION

Kershaw's Division was composed of the brigades of Humphreys, Henagan, Wofford, and Bryan. This organization played a prominent role in most of the earlier campaigns and major battles of the Army of Northern Virginia and, at this stage of the war, was one of its best divisions. The division, in particular, performed competently at the Battles of Fredericksburg, Chancellorsville, and Gettysburg. Prior to 1864, the commander was Maj. Gen. Lafayette McLaws. After Gettysburg, the division was sent with its corps commander, Lt. Gen. James Longstreet, to northern Georgia to assist the Army of Tennessee. While in northern Georgia and eastern Tennessee, the division took part in the Battle of Chickamauga, the siege of Chattanooga, and the East Tennessee Campaign, including the siege of Knoxville.

During the East Tennessee Campaign, Longstreet preferred charges against McLaws. Specifically, an officer on Longstreet's staff informed McLaws that "you [McLaws] have exhibited a want in confidence in the efforts and plans which the commanding officer [Longstreet] has thought proper to adopt." Following a bitter court-martial and an eventual exoneration, McLaws left the corps and took an assignment in his home state of Georgia.[1] The senior brigadier general, Joseph B. Kershaw, was then assigned to command the division. Kershaw was promoted to major general in late May.

Kershaw's Division returned to Lee's army in mid-April with a somewhat diminished strength of about 5,180 men and a worn condition. The campaign in eastern Tennessee was ultimately a failure. This result was compounded by a severe winter and limited supply and foraging conditions.[2] By all accounts, the veterans of this division were pleased to be returning to Virginia. The deficiency in personnel in late April–early May improved with the arrival of the trail (or rear) elements of the division in May and the return of numerous veterans from wounded furlough throughout the campaign. In addition, a new unit, the 20th South Carolina Regiment, was assigned to the division in late May.

Kershaw's men arrived at the Wilderness on the morning of May 6. At this point of the battle, Federal forces led by Maj. Gen. Winfield Hancock were driving Heth's and Wilcox's Divisions of the Third Corps from the battlefield. Kershaw's men were rushed into this action and deployed on the southern side of the Orange Plank Road. The bulk of the division was committed in a timely manner and achieved success in halting the Federal advance and regaining some of the lost ground (see Map 6, Appendix B).[3]

Following the repulse of the Federal advance, a lull in the fighting occurred for several hours. A member of Longstreet's staff found an unfinished railroad cut in the woods south of the Confederate line that provided an open but concealed lane through the dense woods to the left, or southern, flank of the Union forces. Longstreet devised a creative plan to attack the enemy flank using this lane as an approach and, thereafter, directly strike the Federal front. The combined assault was performed during the late morning and was an overwhelming success. All of Kershaw's Division participated in this major action (see Map 7, Appendix B).[4] This attack broke the Union forces and forced a rapid retirement to their original line along Brock Road. Complete Confederate success was frustrated when Longstreet was wounded by friendly fire from the flanking elements.

With the loss of Longstreet, Maj. Gen. Charles Field temporarily assumed leadership of the First Corps. Once Lee became aware of the situation, he appointed Maj. Gen. Richard H. Anderson commander of the First Corps. Late in the day, Confederate forces attempted to gain a complete victory by assaulting and driving the Federals from their breastworks along Brock Road. Kershaw's Division was committed primarily south of the Orange Plank Road. All of the units in the division were again employed in this attack (see Map 8, Appendix B).[5] This assault, the last phase of the battle, was unsuccessful. Judging by the relatively low casualties sustained by the individual brigades, the troops apparently realized the futility of this offensive action and limited their exposure.

Following the conclusion of the Battle of the Wilderness, the Union army attempted to maneuver and force Lee's army into an open battle. The object of this move was the key crossroads at Spotsylvania Court House. Capture of this point would place the Federal army closer to Richmond and likely force the Confederates to battle. During the night of May 7–8, Kershaw's Division led the march of Lee's army to Spotsylvania. Fortunately for the Southern cause, the division got an early start and arrived at the key intersection of the Brock and Fredericksburg Roads just ahead of the Union V Corps. Kershaw's troops were also aided in this vital task by Maj. Gen. James E. B. Stuart's Cavalry Corps, which delayed the parallel enemy march and effort to reach the crossroads.

Upon arrival, part of Kershaw's Division relieved Stuart's cavalry.[6] This force quickly erected barricades on the crest of Laurel Ridge, a slight rise bisecting Brock Road, and repelled hasty Federal attacks upon their position (see Maps 11 and 12, Appendix B). At the same time, the remainder of the division secured and held the intersection at the court house until relieved by Stuart's cavalry.[7] These units then rejoined the rest of the command at Laurel Ridge and repulsed further attacks by the V Corps. The entire division later shifted to the right (or east) to permit deployment of Field's Division of the First Corps on their left (between Brock Road and the Po River). During the night of May 8–9, the Confederates upgraded these improvised barricades to breastworks or earthworks (see Map 13, Appendix B). The success of Kershaw's Division on May 8 in first reaching and then defending this position frustrated the enemy plans and, in part, enabled Lee's army to secure and fortify Spotsylvania.

Elements of the V Corps assaulted Kershaw's position on several occasions over the next five days (May 8–12). Each of these attacks was repulsed with light losses to the defenders (see Map 14, Appendix B). According to available historical mapping, the brigades of the division were arrayed from west to east in the following manner: Wofford, Bryan, Henagan, and Humphreys.[8] During the period May 15–17, Kershaw's Division was shifted from the left of the army to a position between the court house and the Po River on the army's right.[9] This was in response to enemy maneuvers against this portion of Lee's line. The organization was mostly kept in reserve and saw little action at this second position.

The division also was present for the remaining battles of the campaign. At North Anna, only Kershaw's Brigade saw heavy action on one day, otherwise, Kershaw's Division was placed on the corps's left next to the Third Corps sector (see Maps 25 and 29, Appendix B). This line skirted high ground south of the river. The deployment of the units from left to right (west to east) was reportedly as follow: Henagan, Humphreys, Bryan, and Wofford.[10] During the subsequent action at Totopotomoy Creek (Bethesda Church) in late May, the division was posted on the corps's left astride the Shady Grove Road (see Map 31, Appendix B).[11] For most of this engagement and the battle at North Anna, the command participated only in minor skirmishing.

On June 1 at Cold Harbor, Kershaw's Division was shifted to the army's right (southern) flank (next to Hoke's Division). In this new position, the men were embroiled in some of the heaviest fighting of this battle. During the morning of June 1, the organization conducted a reconnaissance in force against Federal cavalry holding Old Cold Harbor. The enemy repulsed this advance (see Map 34, Appendix B). This failure was due to a lack of leadership and coordination by Anderson, Kershaw, and Hoke.[12] The division then took up a position on the corps's right flank and constructed breastworks (next to Hoke's command). The alignment was, from south to north, as follows: Wofford, Bryan, Humphreys, and Henagan.[13]

This section of the Confederate line was heavily attacked during the evening of June 1 and again during the early morning of June 3. During the first of these assaults, the VI and XVIII Corps found a gap between the lines of Kershaw and Hoke astride a small ravine and stream (named Bloody Run) and got in the rear of the southern end of the divisional line (see Map 35, Appendix B). Ultimately, with the assistance of other units in the division and Field's Division, the Confederates were able to restore the position.[14] During the night of June 1–2, the part of the division that had endured the worst of this fighting was pulled out and placed in reserve. It was then, in part, inserted back in the line with Field's Division and actively repulsed a massive Union assault on June 3 (see Maps 39 and 40, Appendix B).

Despite having sustained heavy casualties in May and early June, Kershaw's Division emerged from the campaign in relatively sound condition and strength. One of the brigades, however, had lost heavily in field and line officers, and two others were significantly reduced in numbers. Following the Battle of Cold Harbor, the division moved to Petersburg in mid-June. It would see considerable action during the siege of Petersburg and Richmond in June and July and later was dispatched to the Shenandoah Valley in August and October. In several battles of the latter campaign, the division was roughly handled and sustained considerable losses.

Humphreys's Brigade

This command consisted of four veteran regiments (13th, 17th, 18th, and 21st) from Mississippi. The personnel were raised from the counties around Vicksburg and Jackson and the northern, east-central, and southwestern portions of the state. Humphreys's Brigade was one of the finest infantry units in the Army of Northern Virginia and had compiled a celebrated fighting record during the first three years of the war. As a testament to this, the first two brigade commanders, Richard Griffith and William Barksdale, were both killed in action. Three of its four regiments were present at First Bull Run (Manassas) and the victory at Ball's Bluff in 1861. In 1862 and 1863 the brigade performed splendidly at the Battles of Antietam, Fredericksburg, Chancellorsville, and Gettysburg. On the second day of the latter battle, the Mississippians assaulted and broke the III Corps at the Peach Orchard. This heroic attack nearly caused a total collapse of the entire Union front in the southern portion of the battlefield but cost the brigade its commander, General Barksdale, and nearly one-half of its men.

The Mississippi brigade reported a total of 1,673 casualties for the major battles of 1863, the highest total in the First Corps during this period.[1] This number did include about 340 men captured at Marye's Heights (Chancellorsville Campaign) in May. A compilation of the brigade's CSRs reveals that most of these men were promptly exchanged and rejoined their regiments prior to the Gettysburg Campaign.

Col. Benjamin G. Humphreys of the 21st Mississippi was promoted to lead the brigade after Barksdale's death. He commanded the Mississippians during the Battles of Chickamauga and Knoxville but failed to achieve the same level of success as his predecessors. His performance in these actions was due to a degree of hesitancy at Chickamauga, his inaugural experience as a brigade commander, and the difficulty of the Union defensive position at Knoxville. Humphreys apparently learned quickly from his mistakes, and in the Overland Campaign, his unit demonstrated the same level of competency as in the prior years. There was one increasingly negative trend in the brigade, though. Due to the sheer number of casualties sustained during the previous year, the strength of the command was beginning to wane significantly. In early May 1864, Humphreys's Brigade fielded less than 950 men. The return of rear elements and previously wounded men from leave replaced some of the losses from this campaign. But no new recruits were available to this command, and its overall strength never actually approached this figure.

Humphreys's Brigade was one the first two brigades of Kershaw's Division committed to action on May 6. Along with Kershaw's former brigade (under Henagan), it was deployed in the dense woods adjacent to and directly south of Orange Plank Road (see Map 6, Appendix B). These units first stopped the Federal advance and then drove the enemy back several hundred yards.[2] Humphreys's and Henagan's brigades must have met the stiffest resistance because they clearly sustained the heaviest losses in Kershaw's Division during the Wilderness. This is noteworthy because the enemy had a superior force. Humphreys's men participated in the second phase of fighting at noon and in the unsuccessful assault upon the Federal line of breastworks along Brock Road late in the afternoon (see Map 7, Appendix B).

At the Battle of Spotsylvania, Humphreys's Brigade played a major role in the defense of the Laurel Ridge position on May 8. Along with Kershaw's (Henagan's) Brigade, the Mississippians held off the entire V Corps until the rest of Kershaw's Division, Field's Division, and the Second Corps arrived. Fortunately for these two brigades, this Federal command attacked in an uncoordinated and piecemeal manner as its various units arrived on the battlefield. Part of Humphreys's Brigade contributed significantly to this defense by infiltrating into some woods located to their right-front and firing upon the left flank of the assaulting Federal units (see Maps 11 and 12, Appendix B).[3] The brigade continued to hold this position against several more attacks on May 9–12. During the evening of May 12, the Mississippians were relieved from their Laurel Ridge position and dispatched to the center of the Confederate line. They deployed along a reserve line of breastworks at the Mule Shoe and covered the withdrawal of the frontline units after the onset of darkness.[4]

Humphreys's Brigade saw only minor action at the Battles of North Anna and Totopotomoy during the third and fourth weeks of May. The unit moved to Cold Harbor on June 1 and was attacked that same evening and again during the early morning of June 3 by elements of the XVIII Corps (see Maps 35 and 40, Appendix B). The Mississippians were well entrenched and had little difficulty repulsing these assaults.[5] Following the second of these attacks, their position was subjected to considerable sniping and shelling for the next five to seven days, and the Mississippians sustained some casualties.

At the close of the campaign, Humphreys's Brigade emerged with its unit leadership intact and about two-thirds of its starting strength. The brigade would continue to function effectively but, due to its reduced numbers, would have minimal offensive capability in future battles. With no real replacement system available, the strength of the organization would continue to diminish as the command was again frequently committed to engagements in and around Richmond and Petersburg as well as in the Shenandoah Valley.

Casualty lists covering the period of the Overland Campaign were found in the Richmond newspapers for the 18th and 21st Mississippi Regiments.[6] Despite the fact that similar lists were not found for the 13th and 17th Mississippi Regiments, the compiled casualty figures for this brigade (see Table 20, Appendix A) are considered to be among the most accurate for any of the brigades in Lee's army. The primary reason for this assertion is the relative completeness of the muster rolls for the regiments. One exception is the records for the 17th Mississippi at the Wilderness. The percentage of total casualties for this regiment at this battle appears to be low compared to the other three units (13th, 18th, and 21st). Accordingly, the actual number of casualties for the 17th Mississippi at the Wilderness may have been slightly higher.

Kershaw's Brigade

This brigade of South Carolina troops was formerly Kershaw's command. The core of the brigade—2nd, 3rd, 7th, and 8th Regiments—was present with the army in Virginia since First Bull Run (Manassas). The remaining two units, the 15th South Carolina Regiment and the 3rd South Carolina Battalion, joined in 1862. For the most part, the personnel of this brigade were recruited from the interior portion of the state in a wide band stretching from Georgia to North Carolina. Kershaw's Brigade had forged an excellent combat record, participating in all of the major battles in 1862 and 1863; it also was present at the Battles of Chickamauga and Knoxville. The total reported number of casualties for the major battles in 1863 was 1,395 men.[1] Most of this significant loss was sustained at Gettysburg and Chickamauga.

With the promotion of Kershaw to command of the division, Col. John W. Henagan of the 8th South Carolina assumed temporary command of the brigade. Its six units normally fielded more than 2,000 men in the ranks and was the largest brigade in the division. As a result of the heavy losses experienced in the aforementioned battles in 1863, though, it entered the campaign of 1864 with a strength of under 1,600 men. The return of furloughed wounded veterans and rear elements in the move from eastern Tennessee helped compensate for some of the losses in the Overland Campaign.

Kershaw's (Henagan's) Brigade played a major role in the success of the First Corps at the Wilderness. Along with Humphreys's Brigade, it was one of the principal units that halted the Federal onslaught and restored the Confederate line south of Orange Plank Road on the morning of May 6 (see Map 6, Appendix B). Its losses in this action were moderately heavy. Later in the morning, the South Carolinians were part of the forces that successfully attacked the Union front and drove the enemy back to their original line along Brock Road (see Map 7, Appendix B). Lastly, the brigade took part in the unsuccessful assault upon the Federal breastworks lining this road. The 8th South Carolina was apparently posted in the rear supporting some corps artillery and did not participate in these actions (see Table 21, Appendix A).

Along with Humphreys's command, Kershaw's Brigade played a crucial role in the opening round of the Battle of Spotsylvania. The South Carolinians repulsed all the assaults of the V Corps on their position astride Laurel Ridge on May 8 and later on May 10 and 12 (see Maps 11–14, Appendix B). Most of the casualties sustained by the brigade at Spotsylvania appear to have occurred on May 8. As a part of Kershaw's Division, Henagan's command was shifted to the right of the main army front on May 15 but saw no further significant action during this battle.

At North Anna, Kershaw's (Henagan's) Brigade was initially posted on the northern side of the river to guard the Chesterfield Bridge (of Telegraph Road). During the afternoon of May 23, the main Confederate army retired to the southern side of the river, but four of the brigade's units (the 2nd, 3rd, and 7th South Carolina Regiments and the 3rd South Carolina Battalion) were left to cover and hold this span (see Map 25, Appendix B).[2] The men constructed earthworks and were supported by artillery posted on the higher southern riverbank. During the evening, however, they were assaulted by a superior enemy force (from the II Corps) and were driven in an expeditious manner across the river. For the remainder of the battle, Kershaw's Brigade was posted along the main Confederate line and took part in only minor skirmishing.

On May 31, the 20th South Carolina Regiment was assigned to the brigade. This veteran unit had previously served exclusively in South Carolina but had very little combat experience. The ranks of the regiment nearly doubled the strength of the entire brigade. Its leader, Col. Lawrence M. Keitt, was the ranking officer in the brigade at that time and, accordingly, was given command. Kershaw's Division moved from Totopotomoy to Cold Harbor during the morning of June 1 and assigned to capture the intersection at Old Cold Harbor. Federal cavalry had been ordered to hold this strategic point to permit the arrival and deployment of Union infantry. Unfortunately, Kershaw elected to place his former brigade in the forefront, and in turn Keitt chose his new unit to lead the advance of the entire division. The colonel deployed his troops in a compact formation in an open field and posted himself on his mount in the front (see Map 34, Appendix B).[3]

When the enemy cavalry opened fire, Keitt was immediately mortally wounded and the men of the 20th South Carolina either hugged the ground or broke to the rear. The flight of much of this unit caused disorder in the remainder of the brigade. The chaos spread back to the following units and forced a termination of the operation. Kershaw's veterans apparently viewed the behavior and performance of Keitt's regiment in a very harsh manner. James A. Milling, a member of Company G, 3rd South Carolina Battalion, later recorded in his diary that "the 20th [South Carolina Regiment] had disgraced our brigade."[4] With the death of Colonel Keitt, Colonel Henagan again assumed command of the brigade.

During the remainder of June 1, the brigade took up a position on the left of the division and entrenched. Late in the day, the XVIII Corps assaulted the entire divisional front (see Map 35, Appendix B). The South Carolinians had little difficulty repulsing the assault in their sector, however, a difficult situation developed in another section of the line. The Federals had found a gap in the Confederate line beyond the right of Kershaw's line and had moved upon the flank and rear of Wofford's and Bryan's Brigades (see below). The 2nd South Carolina Regiment and the 3rd South Carolina Battalion were quickly dispatched to reinforce these commands. With the assistance of Bryan's men, these South Carolinians halted the Federal onslaught and restored the original line.[5]

On the morning of June 3, Union forces assaulted the entire Confederate line at Cold Harbor. Henagan's South Carolinians easily defended their portion of the line and helped repel this attack. During the remainder of the battle, their sector was subjected to considerable sniping and artillery fire, which caused some casualties.

With the exception of the ill-chosen position at North Anna (on May 23) and the first action at Cold Harbor (the morning of June 1), Kershaw's

(Henagan's) Brigade had performed in its usual reliable manner. The addition of the 20th Regiment raised the strength of the command to its pre-1864 level. Most of the veteran units, however, had lost heavily, especially in line officers. During the rest of 1864, the brigade saw action at Petersburg, outside Richmond, and in the Shenandoah Valley. Throughout each of these operations, the unit continued to function at a high level. Brig. Gen. James Conner was assigned to command of the brigade during the summer, becoming available when Brig. Gen. Samuel McGowan returned from wounded furlough to his brigade in the Third Corps. The 20th South Carolina experienced no further combat failures but, like most units new to Lee's army, did experience during June and July an unusually high rate of sickness.

South Carolina newspapers provided a patchwork of casualty lists for the seven units of this brigade.[6] The May 25 issue of the *(Columbia) Daily South Carolinian* provided the casualty lists for the entire brigade at the Wilderness, though, as shown by an earlier issue of the *Camden Weekly Confederate,* omitting several names of wounded men in the 2nd South Carolina. Presumably, these men returned to their unit in one to two weeks. The compiled total of 315 casualties for the brigade at the Wilderness is slightly lower that the total of 322 men reported in the *Official Records.*[7] The latter source report enumerates 57 killed, 239 wounded, and 26 missing. The difference between the two totals is likely in slightly wounded men. (Considering that the identities and units of the additional men are not known, the compiled total rather than the official report was used for this study.)

Newspapers were found for Spotsylvania, but in some cases these do not cover all the days the units were in action. This especially applies to the 3rd and 7th Regiments and the 3rd Battalion. Lastly, newspaper casualty lists were found only for the 8th Regiment at North Anna and for the 2nd, 3rd, 8th, and 20th Regiments at Cold Harbor. Judging by these gaps, it is likely that the actual casualties in Kershaw's Brigade at these three later battles were slightly higher (see Table 21, Appendix A).

Wofford's Brigade

Wofford's Brigade established a solid fighting reputation with the Army of Northern Virginia. The initial commander was Howell Cobb, a lawyer and well-known citizen of Georgia. He appeared to have limited leadership capabilities, and under his command, the brigade was badly cut up in the

Maryland Campaign in 1862. Cobb then took an assignment in his home state to permit his younger brother, Thomas R. R. Cobb, to assume command. The younger Cobb proved to be a more competent leader but was mortally wounded at Fredericksburg in late 1862. William T. Wofford of the 18th Georgia Regiment was then given command. By this date, the brigade was composed of units exclusively from Georgia, achieved by the transfers of several units into and out of the command. By mid-1863, the brigade was composed of three regiments (16th, 18th, and 24th), two legions (Cobb's and Phillips's), and one battalion (3rd Sharpshooters). The personnel of these units were raised from the counties located primarily in the northern part of the state.

Wofford's Brigade performed very well at the Battles of Chancellorsville and Gettysburg. On the second day of the latter battle, the Georgians followed the initial attack of Barksdale's Brigade, veered to the right, and advanced upon the flank and rear of the Federals battling in the Wheat Field. The resulting retirement of these forces nearly caused a collapse of this portion of the Union line. The brigade arrived too late to participate in the Battle of Chickamauga but was at the forefront of the unsuccessful assault upon Knoxville in December. Overall, the command reported 1,046 casualties for the year.[1] In the spring of 1864, Wofford's Brigade fielded the largest strength in Kershaw's Division (about 1,615 men). This was maintained by the subsequent arrival of men returning from wounded furlough and personnel bringing up the rear in the move from eastern Tennessee.

The brigade was initially posted in corps reserve at the Wilderness on May 6. It was one of the units selected to participate in the flanking attack upon the Federal line south of Orange Plank Road. The Georgians were deployed on the front line to the left of Mahone's Brigade and experienced considerable success in this assault upon elements of the II Corps (see Map 7, Appendix B).[2] Later in the day, Wofford unsuccessfully attacked the Federal breastworks along Brock Road.[3] As noted above, Kershaw's Division achieved little success in this offensive action. Most of the casualties sustained by these Georgians in the Wilderness likely occurred at this time.

On May 8 at Spotsylvania, Wofford's Brigade was initially sent to the key road intersection at the court house until relieved by Stuart's cavalry.[4] At that time later in the day, it moved to Laurel Ridge, where it was posted on the left of the divisional line. In this position, the Georgians successfully repelled assaults by the V Corps over the next several days (see Map 13, Appendix B).

During the morning of May 12, the brigade was dispatched to the assistance of the Second Corps, moving to the support of Daniel's and Battle's Brigades along the western side of the Mule Shoe (see Map 20, Appendix B).[5] Many of the casualties sustained by Wofford's Brigade during this battle likely occurred in this action.

For the remainder of this battle and throughout the subsequent battles of North Anna and Totopotomoy (Bethesda Church), Wofford's Brigade was only lightly engaged. Compared to other units in Kershaw's Division and the rest of Lee's army, the men had, during the month of May, experienced overall considerable fortune in battle. This ended on June 1 at Cold Harbor. On that day, Wofford's Brigade was posted on the right of Kershaw's Division next to the streambed and deep ravine of Bloody Run.[6] The adjacent command, Hoke's Division, had earlier covered this feature and connected with Wofford's right. On his own, Hoke shifted the command to his opposite flank, leaving a gap in the Confederate line.

As battle fortune would have it, the Federals attacked the fronts of Kershaw's and Hoke's Divisions just before sunset on June 1 (see Map 35, Appendix B). Elements of the VI and XVIII Corps advanced through the undefended ravine and reached the flank and rear of Wofford's Brigade. The Georgians quickly realized their predicament and fled to the rear.[7] Nevertheless, they sustained a reported 266 casualties for the battle, most of which were suffered on this day. The total includes 163 unwounded prisoners. Overnight, the brigade rallied and was reinserted in the line. During the massive Union attack on June 3, the Georgians supported Field's Division.

Despite the setback at Cold Harbor on June 1, Wofford's Brigade emerged from the campaign with the second-highest strength in Kershaw's Division and most of its leadership intact. The command saw considerable action during the siege of Petersburg and Richmond and in the Shenandoah Campaign. During the latter operation, the Georgians lost very heavily near Front Royal in August and at Cedar Creek in October.

There are several significant problems in accurately determining the casualties for Wofford's Brigade during the Overland Campaign. The June 4 issue of Atlanta's *Daily Intelligencer* published a list of casualties for all the units of the brigade for the period May 6–16.[8] This comprehensive list unfortunately fails to provide a breakdown of losses by battle or by day. Any attempt to separate or identify the casualties at each of Wilderness and Spotsylvania is clearly subject to some conjecture. Several other newspapers in Georgia and

Richmond, Virginia, published casualty lists for the 16th and 24th Georgia Regiments for periods ranging from May 6 through May 20, 26, or June 5; these again provide no breakdown by battle or day.[9] A second difficulty is the lack of newspaper casualty lists for the bulk of the brigade at Cold Harbor. With the exception of the list published for the 24th Georgia Regiment for the period May 6–June 5, nothing was found covering the losses at this battle.

One major source for Georgia troops, Lillian Henderson's *Roster of the Confederate Soldiers of Georgia* omits Cobb's Legion, Phillips's Legion, and the 3rd Georgia Sharpshooter Battalion from Wofford's command.[10] These three units represented about 40 percent of the brigade's strength. This source was found, on occasion, to be of benefit in resolving difficulties from the rolls and the newspapers (such as the aforementioned *Daily Intelligencer*). Judging by these difficulties, it is likely that the total loss of this brigade during the campaign and especially at Cold Harbor could have been slightly higher (see Table 22, Appendix A).

Bryan's Brigade

This brigade was also composed of Georgia units. The 10th and 53rd Regiments were enlisted from the counties surrounding Augusta and Columbus and on the southern outskirts of Atlanta, while the 50th and 51st Regiments were recruited from the counties in the extreme southern to southwestern part of the state. The brigade's original commander was Paul J. Semmes of Georgia, who was mortally wounded at Gettysburg. Goode Bryan of the 16th Georgia Regiment (of Wofford's Brigade) was assigned to command after Semmes's death. Bryan's Brigade had historically been the smallest command in the division but was a veteran and reliable unit. It sustained heavy casualties at the Battles of Chancellorsville, Gettysburg, and Knoxville (having arrived too late to participate in the Battle of Chickamauga). The total reported casualties for the year 1863 reached 1,247 men.[1] This loss diminished the strength of the brigade for the following year. At the start of the Overland Campaign, the unit could field only about 1,025 men.

Bryan's Brigade followed Humphreys's and Kershaw's (Henagan's) Brigades in the march to the Wilderness on May 6. It was committed to the right of these two commands south of Orange Plank Road and participated in the successful repulse of advancing elements of the Federal II Corps (see Map 6, Appendix B).[2] Bryan's command sustained numerically and proportionally fewer casualties than Humphreys's Brigade during this action, which may have been due to the heavily wooded character of this portion of the battlefield and possibly less enemy resistance (they were further from the road). The Georgians were involved in the two later phases of the battle. They were part of the forces employed in the late-morning combined frontal-flacking assault (see Map 7, Appendix B), and they participated in the subsequent unsuccessful general assault upon the Federal breastworks along Brock Road.

From this point in the campaign, the involvement of Bryan's Brigade nearly paralleled that of Wofford's Brigade. The Georgians helped hold the key position of Laurel Ridge on May 8, 10, and 12 at Spotsylvania, positioned between Wofford's and Kershaw's Brigades (see Map 13, Appendix B).[3] When Wofford's Brigade was sent to the assistance of the Second Corps during the morning of May 12, Bryan's command took over a portion of its sector of the earthworks. For the remainder of this battle and the following engagements at North Anna and Totopotomoy, these Georgians saw minimal action.

When Kershaw's Division moved to Cold Harbor on June 1, Bryan's Brigade was deployed on the left (north) of Wofford's Brigade (see Maps 34 and 36, Appendix B). In concert with the other Confederate units, the brigade quickly constructed breastworks along their position. As discussed above, the Federal forces assaulted the entire fronts of Kershaw's and Hoke's Divisions during the late hours of this day. Bryan's men had little difficulty repulsing the troops in the front, though the penetration of Union forces into the rear of Wofford's adjacent command presented a perilous situation. The Georgians had to re-fuse their right flank and engage in some desperate fighting in order to avoid encirclement and capture.[4] The arrival of troops from Kershaw's Brigade helped repulse the Federals and restore the line at dusk. In any event, Bryan's command lost 66 men as prisoners and sustained 153 casualties overall from this action. Thereafter, the brigade was pulled out and placed in reserve for much of the rest of the battle.

Although the casualties sustained by Bryan's Brigade during the Overland Campaign were the lowest in Kershaw's Division, the strength of the command was significantly diminished. Like Humphreys's Brigade, this brigade would never again field a strength approaching its numbers earlier in the war. During the remainder of 1864, the Georgians continued to see action during the siege of Petersburg and Richmond and in the Shenandoah Valley.

Newspaper casualty listings for Bryan's Brigade provide a variable patchwork of information.[5] Although they often do not provide a breakdown of casualties by battle, they are generally comprehensive. This especially applies to the 10th, 50th, and 51st Georgia. The only glaring omission is a casualty list for the 53rd Georgia at Cold Harbor. Lillian Henderson's roster of Georgia troops was also beneficial for the study of the personnel in this brigade.[6] It should be mentioned that General Bryan reported that the losses in his brigade at the Wilderness were 31 killed and 103 wounded.[7] These numbers pale in comparison to the compiled casualties for this battle (see Table 23, Appendix A). These figures were primarily obtained from newspapers.

FIELD'S DIVISION

The original commander of this division was Maj. Gen. William H. C. Whiting. Following the Seven Days' Battles outside Richmond in 1862, Whiting became ill and received a medical furlough. The senior brigadier general, John B. Hood, then was given command, and the division thereafter was recognized as Hood's. Born in Kentucky, Hood served with the U.S. Cavalry in Texas just prior to the war. He was an aggressive and disciplined officer and quickly rose to the rank of major general. His division reflected his character and was an aggressive and hard-hitting outfit.[1]

Hood was severely wounded at both Gettysburg and Chickamauga in 1863. While convalescing from the second wound, he transferred to the Army of Tennessee (and command of a corps). Micah Jenkins, the senior brigadier general, then temporarily assumed command of the division for the remainder of the year.[2] He was apparently a favorite of First Corps commander James Longstreet. A second brigadier, Evander Law, also publicly expressed an interest in being promoted to command of the division and was the choice of the other brigade commanders.[3] The Confederate War Department resolved the issue in early 1864 by assigning Maj. Gen. Charles W. Field to the command.[4] Field was an experienced officer, having been wounded in 1862 while leading a brigade in A. P. Hill's Division. Under his leadership, his new command would continue to display an aggressive and tenacious manner and maintain a reputation as one of the best infantry units in Lee's army.

Field's Division consisted of the brigades of Gregg, Benning, Law, Anderson, and Jenkins. The latter brigade was transferred from Pickett's Division in August 1863 in part to compensate for heavy losses sustained by the division at Gettysburg but also because it was fresh and available. Hood's former division participated with Kershaw's command in the Chickamauga and

East Tennessee Campaigns in the fall and winter of 1863–64. Like Kershaw, Field's Division rejoined Lee's army in April 1864 with a somewhat diminished strength (of less than 6,100 men). Its men were likely relieved to be out of Tennessee. The arrival of straggling personnel and the return of a considerable body of men from wounded furlough in both May and June combined to raise the strength of the division and offset heavy casualties during the Overland Campaign.

In the early hours of May 6, Field's Division marched alongside of but slightly behind the lead elements of Kershaw's Division on Orange Plank Road. As these units neared the battlefield, they could hear an increasingly louder volume of musket fire from the dense woods on both sides of the road. At this point in the battle, Federal forces consisting of the II, V, and VI Corps were driving units of A. P. Hill's Third Corps in confusion from the battlefield.[5] Like Kershaw's command, Field's Division was similarly rushed into action but deployed on the northern side of this road (see Map 6, Appendix B). Its lead elements, over half of the division, halted the advance of the opposing Union troops but in the process lost heavily.[6]

Following this action, there was a lull in the fighting for several hours. Through the aid of his staff, General Longstreet devised a plan to attack the Federals' unguarded southern flank and their front simultaneously.[7] The remaining portion of Field's Division was committed to this operation (see Map 7, Appendix B). The combined attack broke the Union line and forced the enemy troops to retreat to their original line along Brock Road. A complete success in this part of the battlefield was lost when men from the flanking column mistakenly fired upon friendly troops and seriously wounded Longstreet.[8]

A second lull in the fighting then occurred. General Field initially took command of the First Corps. Once General Lee was informed of the loss of Longstreet, he assigned corps command to the ranking officer, Richard H. Anderson. During the midafternoon hours, Federal forces tried to regain the initiative. Elements of the IX Corps advanced through dense woods upon the northern flank of the Confederate forces facing the main (Brock Road) line. Part of Field's Division and one brigade of Anderson's Division (now led by Brig. Gen. William Mahone) were posted in this area (see Map 8, Appendix B). These units experienced considerable difficulty holding their ground and were nearly overwhelmed by this superior force.[9] Elements of the Third Corps were dispatched from reserve to help repulse this enemy attack.

In the late afternoon, the Confederates assaulted the Union line of breastworks along Brock Road. Lee hoped to build on his army's earlier success and gain a decisive victory. Only part of Field's Division participated in this attack.[10] The Federals successfully stopped this advance short of and at the breastworks.

Field's Division followed Kershaw's command in the march to Spotsylvania during the night of May 7–8. Upon its arrival, the division was placed on the left of Kershaw's men along the crest and western slope of Laurel Ridge from Brock Road southward to the Po River (see Map 13, Appendix B). The alignment of the brigades in this position was, from west to east, as follows: Gregg, Anderson, Perry (Law), DuBose (Benning), and Bratton (Jenkins).[11] Field's Division repulsed numerous Federal assaults by the elements of the V and II Corps on May 8, 10, and 12 with little loss and remained in this position until May 15 (see Maps 14 and 15, Appendix B). On this date, the division was shifted to the extreme right of the army, between Massaponax Church Road and the Po River. The alignment of the brigades in this position was, from north to south, as follows: Gregg, Bratton, Perry, Anderson, and DuBose.[12] Field's men engaged in only light skirmishing in this position for the remainder of the battle.

During the next two battles of the campaign, Field's Division was only lightly engaged. At North Anna, the division was posted on the right of the First Corps next to the Second Corps south of the river (see Map 29, Appendix B).[13] Several of its brigades participated in some skirmishing against elements of the II Corps on May 24.[14] The division was again placed on the corps's center and right during the Battle of Totopotomoy (Bethesda Church) in late May (see Map 31, Appendix B).[15] During this action, the units again engaged in only limited skirmishing.

On June 1, Field's Division was moved southward to Cold Harbor and was placed on the left of the corps's front next to the Second Corps (see Map 36, Appendix B). With the exception of lending some support to a limited offensive movement conducted by the latter command the following day, this section of the battlefield remained relatively quiet. As a result, part of the division was shifted to the corps's right to support and ultimately relieve elements of Kershaw's Division on June 1 and 3 (see Maps 39 and 40, Appendix B).[16] These troops assisted in repulsing the massive Federal assault upon this section of the Confederate main line on the third with comparatively light loss.

Field's Division overall sustained heavy casualties during this campaign. Approximately two-thirds of these battle losses occurred at the Wilderness.

The division, however, recovered during June as many of the slightly wounded men returned to the ranks. Following Cold Harbor, Field's Division moved to Bermuda Hundred and relieved part of Bushrod Johnson's division (of Beauregard's Department of North Carolina and Southern Virginia). During the remainder of the year, it thwarted several Union attacks along the eastern approaches to Richmond and also participated in several battles in and around Petersburg.

The *Official Records* provide some information regarding the casualties in Field's Division during this campaign in the form of a table for the casualties in the brigades of Jenkins, Law, Benning, and Anderson.[17] These numbers are listed in the form of killed, wounded, and missing for officers and for enlisted men in the nineteen regiments of these brigades. The difficulty is that there is no notation regarding a dated period for these losses. At first glance, it appears that the list applies to the casualties at the Wilderness only. A comparison of the numbers with the compiled rosters of these units reveals that these numbers represent the losses for the first part of the campaign (the Wilderness through Spotsylvania). The casualty figures were derived from the report prepared by the chief surgeon for the division near the end of 1864.[18] It is important to note that the surgeon's report or list does not contain the names of officers and enlisted men slightly wounded during this period; these men returned to the ranks within one to several weeks. The wounded men noted in the surgeon's report were either furloughed and absent for months or were permanently disabled.

Gregg's Brigade

This organization, originally known as Hood's Texans or the Texas Brigade, was one the most famous units in the Army of Northern Virginia. The 1st, 4th, and 5th Texas were its core regiments. During the previous two years of the war, the brigade demonstrated a striking capability unmatched in Lee's infantry. On five occasions, this brigade assaulted and broke or drove back the opposing Federal forces. On several of these instances (for example, Gaines' Mill, Second Bull Run, and Chickamauga), the effort directly led to a Confederate victory. On the other two occasions, namely the cornfield at Antietam and Devil's Den at Gettysburg, its actions procured a temporary gain.

During much of 1862, Hood's Brigade actually had a mixed composition. The 18th Georgia Regiment was assigned in early 1862; the infantry component of Hampton's (South Carolina) Legion was added in June of the same year. After Antietam, these two non-Texan units were transferred to Wofford's and Jenkins's Brigades (respectively). In their place, the 3rd Arkansas was assigned. This regiment was the only unit in Lee's army from the state of Arkansas, and considering its geographic location (west of the Mississippi River adjacent to Texas), the assignment seemed like a natural arrangement. This brigade composition would persist for the rest of the war.

For most of 1863, Brig. Gen. Jerome B. Robertson led this brigade. During the ill-fated East Tennessee or Knoxville Campaign, General Longstreet filed charges against Robertson for apparent negative comments expressed regarding the corps commander's leadership. This action was apparently part of larger effort to remove disgruntled officers under his command, including General McLaws and Evander Law. In any event, the charges against Robertson failed to stand under scrutiny, but he transferred to a command in his home state of Texas.[1] In his place, John Gregg was assigned to command the brigade. Gregg, also a native of Texas, had previously served as a brigade commander in the Army of Tennessee.[2] He became available in late 1863 when his brigade was consolidated with other units in that army.

The Texas Brigade sustained a reported total of 1,215 casualties in 1863 (from the Battles of Gettysburg, Chickamauga, and Knoxville).[3] A study of available sources reveals that the command lost an additional 29 men during the siege of Suffolk in the spring.[4] This total loss of 1,244 men left the brigade significantly reduced in numbers. Gregg reportedly brought about 880 men in April 1864 from eastern Tennessee. Of this number, about 850 were committed to battle on May 6, the smallest strength in Field's Division. Judging by the muster rolls, another 80 men brought up the rear of the move from Tennessee and rejoined their units in May. This was the limit of the manpower reservoir for this brigade. There were virtually no new recruits.

On the morning of May 6, Gregg's Brigade was the second unit in Field's Division to arrive on the Wilderness battlefield. By the fortunes of war, however, it was the first of its brigades to be committed into action. The command deployed north of Orange Plank Road on the western edge of the Widow Tapp field (see Map 6, Appendix B). During this deployment, Federal forces, fresh from their rout of Hill's corps, began emerging from the dense woods at the opposite (eastern) edge of this field. General Lee was present at this critical moment and was determined to observe the advance of the Texans and Arkansans. The rank and file of the brigade responded by shouting, "General Lee to the rear," and refused to advance until he complied with their pleas. Lee resolved to follow their direction and moved out of danger.[5]

Gregg's Brigade then charged the massing Federals and halted their advance.[6] In the process, its regiments lost over one-half of their men. Although it was not apparent at that time, this assault would be the sixth and penultimate successful charge of the Texas Brigade during the war. Benning's and Law's Brigades from Field's Division arrived at the battlefield next and were committed in the same area. Following this action, the Texans and Arkansans were placed in reserve for the remainder of the battle.

Several pertinent comments regarding the status of Gregg's Brigade at this time are found in a unit history of the 3rd Arkansas by Calvin Collier. In this work, Collier mentions that, in the night march from the Wilderness to Spotsylvania, the brigade's column was discernible from the other elements in the First Corps by the high number of white bandages clearly visible on very slightly wounded men. He also states that the brigade had sustained about 65-percent casualties on May 6 and that, in the 3rd Arkansas, only 90 men were reported unhurt after the charge at the Widow Tapp field. On the following day, the number of men unhurt or very slightly wounded reported present for duty was about 125.[7]

At Spotsylvania, Gregg's Brigade participated in the defense of the Laurel Ridge position on May 8, 10, and 12 (see Maps 13 and 14, Appendix B). Many of the losses sustained at this battle occurred during the evening of May 10, when elements of the II Corps attacked and achieved a short-lived lodgment in the sector held by this command (see Map 15, Appendix B). With the assistance from Anderson's Brigade (also of Field's Division), the Texans and Arkansans repulsed these enemy forces.[8] The brigade was very lightly engaged at North Anna and Totopotomoy (Bethesda Church).

But Gregg's Brigade saw action on June 1 and 3 at Cold Harbor. On the first of these days, elements of the brigade were dispatched to the relief of Bryan's and Wofford's Brigades next to Bloody Run (see Map 35, Appendix B).[9] On June 3, the command assisted in the repulse of the massive Federal assault during the early morning hours.[10] The brigade had relieved Kershaw's Division and held a sector between Bloody Run and Central Ravine (see Maps 39 and 40, Appendix B). The attacking troops were part of the VI and XVIII Corps. For the balance of this day and the following approximately six days, this portion of the line was subjected to considerable enemy sniping and artillery fire.

Gregg's Brigade emerged from this campaign with slightly more than 500 men, a number early in the war considered a typical size for one regiment. The strength of the command rose to about 600 in a few weeks as the slightly wounded from the Wilderness returned. During the remainder of 1864, the brigade participated in battles associated with the siege of Petersburg and Richmond and endured another 308 casualties. The command continued to perform reliably; however, in view of their diminished strength, the Texans and Arkansans never again solely influenced the outcome of a battle. General Gregg was killed in action on October 8 outside Richmond during the last major charge of the brigade in the war.

The casualties for this historic command during the Overland Campaign are provided in Table 24, Appendix A. The accuracy and competency of the casualty records for this brigade vary. Two of the Richmond newspapers published the casualties for the two of three Texas regiments at Wilderness and Spotsylvania (May 10 and 12).[11] A more complete tabulation is found in Col. Harold B. Simpson's *Hood's Texas Brigade: A Compendium.* The June 29 issue of the *Petersburg Daily Express* published a list of casualties for the 3rd Arkansas for the period May 6–June 5.[12] This list fails to provide a breakdown of losses by battle and appears to omit many of the slightly wounded men who returned to the unit by this date.

Jenkins's/Bratton's Brigade

Micah Jenkins's brigade was, during the first years of the war, part of Pickett's Division. The command consisted of South Carolina units and, accordingly, was the only non-Virginia element in the division. During the Gettysburg Campaign, Jenkins's Brigade was retained by the War Department to defend the approaches to Richmond. When Lee's army returned to Virginia, the four Virginia brigades in Pickett's Division were sent to Richmond and the southeastern part of the state to provide a garrison force for the capital, reform, and recruit. Jenkins's Brigade then was reassigned to Hood's Division in part to compensate for losses suffered by that command at Gettysburg.

Jenkins's South Carolinians had forged an excellent fighting reputation in 1862, starting with the action at Glendale on June 30, but through no fault of their own, they managed to avoid serious combat for over a year. The brigade held a quiet sector during the Battle of Fredericksburg and missed the subsequent battles of Chancellorsville and Gettysburg. This span of combat misfortune (or fortune) continued into September 1863 with the movement of Hood's Division to Georgia and Tennessee. Although the brigade was clearly the largest and freshest unit in the division, it arrived at Chickamauga after the fighting. By this time, the South Carolinians were spoiling for action. They finally found it on the night of October 28–29 at Wauhatchie, or Lookout Valley (outside Chattanooga). During this engagement, Jenkins's Brigade sparred with elements of the Second Division, XII Corps inconclusively for several hours in the dark.[1] The brigade later participated in the siege of Knoxville.

The reported number of casualties for Jenkins's Brigade for 1863 was 526 men.[2] This figure was significantly below those of the other brigades in Hood's (Field's) Division. As a consequence, Jenkins's command fielded the largest force in the division in the spring of 1864 (almost 1,600 men). That strength was reduced to some degree in early 1864 with the transfer of Hampton's Legion to South Carolina (for conversion to a cavalry unit). The composition of the brigade then was as follows: 1st, 5th, and 6th South Carolina Regiments; 2nd South Carolina Rifles (regiment); and the Palmetto (South Carolina) Sharpshooters Regiment. These units were raised from the central and northern portions of the state. As with the other commands in the First Corps, Jenkins's Brigade was able to recover and maintain its strength throughout the campaign with some new recruits and personnel bringing up the rear in the return from Tennessee. Of side interest, the latter group included the entire band for the 2nd South Carolina Rifles.

On the morning of May 6, Jenkins's Brigade was one of the last in Field's Division to arrive at the Wilderness. The command was first posted in reserve (see Map 6, Appendix B). Late in the morning, though, it advanced astride Orange Plank Road in conjunction with the flanking movement by other Confederate elements against the Federal left flank (see Map 7, Appendix B). This combined assault was very successful. But in the confusion of battle and the heavy woods and underbrush, General Jenkins was killed by the same friendly fire that wounded Longstreet. Col. John Bratton of the 6th South Carolina Regiment then assumed temporary command of the brigade.[3]

In the late afternoon, the South Carolinians assaulted the enemy breastworks along Brock Road. The opposing Federals initially stopped the Confederate advance short of the defenses. In one sector, the woods in front of the Union line caught fire, and the flames spread to the adjacent breastworks. The Federals in this sector, part of the Fourth Division, II Corps, retreated in confusion. Elements of Jenkins's and Anderson's Brigades reportedly rushed into the breach; however, they were counterattacked by elements of the Second Division of the same corps and driven out.[4] There appears to be some confusion regarding the positions and actions of the Confederate units involved in this assault, but the casualty returns reveal that the 5th South Carolina appears to have been one of the units that gained a temporary lodgment in the burning breastworks.

At the Battle of Spotsylvania, Jenkins's (Bratton's) Brigade participated in the successful defense of Laurel Ridge (see Maps 13 and 15, Appendix B). The South Carolinians defended the right portion of the divisional front (next to Kershaw's Division). Elements of the brigade (reportedly the Palmetto Sharpshooters) also helped repel a Union attempt to move on the right flank of Kershaw's Division at dusk of May 8.[5] They were joined by the newly arriving troops of Rodes's Division of the Second Corps. During the evening of May 12, the South Carolinians were posted in a rear defense line at the Mule Shoe. After darkness, they covered the withdrawal of the units that had faced the Federal onslaught for much of that day.[6] Most of the casualties sustained by the brigade during this battle occurred on these two days (May 8 and 12).

For the remainder of the campaign, Bratton's Brigade (now renamed) engaged in only minor skirmishing; this included the Battles of North Anna, Totopotomoy, and Cold Harbor. The casualties in the brigade in each of these actions were very small. At Cold Harbor, it was posted on the left portion of the division and corps sector. On June 2, the command assisted elements of the Second Corps in a reconnaissance astride the Mechanicsville Road against the V Corps. Otherwise, the South Carolinians' sector of the line remained relatively quiet.

Bratton's Brigade emerged from Cold Harbor in a comparatively sound condition. The command still fielded the largest strength in the division. In the subsequent months, it saw considerable action during the siege of Petersburg and Richmond. During these actions, the South Carolinians sustained over 800 casualties, the heaviest in the division.

The degree of coverage of the units of this brigade in the South Carolina newspapers varied widely. Comprehensive casualty lists were found for the 2nd South Carolina Rifles, 5th South Carolina, and the Palmetto Sharpshooters for both the Wilderness and Spotsylvania. The casualty list for the first of these units was not differentiated by battle or date. A casualty list of the 6th South Carolina was found only for the Wilderness.[7] Partial listings for only two companies in the 1st South Carolina were found (see Table 25, Appendix A).

Benning's Brigade

Henry L. "Rock" Benning was a prominent lawyer and judge from Georgia. During 1862 and 1863, he periodically led this brigade of four Georgia regiments in the absence of its original commander, Robert Toombs. When the latter resigned in March 1863, Benning was promoted to brigadier general and permanently assigned to command of the brigade. The men of his original unit, the 17th Georgia Regiment, reportedly gave him the nickname of "The Rock."[1] Under Benning's leadership, the Georgians performed well at Antietam, Gettysburg, and Chickamauga. At the first of these battles, the brigade delayed the advance of Burnside's IX Corps for much of the day, while at the second engagement it stormed and carried the Federal line at Devil's Den (with the Texas Brigade) on the second day. At Chickamauga, it was part of Longstreet's force that routed the Federal right and ultimately led to the Confederate victory. The four Georgia regiments (2nd, 15th, 17th, and 20th) were recruited from widely scattered areas of the state.

These battle triumphs did not come without a price. Benning's Brigade reported a total of 1,003 casualties for the year 1863.[2] As a result of these battle losses in 1863, the command fielded less than 1,000 men at the start of the Overland Campaign. The return of men from wounded furlough and elements bringing up the rear of the move from eastern Tennessee brought about 165–175 more troops to the ranks, but these additions were quickly consumed by the losses in this campaign. The 2nd and 17th Georgia, in particular, were significantly reduced at this stage of the war.

Benning's Brigade followed Gregg's Brigade in the march to the Wilderness on May 6. The Georgians similarly deployed along the same ground on the northern side of Orange Plank Road. As Gregg's command was reeling from its losses, the Georgians then similarly charged into the mass of Federals advancing into the Widow Tapp field (see Map 6, Appendix B). Although less historically publicized than Gregg's charge, Benning's attack also played a key role in stopping the Union advance.[3] As illustrated in Table 26 in Appendix A, the Georgians suffered heavy losses of nearly 30 percent. General Benning was severely wounded during this charge and essentially lost for much of the remaining war. Command of the brigade then devolved upon Col. Dudley M. DuBose of the 15th Georgia Regiment. Following this attack, the brigade was placed in reserve for the balance of the battle.

Benning's Brigade thereafter participated in the remaining battles of the campaign with Field's Division. At Spotsylvania the command assisted in repulsing Federal assaults against the Laurel Ridge position on May 8, 10, and 12 (see Maps 13 and 15, Appendix B). According to a member of the 20th Georgia, much of the brigade's losses in this battle occurred on picket duty or skirmishing in front of the main line of earthworks on May 9–12.[4] At North Anna, Totopotomoy, and Cold Harbor, the brigade was fortunate to be positioned in relatively quiet sectors. At the latter battle, it occupied the middle to left portion of the divisional front (next to the Second Corps).

As mentioned above, Benning's Brigade finished the campaign in a relatively intact but somewhat reduced condition. An examination of the unit rosters indicates that the strength of the command had fallen to about 770 men. Like the other units in Field's Division, the Georgians saw more action during the final year at Petersburg and outside Richmond, sustaining an estimated 275 casualties in these actions.

It is possible that the actual number of casualties sustained by Benning's Brigade at the Wilderness could have been slightly higher (see Table 26). The May 27 issue of Atlanta's *Daily Intelligencer* published a complete list of the casualties for the brigade at these battles by date (through May 12).[5] The losses for the 15th Georgia at the Wilderness appear to be questionable. The percentage loss is substantially below those for the other three units in the brigade, and it lists more men as casualties at Spotsylvania than at the Wilderness for some of the companies. This is somewhat surprising given the record of the brigade at these battles. It is possible that some of these men were erroneously listed by the publisher.

In addition, earlier printed lists for casualties for the 17th and 20th Georgia at the Wilderness were found in two other Georgia newspapers (*the Macon Daily Telegraph* and the *Daily Columbus Enquirer*).[6] These sources list several slightly wounded men not included in the subsequent Atlanta newspaper's issue. In light of these observations and findings, Table 26 assumes that the 15th Georgia sustained an additional loss of seven slightly wounded men at the Wilderness. Henderson's roster of Georgia troops was also beneficial for the study of this brigade.[7]

Law's Brigade

This command of Alabama troops was the last brigade in the First Corps to be organized on a state or regional basis. It was formed after Antietam and Fredericksburg by the transfer of regiments from three other brigades. Specifically, the 44th, 47th, and 48th Alabama Regiments had served with other divisions in the corps, while the 15th Alabama Regiment had been an integral part of Trimble's mixed brigade (of Ewell's Division) in Lt. Gen. Thomas "Stonewall" Jackson's Second Corps. These units joined the 4th Alabama Regiment. All had been recruited from the eastern and central portions of the state. Col. Evander M. Law of the 4th Alabama led the parent brigade for most of 1862 in first Whiting's and then Hood's Division. Law was actually a native of South Carolina and was promoted to brigadier general and permanent command in late 1862.

Following this reorganization, Law's Brigade established a solid fighting reputation. The brigade lost heavily at Gettysburg and Chickamauga and was engaged later at Wauhatchie and Knoxville. At Gettysburg the Alabamans tried desperately to take Little Round Top on July 2 from elements of the V Corps led by Col. Strong Vincent and Col. Joshua Chamberlain. The total number of reported casualties for these 1863 battles was 1,044 men. Compilation of the unit rolls reveals that the brigade sustained another 110 casualties during the siege of Suffolk in the spring of 1863.[1]

During the East Tennessee Campaign the following winter, the siege of Knoxville went poorly for the Confederates. In its aftermath, James Longstreet looked for failure in the performance of some of his subordinates. Law was one of the men singled out for complaint. In response, Law composed a letter of resignation and journeyed to Richmond to file it with the War Department. His superior, Major General Hood, was convalescing from wounds in the capital city and came to his support, persuading Law to relent.[2] In several months the conflict died down, and Law returned to his command during the third week of May 1864.

During the absence of General Law, Col. William F. Perry of the 44th Alabama Regiment led the brigade. The strength of the command at this time was only about 1,255 men. On the morning of May 6, the brigade followed Benning's command in the march to the Wilderness. The Alabamians were first committed to attack advancing Union forces north of Orange Plank Road (see Map 6, Appendix B). The 4th and 47th Alabama supported

Benning's Georgians in the Widow Tapp field and met with a similar experience.[3] These two regiments lost heavily but succeeded in halting the Federal advance.

The remaining three regiments in Law's Brigade, the 15th, 44th, and 48th Alabama, veered to the left and entered dense woods north of this field. The 15th collided with elements of Kitching's brigade of heavy artillery serving as infantry and easily routed them; it was these Federals' first experience in battle. The 44th and 48th Alabama, conversely, encountered most of the Fourth Division, V Corps and found themselves in a desperate fight against a superior force. The 15th came to their rescue. After routing Kitching, the regiment wheeled to the right and caught the Fourth Division in the flank.[4] A lull occurred in the battle after this fighting, and Law's Brigade reformed in the woods north-northeast of the Widow Tapp field.

In midafternoon, two divisions of the IX Corps advanced upon the Alabamians' position (see Map 8, Appendix B). Brig. Gen. Edward Perry's Florida brigade (of the Third Corps) was deployed to the left. After a desperate fight in the woods and ravines, this superior Federal force enveloped and routed these two brigades.[5] Both General Perry and Col. William Perry were wounded at this time; Colonel Perry refused to leave the field. The commitment of reserve units from the Third Corps (Perrin's, Harris's, and Stone's Brigades) halted the Federal advance and averted a disaster in this part of the battlefield.

Along with the other units in Field's Division, Law's Brigade participated in the defense of the Laurel Ridge position at Spotsylvania on May 8–12. The Alabamians were the first unit of the division to arrive at this battlefield. They were initially posted to the left of Henagan's brigade (of Kershaw's Division) and assisted greatly in repulsing the second assault of the V Corps (see Map 12, Appendix B).[6] The majority of the casualties sustained by the brigade at Spotsylvania occurred during this action. Later in the day, Law's Brigade moved to the center of the divisional front (see Maps 13 and 15, Appendix B). On May 15, the command shifted to the army's right and was posted next to the Po River facing east. General Law reportedly returned and resumed command on May 18.[7]

Law's Brigade was present at the remaining battles of the campaign but saw action only at North Anna and Cold Harbor. At North Anna the Alabamians were deployed on the right end of the divisional front. Elements of all five regiments engaged in active skirmishing against the II Corps on May

24 (see Map 29, Appendix B).[8] At Cold Harbor the brigade was one of three units sent by General Field to the assistance of Kershaw's Division during the evening of June 1 after the Federals had broken through the main Confederate line. Elements of Law's Brigade helped repel this enemy force at darkness.[9] The Alabamians then relieved a portion of Kershaw's men and constructed a new line of earthworks. This sector was assaulted by elements of the XVIII Corps on the morning of June 3; the Alabamians had little difficulty in repulsing this attack (see Map 40, Appendix B). General Law was seriously wounded on this day; Colonel Perry then resumed brigade command.[10]

Law's Brigade emerged from the Overland Campaign in a sound condition, though for the first time in the war, its strength fell below 1,000 men. Most of the slightly wounded returned to the ranks, but given the need for troops to contend with Sherman's advance through Georgia, there were few if any new recruits. The brigade continued to see considerable action during the rest of the year at Petersburg and outside Richmond. The records are relatively incomplete for these battles, but the cost to the brigade was at least 350 additional casualties.

The degree of coverage of this brigade in the Southern newspapers varied greatly. Casualty lists were found in Alabama and Richmond newspapers for the 4th, 15th, and 47th Alabama, covering the major battles of the brigade (the Wilderness, Spotsylvania, and Cold Harbor).[11] For the remaining two regiments, little to nothing has been found. The *Selma Daily Reporter* provided a correspondence letter with the casualties in the 44th Alabama from May 16 through June 8.[12] Nothing has ever been found in the newspapers regarding the casualties in the 48th Alabama. This unit was originally recruited from the more-mountainous and sparsely populated northern portion of the state.

The casualties for Law's Brigade are provided in Table 27, Appendix A. In view of the lack of newspapers found covering the 44th and 48th Alabama, it is possible that casualties in these units could have been higher. This especially applies to the Battle of the Wilderness. The percentage of total casualties and percentage of wounded to killed in the 48th Regiment appear to be especially low. In view of these observations and the lack of records for this unit, it is estimated that it sustained at least five additional slightly wounded men (raising their total loss to thirty-eight men). Compared to the losses in the other regiments in the brigade, the casualties in the 44th Alabama appear misplaced or somewhat in error. The total for the Wilderness is comparatively low, while that for Spotsylvania appears to be relatively high. The muster rolls for this unit and the 48th Regiment were the worst in the brigade. In view of these factors, some of the casualties reported for the 44th Regiment at Spotsylvania could have occurred at the Wilderness.

Anderson's Brigade

George T. Anderson's Brigade of Georgians had a long history with the Army of Northern Virginia. The lowest-numbered two units, the 7th and 8th Georgia Regiments, fought alongside Jackson's Stonewall Brigade atop Henry Hill and lost heavily at First Bull Run. From that action, the Georgia brigade was a solid mainstay in the army and was present at every major battle. The original commander of the organization was David R. Jones. During most of 1862, Jones temporarily commanded a division in Longstreet's corps. In his absence, George Anderson led the brigade. Jones ultimately had to resign for health reasons, and Anderson was promoted to brigadier general and permanently assigned to brigade command.

Anderson's Brigade originally consisted of five veteran units—1st (Regulars), 7th, 8th, 9th, and 11th Georgia Regiments. In early 1863, the 1st Georgia (Regulars) Regiment was ordered to its home state for assignment and to recruit. The 59th Georgia Regiment replaced it.[1] This unit had been formed from the 7th Regiment, Georgia State Troops and proved to be a worthy addition. These regiments were raised from counties in the western and central portions of the state. In 1863, Anderson's Brigade sustained heavy casualties at Gettysburg; in a follow-up engagement at Funkstown, Maryland; and at the siege of Knoxville. (The Georgians did not arrive in time to participate at Chickamauga.) The total reported number of casualties from these battles was 1,095 men.[2]

The absence of Anderson's Brigade at Chickamauga proved to be beneficial for the organization. In early 1864, it fielded the second largest strength in Field's Division (about 1,390 men, second to Jenkins's Brigade). During May and June, a steady number of men returned to the ranks from detachment in eastern Tennessee and from wounded and sick furlough.

During the morning of May 6, Anderson's Brigade was the lead unit in Field's Division in the march to the Wilderness. Upon reaching the battlefield, General Field deployed the brigade on the southern side of Orange

Plank Road in support of Kershaw's Division.[3] The Georgians stayed in reserve in this position and missed the first phase of desperate fighting in the early morning between the First Corps and the II Corps and the Fourth Division, V Corps (see Map 6, Appendix B). In retrospect, Anderson's Brigade could have been the first unit committed against the Federals on the northern side of this road and gained notoriety by halting their advance. By the chances of war, this experience and accomplishment fell to Gregg's, Benning's, and Law's Brigades.

After a lull in fighting for several hours, Longstreet attacked the Federal forces in this part of the battlefield with a combined frontal and flanking assault. Anderson's Brigade was one of the units chosen to participate in the flanking attack. The Georgians were posted in the front line to the right of Mahone's Brigade (see Map 7, Appendix B).[4] Longstreet's flank attack first routed the Fourth Division, II Corps and then rolled up the entire enemy line. The Federals were forced to retire to their breastworks along Brock Road.

Late in the afternoon, Anderson's Brigade took part in the assault upon these breastworks. The brigade was deployed to the left of Jenkins's Brigade. A portion of the breastworks caught fire during the fighting, and Union troops fell back in disorder. Most of Anderson's men reportedly rushed into the breach.[5] The Georgians soon were repulsed by elements of the Second Division, II Corps, which moved forward from reserve. Judging by the reported casualties (see Table 28, Appendix A), the 8th, 9th, and 11th Georgia experienced the worst of this action. In a letter published by the *Confederate Union* on June 7, an officer in the 8th Georgia revealed that the retirement from the burning fieldworks began with the 9th Georgia, which was forced to retire by enemy enfilading fire.[6] Each of the other units in the brigade was, in turn, subjected to this same fire and similarly forced to retire.

At Spotsylvania, Anderson's Brigade primarily participated in the defense of Laurel Ridge (see Maps 13 and 14, Appendix B). During an enemy assault upon this position on May 10, elements of the brigade assisted Gregg's Brigade in repelling a limited Federal breakthrough in the latter's sector (to the Georgians' left; see Map 15, Appendix B).[7] Like the other units in Field's Division, Anderson's Brigade was lightly engaged at North Anna and Totopotomoy (Bethesda Church).

The brigade saw more action at Cold Harbor. The command was one of the three brigades dispatched by Field on June 1 to assist Kershaw's Division.

Just before dusk, elements of the VI and XVIII Corps attacked Kershaw and Hoke's lines. The enemy forces found a gap between these divisions and routed and partially enveloped the units posted next to this gap. In Kershaw's command, the principal units affected by this Union success were Wofford's and Bryan's fellow Georgian brigades. Anderson's men rushed to the assistance of these commands and helped repel the Federals.[8] The Georgians held a sector of the main line on June 3 and easily repulsed the massive Federal assault upon their front (see Maps 39 and 40, Appendix B).[9]

Compared to the other commands in Field's Division, Anderson's Brigade emerged from this campaign in a relatively effective condition. It continued to field one of the larger strengths in the division. The loss in line officers during May, however, had been very heavy. During the remainder of 1864, the Georgians were frequently ordered into action. They saw combat in June, August, September, and October outside the approaches to both Petersburg and Richmond. The brigade sustained at least 400 more casualties during these engagements, bringing the total loss for the year to over 1,000 men.

The casualties for Anderson's Brigade during the Overland Campaign are provided in Table 28 in Appendix A, with the highest percentage occurring at the Wilderness. The nominal list of casualties in Field's Division reveals that this command sustained additional losses at Spotsylvania from May 8 through 14 and at Cold Harbor from June 1 through 5. As could be expected, the highest daily loss at these battles occurred on May 10 and June 1. The availability of newspaper casualty lists for the units of this brigade varies widely. Casualty lists were found for the brigade sharpshooter battalion (which included men from all five regiments) and the 8th, 9th, and 59th Georgia Regiments, covering the Wilderness through Spotsylvania (or North Anna).[10] For the 7th Georgia, a list was found for only one company. Nothing was found for the 11th Georgia.

The actual casualties in Anderson's Brigade may have been slightly higher. The commander of the 59th Georgia, Col. Jack Brown, filed and provided the casualty reports for his regiment in the *Macon Daily Telegraph.* In a second report (in the June 4 issue), he states that there were a great many more men who were slightly wounded and were back with the regiment. Unfortunately, their names are not mentioned. Brown's statement probably applies not only to his unit but also to the other regiments in the brigade. Lillian Henderson's *Roster* was also checked for the study of this brigade.[11]

PICKETT'S DIVISION

Because of one charge on one day at the Battle of Gettysburg, Maj. Gen. George E. Pickett's Division is regarded among the best-known units in the Army of Northern Virginia. This command is also recognized as being composed exclusively of brigades from the state of Virginia, the only infantry division in the army to have this distinction. The actual historical facts reveal a slightly different picture. Pickett's Division contained one brigade from South Carolina (Jenkins) until the late summer of 1863. After Gettysburg, this non-Virginia unit was transferred to Hood's Division. Pickett's command was then left with the four Virginia brigades of Kemper, Hunton (formerly Garnett), Barton (formerly Armistead), and Corse. It should also be stated that only Kemper, Garnett, and Armistead participated in the famous charge at Gettysburg. Before Lee's march north, the War Department (that is, Pres. Jefferson Davis) had detached the brigades of Jenkins and Corse from the army to safeguard Richmond. Following the retreat from Gettysburg, the four Virginia brigades spent most the remaining portion of 1863 and the first part of 1864 near Richmond, protecting the capital and recuperating from their recent combat losses.

In the early spring of 1864, Pickett's Division was a division in name only. Two brigades were dispatched to eastern North Carolina to participate in operations against Federal garrisons in coastal ports, while the remaining two brigades were officially part of the Richmond garrison. Pickett was the head of the Department of North Carolina and Southern Virginia, with his headquarters in Petersburg. In view of an impending major Federal threat, General Beauregard was appointed as the head of this department in late April. Pickett was then relegated to a subordinate position at Petersburg with command of a few local troops.

The concentration of Maj. Gen. Benjamin Butler's Army of the James in the eastern approaches to Richmond in early May forced a drastic change in the Confederate command and the rapid return of units from North Carolina and the other coastal states. In the early stages of this Federal concentration, it was not clear if Butler was planning to march upon Richmond or Petersburg. Due to the destruction of a key bridge by a well-coordinated Union cavalry raid, Beauregard was unable to reach Richmond until May 10. The weight of command there thus initially fell upon Pickett, who was able to ward off a weak foray upon Petersburg by scratching together local units and temporarily detaining some of the first regular-army units moving to Richmond. The stress of the situation, however, wore heavily on his health. As soon as Beauregard arrived in the capital, Pickett reported himself sick and declined to accept command of one of the new divisions formed by the department commander.[1]

In any event, three of Pickett's brigades were assigned to separate temporary divisions in Beauregard's new army. They participated in the Battles of Drewry's Bluff and Howlett's House (Bermuda Hundred) in mid-May and shared in the triumphs over Butler's army.[2] The fourth brigade remained with the Richmond garrison and was lightly engaged against Sheridan's cavalry north of the capital during the second week of May.

In response to entreaties from General Lee and the success over Butler, Pickett's Division was reunited and returned to the Army of Northern Virginia on May 20–21.[3] The strength of the division at this stage of the Overland Campaign was about 5,340 men. From this point in the campaign, the division was present at all the battles but provided minor contributions. During the movement to rejoin Lee's army, elements of one brigade were engaged against Federal cavalry at Milford Station on May 21. At North Anna, the division was aligned together for the first time since Gettysburg but was mainly kept in reserve behind Hill's Third Corps on the army's left (see Map 29, Appendix B).[4] At Totopotomoy (Bethesda Church) in late May, the command was deployed astride the Shady Grove Road in the corps's right (see Map 31, Appendix B).[5] The losses to the division at both of these battles were nearly negligible. It should be mentioned that Pickett was ordered to assault the V Corps near Bethesda Church on May 30 in conjunction with an attack by elements of Early's Second Corps (see Map 32, Appendix B). After a weak attempt, though, Pickett and his superior, Richard Anderson, abandoned the effort.[6]

At Cold Harbor, Pickett's Division was again positioned in the center of the corps's line (See Map 35, Appendix B). The arraignment of the division was (from north to south) as follows: Kemper (under Colonel Terry), Barton, and Corse; Hunton's Brigade was posted in reserve.[7] The division remained in this position and alignment during the remainder of the battle. For the most part, this portion of the Confederate line remained a quiet sector, though the division's right wing repulsed the northernmost fringe of the massive Union assault on June 3. The entire division front was subjected to significant sniping and skirmishing for four days thereafter. On the evening of June 1, the divisional reserve was dispatched to the southern portion of the battlefield, where it saw considerable action.

At the conclusion of this campaign, Pickett's Division fielded the largest strength in the First Corps (see Table 3, Appendix A). The division easily maintained this condition or ranking for the remainder of the year. The combat losses were small, especially when compared to Kershaw's and Field's Divisions. In addition, Pickett's brigades were continually supplied with new recruits and conscripts from Virginia.

After Cold Harbor, the division experienced and regained one bit of its past glory. In response to heavy Union attacks by Grant's army against Petersburg in mid-June (after Cold Harbor), Beauregard pulled Bushrod Johnson's Division from the Howlett line at Bermuda Hundred. This strategic move uncovered one of the principal approaches to Richmond for Butler's army. As soon as Johnson withdrew his troops, Butler slowly pushed his advance forces into this line of defenses. Lee, still north of the James River, was initially slow to recognize the Federal intentions. Once he discerned that Grant had left his front for Petersburg, Lee quickly moved to Beauregard's aid. Kershaw's Division and the Third Corps were sent to Petersburg, but Pickett's Division (supported by Field's Division) was assigned the task of recapturing the abandoned works at Bermuda Hundred. Fortunately for the Confederate cause, Butler was slow to recognize the opportunity presented by the removal of Johnson's Division. He advanced tentatively beyond the newly captured earthworks and then made a hasty withdrawal when attacked by Pickett on June 16.[8] The assault to regain this line, which was well directed and executed, cost the division only about 200 casualties.

For the remainder of 1864, Pickett's Division remained in this relatively quiet and inactive sector of the defenses covering the eastern approaches to Richmond and Petersburg. During June–October, Grant's army continually made excursions against critical road and railroad arteries supplying both cities. Despite the facts that Pickett was now the senior divisional commander in the entire army and that his troops were relatively fresh, at no time were his units dispatched to contest these Federal movements and attacks. The tasks of combatting these excursions was left to the often overworked units of Kershaw's and Field's Divisions, most of the Third Corps, and Hoke's and Bushrod Johnson's Divisions.

Starting in May 1864 and continuing through the winter of 1864–65, Pickett's Division had the highest desertion and absence rate in the army. A rough compilation of the available muster rolls indicates that the division lost over 450 men in this manner between May and December 1864. This may have been due to the high percentage of conscripts in the command and other factors such as morale and leadership. It should also be recognized that Pickett's regiments were recruited primarily from the southern part of the Commonwealth in areas located within proximity of Richmond and Petersburg. Compared to the rest of Lee's army, many of the men choosing to desert from these units had a high chance of reaching home safely.

Kemper's Brigade

Although listed on the army rolls as Kemper's Brigade, this organization was actually under the command of the senior colonel, William R. Terry of the 24th Virginia Regiment. Its brigadier, John L. Kemper, was seriously wounded and captured at Gettysburg during the fabled charge on July 3. Kemper was exchanged prior to the start of the campaign, but the severity of his wound kept him from actively serving in the field for the remainder of the war. The general was given a position with the Virginia State Reserves, and soon thereafter, Terry was promoted to brigadier general and permanent command of the brigade.

According to the official brigade report and a recent study, Kemper's Brigade sustained a reported 685 or 779 casualties at Gettysburg.[1] It was the only battle for the unit in 1863 (it was present at the siege of Suffolk in the spring of this year but had no reported casualties in the *Official Records*). The brigade also participated in the siege of Plymouth in the spring of 1864 and sustained a small loss during this successful campaign. Kemper's Brigade was restored to its pre-Gettysburg strength with the return of many of the wounded and exchanged prisoners from that battle and the injection of numerous recruits during the early months of 1864. The charge at Gettysburg had cost the brigade most of its field and line officers and noncommissioned officers. An examination of the unit rolls reveals that the Federals were comparatively slow to exchange these categories of personnel. As a consequence, the regiments had many absent personnel in these leadership positions at the start of the campaign.

The five regiments comprising this brigade were originally recruited from varied parts of the state. The 1st Virginia Regiment was raised in Richmond. The 3rd Virginia Regiment came from the Tidewater region, while most of the 7th Virginia Regiment was recruited from counties in northern Virginia. Lastly, the 11th and 24th Virginia Regiments were raised from the Piedmont region.

At the beginning of May 1864, Kemper's Brigade was still present in North Carolina with the forces led by Maj. Gen. Robert F. Hoke. In response to the concentration of Union forces led by Benjamin Butler east of Richmond and Petersburg in early May, the brigade (less the 3rd Virginia) was moved to Richmond during the second week of May and joined those units being assembled under General Beauregard. Kemper's Brigade was assigned to Maj. Gen. Robert Ransom's division and participated in the battle at Drewry's Bluff on May 15 and 16, losing a confirmed 352 casualties in the four regiments present (the 1st, 7th, 11th, and 24th Virginia).[2]

During the evening and night of May 20, elements of the 1st, 7th, and 11th Virginia were moved by rail to Milford Station on the Mattaponi River. From this point, the force was expected to march to Spotsylvania to rejoin Lee's army. As the troops broke camp in the early morning hours of the twenty-first, friendly cavalry scouts arrived and warned them that a large body of Federal cavalry was advancing upon their camp. The enemy force was actually Brig. Gen. Alfred Torbert's division, and it was the van of the entire II Corps. These Confederates attempted to delay the Federals, but a portion of men from the 7th and 11th Virginia got trapped on the eastern side of the river and were captured.[3] The remainder of Kemper's Brigade along with Corse's Brigade arrived shortly thereafter. These units took up positions to the southeast and south of Milford Station and effectively blocked any further enemy advance.[4]

Kemper's Brigade withdrew the following day and joined Lee's army for the remainder of the campaign. The Virginians were present at North Anna, Totopotomoy, and Cold Harbor but were only lightly engaged in all three of these battles; the only measurable loss occurred at Cold Harbor. The 3rd Virginia rejoined the brigade from North Carolina in late May.

Casualties for this brigade (see Table 29, Appendix A) are well documented. The Richmond newspapers provided comprehensive lists for the battle losses at Drewry's Bluff for each of the four regiments engaged at this battle. The May 26 issue of the *Lynchburg Virginian* provided some casualties and details regarding the units engaged at Milford Station.[5] The respective books of the Virginia Regimental Histories Series were also consulted in the research of this brigade.[6]

Hunton's Brigade

Like Kemper's, this brigade had also sustained very heavy casualties (943 men) at Gettysburg and had spent much of 1863 and early 1864 recovering from this loss.[1] Col. Eppa Hunton of the 8th Virginia Regiment, himself wounded at Gettysburg, had been promoted to the replace the fallen Brig. Gen. Richard B. Garnett. During this period of recuperation, Hunton's Brigade experienced many of the same changes in personnel and deficiencies in line officers and noncommissioned officers as Kemper's Brigade. At the beginning of May, the command actually fielded more men in the ranks than a year earlier at Gettysburg.[2] There also was a minor change to the organization of the brigade at this time. The 18th Virginia Regiment had been temporarily assigned to Corse's Brigade (Pickett's Division), and in its place, the 32nd Virginia Regiment was temporarily assigned from Corse to this command.

The five original units in this brigade came from many areas of Virginia. The 8th Regiment was recruited from the northernmost counties of the state. This area was foremost "Mosby" country, and from 1863, this unit suffered a considerable loss in personnel deserting to join this partisan command. The 18th Regiment was raised from counties in the south-central part of the state, while the 19th Regiment was enlisted from counties in and around Charlottesville. The 28th Regiment was recruited from the Piedmont region, and lastly, the 56th Regiment was raised from the central part of the state.

During the first part of May, Hunton's Brigade was part of the Richmond defenses.[3] As a result, the command was not present at the various battles against Butler's Union forces. The brigade did, however, see some combat during the second week of May. As a part of the overall Federal plan to take the war to Lee's army, the bulk of Sheridan's Cavalry Corps left Grant's main army on May 9 and rode southward toward Richmond. Maj. Gen. Jeb Stuart followed with a portion of his cavalry and contested the Federal advance at Yellow Tavern on May 11. This battle resulted in the mortal wounding of Stuart and a Union victory. Fresh from this success, Sheridan's cavalry moved on to the northern approaches to the capital the next day. Hunton's Brigade, together with others troops from the Richmond garrison and Stuart's cavalry, blocked them. Sheridan skirmished with Hunton's 19th and 32nd Virginia at Brook Church before pulling out to the east (see Map 22, Appendix B).[4] Brook Church was the first action for these regiments in 1864.

On May 20–21, Hunton's Brigade was restored to its original organization and rejoined Lee's army. The brigade saw minor action at North Anna and Totopotomoy (principally the 28th Virginia). During the evening of June 1, the Virginians were dispatched from divisional reserve to the assistance of Hoke's and Kershaw's Divisions at Cold Harbor (see Map 35, Appendix B). Elements of the VI and XVIII Corps had attacked and found a gap in the Confederate line between these two divisions and began to exploit this advantage. Hunton's Brigade arrived just before dusk and aided in sealing the breach and ultimately repelling the Federal advance.[5] For the remainder of the battle, Hunton's Brigade manned this section of the main line adjacent to Hoke's Division and, accordingly, played a major role in repelling the massive Federal assault on June 3 (see Map 39, Appendix B).[6]

In mid-June, Hunton's Brigade led the attack of Pickett's Division to recapture the fortifications at the Howlett House (Bermuda Hundred). The attack cost the brigade about sixty-nine casualties. Overall, though, this brigade experienced comparatively light battle losses during May and June. At the end of Cold Harbor, it fielded the highest strength in the division. But the command had lost at least thirty-nine men to desertion in May. Three of these occurred near Drewry's Bluff. The remaining thirty-six occurred at North Anna and were from the 19th and 28th Virginia Regiments.

Richmond newspapers provided comprehensive casualty lists for the two regiments engaged at Brook Church and four of the five regiments (all but the 8th Virginia) at Cold Harbor.[7] The latter lists cover the period June 1 through June 3, 4, 6, or 8. The respective books of the Virginia Regimental Histories Series were also examined for the study of this brigade and in creating Table 30, Appendix A.[8]

Barton's Brigade

This brigade had sustained 1,223 reported casualties at Gettysburg, the highest in Pickett's Division.[1] Its commander in that battle, Brig. Gen. Lewis A. Armistead, had given his life at the "high-water mark" of the Confederacy during the charge on July 3. Despite these crippling losses, the brigade recovered over the winter of 1863–64 and by May again fielded the largest strength in the division. Most of the regiments had very large enrollments from the date of their enlistments, and the majority of the men were veterans. As in Terry's and Hunton's commands, this brigade had not replaced all of its losses in officers and noncommissioned officers. Brig. Gen. Seth Barton, a veteran of the western theater and recently exchanged after Vicksburg, was appointed its new commander.

Like Terry's and Hunton's Brigade, Barton's Brigade came from varied regions of the state. The 9th Virginia Regiment was raised primarily in the Tidewater area, while the 14th, 38th, and 57th Virginia Regiments were recruited principally from the south-central portion of the state. The last unit, the 53rd Virginia Regiment, was originally formed in 1861 by the consolidation of two independent battalions and a separate company. The original enlistments reflected this organization. About one-half of the regiment was recruited from the south-central part of the state; the remaining half was raised from counties east of Richmond.

At the beginning of May 1864, Barton's Brigade was posted in the defenses of Richmond. It joined the forces of General Beauregard confronting Butler's Army of the James and was assigned to Ransom's Division.[2] It participated in the fighting at Chester Station on May 10 and Drewry's Bluff on May 16.[3] These actions cost the brigade a confirmed 614 casualties or about one-third of its original strength.[4] A comparison of this battle loss with those of the other brigades in the First Corps reveals that it was the highest in Pickett's Division and similar in magnitude to the casualties sustained by many of the units in Kershaw's and Field's Divisions during the same period.

Barton's Brigade returned to its parent division and Lee's army at Spotsylvania on May 20–21.[5] The Virginians were present at the remaining battles of the campaign but saw very minor action. Like Hunton's command, Barton's Brigade experienced some desertion during this period. About twenty-one men deserted while serving under Beauregard, and another twenty-eight men left on or about May 20. The majority of these came from the 14th and 38th Virginia Regiments.

The casualties for this brigade in both the Drewry's Bluff and Overland Campaigns are shown in Table 31, Appendix A. Richmond newspapers provided a fragmented patchwork of casualty lists for this brigade in the battles on May 10 and May 16.[6] Casualty lists were provided for the 53rd Virginia for both of these days. For the 14th and 57th Virginia Regiments, lists were published only for May 10. Similarly, a roster was published only for May

16 for the 38th Virginia. Nothing had been found for the 9th Virginia. In view of the gaps in newspaper coverage for most of these units, it is possible that their casualties in the Drewry's Bluff campaign could have been slightly higher. The respective books of the Virginia Regimental Histories Series were similarly consulted during the research for this brigade.[7]

Corse's Brigade

Corse's Brigade was formed after the Battle of Antietam (Sharpsburg) by the transfer of four Virginia regiments into a new organization led by Col. Montgomery D. Corse (of the 17th Virginia Regiment). In 1863 the 29th Virginia was assigned to the brigade, giving it five regiments. The 29th had been raised and formed in the mountainous southwestern portion of the Commonwealth; historical evidence reveals that the morale of its men improved with its assignment outside its home district.[1] The other four regiments (the 15th, 17th, 30th, and 32nd Virginia) were recruited from counties in and around Richmond, northernmost Virginia, in and around Fredericksburg, and the Hampton Peninsula, respectively.

Due to the chances of war and the intervention of the War Department, Corse's Brigade was never seriously engaged during all of 1863. In the spring of that year, Pickett's and Hood's Divisions took part in the siege of Suffolk and missed the Battle of Chancellorsville. Corse's Brigade was then held back in June to safeguard Richmond and, as a result, missed the Battle of Gettysburg. One regiment, however, the 17th Virginia, engaged in a minor action after this battle at Manassas Gap on July 21–22. The total brigade losses in these engagements were about fifty men.[2] When Pickett's Division was assigned to Richmond and southeastern Virginia to recuperate after Gettysburg, Corse's Brigade fortuitously accompanied the other three brigades and again missed several other battles. In an apparent effort to gain some usage out of this command, a portion of the brigade was temporarily assigned to the Department of Southwest Virginia and East Tennessee over the winter of 1863–64. This detachment again saw minimal action and was returned to southeastern Virginia in January 1864.

As a result of this lack of combat, Corse's Brigade was in comparatively excellent condition at the start of the Overland Campaign. During part of April and early May, the brigade was temporarily assigned to the forces of Robert Hoke in eastern North Carolina. The Virginians were quickly moved back to

Richmond and served with the forces of General Beauregard against the Federal Army of the James. The brigade was assigned to Hoke's Division and was heavily engaged at Drewry's Bluff and Howlett House on May 14–18.[3] During these actions, the command sustained at least 420 casualties. These were the first battles for the organization in over one and one-half years of service.

Corse's Brigade was ordered to rejoin the Army of Northern Virginia on May 20. The brigade reached Penola Station (south of Milford Station) during the morning of May 21. Corse then coordinated with Col. William Terry (commanding Kemper's Brigade) and moved to block the Federal advance from Milford Station that day.[4] The following day it marched southward and joined Lee's army and the rest of Pickett's Division at the North Anna. Corse's Brigade was present at the remaining battles of the campaign but saw action only at Cold Harbor. There the command was positioned on the right of the divisional front and assisted in repulsing the northernmost fringe of the massive Federal assault on June 3.[5]

There was one organizational change to the composition of the brigade during this period. The 18th Virginia Regiment had been temporarily assigned earlier to Corse's Brigade from Hunton's Brigade. In exchange, the 32nd Virginia Regiment had been assigned from Hunton to Corse. These two units returned to their former commands in late May after the brigade's return to Lee's army.

The casualties for Corse's Brigade during the Drewry's Bluff and Overland Campaigns are provided in Table 32, Appendix A. Richmond newspapers provided comprehensive lists of the casualties sustained by this brigade at the battles at Drewry's Bluff (May 14–16) and at Cold Harbor (June 1–6).[6] These lists also accurately reflect the above-noted changes in the composition of the brigade. In addition to the book written on the 29th Virginia, the respective volumes of the Virginia Regimental Histories Series for the other four units of this brigade were included in the study of this brigade.[7]

ARTILLERY

The artillery arm of the First Corps consisted of the battalions of Col. Henry C. Cabell, Lt. Col. Frank Huger, and Maj. John C. Haskell. The overall commander of the corps artillery was Brig. Gen. E. Porter Alexander. All of these units and leaders had a long association with the First Corps. Cabell's Battalion consisted of Callaway's (Troup) and Carlton's (Pulaski) Georgia Batteries, Manly's (Ellis, or A, 1st) North Carolina Battery, and McCarthy's (1st

Richmond Howitzers) Virginia Battery. Huger's Battalion featured Moody's (Madison) Louisiana Battery, Fickling's (Brooks) South Carolina Battery, and the Virginia batteries of Parker (Richmond), Smith (Bedford), Taylor (Bath), and Woodfolk (Ashland). Lastly, Haskell's command consisted of the North Carolina batteries of Flanner (Branch, or F, 13th) and Ramsay (Rowan, or D, 1st), Garden's (Palmetto) South Carolina Battery, and Lamkin's (Nelson) Virginia Battery.

The First Corps artillery was not engaged at the Wilderness. All three battalions played a major role at Spotsylvania, though. Haskell's Battalion arrived at the battlefield with the first units of Kershaw's Division and was posted near Brock Road. It contributed to the repulse of the initial assaults of the V Corps upon the position of Laurel Ridge on May 8.[1] Later in the day, elements of the other two battalions were posted on this line. Huger's Battalion (principally Parker's Battery) replaced Haskell astride Brock Road. Haskell moved some elements to the center of the corps's line. Cabell (mainly Manly's Battery) was deployed on the left of Field's Division.[2] All of the batteries in the First Corps assisted in the repulse of Union attacks upon this position on May 9, 10, and 12. There is reason to believe that the individual batteries were rotated in and out of these positions.

During May 15–16, the First Corps shifted from the left to the right of the army facing east. Huger's Battalion was deployed facing the Massaponax Church Road. Haskell's Battalion was posted on the far right next to the Po River. Cabell was held in reserve with Kershaw's Division.[3] The position reportedly was excellent for defense and was not assaulted or even probed by the opposing Federals.

At the North Anna, elements of all three battalions dueled with Federal artillery posted on the northern side of the river. Parker's Battery, a second undetermined battery from Huger's Battalion, and Callaway's Battery sparred on May 23 in a preliminary to the Union assault upon the Chesterfield Bridge position.[4] Ramsay's and Lamkin's Batteries appeared to have been involved in a similar action on May 25. The First Corps artillery was present at Totopotomoy in late May. Huger's and Cabell's Battalions were posted to the immediate right of Breckinridge's front and assisted his command and artillery in the defense of their position.[5]

All three battalions of the First Corps artillery were posted along the main Confederate line at Cold Harbor. Cabell's Battalion was assigned to Kershaw's front and, accordingly, sustained the highest casualties among the artillery. Most of this loss occurred on June 1 and 3 and fell upon Callaway's and Manly's Batteries. Huger's and Haskell's Battalions were deployed farther north in support of Field and Pickett's Divisions.[6] These sectors of the Confederate line were not assaulted, and the casualties in these commands were negligible.

The records for these artillery units vary widely. The muster rolls for Huger's and Haskell's Battalions are nearly complete but are backdated to a degree. Conversely, the rolls for Cabell's Battalion are very deficient. Fortunately, newspaper casualty lists were found for nearly all the units. The casualties in Haskell's and Cabell's Battalions are well covered in the Richmond newspapers.[7] The losses in Huger's Battalion are covered only to May 20 (Spotsylvania).[8] In addition to the newspapers, the respective books of the Virginia Regimental Histories Series and volume 1 of the North Carolina troops series were included in the research for these artillery battalions.[9] For a breakdown of casualties in the First Corps artillery, see Table 33, Appendix A.

CHAPTER 5

Second Corps

JOHNSON'S/GORDON'S DIVISION

The core of Johnson's Division was originally Thomas J. "Stonewall" Jackson's command in 1862. This division performed with distinction in the Shenandoah Valley during the spring of 1862. Since that period of the war, it had, under a number of leaders, performed reliably but with less notoriety. With the assignment of Maj. Gen. Edward Johnson in May 1863, the division gained its first extended period of command consistency in over a year. At the start of the Overland Campaign, this unit consisted of four brigades: Steuart's, Walker's (or Stonewall), Jones's, and Stafford's. The strengths and morale of these brigades varied significantly. The overall divisional strength was slightly less than 5,500 men.

Johnson's Division led the march of the Second Corps to the Wilderness on Orange Turnpike on the morning of May 5. The division was the first major infantry unit of Lee's army to become engaged in this battle. The four brigades were initially deployed astride this road from north to south in this manner: Walker, Stafford, Steuart, and Jones (see Map 1, Appendix B).[1] In the early afternoon, the First Division, V Corps assaulted the front of Johnson's Division.[2] The action was very intense and confused in the dense woods and underbrush, and one portion of the command was broken. With the assistance of units from the other two divisions of the Second Corps, Johnson's men ultimately were able to repel this assault and hold their ground.

Following this opening action, Johnson's Division moved to the left (northern) side of Orange Turnpike. In the midafternoon, a portion of the division moved forward on the corps's left. These units got embroiled in the underbrush and dense woods against assaulting elements of the First Division, VI Corps (see Map 2, Appendix B). The Confederates received the worst of this encounter and had to withdraw to their original line to reorganize and establish their positions.[3] During the remainder of the battle, Johnson's Division remained in a defensive position at the relative corps center and participated only in skirmishing. A check of the casualty figures reveals that the division sustained nearly half of the losses for the entire Second Corps in this battle.

In the march to Spotsylvania Court House on May 8, Johnson's Division followed that of Maj. Gen. Robert E. Rodes and arrived on the battlefield at dusk. The lead units assisted the latter division in driving off elements of the V and VI Corps (see Map 13, Appendix B).[4] Upon arrival, Johnson's men were posted to the north and east of Rodes's line on the crest of a broad and gently sloping ridge facing to the north.[5] The eastern edge of the line was bent back toward the south to avoid a streambed beyond the ridge. The result of this deployment yielded an extended narrow horseshoe-shaped salient in the army's line. This unusual configuration was dubbed the "Mule Shoe" by the combatants.[6] Johnson's brigades were deployed along the face of this salient, from west to east: Walker's, Hays's, Jones's (under Col. William Witcher), and Steuart's. In part to make up for some of the losses suffered at the Wilderness and in part due to a command shuffling ordered by General Lee, Hays's Brigade was transferred at this time from Early's Division to Johnson's Division. Brig. Gen. Harry T. Hays assumed command of both his brigade and that of Stafford.[7] These two brigades were relatively small and were both composed of regiments from Louisiana.

The sector held by Johnson's Division remained relatively quiet until the evening of May 10. Several hours before dusk, the Fourth Division, II Corps advanced upon the front of the salient (see Map 16, Appendix B). This poorly timed and coordinated assault was easily repulsed.[8] Elements of the VI Corps under Col. Emory Upton then assaulted and broke the adjacent portion of the line to the left and southwest, held by Rodes's Division, shortly before dusk. A significant portion of Johnson's Division was employed to restore this breach.[9]

In response to this short-lived Union success, the deployment of Johnson's Division was adjusted on May 11. General Hays had been wounded two days earlier, and the Louisiana brigades were again separated. The regiments of Hays's original brigade (under Col. William Monaghan) were moved to the divisional left between Walker's Brigade and Daniel's Brigade of Rodes's Division. The units of Stafford's original command (now under Col. Zebulon York) remained in their original position. On the morning of May 12, the divisional alignment from west to east was Hays's (under Monaghan), Walker's, Stafford's (under York), Jones's (under Witcher), and Steuart's Brigades.[10]

In the early hours of that day, the entire II Corps assaulted the center of Johnson's front (see Map 18, Appendix B). Weather conditions at this time consisted of a misty rain and dense fog. Higher command had removed the artillery batteries originally positioned nearby overnight and, despite the requests and warnings of General Johnson and his corps commander, Lt. Gen. Richard S. Ewell, they were not returned in time to assist in the defense of this position. In addition, the forward picket line was swallowed up by the rapid Federal advance through the dense fog without providing the usual early warning, and in some cases, the men behind the breastworks experienced difficulty in firing their arms in the damp conditions.

As a result of these unfortunate factors, the Union assault broke through and overwhelmed most of Johnson's Division. The location of the initial breach has historically been placed with Witcher's ill-fated brigade, but new research reveals that it could have occurred in York's command or at the junction of these two units. (See the following discussions for these two brigades.) After gaining an initial penetration of the main Confederate line, the Union troops moved laterally to the east and west in the rear of the breastworks and successively encircled adjacent units. In this manner, the Confederates to the east-southeast were quickly captured with little trouble. Those to the west appear to have offered substantial resistance before being overcome.[11] Portions of these commands escaped by fighting their way toward the west and Rodes's line. During this Federal attack, Walker was wounded and Johnson and Steuart were captured.

After this disaster, the survivors of the division were sent to the rear to rally and reform. They spent the remainder of May 12 helping prepare a new line of entrenchments across the base of the salient. The remnants of Johnson's command were thereafter reorganized. The fourteen Virginia regiments from Walker's, Jones's (Witcher's), and Steuart's Brigades were consolidated to form one brigade under the command of Col. William Terry. The two North Carolina regiments formerly in Steuart's Brigade (the 1st and 3rd) were transferred to Ramseur's Brigade in Rodes's Division. The two Louisiana brigades were again consolidated into one unit.

The extent of the disaster to Johnson's Division can be gauged by a quick glance at the respective numbers. The brigades of Walker, Jones, and Steuart started the campaign with about 4,780 men. Newspaper accounts after May 12 reported that the 1st and 3rd North Carolina of Steuart's Brigade were each left with about 30 men.[12] Terry's newly consolidated Virginia brigade could similarly field only 600 men in the ranks, though it is likely that this figure could have been more (probably closer to 700, including officers). Combined then, these three brigades of Johnson's Division could only field on May 13 about 750 men. Similar figures for the two Louisiana brigades were not found, but it appears that on May 13 they numbered no more than 700 men. Including losses to sickness and taking into consideration some increases in personnel to the ranks between May 5 and 12, it is clear that Johnson's original division lost about 4,300 men (out of an initial 5,490) between these dates. It was a sad end to a proud force once known as Jackson's Division.

With the loss of Generals Johnson, Steuart, and Walker, none of the original commanders were left. The newly consolidated Virginia and Louisiana brigades were gathered with the brigade of Col. Clement A. Evans (from Early's Division) to form a new division under Brig. Gen. John B. Gordon. This cobbled division was next engaged on May 18 and May 19 at Spotsylvania. On the eighteenth, it easily repulsed a Federal assault on the new line of entrenchments at the base of the original salient. The next day the division took part in the action at Harris Farm.[13]

Now known as Gordon's Division, it participated in the remaining battles of the Overland Campaign. At North Anna, it was held in corps reserve on the army's right (see Map 24, Appendix B).[14] At Bethesda Church and Cold Harbor, the position of the division was shifted along the corps's front (see Maps 31 and 32, Appendix B). Its only substantial fighting was against elements of the V and IX Corps on June 1–3 between the Shady Grove and Mechanicsville Roads (see Maps 36, 37, and 41, Appendix B).[15]

Walker's (Stonewall) Brigade

The Stonewall Brigade (sometimes referred to as the First Brigade), originally commanded by Brig. Gen. Thomas J. Jackson, was one of the most famous infantry units of the war. The personnel were recruited principally from the Shenandoah Valley and neighboring counties to the west and southwest. Having earned the title "Stonewall" for its performance at First Bull Run (Manassas) in 1861, the organization had not quite lived up to this appellation in several subsequent actions in 1862. During 1862 and 1863, this Virginia brigade had several commanders killed in action, and many of the original personnel were lost to battle and sickness or transferred to the cavalry or artillery. Despite these changes, the brigade had performed acceptably in 1863, losing a reported combined 1,035 casualties at the Battles of Chancellorsville, Second Winchester, Gettysburg, and Mine Run.[1] After Chancellorsville, Brig. Gen. James A. Walker was assigned to the command. Prior to the war, Walker had been a student at the Virginia Military Institute (VMI) and personally had a run-in with Jackson. During 1862 and 1863, he had proven himself capable as a temporary brigade leader in Early's Division and was a solid choice for command.[2] By the spring of 1864, the strength of this famous unit had been somewhat restored with returning convalescents and new personnel (to about 1,320 men).

In the opening phase of the Battle of the Wilderness on May 5, the Stonewall Brigade was posted on the division's left and, for all purposes, not engaged (see Map 1, Appendix B). Later in the afternoon, it was advanced forward into dense woods and undergrowth and collided with elements of the First Division, VI Corps (see Map 2, Appendix B). The regiments posted on the right (the 4th, 5th, and 27th Virginia) received considerable enemy fire and took some casualties. At nearly the same time, the leftmost regiment, the 33rd Virginia, was struck by the advancing Federals and similarly affected.[3] General Walker then had to order the entire brigade to withdraw to their original line to reorganize. The Virginians remained in this position for the remainder of the battle, thereafter engaging in only skirmishing.

Walker's Brigade led the march of Johnson's Division to Spotsylvania Court House on May 8. Portions of the command came to the assistance of Rodes's Division at dusk against elements of the VI Corps.[4] From the night of May 8 through the morning of May 12, the brigade front covered a portion of the divisional line at the face of the Mule Shoe. According to an available report, the alignment of the regiments in the brigade, from west to east, was as follows: the 2nd, 33rd, 27th, 5th, and 4th (see Map 16, Appendix B).[5] Doles's Brigade of Rodes's Division was positioned on the immediate left of the 2nd Virginia. On the evening of May 10, elements of the VI Corps struck and broke through Doles's line. Initially, the 2nd and 33rd Virginia fired into the flank of the assaulting forces. Once the Federals overwhelmed most of Doles's Brigade, a portion of them moved upon the Virginians' left-rear and routed the two regiments. Walker rallied these units about 100 yards to the rear and brought up the rest of his troops.[6] He was, through this effort, able to form a solid front along the northern edge of the breakthrough and thereby contribute to the ultimate repulse of this Union attack.

On May 12, the Stonewall Brigade was nearly destroyed in the early morning assault by the entire II Corps. The Federals gained a breakthrough in the main Confederate line at a point several hundred yards to the east and then successively enveloped the entrenchments to the left and right (see Map 18, Appendix B). The initial assault on the brigade nearly destroyed its right regiment (the 4th). As the Federal onslaught moved west, the remnant of each regiment fell back upon the unit to its west.[7] As could be expected, the left regiment, the 2nd, sustained the least loss. Ultimately, the survivors of the Stonewall Brigade fell back upon Hays's and then Daniel's Brigades. An examination of the compiled casualties reveals that Walker's command lost 577 prisoners on May 12; of this total, at least 25 were wounded. Judging by these numbers, it appears that Walker's Brigade put up a fight before succumbing to superior forces. In this action, the brigadier was severely wounded and lost for almost a year's service.

The extent of the casualties in Walker's Brigade on May 12 can be clearly expressed with an excerpt published in the issue of the *Staunton Spectator and Advertiser* dated May 24: "Three hundred and thirty-nine men left in the Stonewall Brigade." A detailed study of the individual records of the regiments yield about 340–350 men present at this time. The balance or excess numbers of men were probably absent sick or slightly wounded (unreported) in field hospitals. Thereafter, the remnant of the command was amalgamated with the other Virginia regiments in Johnson's Division under the command of Col. William Terry (promoted to brigadier general on May 20), and the Stonewall Brigade ceased to exist independently. General Terry's new command subsequently saw action on May 18 and 19 at Spotsylvania, on May 23–25 at North Anna, on May 30 at Bethesda Church, and on June 1–3 at Cold Harbor.

Terry's composite brigade performed poorly at Harris Farm. When first fired upon, many of the troops broke for the rear, exposing a neighboring brigade to enfilading fire.[8] At North Anna, this new command was largely posted in the rear, while at Bethesda Church it held a portion of Gordon's line. At Cold Harbor, it participated in the maneuvers and actions executed by the Second Corps (see Maps 36, 37, and 41, Appendix B).[9] In most of these actions, the unit was lightly engaged; however, a check of the compiled casualties reveals that its component regiments took some losses at Harris Farm (Spotsylvania) on May 19 and at Cold Harbor on June 1–3.

Accurately determining the strength and losses of Walker's (Stonewall) Brigade during the Overland Campaign was one of the more challenging aspects of this study. Limited casualty lists were recorded and published in local newspapers in mid-May. The only complete listings found were for the 2nd Regiment on May 5 at the Wilderness and for the 5th Regiment at the Wilderness and its killed and wounded at Spotsylvania on May 10 and 12. The available listings for the 4th and 27th Regiments cover men principally from Rockbridge and Wythe Counties for these same battles. No similar record for the 33rd Virginia Regiment has been found.

Casualty lists for battles in 1863 in the Stonewall Brigade were provided in the Staunton, Harrisonburg, and Lexington newspapers and are available for study. Judging by the accuracy and thoroughness of these earlier listings (principally those in the *Staunton Spectator and Advertiser* and the *Rockingham Register & Virginia Advertiser*), complete lists for the brigade would have likely been provided in late May or early June 1864. Some casualty lists were published in May 1864 in Staunton, Lexington, and Wytheville.[10] The 5th Virginia Regiment received the most coverage at this time. Later, possibly more-comprehensive issues (in June) were never published due to an unfortunate event linked to the war. During late May and early June, a Union force under Maj. Gen. David Hunter advanced through the Shenandoah Valley. Upon Hunter's orders, all printing presses and offices were destroyed or confiscated. For researchers and historians, the casualty information for this historic brigade was permanently lost at this time. In the case of the Rockingham newspaper, no copies of any of the issues published between April 29 and August 12 have yet been found.

As described in an earlier section, the rosters of the men in this brigade were compiled and recorded from the CSRs. With the completion of this task for the Stonewall Brigade, it appeared that the derived casualty totals were relatively low. The total loss in the Overland Campaign for the 5th Virginia Regiment was about 250 men; the corresponding losses for the other four regiments ranged between 110 and 150. The total casualties for the campaign for the entire brigade came to about 750 (out of an estimated starting strength of 1,300–1,320). A deduction of this total loss from the estimated strength of the brigade at the start of the campaign failed to account for all the personnel, especially when compared to the number of men reportedly left in the brigade (339) and the total for the fourteen Virginia regiments in

Johnson's Division (in excess of 600) after May 12. In particular, there were limited numbers of killed and wounded.

The CSRs revealed some inconsistent records that could, in part, account for some of the discrepancies. Each of the regimental records was found to have numerous men who appeared to be present on or before April 30 and then vanished from the records afterward. One might judge that these men were transferred to another unit, deserted, died on the battlefield, or were wounded and furloughed never to return. But most of these men with no later record belonged to companies that were consolidated or discontinued after May 12. After that date, each of the regiments was reduced to typically one to four companies. These consolidated companies have muster rolls for later months in 1864, whereas the rolls for the discontinued companies end on April 30. On this basis, then, men in the discontinued companies who were killed or wounded in the campaign are not reported in the CSRs.

At this stage of research, it was clear that additional sources would be needed. County histories, the respective books of the Virginia Regimental Histories Series, listings from the Confederate Cemetery at Spotsylvania, and records at the Virginia State Archives were all examined.[11] These sources provide a higher number for the brigade's casualties, but this new total still did not fully account for the difference in the above figures. In addition, the total number of casualties for most of the units in the brigade was still proportionally much lower than the numbers for the 1st and 3rd North Carolina Regiments in Steuart's Brigade as well as the new totals for the 5th Virginia Regiment and Company A, 4th Virginia Regiment (from Wythe County) in the Stonewall Brigade. Newspapers casualty lists were found for each of these commands.

Details from two diaries proved very useful. James Bosang of the 4th Regiment reported in his diary that his unit lost five killed and forty-five wounded on May 5 at the Wilderness.[12] These figures seemed to be consistent with the totals provided in the newspapers for the 2nd and 5th Regiments. The diary of George D. Buswell, Company H, 33rd Virginia Regiment, provided a further breakthrough.[13] This officer listed the names and dates of all the men who became casualties at the Wilderness and Spotsylvania, amounting to five killed and six wounded on May 5, one wounded on May 6, three wounded on May 10, and one killed, one wounded, and ten captured on May 12. As a basis for comparison, other primary sources listed only one man killed (Capt. Michael Shuler at the Wilderness) and the same ten men captured for this company during the entire campaign.

This sample, although admittedly rather small in size compared to the total number of companies in the brigade, is considered an accurate representation of the events and patterns of casualties that occurred in the Stonewall Brigade. Clearly, the number of killed and wounded at both the Wilderness and Spotsylvania are higher than those indicated in the CSRs and other available sources. Based on the information contained in these diaries and the newspapers, the casualty total for the brigade at the Wilderness was raised from 214 to 246, while that for Spotsylvania was raised from 746 to 775 (see Table 34, Appendix A). The total estimated increase in casualties was 61 men, or about 6 percent of the brigade total. These estimated increases are conservative, though, and the actual losses may have been slightly higher.

Table 34 indicates that the Stonewall Brigade lost 775 men at Spotsylvania. A research of the muster rolls and other sources reveals the following breakdown by day: 46 on May 10; 666 on May 12; 5 on May 18; and 58 on May 19. The losses for May 19 are somewhat surprising and demonstrate that the command had not lost all of its fighting capability on the twelfth. The Buswell diary and the newspaper listing for the 2nd Virginia also provide other interesting facts. Some men listed as casualties in these references are not contained in the muster rolls in the CSRs. A check of these revealed that some of these men had been present earlier in the war but had no record in 1864. Others had no record at all but featured surnames the same as other men in the same company. These findings tend to indicate that the total number of men in the brigade was slightly higher and that the corresponding number of casualties should also be higher. Furthermore, in discussions with Robert J. Driver, Civil War historian and author in the Virginia Regimental Histories Series, Driver noted that, in his extensive research of Virginia units in the Second Corps, he had found the same pattern.

Jones's Brigade

Jones's Brigade consisted of six Virginia regiments (the 21st, 25th, 42nd, 44th, 48th, and 50th) that were raised principally from the south-central and southwestern mountainous portions of the state. This organization, sometimes referred to as the Second Brigade, served under Jackson in his Valley Campaign of 1862. Like the Stonewall Brigade, this unit had since 1862 seen a number of commanders. Its performance during this period was at times mediocre. In an effort to improve this, John M. Jones was promoted to brigadier general and given command after Chancellorsville. In the battles of 1863, the brigade had sustained a reported 993 casualties.[1] During the winter months of 1863–64, the strength of Jones's Brigade was raised to the largest in the division (about 1,850 men) with the assignment of a considerable number of new personnel.

On the morning of May 5, Jones's Brigade led the corps and division march into the Wilderness. It was accordingly the first infantry unit of the army to be seriously engaged in this battle. Jones's superiors, Richard S. Ewell and Edward Johnson, deployed the brigade south of Orange Turnpike on the western edge of Saunders's Field. In this position, it was assaulted at midday by elements of the First Division, V Corps (see Map 1, Appendix B). The southern portion of the attacking force extended beyond (or south of) Jones's line and also had the cover of dense woods just outside the edge of this field. As a result, the right end of the brigade was partially enveloped and overwhelmed. Thereafter, the entire command broke in disorder toward the rear. General Jones was killed trying to rally his fractured line.[2] The 25th Virginia Regiment was reportedly on the brigade picket line during this action.[3] Information regarding the alignment of the rest of the regiments during this engagement has not been found, but judging by the compiled casualty figures (see Table 35, Appendix A), the 48th and 50th Virginia Regiments appear to have received the worst of this action.

The brigade was thereafter rallied and reorganized in the rear and placed in reserve for the balance of the day. The 25th Virginia was temporarily attached to Hays's Brigade (of Early's Division) in midafternoon. Hays's composite command got embroiled with elements of the First Division, VI Corps in dense woods and underbrush on the Confederate left and had to fall back to the original line to avoid being encircled (see Map 2, Appendix B). The 25th Virginia was posted on the extreme left of Hays's Brigade. This area of the battlefield contained a ravine, and the vegetation was especially dense. When the main portion of the Confederate line fell back, the majority of this regiment was trapped by enemy skirmishers and captured.[4] On the morning of May 6, Jones's Brigade, now under the command of Col. William A. Witcher of the 21st Regiment, was reinserted in the front line near its former position. The Virginians then engaged primarily in skirmishing for the remainder of the battle.

Jones's (Witcher's) Brigade arrived at Spotsylvania with the rest of the division on the evening of May 8. The command was deployed on the east-central sector of the divisional front between Hays's Brigade on the left and Steuart's Brigade on the right (see Map 16, Appendix B).[5] This entire front covered the apex of a narrow salient facing toward the north and northeast. On the evening of May 10, Federal forces led by Col. Emory Upton of the VI Corps successfully assaulted and overwhelmed a section of the Confederate breastworks along the western side of the salient. A small portion of Witcher's command was dispatched to assist the forces counterattacking and restoring this broken section of the line.[6]

On the morning of May 12, Witcher's men still occupied the right center of the division line. That previous evening or the night, most of the 21st and part of the 42nd Virginia Regiments had been posted on a picket line about 900–1,200 yards in front of the main line. The 42nd was placed on the left facing north, the 21st on its right facing more to the northeast. A portion of the 48th Virginia was detailed to relieve the 42nd and was in the process of completing this assignment by the early morning hours.[7] As a result of this detachment, about two-thirds of the brigade covered Witcher's front in the main line. Two of these, the 25th and the 50th, had been badly cut up in the Wilderness.

The early morning assault by the entire II Corps in the dense fog and mist quickly engulfed the 42nd and 48th Virginia on the picket line. These regiments were deployed in the direct path of the assault and scarcely had a chance to put up any resistance. The Federal column largely passed to the left, or west, of the sector covered by the 21st Virginia. Most of the men in this unit moved to the east in the fog, circumvented around the eastern side of the salient, and eventually reached friendly forces through the sector held by Heth's Division.[8] In the meantime, the main impetus of the assault struck the area held by Witcher's reduced regiments and the two brigades to the west (see Map 18, Appendix B). At some point, the Union forces created a gap and broke through the main line of entrenchments.

The blame for this enemy success, which ultimately led to the loss of most of Johnson's Division, was historically placed upon Witcher's regiments. Some reports stated that these troops acted with cowardice, hardly fired several rounds, and then broke to the rear. The surgeon for the 25th Regiment, Maj. Abram Schultz Miller, wrote to his wife a series of letters during this period. In one he declared, "our Brigade was to blame for the most of it" (meaning the disaster to Johnson's Division on May 12). He further mentioned that although his regiment was one of the best in the service, several others in the brigade "run all the time." In his wartime diary, George D. Buswell of the 33rd Virginia Regiment (Stonewall Brigade) also blamed the "2nd Brigade."[9] A report published in the May 23 issue of the *Daily Richmond Enquirer* stated that Walker's (Stonewall) and Jones's Brigades had faltered and given way but that the break in the main line occurred 300 yards to the right of the Stonewall Brigade.

But Col. Robert W. Withers (who survived the battle) of the 42nd Virginia Regiment wrote in correspondence dated May 16 (and published in the *Lynchburg Virginian*) that the 50th Virginia Regiment on the brigade's left (next to Stafford's Brigade) had held its ground until being essentially overwhelmed by vastly superior numbers.[10] General Terry (commander of the consolidated Virginia brigade from May 13) in a reply dated June 7 to the account in the *Enquirer* came to the defense of the Jones's Brigade. He stated that this command had been erroneously and unjustly blamed, that a full knowledge of the facts would prove sufficient vindication. The 44th Virginia was apparently posted in the brigade center, with the remnants of the 25th Regiment on the right. A postwar article written by Robert A. Marshall of the 25th Virginia reported that his regiment held its portion of the line until being suddenly surrounded by enemy troops approaching from the left rear.[11]

A check of the unit rosters reveals that the entire brigade had only about 305–310 men left after May 12. Of this total, the 21st Regiment, which largely escaped the onslaught, fielded 173 men.[12] The 50th Virginia Regiment had the next largest total at about 40 men present. Records indicate that the brigade lost 817 prisoners, 36 of whom were wounded. These numbers would tend to indicate that most of the troops in this brigade put up a fight and held out until being overwhelmed and captured. Following May 12, the survivors of the six regiments were grouped into one unit in the consolidated brigade of William Terry. This consolidated unit subsequently participated in the remaining battles of the campaign in the division of Brig. Gen. John B. Gordon. (For a discussion of the actions and events pertinent to Terry's command, see the above summary for the Walker's (Stonewall) Brigade.)

The compiled casualties for Jones's Brigade are provided in Table 35. Along with the Stonewall Brigade, obtaining an accurate determination of the strength and casualties of this command during the Overland Campaign has been one of the more challenging and frustrating aspects of research.

Three of the regiments (the 42nd, 44th, and 48th) have no muster rolls for the first part of 1864. One other unit (the 50th) has no rolls after 1861. Accurately determining the names and number of men who were or could have been present at April 30 or even May 5 is a near-impossible task. For each of these units, heavy reliance was placed upon clothing issues (in the CSRs). Fortunately, Colonel Withers of the 42nd Regiment, in the aforementioned correspondence to the *Lynchburg Virginian,* mentioned that the brigade had about 1,700 "muskets" at the start of the campaign.[13] Estimating about 150 for officers, the estimated total strength would about 1,850 men on May 5.

As for casualties, the muster rolls for the regiments in this unit feature the same types of problems and omissions as those described above for the Stonewall Brigade. Newspaper casualty listings were found for the 21st, 44th, 48th, and 50th Virginia and a part of the 25th Virginia.[14] Similar complete newspaper listings were never found for the remaining regiment, the 42nd Virginia. Some men listed in the newspapers have no entries in the CSRs and many names found in other sources, such as county histories and state postwar records, are not in the newspapers. Except for the 21st Regiment, these observations apply to all the units of Jones's Brigade. The newspaper reference for the 50th Regiment is especially weak. For example, the entry for Company I provides the names of the men killed and wounded (through May 12) and the men who escaped on May 12. The remaining personnel are addressed with a statement that everyone else was missing and believed captured (with no names mentioned).

Fortunately for this study, other sources were found or provided. A letter written by Pvt. John S. Holley of the 48th Virginia Regiment indicates that his unit sustained 88 casualties in the Wilderness, 80 on May 5 and 8 on May 6. A detailed check of the roster and a newspaper casualty list (from the *Abingdon Virginian*) could account for only about 79 of these men.[15] Although not listed by name, Colonel Withers's correspondence reported the number of killed and wounded in his regiment (42nd Virginia) through May 12. Some information was obtained from the respective volumes of the Virginia Regimental Histories Series.[16] The books written by Richard Armstrong, John Chapla, and Kevin Ruffner on five of the six regiments were very beneficial.

Accurately determining the names and numbers of men captured from the 25th and 50th Regiments on May 5 at the Wilderness and on May 12 at Spotsylvania was also considerably difficult. As discussed above, both of these regiments sustained heavy losses in prisoners on May 5. The muster rolls, for the most part, are missing, and the Federal POW records are not very clear. Specifically, the date of capture for many of the enlisted personnel is given only as May 12, while for some men the dates of both May 5 and May 12 (or both May 12 and 19) are given. Officers, in general, are listed as all being captured on May 10. The letters written by Surgeon Miller are beneficial for gauging the numbers of prisoners taken from the 25th Regiment on these dates. He mentions that the regiment started the campaign with 269 "muskets." On May 7, the regiment could field only 75 similar personnel. After May 12, this number had fallen to 20. For the 50th Regiment, there are no similar sources. The newspaper does not differentiate the captured by battle, and admittedly, estimates were made.[17]

In view of these findings, the number of wounded in the 42nd and 48th Regiments at the Wilderness were increased by four and nine, respectively, to account for the numbers given in the report and letter. Additionally, some of the men reported captured by the Federals from the 25th and 50th Regiments on May 12 were shifted from the totals for Spotsylvania and assigned to the totals for those captured at the Wilderness. Lastly, the figures for wounded in the 50th Regiment were increased by ten for the Wilderness and by five for Spotsylvania. Judging by the poor quality of the muster rolls for this regiment and the omissions in the newspaper, these increases are considered representative and appropriate. The actual casualties for the 50th Virginia may even have been higher.

In any event, it is possible to provide a breakdown of the casualties in Jones's Brigade at Spotsylvania by day. Based upon the available information, these are as follows: 23 on May 10; 869 on May 12; and 24 on May 19. The majority of the loss on May 19 occurred, as could be expected, in the 21st Regiment. One officer from the brigade staff was captured at the corps field hospital at Spotsylvania on June 10. He apparently had taken ill during the battle in May and was left behind when the army moved south to the North Anna.

Steuart's Brigade

This brigade was one of the few in the Army of Northern Virginia that featured a mixed composition. Its commander, Brig. Gen. George H. Steuart, was a native of Maryland. Two of the regiments (the 1st and 3rd) were raised primarily from eastern North Carolina; the remaining three (the 10th, 23rd, and 37th) were enlisted from the same areas of Virginia as Walker's and Jones's Brigades. The Virginia units served since the earliest days of the division under Jackson and were often referred to as the Third Brigade. The North Carolina regiments were assigned to the brigade after Antietam, having served in D. H. Hill's (later Rodes's) Division with distinction. The record of this brigade at the Battles of Chancellorsville, Second Winchester, Gettysburg, and Mine Run indicates that at this stage of the war, it was one of the best commands in the Second Corps and certainly in Johnson's Division. During these 1863 battles, the five units in this brigade had sustained the highest reported number of casualties (1,593) in the division.[1] This figure almost equaled its strength (1,610 men) at the start of the Overland Campaign.

In the opening phase of the Wilderness on May 5, Steuart's Brigade was posted on the western edge of Saunders's Field on the northern side of Orange Turnpike (between Stafford's and Jones's Brigades; see Map 1, Appendix B). The alignment of the regiments was, from north to south: 23rd Virginia, 10th Virginia, 3rd North Carolina, and 1st North Carolina.[2] The 37th Virginia was detached from the brigade to remain in the rear to guard Raccoon Ford on May 4.[3] In the early afternoon, Steuart's position was assaulted by elements of the First Division, V Corps (see Map 2, Appendix B). This attack was handily repulsed, with the Union forces sustaining heavy losses.[4] The brigade repelled a second assault, made by elements of the First Division, VI Corps, during the late hours of the day.[5] It then remained in this position for the rest of the battle and saw no more significant action. The 37th Virginia rejoined the command either late on May 5 or during the morning of May 6.

On the march to Spotsylvania on May 8, Steuart's Brigade apparently brought up the rear. As the various units of Johnson's Division arrived at the northern end of the Confederate line, they were posted in the order of their march. Steuart's Brigade thus was deployed at the eastern end of the division facing northeast (see Map 16, Appendix B). During the first several days of this battle, the command constructed breastworks and improved its defensive position. Near dusk on the evening of May 10, elements of the VI Corps broke into and overwhelmed a substantial portion of the line of Doles's Brigade of Rodes's Division. Steuart's Brigade was one of the principal units called upon to counterattack and restore this section of the line. The command faced to the rear and advanced across the rear of the salient to reach the location of the Union breakthrough.[6] It was near dark at the time contact was made with enemy forces, but the men performed very capably under these circumstances.

During the massed Union assault upon Johnson's Division in the early hours of May 12, Steuart's Brigade was effectively destroyed. Only the western portion of the brigade's front, held by the two North Carolina regiments, was actually attacked (see Map 18, Appendix B).[7] These regiments initially held their position until Federal forces broke through the approximate center of the divisional front to the northwest. Elements of the First Division, II Corps then moved quickly to the east-southeast, enveloping this brigade from behind. Only those men who quickly realized the extent of the impending disaster and broke immediately to the rear escaped. General Steuart was also captured.

Following this disaster, Steuart's Brigade was broken up. The survivors of the 1st and 3rd North Carolina were transferred to Ramseur's Brigade in Rodes's Division. (The rest of their story in the campaign can be found in the discussion for that brigade below.) The remnants of the 10th, 23rd, and 37th Virginia Regiments were grouped into one command and consolidated with the other Virginia units in a brigade under William Terry. (A description of their subsequent participation in the campaign can be found under "Walker's (Stonewall) Brigade" above.)

The casualties for Steuart's Brigade during the campaign are provided in Table 36, Appendix A. A check of the available records indicates that the brigade sustained a total of 1,235 casualties at Spotsylvania. These can be broken down by day in the following manner: 3 on May 8; 78 on May 10; 1 on May 11; 1,126 on May 12; 2 on May 16–17; and 21 on May 19. Additionally, four men, who were apparently very ill and left at the corps field hospital, were captured on the battlefield on June 10. As for May 12, the brigade lost 1,091 prisoners (17 of whom were wounded).

The quality and accuracy of the compiled records for this brigade vary widely. The muster rolls, rosters from Manarin and Jordan's work on North Carolina troops, and newspaper casualty lists for the 1st and 3rd North Carolina are very good and provide a solid basis for comparison with other units in the division.[8] In contrast, the records for the three Virginia regiments display many of the same difficulties as the units from Walker's and Jones's Brigades. Newspapers providing casualty lists were found for all three units, however, they cover only selected companies or appear to be partial lists.[9] The pertinent books from the Virginia Regimental Histories Series were also examined.[10] In view of the apparent limitations of the newspaper lists, twelve more wounded were added to the totals for the brigade. Of these twelve, three were assigned to the 23rd Virginia at the Wilderness and two were assigned for the same unit at Spotsylvania. The remaining seven were assigned to the 10th Virginia at Spotsylvania.

Stafford's Brigade

This unit was often referred to as the Fourth Brigade. It consisted of the 1st, 2nd, 10th, 14th, and 15th Louisiana Regiments, raised primarily from the city of New Orleans and the surrounding parishes of southeastern Louisiana. Earlier in the war, the men of this command had formed a reputation for drinking, pillaging, and hard fighting.[1] Leroy A. Stafford was promoted to brigadier general and transferred from Hays's Brigade after Gettysburg to replace the brigade's previous commander, Francis T. Nicholls, who was seriously wounded at Chancellorsville. The brigade had performed credibly in 1863, losing a reported 847 casualties in the major battles.[2]

During the winter of 1863–64, however, a substantial number of men from this brigade deserted the ranks. In correspondence from early 1864, Lee stated that he was aware of the extensive number of desertions in this brigade and that he as well as Generals Ewell and Johnson were unable to gauge the cause.[3] One factor may have been that much of the populated portion of Louisiana was occupied by Federal forces and had been since 1862–63. In addition, the regiments of this brigade had largely been unable to recruit new personnel since 1862. In any event, the strength of Stafford's Brigade had diminished to such a point that it was clearly the smallest brigade in the division and the Second Corps (having only about 705 men).

At the start of the Battle of the Wilderness on May 5, Stafford's Brigade was placed on the division's left (see Map 1, Appendix B). In the early afternoon, it assisted in repulsing the initial assault in Saunders's Field by the V Corps.[4] A few hours later, the Louisianans and the Stonewall Brigade advanced forward into dense woods and underbrush in front of the main line of entrenchments and collided with advancing elements of the First Division, VI Corps (see Map 2, Appendix B). In this action, the brigade was subjected to heavy frontal and flanking fire and had to retire to the original line to reorganize and reform. General Stafford was mortally wounded at this time while trying to rally and hold the advanced position.[5] His brigade then remained behind entrenchments on the division's left for the balance of the battle and engaged primarily in skirmishing.

On May 8, this small force was amalgamated with the Louisiana command of Brig. Gen. Harry T. Hays to form a more-typical-size brigade.[6] The combined unit arrived at Spotsylvania on the evening of May 8 and was posted on the divisional left-center between Walker's and Jones's (Witcher's) Brigades (see Map 16, Appendix B).[7] General Hays was wounded the next day. The combined brigades were again separated, with Col. Zebulon York of the 14th Louisiana taking command of Stafford's original units.[8] There is little evidence in available records to indicate that this brigade was seriously engaged on May 10. During the night of May 10–11, the units of Hays's original brigade were shifted to the division's left to cover part of the line formerly held by Rodes's command.[9] The five regiments under Colonel York continued to occupy the section between Walker and Witcher.

The massive assault by the II Corps on the morning of May 12 struck York's command head on (see Map 18, Appendix B). As with the other units in the division, these Louisiana troops were likely hampered by the dense fog and wet gunpowder in the rainy mist. The men who tried to hold the brigade line were clearly overwhelmed by far-superior numbers.[10] A check of the personnel records from the muster rolls indicates that, with the exception of the 10th Louisiana, the regiments of this brigade lost about 36–52 percent of their men this day. This percentage loss is far below the numbers for the other units in the division, though. The 1st Louisiana Regiment, in particular, suffered the lowest percentage loss.

Judging by this and comparable data from the remaining brigades in the division, it appears that the men in this command were afforded more time to react and thus escape the impending disaster than the other brigades in Johnson's Division. At the first sign of the coming catastrophe, there may have been an order from someone in the 2nd Louisiana to fall back.[11] But it could be concluded that the proportionally high number of survivors indicates that a significant number of men in York's command may have quickly fled to the rear. The original break in the Confederate line may have occurred in the left portion of Jones's Brigade or even at the junction of the two brigades. Regardless, with so many of York's men apparently fleeing the line for the rear, this gap quickly became a wide chasm.

Following the action on May 12, the two original Louisiana brigades were again combined into one force under York's command in the new division led by General Gordon.[12] Stafford's original five regiments provided only a small portion of this new brigade. These units were present at the remaining battles of the campaign, principally seeing action on May 19 at Harris Farm (Spotsylvania) and on June 1–3 at Cold Harbor (see Maps 36, 37, and 41, Appendix B). Stafford's Brigade lost a recorded 338 men at Spotsylvania (see Table 37, Appendix A). A breakdown of this loss on a daily basis is as follows: 290 on May 12; 47 on May 19; and 1 on May 21.

The June 16 issue of the *Richmond Whig* provided a list of the casualties for all of the units in the brigade for the entire campaign.[13] The date of this issue was almost a full month after the Battles of the Wilderness and Spotsylvania. A close check of the CSRs provided several additional wounded men not listed in this newspaper. It is possible that the published list did not include all of the slightly wounded from these battles and that the brigade loss for the campaign was higher (see Table 37).

EARLY'S/RAMSEUR'S DIVISION

This second division of the Second Corps achieved a reputation as a reliable and hard-fighting outfit under the command of first Richard S. Ewell and then Jubal A. Early. Major General Early had led the division since the Battle of Antietam and was the senior-ranking divisional officer in the corps. His command consisted of four brigades: Gordon's, Hays's, Pegram's, and Hoke's. In November 1863, most of Hays's and Hoke's Brigades were overrun and captured in a limited engagement along the Rappahannock River.[1] The latter brigade was then sent to its home state of North Carolina to recruit and reform, leaving the division with only three brigades at the start of the Overland Campaign.

At the beginning of the Battle of the Wilderness on May 5, Early's Division was placed in corps reserve (see Map 1, Appendix B). In response to the success of the initial Federal assault on Johnson's Division, one part of Early's command was quickly dispatched to counterattack and restore that part of the original line.[2] The entire division was subsequently shifted to the corps's left (northern end). In this second position, the brigades saw action on both days of the battle (see Maps 2 and 9, Appendix B).[3]

At the Battle of Spotsylvania, Early's Division was again initially posted as corps reserve. This allowed it to avoid the disasters that befell other elements of the Second Corps. In any event, the division was twice employed to counterattack and restore broken portions of the front (on May 10 and 12; see Maps 16, 18, and 19, Appendix B).[4] The action on the latter day, in particular, was a severe but heroic affair that cost a substantial number of casualties. Following several days of minor skirmishing, the division was again engaged on May 18 and 19.[5] It played a principal role in the fighting on both of these days (see Map 24, Appendix B).

The division experienced several organizational and command changes while at Spotsylvania. On May 8, Early was temporarily placed in command of the Third Corps (Lt. Gen. A. P. Hill being sick). Wanting Brig. Gen. John B. Gordon to command the division, Lee transferred Brig. Gen. Harry T. Hays, who outranked Gordon, along with his brigade to Johnson's Division. Robert D. Johnston's command was transferred from Rodes's Division to provide Gordon with three brigades.[6] On May 13, the remnants of Johnson's Division were added to Gordon's command.[7] This unit was divided on May 22 when Hill returned to duty. At that time, Early resumed command of his division and Gordon was assigned as permanent commander of Johnson's former division. Gordon's and Hays's Brigades were permanently transferred to Gordon's Division. Hoke's Brigade (under Lt. Col. William G. Lewis) returned on May 20 after an absence of almost seven months. This unit, along with Pegram's and Johnston's Brigades, now constituted Early's Division.[8]

During the movement from Spotsylvania to North Anna, elements of Early's Division had a small number of men captured at Milford Station on May 21 and at Hanover Junction on May 22–23. Most of these losses occurred due to straggling. At North Anna, the division was posted on the corps's (and army's) right (see Map 29, Appendix B). In this position, the units engaged only in skirmishing and sustained very small losses. On May 27, Ewell reported sick and Early was promoted to command of the Second Corps. Stephen D. Ramseur was then promoted from Rodes's Division to take command of this division.[9]

In late May, the division moved to the Bethesda Church area outside Richmond and was deployed on the corps's right astride Mechanicsville Road (see Map 31, Appendix B). On May 30, Ramseur committed part of his new command to conduct an aggressive reconnaissance against a portion of the line held by the V Corps at the junction of Shady Grove and Old Church Roads (see Map 32, Appendix B).[10] The operation was a hasty, ill-conceived affair and ended badly. Otherwise, the division was lightly engaged at this battle. It remained in this general portion of the Second Corps's front during the next two weeks (including Cold Harbor). On June 1–3 and 6–7, elements of the division executed several offensive movements against Federal positions (see Maps 36, 37, and 41, Appendix B).[11] For the most part, these were limited operations incurring light casualties.

Hays's Brigade

This brigade, also known as Lee's "Louisiana Tigers," was one of the hardest-fighting and reliable units in the Army of Northern Virginia. It was composed of the 5th, 6th, 7th, 8th, and 9th Louisiana Regiments, recruited from New Orleans and its outlying parishes. The fame of the brigade started in the spring of 1862 with its role at the Battle of Port Republic during Jackson's Valley Campaign. At the Battles of Chancellorsville, Second Winchester, Gettysburg, and Mine Run, the brigade performed well while sustaining a reported total of 798 casualties.[1] Its fortune changed in late 1863 when most of the brigade was overrun and captured by the VI Corps at Rappahannock Bridge on November 7.[2] The recorded total loss from this single incident was 702 men, most of whom were captured.[3] Only the brigade commander, Brig. Gen. Harry T. Hays, and several hundred of the men escaped disaster.

Hays's Louisiana Brigade spent the winter recovering from this loss. A check of the service records reveals that the Federals exchanged most of the enlisted personnel captured at Rappahannock Bridge in mid-March 1864. Following an examination at a Confederate hospital and a thirty-day furlough, these men principally returned to their units during the last week of April and the first two weeks of May. A check of the available records, however, indicates that the Federals retained in captivity most of the line officers and noncommissioned officers. Thus, Hays's Brigade embarked into the campaign missing much of its veteran leadership and at an overall low strength of about 900 men.

At the Wilderness, the Louisianans were initially posted in reserve with Early's Division (see Map 1, Appendix B). During the middle to late afternoon of May 5, the command was shifted to the corps's left and advanced to engage elements of the First Division, VI Corps (see Map 2, Appendix B). The brigade was somewhat roughly handled during this action and sustained most of its losses at this battle at this time.[4] Two of its five regiments, the 5th and 6th Louisiana, experienced heavy losses (see Table 38, Appendix A). Thereafter, the brigade was deployed as the right of Early's Division on the corps's left. With the exception of a small contribution in repelling an attack by elements of the Third Division, VI Corps against the corps's left late in the day, the command was limited to skirmishing for the remainder of the battle (see Map 9, Appendix B).[5]

On May 8, Lee ordered an organizational change in the Second Corps. Hays's Brigade was transferred to Johnson's Division. General Hays assumed command of both his and the Louisiana brigade of Leroy Stafford (that general having been mortally wounded on May 5).[6] This combined unit then marched to Spotsylvania, arriving at dusk on May 8. Hays himself was seriously wounded the following day, probably by artillery or by a sniper.[7] Leadership of the Louisiana units was again divided, with Col. William Monaghan of the 6th Louisiana Regiment assuming command of the five regiments of Hays's original brigade.[8]

Hays's (Monaghan's) Brigade was initially posted between Walker's and Stafford's (under Colonel York) Brigades in a portion of the Mule Shoe salient (see Map 16, Appendix B). After the limited success of the Federal attack upon Doles's Brigade of Rodes's neighboring division on May 10, the next day Monaghan's command was shifted to the left of Walker's Brigade next to Daniel's Brigade (of Rodes's Division).[9] This was likely done to replace the losses suffered by Doles on the tenth. This fortuitous change permitted the brigade to escape the worst of the disaster experienced by Johnson's Division on the morning of May 12 (see Map 18, Appendix B). When Union forces broke through Johnson's line and tried to envelope Monaghan's sector, each of the regiments was able to fall back and rally on Daniel's Brigade to the left (or west).[10] Judging by the recorded losses at Spotsylvania, the 7th and 8th Louisiana were posted on the brigade's right and sustained the worst of the Union assault. Conversely, the 9th Louisiana was apparently deployed on the left and escaped with the lowest relative loss.

After May 12, the two Louisiana brigades were again consolidated into one brigade, this time under the command of Colonel York (of the 14th Louisiana), and placed in the division of John Gordon. Although both of these brigades were, by this point in the campaign, relatively small in number, Hays's Brigade comprised about 70 percent of the new unit's strength. For the rest of the campaign, the participation of the units of Hays's former brigade mirrored that of Stafford's (and can be found above in the discussion of that unit). There was one minor exception. For some reason, Hays's old brigade appears to have missed the engagement of May 19 at Harris Farm (Spotsylvania). Possibly, they were kept in reserve or were left behind to cover the original entrenchments.

The casualties for Hays's Brigade during the Overland Campaign are provided in Table 38. There is reason to conclude that these regiments may have sustained a slightly higher number of casualties in the campaign. A Richmond newspaper published a list of the losses in the main battles for the 5th Louisiana.[11] As for the rest of the brigade, a second Richmond newspaper provided a list of casualties for the entire brigade. This principal newspaper listing was published at the close of the campaign and does not provide a breakdown by battle.[12] Thus, it is possible that there may have been additional men slightly wounded in some of the earlier engagements.

Gordon's/Evans's Brigade

Under the superb leadership of its commander, Brig. Gen. John B. Gordon, this brigade became one of the best organizations in the Second Corps. The command consisted of six regiments from Georgia (the 13th, 26th, 31st, 38th, 60th, and 61st). These units were raised from nearly every part of the state. At the Battle of Gettysburg, the brigade had performed especially well on the first day, overrunning and routing elements of the XI Corps. During 1863, Gordon's command had sustained a reported total of 841 casualties.[1] At the commencement of the Overland Campaign, it was in excellent condition and, at 2,270 men, fielded the largest strength in the corps.

Judging by the extent of casualties, these Georgians were heavily involved in nearly every action of the campaign. At the Wilderness on May 5, Gordon's Brigade was at first placed in reserve behind elements of Johnson's and Rodes's Divisions. In the early afternoon, the First and Fourth Divisions of the V Corps broke a portion of the Confederate front (specifically Jones's Brigade of Johnson's Division) on the south side of Orange Turnpike. Gordon's men moved quickly into the breach and with assistance by two units of Rodes's Division, repulsed the Federals (see Map 1, Appendix B).[2]

Following this opening action, the Second Corps consolidated its line and entrenched. Gordon's Brigade was deployed at the extreme right of the corps's line (see Map 2, Appendix B). In this second position, the brigade repulsed a reconnaissance executed later in the day by elements of the Third Division, V Corps.[3] On the morning of the following day (May 6), the brigade was relieved and shifted to the extreme left of the divisional and corps line. At dusk, it participated in a flanking attack upon the VI Corps (see Map 9, Appendix B).[4] This movement and attack yielded the capture of two opposing generals and about 600 prisoners. Gordon had urged this attack throughout the day and was eventually sanctioned by General Lee in the evening.

Nevertheless, Gordon was promoted to command Early's Division after the Battle of the Wilderness and ultimately both Early's and Johnson's Division during the period May 12–20. Col. Clement A. Evans of the 31st Georgia Regiment was thereafter assigned command of this brigade.[5] Under Evans's leadership, it reached the Spotsylvania battlefield during the night of May 8–9 and was again posted in reserve behind Rodes's Division (see Map 16, Appendix B). The brigade was first engaged during the evening of May 10 in response to an assault on Doles's Brigade (Rodes's Division) by elements of the VI Corps. In this action, Evans's command was one of several units that successfully halted the Union breakthrough and drove enemy forces from the captured earthworks.[6]

Two days later, on May 12, Evans's men similarly restored a section of the Confederate line following the breakthrough and capture of most of Johnson's Division by the II Corps (see Map 19, Appendix B). Once the extent of the Federal success was realized, General Gordon had Evans initially move three regiments forward to stem the breach. These units (the 31st and likely the 38th and 60th Georgia) moved through the dense fog and collided with a superior force. They were nearly surrounded and had to withdraw in order to rally.[7] The Federal advance was, however, halted by their effort.

While Evans rallied the three regiments, Gordon deployed the remaining units of the brigade (the 13th, 26th, and 61st Georgia) with Pegram's Brigade south of the breakthrough location. Lee was present to observe this deployment, and these troops as well as Gordon had to implore and convince him move to the rear. These regiments, along with rallied portions of the 31st, 38th, and 60th and Pegram's Brigade, then moved forward in a northeasterly direction and regained the eastern portion of Johnson's original defensive line.[8] During this advance, the first three regiments advanced beyond the original line and suffered substantial casualties.[9] The 61st Georgia, in particular, lost heavily in prisoners.

Evans's command was next engaged on May 18. During this action, the brigade easily repulsed an assault by the II and VI Corps upon the new line south of the Mule Shoe earthworks.[10] The following day the Georgians advanced with most of the Second Corps at Harris Farm against newly arrived Federal heavy-artillery units (serving as infantry).[11] As listed in Table 39, Appendix A, this brigade lost a recorded 690 casualties at Spotsylvania. This total can be broken down by day in the following manner: 52 on May 10; 1 on May 11; 509 on May 12; 27 on May 18; and 101 on May 19. This total also includes 285 unwounded prisoners, 210 of which were taken on May 12 and 74 captured during the night of May 19–20 (at Harris Farm).

Evans's Brigade (Gordon being promoted to major general on May 14) was present at North Anna, Bethesda Church, and Cold Harbor as part of Gordon's (formerly Johnson's) Division. Most of the small loss from the first of these battles consisted of captured stragglers on the march from Spotsylvania. The only major actions experienced by the command occurred at Cold Harbor on June 1–2 in the area of Beaver Dam Creek and Old Church Road (south of Bethesda Church; see Maps 36 and 37, Appendix B). In these actions, the Georgians successfully attacked elements of the V and IX Corps.[12]

During late May, the brigade received a reinforcement of about 450–500 men with the assignment of the 12th Georgia Battalion and an independent company (N) to the 38th Regiment.[13] Company N had five men captured at Milford Station on May 21 by Federal cavalry. These new units sustained over 40 percent of the entire brigade loss at Cold Harbor. Despite losing in excess of 1,200 men during the campaign, Evans's Brigade was still very much intact and could, after Cold Harbor, field the largest strength in the corps.

The casualty listings in the newspapers for the six regiments comprising this brigade are a variable patchwork of information.[14] Some units (for example, the 13th and 38th Georgia Regiments and 12th Georgia Battalion) were well reported, with listings for each battle. Other units (the 31st and 61st Georgia) had limited or no newspaper listings. Outside sources, such as Lillian Henderson's work on Georgia troops and individual unit histories on the 26th and 61st Regiments, helped fill the voids.[15] Considering the extensive number of casualties sustained by this brigade, it is difficult to imagine that more battle losses occurred or could be found in the brigade.

Pegram's Brigade

This brigade of five Virginia regiments, initially commanded by Arnold Elzey and subsequently by Jubal Early, was part of Jackson's Valley Army in 1862.

Under Early's command, it established a solid and reliable fighting reputation. When he was promoted, the command devolved upon former governor William Smith. Under his leadership, the morale and combat performance of the unit appeared to decline. At Chancellorsville, the brigade played a minor role. At Gettysburg, the command was kept in reserve or guarding the army's flank for much of the battle. Two of the regiments (the 13th and 58th Virginia) were actually left to guard prisoners captured at Second Winchester and missed the fighting. The remaining three regiments (the 31st, 49th, and 52nd Virginia) were present and were engaged at Culp's Hill on July 3. The total number of reported casualties for battles in 1863 was only 312.[1]

General Smith was reassigned that October. Brig. Gen. John Pegram was brought back to his home state of Virginia from the western theater to take over command of this brigade. Under his leadership, the morale, condition, and strength of the command improved significantly. During the Overland Campaign, this brigade demonstrated on as many as four occasions that it was again a solid and reliable fighting force and as good as any other unit in the Second Corps. Its strength at the commencement of the campaign was slightly more than 1,500 men. The component regiments were recruited from counties located in the Shenandoah Valley, east of modern-day Roanoke, and the northern and western (mountainous) regions of Virginia and modern-day West Virginia.

At the start of Battle of the Wilderness, Pegram's Brigade was again posted in corps reserve and was the last unit committed to action on May 5.[2] During the late afternoon, it was moved to the divisional and corps left opposite elements of the First Division, VI Corps (see Map 2, Appendix B). Pegram's Brigade followed Hays's Brigade in this movement. Its arrival was fortunate for the Confederate side, for Hays's men had gotten into considerable difficulty. The Virginians helped repulse the enemy advance and thereby permitted Hays to withdraw from an exposed position.[3] Pegram was wounded during this engagement, and leadership of the brigade fell upon the senior-ranking colonel, John S. Hoffman of the 31st Virginia.[4] During the next day, the brigade remained on the corps's left flank and repulsed one Union assault.[5] At dusk, it supported Gordon's successful flank attack upon the VI Corps (see Map 9, Appendix B).[6]

Pegram's Brigade arrived at the Spotsylvania battlefield during the night of May 8–9 and was again placed in corps reserve (see Map 16, Appendix B). The command was lightly engaged near dusk the following day. In this action, it assisted in repelling the assault and breakthrough by Upton's units of the VI Corps.[7] During the early hours of May 12, the II Corps massed, broke through, and overran most of Johnson's Division. Pegram's Brigade, along with a portion of Evans's Brigade, was posted at that time in a second line of breastworks behind the left of Johnson's position (see Map 18, Appendix B). They initially kept the Federals from advancing southward following their conquest of the Stonewall Brigade.[8] Gordon pulled these units back to reform and were then called upon by none other than General Lee to restore the broken front. A situation occurred at this time similar to that involving the Texas Brigade on May 6 at the Wilderness. Amid repeated calls for Lee to move to the rear and out of danger, a sergeant of the 49th Virginia grasped the bridle of the army commander's horse and led him to the rear.[9]

Pegram's Brigade then responded by advancing to the northeast and clearing the enemy from the breastworks originally held by Jones's Brigade and a portion of Steuart's Brigade (see Map 19, Appendix B). In the process, the command confronted and pushed back a substantially larger enemy force. Based upon available information, it appears the alignment of the brigade during this charge was, from left to right: the 13th, 52nd, 58th, 31st, and 49th Virginia.[10] The 58th Regiment likely advanced beyond the original earthworks and, as experienced by several elements of Evans's Brigade, lost heavily in prisoners as a result.

For the remainder of May 12, Pegram's Brigade held the eastern side of the Mule Shoe salient.[11] The unit was next engaged on May 18, when it easily repulsed an assault by elements of the II and VI Corps. On May 19, the Second Corps participated in a maneuver against the right-rear of the Federal army at Harris Farm. Colonel Hoffman's men were again initially placed in reserve. When elements of Rodes's Division (principally Ramseur's Brigade) became overextended against a numerically superior force, the Virginians moved up to the left portion of the front and assisted in holding off the enemy long enough to permit a withdrawal of the entire corps (see Map 24, Appendix B).[12] Of the recorded 470 casualties at Spotsylvania for the brigade (see Table 40, Appendix A), 1 occurred on May 8; 13 on May 10; 1 on May 11; 2 on May 14; 1 on May 17; 9 on May 18; and 103 on May 19. Four men also deserted and were captured at the end of Spotsylvania, and one man was likely left as a nurse with the wounded and captured on June 10. The balance (334) likely were incurred on May 12.

Pegram's Brigade was present at the remaining battles of the campaign. It was only slightly engaged at North Anna. Most of the minor losses in this battle actually were stragglers captured during the march from Spotsylvania. In late May, General Early was promoted to command of the Second Corps, and Brig. Gen. Stephen D. Ramseur was given command of Early's former division. At the same time, Early placed Col. Edwin Willis of the 12th Georgia Regiment in temporary command of Pegram's Brigade.[13] Willis's unit was probably the best brigade in Ramseur's new division at this stage of the campaign.

At Bethesda Church on May 30, Ramseur ordered Willis to take his men and "feel the enemy and ascertain his strength." The approval for this aggressive reconnaissance was obtained by Ramseur over the initial protests of the corps commander. The overall intent of the plan was that additional support was to be provided by the rest of the division as well as by Pickett's Division of the First Corps. These other units were never ordered forward or failed to execute their planned assignment, and the Virginians advanced unsupported against a superior and well-entrenched enemy force belonging to the Third Division, V Corps (see Map 32, Appendix B). In this ill-advised attack, Pegram's Brigade suffered heavily, and Colonel Willis was killed. The 49th and 52nd Regiments, which advanced over mostly open ground, were especially hard hit. Available historic information reveals that the personnel of the brigade quickly realized their predicament. Nevertheless, they maintained their alignment and continued forward. Some men actually reached the Federal entrenchments before being shot down or captured.[14]

Following this battle, command of the brigade again fell to Colonel Hoffman. In June, however, the command was given to Lt. Col. Robert D. Lilley, promoted to brigadier general, of the 25th Virginia Regiment. Lilley had just returned from furlough, but his regiment had been decimated earlier at the Wilderness and Spotsylvania. Lilley's command then participated in the fighting at Cold Harbor (primarily on June 1–3).[15] At the close of the campaign, the brigade was severely reduced and could only field about 40 percent of its original strength.

The casualties for Pegram's Brigade during the campaign are provided in Table 40. Newspaper casualty lists as well as other sources found for this brigade were, on the whole, similar in scope to those found for Gordon's Brigade, providing a variable patchwork of data with some gaps.[16] For example, a listing of the losses for the 13th Virginia on May 19 at Spotsylvania was not found. Similarly, a listing for the 31st Virginia at Bethesda Church (May 30) was not found. The respective books from the Virginia Regimental Histories Series for the units of this brigade were also found to beneficial.[17] Judging by the available information, it is difficult to imagine that there could have been additional losses in this brigade.

Hoke's Brigade

This brigade of four North Carolina regiments, which were raised principally from the west-central (Piedmont) portion of that state, was formed late in the spring of 1863 by the transfer of several units from other organizations within the Army of Northern Virginia. The ranking officer, Col. Robert F. Hoke of the 21st North Carolina, was promoted to brigadier general and assigned command. Hoke was wounded at Chancellorsville in May 1863. From that date, the brigade experienced a continuous number of command changes. The senior-ranking officer, Col. Isaac E. Avery of the 6th North Carolina, then assumed command. He was mortally wounded on July 2 at Gettysburg. The command was then transferred to Col. Archibald C. Godwin of the 57th North Carolina.

The brigade then had the misfortune to be placed with most of Hays's Brigade on the northern side of Rappahannock Bridge in early November 1863. On November 7, elements of the VI Corps overran and captured most of these two brigades.[1] Of the four component regiments, only the 21st North Carolina happened to be posted on the southern side of the river and thus escaped this disaster. The remaining three (the 6th, 54th, and 57th) and Colonel Godwin were captured. Before this date, the brigade had sustained a reported 657 casualties in battles in 1863. An additional 927 men were lost at Rappahannock Bridge.[2]

Following this debacle, the much-reduced brigade was transferred to North Carolina to recruit and reorganize. A check of available service records reveals that, unlike Hays's Brigade, the personnel captured at Rappahannock Bridge were not, for the most part, exchanged during the early spring of 1864. As a result, the three decimated regiments had to restore their ranks with new recruits and conscripts along with the usual number of returning veterans. In the spring of 1864, the 21st North Carolina had the highest strength in the brigade and was composed primarily of veteran personnel. The other three regiments (the 6th, 54th, and 57th) were smaller and contained a high percentage of new personnel. In addition, their individual companies typically had only one officer and one or two noncommissioned officers in the ranks. Most of the absent leadership of these units were still prisoners of war.

General Hoke returned to duty in late 1863 or early 1864 and was temporarily assigned to eastern North Carolina. In April 1864, he planned and directed a successful recapture of the coastal town of Plymouth. Among the forces in his command was his old brigade. As reward for this operation, Hoke was promoted to major general and given command of a division.[3] The command of his former brigade was given to Lt. Col. William G. Lewis of the 43rd North Carolina.[4] This regiment was temporarily attached to the brigade from Daniel's Brigade (of Rodes's Division). As an indication of the earlier loss of officers at Rappahannock Bridge, there were no other officers in the brigade at this time above the rank of captain.

With the commencement of active operations by Union forces in Virginia in early May, Hoke's (Lewis's) Brigade was quickly transported to Richmond and joined the army forming under General Beauregard. These units confronted General Butler's Army of the James. At this time, Lewis's command could field about 1,440 men. The 21st, 54th, and 57th North Carolina Regiments all were engaged at Drewry's Bluff on May 16.[5] These three units sustained a reported eighty casualties in this battle.[6]

In response to urgent entreaties made by General Lee to Richmond, Hoke's Brigade was returned to the Army of Northern Virginia, arriving at Spotsylvania on or about May 20–21.[7] The brigade was present at the remaining battles of the campaign but not seriously engaged until Bethesda Church and Cold Harbor. In fact, with one exception, all of the minor losses recorded at Spotsylvania, Milford Station, and North Anna consist of missing personnel or stragglers captured during marches from and to the various battlefields. The 6th North Carolina was lightly engaged at Bethesda Church on May 30. The entire brigade participated in a corps assault upon elements of the V Corps on June 2 and led a divisional reconnaissance upon the front of the IX Corps on June 6–7.[8] During these last several days, Hoke's Brigade sustained most of the limited casualties in Ramseur's Division.

Although, some of the above-detailed deficiencies in leadership and experienced personnel still lingered, Hoke's Brigade emerged from the Overland Campaign with the largest strength in the division. Colonel Godwin was exchanged and returned to duty after this campaign. He was promoted to brigadier general and placed in command of the brigade. Godwin was killed in September at Third Winchester.

The casualties in the brigade at Cold Harbor were published in North Carolina and Virginia newspapers.[9] Manarin and Jordan's volumes on North Carolina troops were also checked for this study.[10] For the brigade's losses during the Overland Campaign, see Table 41, Appendix A.

RODES'S DIVISION

This division, initially organized and commanded by Daniel H. Hill, became a solid fixture in the Second Corps. Under the leadership of the young and spirited Maj. Gen. Robert E. Rodes, it continued to perform reliably in 1863. In the spring of 1864, the division consisted of the following five brigades: Battle's, Doles's, Ramseur's, Daniel's, and Johnston's. Two regiments, one each from Doles and Daniel, were absent from their respective commands, attached to and serving with Hoke's Brigade in North Carolina and southeastern Virginia.[1] Nevertheless, these five brigades fielded the largest and, by many accounts, the best division in the corps.

At the start of the Overland Campaign, Johnston's Brigade was detached near Hanover Junction in the army's rear.[2] Ramseur's Brigade and one regiment of Battle's Brigade were, in addition, temporarily left at Raccoon Ford on May 4–5 to cover the rear of the corps as it moved toward the advancing Federal army.[3] As a result of these detachments, Rodes's Division entered the Wilderness on May 5 with less than three of its brigades and slightly more than one-half of its overall strength.

During the opening stages of this battle, Rodes's available units were initially deployed to the right of Johnson's Division south of Orange Turnpike on a low-lying ridge (see Map 1, Appendix B). Battle's Brigade was posted to the right-rear of Jones's Brigade (Johnson's Division). Doles's and Daniel's Brigades extended the line to the right (south).[4] In the early afternoon, the V Corps assaulted this position.[5] Rodes's Division was hard pressed to hold this line but succeeded, with some assistance from reserve elements of the Second Corps.

For the balance of the battle, Rodes remained in the same position on the southern side of Orange Turnpike and engaged in primarily skirmishing and sniping. Ramseur's Brigade and the detached regiment of Battle's Brigade arrived on the battlefield during the night of May 5–6.[6] Johnston's Brigade was relieved from its assignment in the rear on the fifth, hastily marched toward the battlefield, and arrived in the early afternoon of the sixth. Both of these brigades participated in the fighting on May 6.

The next day Rodes's Division was reduced to four brigades with the transfer of Johnston's Brigade to Early's Division, then commanded by Gordon. (For a discussion of the actions experienced by this unit, see the above summary for Early's Division as well as the brigade summary to follow.) Rodes's Division led the march of the Second Corps to Spotsylvania during the late afternoon of May 8 and near dusk was rushed into action against units of the V and VI Corps (see Map 13, Appendix B). These enemy forces were threatening the right (or eastern end) of the line held by Kershaw's Division of the First Corps. In the rapidly waning hours of daylight, the fighting quickly developed into a desperate melee-style action. Battle's Brigade, followed by the commands of Ramseur, Daniel, and Doles, all participated.[7] During the night and early hours of May 9, these units dug in on a line generally facing west between the First Corps and Johnson's Division. The brigades were arrayed from south to north in the same order as their arrival on the battlefield.

During most of May 9 and 10, Rodes's men principally engaged in skirmishing and sniping. In the evening hours of the tenth, elements of the VI Corps rushed upon and overwhelmed a significant portion of the divisional line (see Map 16, Appendix B).[8] For the Federals, this attack unfortunately was not supported and ultimately was repulsed. The Confederate commanders (Ewell and Rodes) reacted quickly to halt the breakthrough. With considerable assistance from both Johnson's and Early's Divisions, Rodes's men repulsed the Federals and restored the original line.

During the early hours of May 12, the II Corps executed a massive assault upon the portion of the Confederate line held by Johnson's Division. This assault was highly successful, breaking and destroying most of that division. Rodes's brigades, deployed to the immediate southwest of Johnson's front, were again embroiled in this conflict. The northern portion of the division formed a solid front on the western edge of the break and provided a refuge upon which the adjacent remnants of Johnson's command could escape and rally (see Map 18, Appendix B). Shortly thereafter, Rodes dispatched another portion of his division to resist a main portion of the breakthrough (see

Map 19, Appendix B). For the remainder of the day, these units held the line against Federals of the II and later the VI Corps massed on the opposite side of the earthworks.

The participation of Rodes's Division at Spotsylvania did not end with the close of the battle on May 12. On May 18, the division was lightly engaged repelling a costly Union attack on the new line held by the Second Corps (along the base of the Mule Shoe salient).[9] During the following day, General Ewell committed most of his corps to conduct a reconnaissance around the Federal right flank. The lead force of the column, Rodes's Division, collided unexpectedly with heavy artillery units posted in the rear of the Union army (see Map 24, Appendix B).[10] These particular units had been converted to infantry and had just arrived at the battlefield from Washington, D.C. The resulting action, referred to by historians as Harris Farm, deteriorated into an all-out conflict. Ewell's force quickly found itself outnumbered and without any artillery support. With considerable effort, the Confederates were able to extricate and withdraw all of their units.

At the close of the Battle of Spotsylvania, the two absent regiments serving with Hoke's Brigade rejoined their respective commands, bringing a much-needed reinforcement. At North Anna, Rodes's Division received a well-deserved respite. The Second Corps was deployed on the army's right. As part of this line, Rodes was posted on the corps's left (next to the First Corps). For the most part, this was a relatively inactive portion of the battlefield. The only noted action for the division occurred during the evening of May 24 (see Map 29, Appendix B). In this encounter, the sharpshooters of the division engaged with enemy skirmishers just east of the Richmond, Fredericksburg, and Potomac Railroad.[11]

Rodes's Division was heavily engaged in the battles outside Richmond in late May and early June. On May 30 at Bethesda Church, the division sparred with elements of the V Corps astride Old Church Road and drove them back about one-half mile before being forced to retire (see Map 31, Appendix B).[12] The next day this command was shifted to the corps's left astride and north of Shady Grove Road (see Map 32, Appendix B). Rodes's Division remained in this same general position and participated in several phases of heavy but inconclusive fighting against the V and IX Corps on June 1–3 (see Maps 36, 37, and 41, Appendix B).[13]

During the Overland Campaign, Rodes's Division saw more than its fair share of fighting and paid a heavy price for its continued usage. Each of the five original brigades lost at least 50 percent of its initial strength, and the total loss for these commands actually exceeded the corresponding total loss for Johnson's Division. Unlike the latter, which was mostly captured, Rodes's Division sustained a much higher proportion of killed and wounded. In particular at Spotsylvania, Rodes's Division engaged in more heavy and desperate fighting than any other unit (of similar size) in Lee's army. Together with Gordon's/Evans's and Pegram's Brigades, they clearly formed the backbone of the Second Corps and determined the outcome of this battle.

Ramseur's Brigade

Stephen D. Ramseur, a young and aggressive officer, commanded this brigade of North Carolinians from early 1863. Under his leadership and training, this unit became one of better brigades in Rodes's Division and the Second Corps. It especially performed very well in the Battles of Chancellorsville and Gettysburg. The total number of reported casualties during 1863 was significant, reaching 1,373 men for the units of this brigade, the 2nd, 4th, 14th, and 30th North Carolina Regiments.[1] They were recruited from the eastern and west-central portions of the state. The heaviest brigade losses were incurred at Chancellorsville in May and at Kelly's Ford on November 7. During the latter action, portions of the 2nd North Carolina and 30th North Carolina Regiments were overwhelmed and captured by elements of the III Corps. As a result of these losses, Ramseur's Brigade entered the Overland Campaign at a somewhat diminished strength of 1,440 men.

On May 5, Ramseur's Brigade was temporarily left to cover the rear of the Second Corps as it moved into the Wilderness and to scout and confirm enemy intentions. Once it was clear that the entire Federal army was committed at the Wilderness, the unit was quickly ordered to rejoin its division. The North Carolinians arrived at the battlefield during the night of May 5–6 and were first placed in corps reserve. The following day, May 6, the brigade was shifted to the corps's right. In this movement, it blunted an advance by the IX Corps toward the high ground around the Chewing Farm.[2] At this stage of the battle, a large gap separated the two wings of Lee's army. But with this action, Ramseur's Brigade prevented the enemy from reaching and exploiting this weakness.

On the march to Spotsylvania on May 8, Ramseur's Brigade followed Battle's command. Upon arrival, the North Carolinians were quickly dispatched to combat enemy forces threatening the right of the First Corps.[3] The men then constructed breastworks in this position for the next two days. On the evening of May 10, the brigade participated in the successful counterattack against enemy forces that had overwhelmed Doles's front on the division's right (see Map 16, Appendix B).[4] So far in the campaign, Ramseur's command had been engaged on three occasions but had not sustained serious losses. This would dramatically change on May 12.

In the early hours of that day, the II Corps assaulted and overwhelmed adjacent portions of the Confederate line held by Johnson's Division to the northeast. In response to this disaster, Ramseur's Brigade was ordered to counterattack and restore a portion of the lost defenses. Ramseur pulled his men out of line, faced to the north, and advanced toward the enemy forces occupying the left portion of Johnson's front held previously by Hays's and Walker's Brigades (see Map 19, Appendix B). During this advance, the North Carolinians were subjected to heavy fire but did not falter. The regiments of the command were arrayed from west to east in the following manner: the 14th, 4th, 2nd, and 30th. This attack successfully pushed the enemy over two lines of breastworks to the outer face of the main line. During this assault, General Ramseur was painfully wounded. He refused to leave the field but was temporarily absent for a short period. Col. Bryan Grimes of the 4th North Carolina commanded the brigade in his absence.[5]

After capturing the outer line of earthworks, Grimes recognized that his right flank was exposed. The 30th North Carolina, in particular, was subjected to a continual flanking fire and envelopment and lost heavily.[6] General Lee then dispatched several brigades of the Third Corps from other areas of the Confederate line to advance and cover Ramseur's eastern flank. At the same time, the Federals committed the VI Corps to this sector, joining the men of the II Corps massed and hunkered down along the outer face of the main line of breastworks. The fighting was of a close-order, desperate nature and continued throughout the rest of the day amid a driving rainstorm.[7] This portion of the battlefield and the sector to the east became known as the "Bloody Angle." After darkness, the Ramseur's men withdrew to a newly constructed line in the rear.

Ramseur's Brigade was subsequently engaged at Spotsylvania on May 18 and 19. The participation of the command on the eighteenth was very slight, given the quick nature and failure of the Federal assault. But the following day, the brigade led the march of Ewell's corps and actually initiated the fighting at Harris Farm.[8] The price paid for this involvement was relatively high, especially when viewed in light of the casualties sustained on May 12 (detailed below). After the twelfth, the command had received a small reinforcement in the form of the 1st and 3rd North Carolina Regiments from Steuart's (discontinued) Brigade. These units had been practically destroyed at the Mule Shoe salient, and the reinforcement amounted to only about sixty men.

As mentioned above, Ramseur's Brigade was present at the remaining battles of the campaign. The North Carolinians engaged enemy forces at North Anna on May 24, at Bethesda Church on May 30, and at Cold Harbor on June 1–3.[9] The loss in the brigade on May 30 was again proportionally high. On this day, the brigade probably supported Grimes's Brigade (described below). General Ramseur was assigned to command Early's Division in late May, and command of the brigade went to the senior-ranking colonel, Risden T. Bennett of the 14th North Carolina. Bennett was seriously wounded at Cold Harbor on June 2, and Col. William R. Cox of the 2nd North Carolina then was given command.[10] At the close of the campaign, Ramseur's Brigade was still an intact and competent fighting unit, though significantly reduced in strength.

See Table 42, Appendix A for the casualties sustained by Ramseur's Brigade during the campaign. The command sustained a recorded 653 casualties at Spotsylvania. An estimated daily breakdown of this total loss is as follows: 54 on May 8; 39 on May 10; 392 on May 12; 1 each on May 14, 15, and 18; and 160 on May 19. Five men, probably ill and left at the corps hospital when the army moved on to North Anna, were also captured on this battlefield on June 10. The number of casualties sustained in the campaign may have been slightly higher. The casualty lists from newspapers provide a patchwork of information with some gaps.[11] No listings for the 2nd North Carolina Regiment were found for battles after May 11. The reported number of casualties for this unit at Spotsylvania appears to be somewhat low. No newspaper casualty lists were found for the 14th and 30th North Carolina Regiments for battles after May 20. As with the other brigades from North Carolina, Manarin and Jordan's volumes were included in the research for this command.[12]

Daniel's/Grimes's Brigade

Junius Daniel's brigade of North Carolinians was a comparatively recent addition to the Army of Northern Virginia, having been assigned to Rodes's

Division after the Battle of Chancellorsville to replace Colquitt's Brigade. But Daniel's unit was not a new command, having served for over a year in eastern North Carolina. At Gettysburg, the unit sustained heavy losses. Its total reported number of battle casualties for 1863 was 956.[1] In the fall of that year, the field strength of the brigade was reduced with the departure of the largest regiment, the 43rd North Carolina, to its home state with Hoke's Brigade. The composition of Daniel's Brigade was then the 32nd, 45th, and 53rd North Carolina Regiments and the 2nd North Carolina Battalion, units raised from the eastern and central part of the state.

Daniel's Brigade was moderately engaged at the Wilderness on May 5. During the early afternoon, the North Carolinians easily repulsed an attack by the Fourth Division, V Corps (see Map 1, Appendix B).[2] This was in contrast to a local Union success on the left of the divisional line. Judging by the compiled brigade casualties, the 45th North Carolina Regiment, positioned on the left (next to Doles's Brigade), was the only unit of the command heavily engaged in this early phase of the Wilderness. For the remainder of this battle, the brigade saw limited action and engaged only in skirmishing and sniping.

Daniel's Brigade was the third unit in the divisional column on the march to Spotsylvania, arriving after Battle's and Ramseur's Brigades. As a result, it appears to have been only lightly engaged on May 8. On May 10, the North Carolinians were not as fortunate. Upton's successful assault against Doles's Brigade on that evening also encompassed part of Daniel's line (see Map 16, Appendix B). The 32nd North Carolina, posted next to Doles's command on the right, was overwhelmed and largely captured. A check of the compiled casualties for this day indicates that this regiment lost nearly 75 percent of its strength. The 45th North Carolina was apparently posted next to the 32nd Regiment and also suffered heavily. Together, they lost more than 300 men as prisoners. The remainder of Daniel's Brigade formed a new line perpendicular to their original position and fought to hold the southern side of the breach.[3] The arrival of other units from the Second Corps ultimately halted the breakthrough and forced the Union forces to withdraw.

On the morning of May 12, Daniel's Brigade held a section of breastworks southwest of and next to Johnson's Division. Following the initial success of the Federal assault upon this division, the North Carolinians blunted the enemy's attempt to expand this breakthrough (see Map 18, Appendix B).[4] The command was thereafter embroiled in the close-order fighting against elements of the II and VI Corps near and west of the Bloody Angle for the rest of the day (see Map 19, Appendix B). Judging by the relatively low number of reported casualties for the brigade, it appears that the men benefited from the constructed earthworks. During this fighting, however, General Daniel was mortally wounded.[5] He apparently died the following day, though one report in the service records lists the date of his death as May 19. At this point in the campaign, there were no colonels left in the brigade's ranks so Col. Bryan Grimes of the 4th North Carolina Regiment (Ramseur's Brigade) was assigned brigade command and soon promoted to brigadier general.[6]

Grimes's Brigade was again engaged on May 18 and 19 at Spotsylvania. On the latter day (at Harris Farm), the command saw heavy combat and lost considerably.[7] The 43rd North Carolina Regiment returned to the brigade after May 19 as a much-needed reinforcement. Along with their division, the North Carolinians saw action at North Anna on May 24, Bethesda Church on May 30, and Cold Harbor on June 1–3 (see Map 29, Appendix B). The brigade was especially successful executing a limited assault on May 30 against elements of the V Corps.[8] The newly arrived 43rd Regiment sustained about one-half to two-thirds of the casualties for the entire brigade in each of these limited engagements. In the view of brigade command, this unit was probably considered the freshest and most combat ready.

The casualties for Daniel's/Grimes's Brigade during the Overland Campaign are provided in Table 43, Appendix A. The command sustained a reported total of 772 casualties at Spotsylvania. A breakdown of this loss is as follows: 14 on May 8; 2 on May 9; 525 on May 10 (including 345 unwounded prisoners); 60 on May 12; 5 on May 14–15; 4 on May 17; 2 on May 18; 148 on May 19; and 4 on May 21–22 (likely stragglers captured on the march from this battlefield). In addition, 6 men were captured on June 10 at the battlefield, probably either ill or left to tend to the sick and severely wounded (as field nurses) at the corps's field hospital. This brigade is well covered in the North Carolina newspapers and in Manarin and Jordan's volumes on North Carolina troops.[9]

Doles's Brigade

This brigade of Georgia troops was viewed by many in the Army of Northern Virginia as one of the better units in Rodes's Division and, for that matter, in the Second Corps. Brig. Gen. George Doles had commanded the brigade since late 1862. He had handled his troops capably at Chancellorsville and superbly at Gettysburg, with comparably fewer losses than the other brigades in the division. The total reported number of combat losses for the brigade in 1863 was 685.[1] As a result of these comparatively light casualties, Doles's Brigade was in excellent condition at the start of the campaign. One regiment, the 21st Georgia (minus one company recently transferred and attached to the 44th Georgia), was detached with Hoke's Brigade and not available for the Wilderness and Spotsylvania. The strength of the remaining three regiments, 4th, 12th, and 44th Georgia (and one company) at this time was about 1,365 men. They had been recruited from counties located in the middle to western portions of the state.

In the opening phase of the Wilderness, Doles's Brigade was initially posted in the division's center. Elements of the V Corps assaulted this position during the early afternoon and temporarily drove back the left portion of this command (see Map 1, Appendix B). Rodes and Doles rallied the retreating personnel and restored the line.[2] The 4th Georgia appears to have sustained particularly heavy losses during this action (see Table 44, Appendix A). For the balance of the battle, the brigade remained in the same approximate position but took part in no additional significant fighting.

Doles's Brigade brought up the rear of Rodes's Division in the march to Spotsylvania on May 8. It was, accordingly, posted last on the division line (on the right) and next to Johnson's Division; it was lightly engaged that day. The arrangement of the three regiments was, from south to north: the 44th, 4th, and 12th.[3] Two days later, Doles's Brigade experienced one of its worst days of the war. Elements of the VI Corps under the command of Emory Upton, in a well-planned and executed operation, attacked and overwhelmed the entire brigade front (see Map 16, Appendix B).[4] The Union forces were aided by the cover of a stretch of woods located close to the main line of breastworks. In addition in the late afternoon hours, Colonel Upton's forces purposefully drove in the brigade's picket line, thus removing and negating any early warning of the concentration and impending assault. Lastly, the attack was designed to occur in the evening hours and appears to have, as intentioned, caught the Georgians somewhat unprepared.

In any event, after a brief period of hand-to-hand combat, Doles's entire brigade was overwhelmed. A compilation of the available records indicates that its regiments lost about 625–650 men, with over 400 prisoners, out of an initial strength of 1,100 troops. It is likely that, in the fading hours of daylight, many of the men escaped capture. Those who were taken by the Federals were moved over the breastworks and then rushed to the rear for incarceration. General Doles was himself initially captured but escaped by pretending to be wounded and lying among the fallen men outside the breastworks.[5] After the firing abated with the end of daylight, the general merely rose up and climbed back over the works to safety. As fate would have it, he personally would have been better off remaining a prisoner.

For the rest of the battle, the brigade was again in action on May 12, 18, and 19. On the first of these days, the remnant of Doles's command supported Daniel's Brigade and also briefly assisted Wilcox's Division of the Third Corps (to the east).[6] This small force was also heavily engaged at Harris Farm on May 19 with the rest of Rodes's Division.[7] The main portion of the 21st Georgia rejoined the brigade after this engagement, nearly doubling its strength at that time. Despite the crippling losses at Wilderness and Spotsylvania, the unit continued to function as a separate command.

Doles's Brigade was next lightly engaged at North Anna on May 24 and at Bethesda Church on May 30. On June 1–3, the Georgians participated in the divisional operations at Cold Harbor against elements of the V Corps (see above). As could be expected, the relatively fresh 21st Georgia Regiment sustained the bulk of the small losses incurred during these latter actions of the campaign. General Doles, though, was killed along Shady Grove Road on June 2. Phillip Cook of the 4th Georgia Regiment, the ranking colonel present, then assumed command of the brigade.[8] As discussed earlier, Col. Edward Willis of the 12th Georgia Regiment had been assigned to temporarily command Pegram's Brigade (Ramseur's Division) on May 30; he was mortally wounded that same day and died May 31.

The casualties for Doles's Brigade during the Overland Campaign are provided in Table 44. The Georgians sustained a reported 724 battle casualties at Spotsylvania; 674 of these occurred on May 10 and 12. Although the records do not clearly separate the losses on these two days, it is likely that approximately 650 were incurred on May 10. The number of unwounded prisoners lost on that day was 411. A breakdown of the remaining losses for Doles's Brigade at Spotsylvania is as follows: 23 on May 8; 1 on May 18; 20 on May 19; and 6 on May 21–22. The *Macon Daily Telegraph* published a casualty list for the entire brigade at the Wilderness and Spotsylvania in early June.[9] The research for this brigade was supplemented with one limited casualty list from a Richmond newspaper and Lillian Henderson's rosters.[10] No newspaper listings were found for battles after May 21. In any event, it is difficult to imagine how this command could have sustained any further casualties during the campaign.

Battle's Brigade

Under the leadership of its original commander, Robert Rodes, this brigade of five Alabama regiments forged a solid fighting record in 1862. With the promotion of Rodes to lead the division in 1863, the command of the brigade fell to the senior colonel present at that time, Edward O'Neal of the 26th Alabama Regiment. O'Neal led the brigade at the Battles of Chancellorsville and Gettysburg with little distinction and incurring heavy losses. The total reported number of casualties for the brigade during 1863 was 1,548 men.[1] Most of these occurred at the two major battles under O'Neal's leadership.

In view of O'Neal's performance, the corps and army command looked for a change. Col. Cullen A. Battle, the commander of the 3rd Alabama Regiment, was considered a promising young officer in the mold of Robert Rodes. General Lee arranged for the desired change by transferring O'Neal and his regiment to their home state to recruit and reorganize, thereafter promoting Battle.[2] The 61st Alabama, a relatively inexperienced regiment serving on garrison duty in it home state, took the place of the departing 26th Alabama. Soon after joining the army in early 1864, this regiment, like many new units, initially experienced a significantly high rate of sickness. Despite this impediment, the brigade could field at the start of the Overland Campaign slightly more than 1,800 men. The other units comprising this organization were the 3rd, 5th, 6th, and 12th Alabama Regiments, all of which had been recruited from counties located primarily in the southern half of the state.

Battle's Brigade was heavily engaged in the initial phase of the Battle of the Wilderness. It was arrayed with the 3rd and 5th Alabama Regiments on the left and the 6th and 61st Alabama on the right.[3] There are reports that, when the Federal forces first attacked, some of the men of the first two units were under the impression that they were not to bring on a major engagement at this time. Others stated that they were ordered to retire by an unnamed officer in Jones's Brigade.[4] In any event, this portion of the brigade withdrew in confusion (with Jones's Brigade) before being rallied and moved back into the action (see Map 1, Appendix B). The 12th Alabama Regiment, which had temporarily been left at Raccoon Ford with Ramseur's Brigade, rejoined Battle's Brigade late that night. For the remainder of the battle, Battle's command occupied the left portion of the divisional sector and was involved in only skirmishing and sniping. As a side note, the veterans in the older four regiments expressed satisfaction with the performance of the 61st Alabama.[5]

Battle's Brigade led Rodes's Division in the march to Spotsylvania. As a result, it was the first to become engaged in the melee-style action against elements of the V and VI Corps at dusk on May 8 (see Map 13, Appendix B).[6] General Battle was slightly wounded in this action but remained on the field. His Alabama troops were subsequently engaged in the fighting on May 10, 12, 18, and 19. On the first of these days, the brigade was heavily involved in halting the breakthrough of Upton's Union forces (see Map 16, Appendix B).[7] On May 12, it supported Ramseur's and Daniel's Brigades at and west of the Bloody Angle (see Map 18, Appendix B).[8] On May 19, the command was one of the principal units that forced the action at Harris Farm.[9]

Battle's Brigade was lightly engaged at North Anna on May 24 but took part in the heavier fighting at Bethesda Church on May 30 and Cold Harbor on June 1–3. Although the campaign had been an experience of steady attrition resulting in a loss of more that 50 percent, Battle's Brigade emerged from Cold Harbor with most of its command structure intact and a combat strength higher than the corps average.

The casualties for Battle's Brigade during the campaign are provided in Table 45, Appendix A. The analysis to compile this information encountered some obstacles but, at the same time, some revealing and beneficial information for this study. A tabulation of the personnel casualties recorded in the CSRs yielded the following minimal totals for the individual regiments: 148 for the 3rd Alabama; 177 for the 5th Alabama; 178 for the 6th Alabama; 111 for the 12th Alabama; and 153 for the 61st Alabama. In addition, a number of men in each regiment entered a hospital following the commencement of the campaign with an unrecorded ailment. Initially for this study, it was considered that they could have been wounded.

Clearly, additional, more-detailed sources were needed. Several newspapers published in Alabama, in part, filled this need.[10] These sources listed some of the most detailed information found for this study and shed considerable light upon the research to accurately determine the brigade's battle casualties during the campaign. The vast majority of new men found to be casualties were wounded at either the Wilderness or Spotsylvania. Many of these were individuals suspected earlier from the uncertain hospital records. Unfortunately, no newspaper lists were found for the most of the 5th and all of the 61st Alabama Regiments.

With the inclusion of this additional information, the increase in the 3rd and 6th Alabama Regiments and one company of the 5th Alabama Regiment was about 16–18 percent. For the 12th Alabama Regiment, which missed the May 5 action at the Wilderness, the increase was even greater (about 31 percent). On this basis, the conclusion was that the total casualties for the remainder of the 5th and 61st Regiments were also greater. Most of these men were likely slightly wounded and returned to the ranks in May or June.

One additional reference was found in the newspapers. The *Montgomery Daily Advertiser* reported that the 12th Alabama Regiment had lost 78 men at Spotsylvania between May 8 and 12 and that the entire brigade had sustained 614 casualties up to and including May 12.[11] A careful examination of the compiled personnel losses to this point revealed that there was a deficit and that the required increase (attributable to the 5th and 61st Regiments) would be in the same proportion or percentage as the confirmed increases to the 3rd and 6th Regiments. On this basis, the casualty totals for the two listed regiments were increased as follows: the 5th Alabama Regiment, 10 more wounded at Wilderness and 2 more wounded at Spotsylvania; and 61st Alabama Regiment, 6 additional wounded at Wilderness (see Table 45). The actual number of battle casualties sustained by the 5th and 61st Regiments probably was higher.

Battle's Brigade lost a total of 483 casualties at Spotsylvania. Using the available newspaper sources and the other available information, this loss can be broken down on a daily basis in the following manner: 113 on May 8; 44 on May 10; 161 on May 12; 1 on May 16; 4 on May 18; and 157 on May 19. In addition, 3 men were captured on the battlefield on June 10 who were either very ill or were left as nurses at the corps field hospital. It is possible that some of the casualties listed for May 12 could have occurred on May 10.

Unlike the other brigades in Rodes's Division, Battle's Brigade did not lose a significant number of casualties in one battle or on one day of Spotsylvania. As shown above, this command experienced moderate but continuous combat losses in nearly every engagement. The total and proportion of casualties matched any unit in the rest of the corps and demonstrates the competency of this brigade.

Johnston's Brigade

This brigade of four North Carolina regiments was a solid component in D. H. Hill's (later Rodes's) Division for almost two years, though it seemed to be an ill-fated and hard-luck outfit. The brigade served valiantly but lost severely during the Peninsula Campaign. Several months later, the organization lost its young and aggressive leader, Brig. Gen. Samuel Garland, at South Mountain, sustaining additional heavy casualties at this engagement and at the subsequent Battle of Antietam. Thereafter, Alfred Iverson Jr. of the 23rd North Carolina Regiment was promoted to command of the brigade.

The major problem with this assignment was that Iverson was a native of Georgia and not North Carolina. During the Battle of Gettysburg, much of the brigade was decimated on the first day in a reckless attack. Iverson, who played a role in the flawed deployment of the command and stayed in the rear, was heard to make some disparaging remarks regarding the conduct of the troops.[1] Word of his comments spread like wildfire through the ranks, and in the aftermath of this battle, the men refused to continue serving under his command.[2] Iverson was conveniently transferred to another assignment, and Robert D. Johnston of the 23rd North Carolina Regiment, a North Carolinian, was promoted to brigade command.[3]

The reported battle losses for 1863 in the brigade were 1,423 men.[4] During the winter of 1863–64, Johnston worked to restore the morale of his unit. The strength of the organization improved with the return of many of the men wounded in 1863. But with only about 1,320 men at the start of the Overland Campaign, Johnston's Brigade was the smallest command in the division. The personnel of its four regiments (the 5th, 12th, 20th, and 23rd North Carolina) were raised from the southeastern, east-central, and west-central portions of the state.

At the beginning of May, Johnston's Brigade was stationed in the army's rear at Hanover Junction. The North Carolinians joined the army at the Wilderness battlefield during the afternoon of the second day (May 6) and participated in Gordon's successful flanking attack upon the VI Corps at dusk (see Map 9, Appendix B).[5] After this battle, Johnston's Brigade was transferred to Early's (soon Gordon's) Division.[6]

Early's Division (and Johnston's Brigade) was initially posted in corps reserve at Spotsylvania. The North Carolinians were committed on four separate occasions during this battle. In several of these actions, the past misfortune again returned. On May 9, Confederate cavalry pickets observed enemy activity along Fredericksburg Road northeast of Spotsylvania Court House. Johnston and a portion of his brigade were sent to reconnoiter. They encountered a superior force of the IX Corps and sustained more than 40 percent casualties in the engagement.[7] On May 10, the brigade took part in a successful counterattack against the enemy force that broke and overwhelmed Doles's Brigade.[8]

On May 12, Johnston's Brigade was the first unit committed by General Gordon to counterattack the Union forces that had captured most of Johnson's Division. The North Carolinians advanced into the dense fog and encountered a sizeable portion of the II Corps (see Map 19, Appendix B). The brigade was nearly overwhelmed and badly cut up. During this advance, General Johnston was wounded. His successor, Col. Thomas M. Garrett of the 5th North Carolina Regiment, was then killed. The leadership of the brigade thereafter fell to Col. Thomas F. Toon of the 20th North Carolina Regiment. Gordon pulled the North Carolinians back to a new line. Although they failed to regain the lost ground and suffered severely, they had halted the Union advance and temporarily threw the enemy into some confusion. Elements of Johnston's Brigade then supported Pegram's and Gordon's (Evans's) Brigades in their successful attack in regaining the lost ground.[9] Lastly, the brigade took part in the fighting at Harris Farm on May 19.[10]

Johnston's Brigade, still under Toon's command, was present at North Anna but sustained no recorded casualties. It was also lightly engaged at Bethesda Church on May 30 and at Cold Harbor on June 1–3. At the close of the campaign, the command was severely reduced in both numbers and leadership.

The battle losses for Johnston's Brigade during the campaign are provided in Table 46, Appendix A. The command suffered a reported total of 739 casualties at Spotsylvania. A daily breakdown of this total loss is as follows: 150 on May 9; 54 on May 10; 2 on May 11; 401 on May 12; 2 on May 15; 2 on May 16–17; and 122 on May 19. In addition, 6 men were captured at Spotsylvania on June 10; some of these were ill, while others were reported as being musicians and left as nurses with the severely wounded and sick at the corps field hospital.

It is possible, even likely, that the losses sustained by this brigade in the campaign were slightly higher. The recently published volumes by Manarin and Jordan on North Carolina troops were included in the research for this brigade.[11] Several additional casualties were found in this source. Newspaper listings for the full campaign were found for only two of the regiments (the 12th and 20th North Carolina).[12] For the 5th North Carolina, a listing for only one company was found, covering the period of May 6–19. Nothing was found for the 23rd North Carolina.

ARTILLERY

The artillery component of the Second Corps consisted of eighteen batteries in five battalions. Lt. Col. Robert A. Hardaway's battalion consisted of the batteries of Jones (Virginia, 2nd Richmond Howitzers), Smith (Virginia, 3rd Richmond Howitzers), Graham (Virginia, 1st Rockbridge), Dance (Virginia, Powhatan), and Griffin (Virginia, Salem/Roanoke). Maj. Richard C. M. Page's battalion was composed of the batteries of Reese (Alabama, Jeff Davis), Carter (Virginia, King William), Fry (Virginia, Orange), and Montgomery (Virginia, Louisa). The remaining three battalions fielded only three batteries. Maj. Wilfred E. Cutshaw commanded the batteries of Garber (Virginia, Staunton), Carrington (Virginia, Charlottesville), and Tanner (Virginia, Richmond Courtney). Lt. Col. Carter M. Braxton led the batteries of Carpenter (Virginia, Alleghany), Cooper (Virginia, Stafford), and Hardwicke (Virginia, Lynchburg). Lt. Col. William Nelson's battalion consisted of the batteries of Milledge (Georgia Regulars), Kilpatrick (Virginia, Amherst), and Massie (Virginia, Fluvanna).

As can be perceived, nearly all of the artillery batteries in the Second Corps were composed of Virginians. Like the artillery arm of the First Corps, all of the units and their leaders were veterans. The commander of the corps artillery was Brig. Gen. Armistead L. Long. At the start of the campaign, Hardaway's, Braxton's, and Nelson's Battalions were under the direction of Col. William H. Carter. Similarly, Page's and Cutshaw's Battalions were led by Col. J. Thompson Brown.

For the most part, the artillery of the Second Corps was not engaged at the Wilderness. This was due primarily to the heavily wooded character of the northern portion of the battlefield. The artillery, however, reported four casualties in action. Chief among this loss was the combat death of Colonel Brown.

In contrast to the Wilderness, the Second Corps artillery was heavily engaged and suffered severe losses during the Battle of Spotsylvania. The infantry of the Second Corps took up a position to the right of the First Corps during the night of May 8–9. The artillery battalions were deployed at various points along this line where they could cover the approaches to the front and command a clear field of fire. Initially, on May 9, Page's and Braxton's Battalions were placed on the front line and the remaining battalions were held in reserve. On May 10, the corps command shuffled these units. Nelson's Battalion replaced Braxton's and was deployed with Johnson's Division. Jones's and Smith's Batteries (of Hardaway's Battalion) relieved Page and were posted with Rodes's Division. The remaining three batteries of Hardaway's Battalion and Cutshaw's Battalion were kept in the immediate rear with Gordon's improvised division. Braxton's and Page's Battalions were sent back to the rear near Spotsylvania Court House.

In the late afternoon of May 10, the Fourth Division, II Corps assaulted the portion of the front held by Johnson's men. Nelson's and Page's Batteries (along with the infantry of Hays's Brigade) were chiefly responsible for repulsing this attack (see Map 16, Appendix B).[1] Elements of the VI Corps assaulted the portion of the line held by Doles's and Daniel's Brigades of Rodes's Division just before dusk on the same day. The batteries of Smith and Jones were posted in this sector. Initially, the Federals captured Smith's four guns and about a quarter of the battery's personnel.[2] The Second Corps command then brought up reserve units and counterattacked. In the confusion of the battle and in concert with the counterattack, the surviving men of the battery, with some men of Jones's Battery, were able to regain the guns and contribute to the eventual repulse of the Federals.[3] Overall, this fighting cost Smith's Battery 40 casualties.

Overnight and during the following day, the deployment of the corps artillery was again changed. Smith's Battery was relieved by the remaining batteries of Hardaway's Battalion and sent to the rear. In the sector of Johnson's Division, Cutshaw's Battalion was added to Nelson's and Page's Battalions. During the night of May 11–12, General Lee concluded that the Federal army would be retreating from the battlefield in the morning. He wanted to pursue the enemy forces promptly in an effort to gain a tactical advantage. Accordingly, he ordered General Long to remove the artillery (Page's and Nelson's Battalions) from most of the section held by Johnson's Division. In the view of the army commander and his staff, the access trail leading to this area was too narrow and somewhat obstructed by woods.[4]

In response to pleas by the respective corps and division commanders, Richard S. Ewell and Edward Johnson, this artillery was returned at daybreak on May 12. Cutshaw's Battalion had not been removed and was still positioned along the western side of the Mule Shoe salient. This deployment consisted of Garber's Battery with Daniel's Brigade of Rodes's Division and Tanner's and Carrington's Batteries with the Stonewall Brigade and York's Brigade. Page's four batteries were dispatched and returned to the eastern side of the salient to join Jones's (under Witcher) and Steuart's Brigades. The positioning of these batteries, from north to south, was: Montgomery's, Carter's, Fry's, and Reese's.[5] During the movement to the front, one gun of Montgomery's Battery sustained a breakdown and was left in the rear. One section (two guns) of Fry's Battery was absent detached at the time.[6]

Thus, the Second Corps had twenty-one guns deployed with Johnson's Division. Unfortunately for the Confederate cause, the thirteen guns of Page's Battalion were unlimbered just minutes before the entire II Corps assaulted and broke through a portion of the division's line. As the Federal forces enveloped each of Johnson's brigades, all twenty-one guns as well as 204 men from Cutshaw's and Page's Battalions were captured.[7] Overall, these six batteries sustained 250 casualties. Following the initial enemy success, Rodes and Ewell faced the batteries of Garber and Jones toward the north and kept the Federals from advancing farther into the salient.[8]

Following the retirement of the Confederate forces from the Mule Shoe during the night of May 12–13, the artillery of the Second Corps was reformed and posted along the new line of earthworks constructed along the base of the salient. This line was assaulted by elements of the II and VI Corps on May 18. The batteries (of principally Hardaway's, Nelson's, and Braxton's Battalions) quickly broke up this attack and inflicted heavy casualties with little loss to the Southern ranks.[9]

For the most part, the corps artillery was lightly engaged or not engaged at the Battles of North Anna and Totopotomoy Creek (Bethesda Church). During the first three days of June at Cold Harbor, most of the batteries sparred with Federal artillery and supported limited offensive excursions by Gordon's and Rodes's Divisions against the V and IX Corps. Most of this action fell upon Nelson's and Hardaway's Battalions. Kirkpatrick's Battery, in particular, appears to have been roughly deployed and handled, losing twenty-nine men on June 3.

The accuracy of the records for these batteries varies widely. The muster rolls for Page's and Cutshaw's Battalions are very good. Those for Hardaway's and Nelson's Battalions are acceptable. Conversely, the muster rolls for Braxton's Battalion have many gaps. Additionally, the records for most of the batteries in Page's and Nelson's Battalions contain inspection reports. These detail the activities and casualties for the respective battery for all of 1864 and are, accordingly, an excellent source. Lastly, newspaper casualty lists were found for all eighteen batteries. These principally cover the major engagements (and casualties) at Spotsylvania and Cold Harbor. Lastly, the respective books of the Virginia Regimental Histories Series were included in the research for this study.[10] See Table 47, Appendix A, for the casualties sustained by the Second Corps artillery during the Overland Campaign.

CHAPTER 6

Third Corps

HETH'S DIVISION

This division was formed after the Battle of Chancellorsville by combining Brockenbrough's and Archer's Brigades of Maj. Gen. A. P. Hill's Light Division with the brigades of Pettigrew and Davis. The latter two units were new only to the Army of Northern Virginia, having previously served in southeastern Virginia and North Carolina. At Gettysburg, Maj. Gen. Henry Heth's Division obtained two notable distinctions. It was the first unit of Lee's army to be engaged in this battle and, over the course of the three days, sustained the highest divisional losses. These casualties resulted from heavy fighting on July 1 and participation in Pickett's/Pettigrew's/Trimble's Charge on July 3. Heth's command received a needed reinforcement with the assignment of Cooke's Brigade in August 1863, but on October 14 a portion of the division was badly cut up at Bristoe Station.

Heth's Division recovered from these battle losses over the winter of 1863–64 with the influx of wounded veterans, exchanged prisoners, and new recruits. In addition, it received some reinforcements in April 1864 in the form of a regiment and a battalion from Mississippi to Davis's Brigade. By the start of the Overland Campaign, the strength of Heth's Division had increased significantly and was the second highest in the army (exceeded only by Wilcox's command). The division at this time consisted of the brigades of Kirkland, Cooke, Davis, and Walker. The first three brigades were solid organizations. The latter was an amalgamation of the former brigades of Archer and Brockenbrough. These organizations were from different states and had separate identities and battle histories. The merger would ultimately prove to be a problem.

Heth's Division led the advance of the Third Corps into the Wilderness.[1] With the first enemy contact, it was deployed during the afternoon of May 5, with Davis on the left, Cooke in the center (astride Orange Plank Road), and Walker on the right.[2] Kirkland's Brigade was initially held in reserve. In the later part of the afternoon, the II Corps, assisted by most of the Second Division, VI Corps, began engaging these units. This Union force increased and maintained the pressure for the remainder of the day (see Map 3, Appendix B).[3] Most of the landscape consisted of dense woods with thick underbrush, and in many cases, it was difficult to distinguish friend from foe. Heth's Division managed to hold its position, but in the process lost heavily. The arrival of Wilcox's Division during the latter hours of the day provided a well-needed reinforcement and relief.

At this stage of the battle, the men were exhausted and their lines intermixed. The darkness and dense character of the woods contributed to the confusion. In some areas, enemy forces were a stone's throw away, and their conversations could be clearly heard. Both Wilcox and Heth expressed a serious concern to A. P. Hill, the Third Corps commander, regarding the state of the Confederate position. They attempted to reorganize the line, with Wilcox's Division primarily moving to the southern side of Orange Plank Road and Heth's Division shifting to the northern side. Hill, with Lee's approval, elected to forego any further improvements to the line (such as breastworks).[4] Reinforcements in the form of Longstreet's First Corps were expected early the next day.

The opposing Federal forces of Maj. Gen. Winfield Hancock got the jump on these two Confederate units in the early morning hours of May 6.[5] Hancock unleashed an overwhelming force in a massive assault across the entire front of both Wilcox's and Heth's Divisions (see Map 5, Appendix B). The bulk of the latter initially withstood the First Division, V Corps, but the defeat and retirement of Wilcox's Division (to the right) forced its withdrawal as well.[6] Following the arrival of Longstreet's corps, Heth's Division was rallied and shifted to the corps's center between Wilcox's and Anderson's Divisions.[7] In this position, the division saw little further action. Davis's Brigade, however, somehow got separated and engaged in addition combat that day.

Heth's Division moved to Spotsylvania on May 8–9 and was initially posted in reserve.[8] In response to a Federal move against the Confederate left flank south of the Po River at Block House Bridge during the afternoon of May 9, General Lee ordered Heth's and Mahone's Divisions to meet this threat.[9] The level of the Po River was very high at this time due to heavy rains. For this reason and other considerations, Union commanders decided overnight to cancel this operation and began withdrawing their units at midday on May 10. Heth's Division had to march behind the Confederate line from the right to the extreme left (see Map 14, Appendix B). When the men arrived at the high ground overlooking the river at midafternoon, most of the Union units had completed their crossing back to the north side. Heth deployed the brigades of Davis and Kirkland in the front and the commands of Cooke and Walker in a second line and quickly advanced upon the remaining enemy troops.[10] All four brigades were ultimately committed in this attack. The last Federal unit, the First Division, II Corps, was caught in the process of retiring across the river and, as a result, sustained significant losses.

Thereafter, Heth's Division was shifted back to the eastern portion of the battlefield and deployed along the line of breastworks facing east-northeast.[11] The following day (May 12), the command successfully defended this position against an attack by the IX Corps in the afternoon (see Map 21, Appendix B). For the remainder of the battle, the division engaged in only skirmishing and sniping.

Heth's Division was ordered to support Wilcox's Division during the engagement at Jericho Ford at the North Anna on May 23 but arrived too late to have any significant influence. As requested by Wilcox, Heth deployed his troops to the right of his forces. In this position, they were unable to contribute to the overall battle situation but were subjected to considerable enemy artillery shelling.[12] Following the conclusion of the fighting, Heth's Division retired to the main Confederate line at Anderson's Station (between the Virginia Central Railroad and the Little River).[13]

Heth's Division was present at Totopotomoy with the Third Corps but saw no significant action (see Map 31, Appendix B). Unlike the other units in the corps, the division remained on the army's overall left (or northern) flank during the Battle of Cold Harbor. With the movement of the VI and II Corps to the southern portion of the battlefield on June 1–2, Heth moved forward and took up a position along Shady Grove Road facing southward (next to the Second Corps). The brigades of Davis, Kirkland, and Cooke were deployed (from west to east) on this line (see Map 36, Appendix B). They were lightly engaged on June 2 and more heavily engaged on the third, repulsing limited attacks by elements of the IX Corps (see Maps 37 and 41, Appendix B).[14] Walker's Brigade was posted to cover the rear of the division at this time. As luck would have it, they skirmished with elements of the Third Division, Cavalry Corps on this and the following day (June 4).[15]

Although a bit more fortunate than Wilcox's Division, Heth's Division also sustained heavy casualties during the campaign. Most of these losses occurred at the Wilderness, though a significant percentage were of a slight nature. Many of these men returned to the ranks in several weeks or one to two months at most. As a result, Heth's Division recovered quickly and went on to play a considerable role in later actions in and around Petersburg.

Cooke's Brigade

The brigade of John R. Cooke was a veteran outfit that in 1862 was part of Longstreet's First Corps. Following the Battle of Fredericksburg (in December), this command was assigned to the Department of Richmond and Southeastern Virginia in compliance with a request of President Davis that, when Lee's army campaigned in northern Virginia, troops be continuously maintained in this department to safeguard the Confederate capital. For the better part of 1863, Cooke's Brigade became a pawn in a process of continual negotiation and political maneuvering between Lee and Davis over this directive. During this year, the general frequently reminded the president that Cooke's Brigade was a part of the Army of Northern Virginia. This issue was partially resolved after the Battle of Gettysburg, with George Pickett's division being sent to Richmond and southeastern Virginia to refit; in exchange, Cooke's command was released to Lee. The army commander assigned the North Carolinians to Heth's battered division.

Cooke's Brigade was thereafter bloodied at Bristoe Station in October 1863 (suffering about 700 casualties) but recovered over the winter.[1] Four regiments comprised this command—the 15th, 27th, 46th, and 48th North Carolina—recruited from the eastern to west-central portion of the state. At the start of the Overland Campaign, Cooke's Brigade was, compared to many other units in Lee's army, in excellent condition. Its morale was high and the ranks were nearly full, with about 1,960 men present for duty. At the Wilderness, the North Carolinians experienced more action than they were likely seeking.

During the afternoon of May 5, Cooke's Brigade led the advance of Heth's Division into the Wilderness on Orange Plank Road.[2] After contact was made with enemy infantry, Heth deployed Cooke in the divisional center astride this road (see Map 3, Appendix B). The 15th and 46th North Carolina Regiments were posted to the south, while the 27th and 48th North

Carolina Regiments were positioned to the north.[3] This position became the focus of repeated attacks and heavy musket fire from three separate enemy divisions throughout the remainder of the day.[4] Cooke's Brigade held firm but sustained a loss of close to 40 percent of its original strength. The 46th North Carolina, in particular, suffered severely on this date. With such a loss in personnel, an effective volume of fire could not be maintained indefinitely. Generals Heth and A. P. Hill recognized the problem and, in the early evening, reinforced and ultimately relieved Cooke's command with McGowan's Brigade from Wilcox's Division.[5]

Overnight, Cooke's Brigade was shifted to the northern side of Orange Plank Road and posted on the division's (and corps's) left (see Map 5, Appendix B). Contrary to orders, the North Carolinians attempted to construct breastworks. This defensive improvement helped the men withstand the initial Federal assault at daybreak on May 6.[6] As described above, many of the units in the Third Corps to the south or right failed to hold their position and were driven from the field. This uncovered Cooke's position and ultimately led to a similar retreat. After the arrival of the First Corps, the North Carolinians were reformed in the rear and posted in the corps's center between Kirkland and Walker's Brigades.[7] This area of the battlefield, between Orange Plank Road and Orange Turnpike, thereafter remained relatively quiet, and the command saw no further major action in this battle.

At Spotsylvania, Cooke's Brigade participated in the assault upon the Union forces crossing the Po River on May 10 and again lost heavily.[8] Two days later, the command played a very minor role in the repulse of the attack upon the eastern side of the Confederate line by elements of the IX Corps and later supported Mahone's Brigade in a reconnaissance in force against the enemy entrenchments.[9] The North Carolinians next were slightly engaged at North Anna (Jericho Mill). As described above, they arrived near the end of this battle and saw limited action. Cooke's Brigade was present at Totopotomoy and Cold Harbor but was actively engaged only on June 2 and 3 at the latter (see Maps 37 and 41, Appendix B).[10] The 48th North Carolina Regiment sustained the most losses of the brigade at this battle.

Cooke's Brigade sustained by far the heaviest losses in Heth's Division during this campaign (see Table 48, Appendix A). This was due primarily to the unit's role on May 5 at the Wilderness. By the close of the campaign, its strength was significantly reduced. Yet the command and leadership elements remained intact, and the brigade recovered quickly. This was due to the fact that many of the casualties sustained at the Wilderness fell into the "slightly wounded" category. An examination of the rolls of one regiment (the 46th North Carolina) reveals that about 32 percent of the wounded from the campaign were discharged from hospitals and returned to the unit within one to five weeks.

The reported number of casualties for this brigade appears to be comprehensive and accurate. All four regiments were well covered in the North Carolina newspapers.[11] The only limitation was found in the listing for the 48th North Carolina Regiment in the *(Raleigh) Daily Confederate* issue of June 26, 1864, which failed to provide a breakdown by battle. Manarin and Jordan's series on North Carolina troops was also examined and included among the sources for this brigade.[12]

Kirkland's Brigade

By the spring of 1864, the North Carolina brigades of Kirkland and Cooke comprised the core of Heth's Division. The original commander of Kirkland's Brigade was Brig. Gen. J. Johnston Pettigrew. The history and fighting record of Pettigrew's Brigade was quite different from those of the rest of the division. It was formed in late 1862 and served principally in eastern and central North Carolina until the spring of 1863. Following the Battle of Chancellorsville, the organization was transferred to Lee's army and assigned to Heth's newly forming division. Three of its regiments, the 44th, 47th, and 52nd North Carolina, had not yet participated in a major battle or operation. At this time, their strengths (and that of the 11th North Carolina Regiment) ranged between about 550 and 650 men, an unusually high number for this year of the war. The brigade's fifth regiment, the 26th North Carolina, fielded about 900 men in mid-1863. This unit had been a favorite of Zebulon Vance, governor of North Carolina, and was for several months kept near Raleigh and afforded an opportunity to recruit to the maximum limit. These five units were originally raised from throughout the state.

During the Gettysburg Campaign, the 44th North Carolina was detached and kept in Virginia to protect the northern approaches to Richmond. While Lee's army was locked in battle in Pennsylvania, this unit managed to lose about 100 men in a small action near Hanover Court House.[1] Despite this detachment, the strength of Pettigrew's Brigade at Gettysburg was about 2,700 men, the largest in the army. It was heavily engaged on both the first and third days of this battle and sustained a reported 1,105 casualties. Recent studies have found that this number likely represented the loss only on the first day (July 1) and that the total for the battle was more likely in excess of 1,700 or even 1,800 men.[2] The 26th North Carolina alone lost approximately 800 men.

General Pettigrew was mortally wounded on July 14 at Falling Waters, Maryland, during the retreat from Gettysburg. Col. William W. Kirkland of the 21st North Carolina Regiment (of Hoke's Brigade) was promoted to fill the vacancy. Like Cooke's Brigade, Kirkland's command was badly cut up at Bristoe Station in October 1863 (losing an additional 600 men).[3] Over the winter, the strength and morale of the organization improved. Many personnel wounded and/or captured at Gettysburg and Bristoe Station returned, and some new recruits were added to the ranks. At the start of the campaign, the brigade again fielded the highest strength in the division (about 2,150 men).

Kirkland's Brigade initially led Heth's Division in the march to the Wilderness on May 5.[4] Once the division paused to rest at midday, Cooke's Brigade relieved Kirkland, and the latter then brought up the rear. When contact was made with enemy infantry, Kirkland's command was initially posted in reserve behind Cooke's line (see Map 3, Appendix B). There are few reports detailing the actions of the brigade on this day, but judging by the casualty figures, it appears that the various regiments were parceled out individually as reinforcements to the other three brigades posted in the front line. It appears that the 26th, 44th, and 47th Regiments were sent to Cooke's Brigade. The 52nd North Carolina remained in the rear, guarding the division trains until late in the day. The role of the 11th North Carolina during this battle is not clear.

Kirkland's Brigade was apparently regrouped and shifted overnight to the northern side of Orange Plank Road next to McGowan's Brigade (Wilcox's Division).[5] In this position, the brigade was posted on the left of the front line (see Map 5, Appendix B). The Federal onslaught in the early morning hours of May 6 apparently caught it by surprise and quickly routed the entire unit.[6] A near disaster for the Confederate cause was averted by the timely arrival of Longstreet's corps. Kirkland's Brigade was subsequently rallied and sent to the corps's center. The North Carolinians saw no further major action for the rest of the battle.

At the Battle of Spotsylvania, Kirkland's command was first engaged on May 10 against elements of the II Corps on the southern side of the Po

River.[7] The brigade returned to its former position on the army right following this action. The North Carolinians were slightly engaged in this defensive position during the afternoon of May 12, repulsing an attack by the IX Corps (see Map 21, Appendix B). For the remainder of this battle, the men participated in only minor skirmishing. Subsequently, Kirkland's Brigade was slightly engaged at North Anna on May 23 and at Totopotomoy on May 30 but more heavily engaged at Cold Harbor on June 2 and 3 (see Maps 37 and 41, Appendix B).[8] The fighting at Cold Harbor occurred against elements of the IX Corps along Shady Grove Road. General Kirkland was seriously wounded on June 2.[9] Col. George H. Faribault of the 47th North Carolina Regiment temporarily assumed command of the brigade.

Kirkland's Brigade emerged from the Overland Campaign relatively intact and with the highest strength in the division. Within several weeks, Col. William McRae of the 15th North Carolina Regiment (of Cooke's Brigade) was promoted and given command of this brigade. Douglas Southall Freeman has stated that the morale and attitude of the North Carolinians flourished under his leadership.[10] The historic record reveals that McRae's Brigade performed solidly at Petersburg. William Kirkland later returned from wounded furlough and was assigned to another brigade.

The casualty lists published for this brigade have been a continual source of frustration. See Table 49 in Appendix A. Outside of lists for the officers and one company, nothing was found for the 11th North Carolina Regiment.[11] The reported number of killed and mortally wounded for the regiment is very low for both the Wilderness and Cold Harbor. Judging by the comparatively low reported casualties, one is tempted to assume that this unit was continually held in reserve or was somehow frequently detached during critical moments. Perhaps the truth lies somewhere in the middle. It could have been very fortunate in its battle assignments, or the actual number of casualties could have been slightly higher. Similarly, no newspaper listing was found for the 52nd North Carolina Regiment. Given its initial assignment in the rear on May 5, this omission does not appear to be as glaring.

As for the 26th North Carolina Regiment, a casualty list was published in a June issue of the *Fayetteville Observer* for the period May 10–June 15. The correspondent mentions that this list was a follow up to a prior list provided for the first battle in the campaign (meaning the Wilderness). This first list has not been found. Individual casualty listings for six of ten companies in this regiment have been found for the Wilderness in other newspapers or issues.[12] In each instance, these added many more men to the casualty numbers. The *Daily Richmond Enquirer* published a list for the 44th North Carolina Regiment, covering the entire campaign, on June 22. This unfortunately failed to provide a breakdown by battle and appears to omit the slightly wounded men. Several North Carolina newspapers also published partial lists for this unit.[13]

In contrast, two issues of Raleigh's *Daily Confederate* provided very beneficial lists of the casualties in the 47th North Carolina between May 5 and May 23.[14] One of these in particular (June 8 issue) listed the casualties in this regiment by day. They are as follows: 95 on May 5; 9 on May 6; 20 on May 10; 2 on May 12; 3 on May 18; and 4 on May 23. These data provide an excellent guidepost regarding the degree of engagement for this regiment, and especially the entire brigade, for the Battles of the Wilderness, Spotsylvania, and the North Anna. In the cases of the 11th, 44th, and 52nd Regiments, this information was considered in apportioning the casualties to the various battles for other regiments in the brigade. As described above, the records and available newspaper lists for these units contained the names of some men who were killed or wounded at an undetermined battle and/or date in the campaign.

Davis's Brigade

Like Pettigrew's/Kirkland's Brigade, Davis's Brigade joined Lee's army and Heth's Division before the Battle of Gettysburg. But there were other notable features with this organization. First, the commander, Joseph R. Davis, was a nephew of President Davis and a relatively inexperienced leader.[1] Charges of nepotism followed and flourished with his assignment.[2] Secondly, the brigade was composed of units from different states, which was unusual in the Army of Northern Virginia. For the most part, the army's infantry and cavalry brigades were composed of regiments and battalions from the same state or, at least, neighboring states. The units initially comprising Davis's command were the 2nd, 11th, and 42nd Mississippi and the 55th North Carolina. The first two regiments were veteran outfits, having been an integral part of Hood's Division for much of 1862. The latter two were relatively inexperienced. The 55th North Carolina Regiment was apparently added in 1863 to increase the strength of the organization to a typical brigade size.

Davis's Brigade also fielded a comparatively high strength of about 2,300 men at Gettysburg and sustained overwhelming casualties at this battle. The command was handled very poorly on the first day and participated in the famous charge on the third day. The reported number of casualties was 897, though this figure includes no missing personnel, a glaring omission since the brigade lost several hundred men captured on July 1. More-recent compilations indicate that the brigade loss was at least 1,500 men. Overall, the total loss for the unit for 1863 was about 1,580 men.[3]

Davis's Brigade attempted to recover during the winter of 1863–64. This was a difficult task given the fact that most of the new enlistees from Mississippi were sent to the Army of Tennessee in northern Georgia. Each of the four regiments was swelled to some extent by the return of wounded veterans and other former absentees. An examination of the CSRs for the 2nd Mississippi Regiment, for example, yielded some pertinent data regarding this process. The estimated starting strength of the unit on May 5, 1864, is 285 men. Of this number, 60 returned from wounds sustained at Gettysburg and 80 returned from other absences. Only eight recruits were added over the winter. The 55th North Carolina Regiment, having a geographically closer home, fared better in this respect than the three Mississippi regiments.

In early March 1864, it was apparently clear that Davis's Brigade would still be severely understrength. President Davis himself attempted to rectify this situation by ordering the transfer of the 26th Mississippi Regiment and the 1st Confederate Battalion from a camp in western Alabama to the Army of Northern Virginia. The main components of these units left Alabama on March 28 and arrived in Virginia on April 12–13. It is possible that some men trickled in over a period of several weeks; Company A, 1st Confederate Battalion appears to have arrived at Cold Harbor in June. Together, the two units appear to have added about 460 men to this brigade, giving the command a total strength of about 1,690 men on May 5.

The four Mississippi regiments were recruited exclusively from the northeastern part of the state. The 1st Confederate Battalion consisted of six companies, four of which were from Alabama and one each from Georgia and Tennessee. The Alabama companies also contained some personnel from neighboring western Florida and were originally part of the 2nd Alabama Regiment, which had been mustered out in 1862 following completion of its one-year enlistment. The 55th North Carolina Regiment was raised from counties in the western and eastern parts of the state.

General Davis was initially absent during the Overland Campaign and, in his stead, Col. John M. Stone of the 11th Mississippi Regiment assumed command. The brigade was heavily engaged on May 5 at the Wilderness. It was posted to the left of Cooke's Brigade and similarly was the target of repeated enemy assaults and fire throughout the afternoon and evening (see Map 3, Appendix B).[4] Thomas's Brigade (Wilcox's Division) provided a much-needed reinforcement and relief in the evening hours.[5] Overnight, Davis's Brigade was moved to the left rear of Kirkland's Brigade on the corps's left. The troops attempted to construct hasty breastworks. Buttressed with this defensive improvement, they repulsed the initial Federal assaults on the morning of May 6 (see Map 5, Appendix B). The withdrawal of units to the right, however, forced the retirement of this mixed command. Elements of this brigade were among the last of the Third Corps to leave the field during this stage of the battle.[6]

Davis's Brigade must have maintained some form of order because within several hours, it was added to a group of other commands performing a flanking movement and attack upon the southern (left) end of Federal units in this area (see Map 7, Appendix B).[7] The counterattack was very successful and forced a retirement of the entire enemy force facing the First Corps. Thereafter, the brigade was moved back to reserve. In the afternoon, it was sent with several brigades of Anderson's Division of the Third Corps to counter an assault by elements of the IX Corps upon other units holding a line north of Orange Plank Road (see Map 8, Appendix B).[8] This operation also proved successful. Overall, Davis's Brigade lost heavily at the Wilderness (see Table 50, Appendix A). The 2nd and 42nd Mississippi and 55th North Carolina, especially, had their ranks significantly reduced.

General Davis returned to duty at Spotsylvania. His brigade participated in the action against the II Corps on the Po River on May 10 and was slightly engaged at the opposite end of the battlefield on May 12 (see Map 21, Appendix B).[9] As with the other units in Heth's Division, Davis's Brigade was lightly engaged at North Anna on May 23 and at Totopotomoy on May 30. But the mixed command was heavily engaged at Cold Harbor on June 2 and 3 (see Maps 37 and 40, Appendix B).[10] Casualties from this engagement were proportionally higher in the 1st Confederate Battalion and the 11th and 26th Mississippi Regiments.

By the end of the campaign, Davis's Brigade was still intact but much reduced in strength. It recovered to some extent and continued to play an active role in operations in and around Petersburg during the summer and autumn of 1864.

The newspaper casualty lists for the units of this brigade provide a patchwork of information. The *Daily Richmond Enquirer* provided periodic and comprehensive lists for the units from Mississippi and the 1st Confederate Battalion.[11] A Mobile newspaper also provided casualties information for the 1st Confederate Battalion.[12] The battle losses for the 55th North Carolina Regiment at the Wilderness were provided in Raleigh's *Daily Confederate*, the *Daily Richmond Enquirer*, and the respective volume of Manarin and Jordan's series on North Carolina troops.[13] No other casualty lists were found in newspapers for this regiment. Thus, it is possible that the North Carolinians could have sustained a few more casualties. Some additional information regarding the Mississippi troops was found in Dunbar Rowland's *Military History of Mississippi*.[14]

Walker's/Fry's Brigade

This unit was, in effect, a merger of Archer's and Brockenbrough's Brigades, two of the original units of Hill's Light Division. The merger was implemented due to a lack of suitable commanders and the relatively small strength of both organizations. Afterward, the combined strength of the new unit was more in line with those of the other three brigades in Heth's Division.

Archer's Brigade had been composed of three regiments from Tennessee (the 1st, 7th, and 14th) and one regiment (13th) from Alabama. A fifth unit, the 5th Alabama Battalion, had been part of this unit for most of the war but prior to the Overland Campaign was transferred to the Third Corps as headquarters guard. The Tennessee units were recruited from counties located in and around Clarksville, east of Nashville, and along the southern border with Alabama. The 13th Alabama Regiment, conversely, was raised from the eastern part of that state.

The brigade had garnered an excellent fighting record in 1862 and 1863. At the Battle of Gettysburg, it suffered heavily, losing General Archer and more than 100 men as prisoners on the first day and more than 500 men and Archer's battlefield successor (Col. Birkett D. Fry of the 13th Alabama Regiment) in the famous charge on July 3. In this assault, elements of the brigade reached the stone wall at the crest of Cemetery Ridge alongside Pickett's Division. In the aftermath, the brigade could field only about 500 men and no experienced commander. Overall, its reported battle losses for all of 1863 were as many as 1,113 men.[1]

Brockenbrough's Brigade consisted of four Virginia units, the 40th, 47th, and 55th Regiments and the 22nd Battalion. The organization also had established a competent battle record, mainly under the leadership of Charles Field and Henry Heth, both of whom were later elevated to division command in Lee's army. Col. John M. Brockenbrough of the 40th Virginia Regiment assumed command of the brigade after Heth's promotion.

At Gettysburg, the fortunes of the brigade plummeted. On the first day, the men fought with little distinction. During the Pickett/Pettigrew/Trimble Charge on the third day, the Virginians (at this point led by Col. Robert M. Mayo of the 47th Virginia Regiment) were posted on the left end of the division.[2] As the massed Confederates advanced toward the main enemy position, a Union regiment (8th Ohio) on picket duty to the north turned and poured fire into the open flank of the brigade. Many of the Virginians responded by breaking ranks, dropping to the ground, or fleeing to the rear. During the retreat to Virginia, the brigade again performed badly and lost more than 200 men as prisoners at Falling Waters. A review of reports and recent roster compilations reveals that this brigade had about 700–750 battle casualties in 1863.[3] This pales in comparison to the losses sustained over the same period by the other three (original) brigades in Heth's Division.

Lt. Col. Henry H. Walker was promoted to brigadier general in the aftermath of Gettysburg and given command of the consolidated brigade. He was actually a junior officer to John M. Brockenbrough of the 40th Virginia Regiment, who in response to this apparent slight, resigned. Over the winter of 1863–64, Walker worked diligently to forge a unified command and improve its morale. Archer's original four units were replenished to some degree (to a combined strength of about 755 men) with the return of wounded veterans and exchanged prisoners and an influx of some new recruits. An examination of the individual rolls reveals that 50–69 percent of the May 1864 strength of these units came from these returning or new personnel.

The four Virginia units provided a somewhat larger force of about 900 men, but questions still lingered regarding their morale and reliability. The 22nd Battalion was actually a converted heavy artillery unit that was raised in Richmond and the surrounding counties. Its battle record was among the worst in the brigade. The three regiments (40th, 47th, and 55th) were raised from the "Northern Neck" and "Middle Neck" areas of eastern Virginia. The army's winter camps were situated just west of this region for several years. Except for the cavalry, it is likely that these men could successfully slip away from camp without authorized leave to visit home and rejoin the army more often than any other brigade in the army. This may or may not have been a contributing factor to the record of this command. Regardless, the ranks of these Virginia units were never full.

As for the Overland Campaign, Walker's Brigade began by being positioned on the right of Heth's Division during the opening phase of the Wilderness on May 5 (see Map 3, Appendix B). It initially repulsed assaults by the Third Division, II Corps. As the enemy fed more troops (First Division, II Corps) into the fighting, Walker's Brigade experienced difficulty holding its position. In the late afternoon and early evening hours, the command was reinforced and ultimately relieved by Scales's and Lane's Brigades.[4] Overnight, Walker's men were shifted to a position on the southern side of Orange Plank Road behind Wilcox's Division (see Map 5, Appendix B).[5] In the early morning hours of May 6, Federal forces unleashed a full and overwhelmingly successful assault upon the entire front of the Third Corps. Along with the rest of Heth's and Wilcox's Divisions, Walker's Brigade was swept to the rear. Later in day, the command was rallied and posted in the corps's center between Kirkland's and Cooke's Brigades.[6] It saw no significant action for the rest of this battle.

Walker's Brigade was next in action on May 10 at Spotsylvania in the operation against the II Corps on the southern side of the Po River. Unfortunately for the men, General Walker was severely wounded during the fighting.[7] Colonel Mayo of the 47th Virginia Regiment then assumed command. Following this action, the brigade returned to its original position on the right of the overall Confederate line, facing east.[8] This sector featured a small salient and was the focus of the attack by elements of the IX Corps on the afternoon of May 12 (see Map 21, Appendix B). The Union forces gained a small penetration in this line before being driven back by other units of the Third Corps.[9] For the remainder of the battle of Spotsylvania, Walker's Brigade engaged principally in skirmishing and suffered very light losses. A check of the casualty figures reveals that about 75–80 percent of its loss at Spotsylvania occurred on May 10, while another 10–15 percent occurred on May 12.

Walker's Brigade was slightly engaged during the fighting at Jericho Mill (North Anna) on May 23. The command arrived at the close of hostilities and had little effect upon the outcome of the battle.[10] Its losses at North Anna were light, though unlike the first two battles of this campaign, they were actually the heaviest in Heth's Division. In the latter part of May, Birkett Fry returned to Lee's army and assumed command of the brigade.[11] He had been convalescing from wounds received at Gettysburg and had been promoted to brigadier general; during the Battle of Drewry's Bluff, he had temporarily led Barton's Brigade.[12] Now known as Fry's Brigade, the command was present at the remaining battles of the campaign but sustained casualties only at Cold Harbor. It was posted in the rear of the division to guard the open eastern flank and sparred with elements of the Third Division, Cavalry Corps during the period June 2–5.[13]

Fry's Brigade saw further but somewhat limited action in 1864 during the siege of Petersburg. In late 1864, the Virginia units were transferred to the Richmond garrison and replaced by Fulton's small Tennessee Brigade. The 2nd Maryland Battalion was assigned to this otherwise all-Tennessee organization to increase its strength. Ultimately, the 22nd Virginia Battalion was merged with another Virginia unit. The records in the CSRs reveal that on several occasions, many of the men of this unit were found cowering in the rear during subsequent battles in 1864.

The casualty figures for Walker's/Fry's Brigade during this campaign tend to provide information leading to these latter charges and changes. They are presented in Appendix A in two tables (51 and 52), one for each original component of this command. The brigade overall sustained a significantly lower percentage of casualties than the other brigades of Heth's Division. This would tend to indicate an actual decline in battle performance by this unit or recognition of a decline by the divisional and corps commanders. The record shows that Walker's Brigade experienced the most difficulty in holding its section of the divisional line on May 5 at the Wilderness. A breakdown of its casualties for the entire campaign also provides some revealing information. The units of Archer's former brigade sustained a compiled battle loss of 311 men, while those of Brockenbrough's former command suffered about 305 casualties. Considering the original strengths of these two components, the proportions in battle loss were 41 percent and 34 percent, respectively.

The newspaper listings for this brigade are somewhat limited. The *Daily Richmond Enquirer* of June 4, 1864, provided a list of the casualties in Archer's former brigade for the Wilderness and Spotsylvania (without a breakdown).[14] Beyond this point in the campaign, nothing was found. The various Richmond newspapers provided a nearly complete patchwork of lists for the four Virginia units.[15] The only major omission from these sources was a listing of the battle losses for the 22nd Battalion at North Anna and Cold Harbor. Some additional information regarding casualties in the Virginia units was found in the respective books of the Virginia Regimental Histories Series.[16]

WILCOX'S DIVISION

This division comprised the core of A. P. Hill's famous Light Division from Stonewall Jackson's Second Corps. This former organization achieved a splendid battle record in 1862. Following Jackson's death after the Battle of Chancellorsville and the promotion of Hill to command of the new Third Corps, the Light Division was split up, with four brigades assigned to William Dorsey Pender and the two remaining brigades given to a new division led by Henry Heth. Pender was mortally wounded at Gettysburg, and the command of his division was given to Cadmus M. Wilcox, formerly of Anderson's Division. Most of the division had been badly bloodied at this battle and at Chancellorsville, but over the winter of 1863–64, many men returned from wounded furloughs. In addition, a considerable number of recruits were added to the ranks. As a consequence, at the start of the Overland Campaign, this organization fielded the highest divisional strength (about 7,295 men) in the army. In the view of many in Lee's command, it formed the backbone of the Third Corps. Wilcox's Division consisted of four veteran brigades: McGowan's, Lane's, Scales's, and Thomas's.

Wilcox's Division followed Heth's brigades into the Wilderness and was heavily engaged on both days of this battle. On May 5, the command was initially posted in reserve but was soon advanced to the left of Heth and north of Orange Plank Road.[1] This latter move was made in an effort to bridge a large gap between this unit and the Second Corps (to the northwest). Heavy Federal attacks upon Heth's Division during the late afternoon forced a second change in the deployment of Wilcox's Division. First, the brigades of McGowan and Scales were committed to shore up Heth's line. In the evening, Thomas's Brigade and then Lane's Brigade were dispatched to assist in holding this front (see Map 3, Appendix B).[2] The fighting in this sector continued until dark.

At this stage, the men of both commands were exhausted, and their lines were poorly prepared for further enemy attacks. Despite urgings by both Wilcox and Heth, General Hill (with Lee's approval) decided against improving their defensive positions and elected to gamble on the arrival of reinforcements in the morning. The division commanders attempted to reorganize their line, with Wilcox's men primarily shifting to the southern side of Orange Plank Road and Heth's moving to the northern side (see Map 5, Appendix B).

The Federals got an early start on the Confederates in the early morning of May 6 and assaulted the entire front of Wilcox's and Heth's Divisions with an overwhelming force. One by one, Wilcox's brigades were enveloped and driven back. In less than an hour, the piecemeal withdrawals evolved into a major retreat of both divisions.[3] At this point, Longstreet's First Corps fortuitously arrived on the battlefield. These fresh troops halted the Union advance and restored the Confederate front. Wilcox's Division was thereafter re-formed in the rear and then posted between the First and Second Corps north of Orange Plank Road.[4] In this position, the command experienced no further action in this battle.

The Confederate Third Corps marched to Spotsylvania on May 8 and 9. Wilcox's Division brought up the rear and, upon arrival, was posted on the right of Johnson's Division (Second Corps).[5] Wilcox's men dug in and constructed breastworks along this line, which faced toward the north-northeast and covered Fredericksburg Road. For the next several days, the command skirmished with elements of the IX Corps.[6] During the early morning hours of May 12, the II Corps assaulted and captured most of Johnson's Division. The impetus of this successful attack spilled over into the leftmost portion of Wilcox's command. In conjunction, elements of the IX Corps soon thereafter attacked the front of the division (see Map 18, Appendix B). Ultimately, Wilcox's troops recovered and repulsed both of these attacks.

At the same time, elements of the Second Corps counterattacked and regained the portion of the line formerly held by Johnson's men. Parts of Wilcox's Division were detached to this part of the battlefield. The remaining elements of this command were pulled out and placed either in reserve or at the extreme southern end of the line. Heth's Division then shifted over to cover most of Wilcox's original line of fortifications. During the midafternoon, elements of the IX Corps again assaulted a portion of the Confederate front now held by Heth's Division. One of Wilcox's brigades, supported by a brigade of Mahone's Division, successfully countered this Federals move. This ended the attacks upon the Confederate right flank on May 12.

Wilcox's Division was involved primarily in skirmishing and sniping for most of the remainder of Spotsylvania. On May 21, however, pickets and scouts noted that the enemy appeared to be leaving the battlefield. During the early evening, two brigades were dispatched to determine the accuracy of these reports. These units were formed abreast Massaponax Church Road and advanced eastward. They encountered elements of the VI Corps and enjoyed a brief success before being repulsed and returning to their own lines.[7]

On May 22–23, Wilcox's Division marched to and crossed to the southern side of the North Anna River. During the early evening of May 23, the command was ordered by General Hill to attack the V Corps at Jericho Mill (Noel Station). This Federal command had just crossed the North Anna and was in the process of deploying its infantry and artillery forces into the bridgehead. Wilcox deployed his brigades from east to west as follows: Lane's, McGowan's (under Brown), Thomas's, and Scales's (under Lowrance; see Map 26, Appendix B). The attack was initially successful, especially on the left (west).[8] Federal artillery and an opportune counterattack by several veteran infantry units ultimately halted this Confederate assault (see Map 27, Appendix B). In the end, Wilcox had little to show for the effort except more than 700 casualties.[9] Thereafter, Wilcox's Division was pulled back to a main Confederate line at Anderson's Station. For the remainder of the Battle of the North Anna, this portion of the front was mostly dormant, and the men experienced a well-earned respite.

Wilcox's Division was present at the later battles of the campaign, Totopotomoy and Cold Harbor, but experienced limited action. At Totopotomoy, the full division was posted on the army's left along the heights above the southern side of the creek (see Map 31, Appendix B).[10] Lane's and Scales's Brigades lightly skirmished with enemy forces on May 31 at Storr's Farm (near Pole Green Church). On June 2, the division was moved quickly to the army's right flank south of Cold Harbor. Wilcox's Division relieved Confederate cavalry and quickly entrenched, extending the main line southward almost to the Chickahominy River. The alignment of the brigades in this position was, from north to south: Lane's, Scales's, Thomas's, and McGowan's.[11] The following day, June 3, the brigades posted at the northern end of the divisional and corps front assisted in repulsing the massive and costly Federal assault upon the main Confederate line. For the remainder of Cold Harbor, the various units engaged in and were subjected to sniping and artillery fire.

A review of the various battles and casualty lists reveals that Wilcox's Division saw more than its fair share of fighting during this campaign. Overall, the command sustained more than 3,800 casualties, the largest loss in the

Third Corps and amounting to about 47 percent of the division's original strength. The loss in regimental- and company-level leadership was even higher. Despite these casualties, Wilcox's Division recovered to some extent over the summer. Two of its brigades, Lane's and McGowan's, consistently were called upon and played crucial roles in thwarting Federal movements and assaults during the siege of Petersburg.

Lane's Brigade

The brigade of Brig. Gen. James H. Lane compiled one of the finest fighting records in the Army of Northern Virginia. This organization was originally led by Brig. Gen. L. O'Brien Branch and saw its first action with Lee's army at the Seven Days' Battles outside Richmond in 1862. Thereafter, this brigade of five North Carolina regiments was actively involved in every major battle of the army in 1862 and 1863. Following the death of General Branch at the Battle of Antietam, Lane was promoted from the 28th North Carolina Regiment to command the brigade. Lane's Brigade sustained over 900 casualties at the Battle of Chancellorsville, the highest in the entire army. At Gettysburg, the North Carolinians participated in the charge of Pickett, Pettigrew, and Trimble on July 3 against Cemetery Ridge. This battle cost the brigade at least another reported 660 casualties; the actual loss may have been as much as 762. The total tally of combat losses for the year 1863, by one report, reached 1,569 men. A more modern compilation reveals that the loss was probably at least 1,671 men.[1]

Despite these battle losses, Lane's Brigade fielded the largest infantry strength in Lee's army in the spring of 1864 (about 2,350 men). This was due to three primary factors. First, the individual regiments had comparatively large enrollments at the time of their enlistments and original formations. This particularly applied to the 28th and 37th North Carolina Regiments. Secondly, a significant number of men wounded in 1862 and 1863 returned to the ranks over the winter of 1863–64. Lastly, the command was successful in recruiting some new personnel. Its five units originally recruited from southeastern and west-central regions of North Carolina.

During the first day of battle at the Wilderness (May 5), Lane's Brigade was committed at about five o'clock in the evening to support Scales's Brigade on the corps's right (see Map 3, Appendix B). The alignment of the command at this time was (from north to south): the 7th, 33rd, 28th, and

18th North Carolina Regiments and the brigade sharpshooters. Its fifth regiment, the 37th North Carolina, was detached to cover the left flank of the brigade and connect with McGowan's Brigade and elements of Heth's Division.[2] This regiment actually saw little fighting on this day. Conversely, the rest of the brigade charged into elements of the II Corps and became heavily engaged in a dense thicket and swamp in its immediate front. After the North Carolinians gained some success, the Federals were reinforced and began to apply considerable pressure on the right of the brigade.[3] The 18th North Carolina Regiment and the sharpshooters were able to deflect this advance to some degree by re-fusing their right, but ultimately this enemy action forced the entire brigade to retire to their original position (with Scales's Brigade). The 7th North Carolina, on the brigade's left, failed to receive the order for this movement and was nearly encircled at dusk. This regiment had to fight its way out of this predicament in order to get back to the main line.

At this stage of the battle, Lane's and Scales's Brigades were intermixed. Overnight, General Lane attempted to form his brigade to the right and rear of Scales's line (see Map 5, Appendix B). As advised by higher command, the troops of the Third Corps did not construct entrenchments or significantly improve their defensive position. During the early hours of May 6, the Federals attacked along the full front and drove both Heth's and Wilcox's Divisions from the field. Lane's Brigade attempted to hold its position, but the retreat of Scales's Brigade and other units to the west forced its retirement too.[4] The 33rd North Carolina Regiment, in particular, tried to maintain its position and lost heavily. After the arrival and relief of Longstreet's First Corps, the North Carolinians rallied and were inserted on the corps's left (next to the Second Corps).[5] The brigade remained in this position for the remainder of the battle and saw little further action.

Lane's Brigade arrived at Spotsylvania about noon on May 9 and was first posted near the court house to the left of Fredericksburg Road. After some shuffling during the next two days, the brigade was posted to the immediate right of Steuart's Brigade (Johnson's Division, Second Corps) facing east. The regiments were aligned, from north to south, as follows: the 18th, 28th, 33rd, 7th, and 37th.[6] The positions of the four northernmost units occupied several bluffs in advance of the main line but was cut by several small swampy ravines (see Map 18, Appendix B).

Soon after daybreak on May 12, a massive assault by the II Corps penetrated and overwhelmed most of Johnson's Division. Lane ordered his northernmost four units to retire to the main line. The 33rd and 7th North Carolina Regiments successfully completed this maneuver, forming to the left of the 37th North Carolina Regiment. The 28th and the 18th North Carolina Regiments, however, were nearly encircled by enemy units advancing from Steuart's captured entrenchments.[7] The 18th North Carolina and the adjacent left portion of the 28th North Carolina had to literally fight their way out of this Federal encirclement. These regiments then formed to the left of the 33rd North Carolina, facing north. With the assistance of reinforcements from Doles's, Thomas's, and Scales's Brigades, they were able to hold this position and prevent any further enemy advance (see Map 19, Appendix B). At the same time, elements of the Second Division, IX Corps attacked the original front of the brigade from the east. The 37th, 7th, and 33rd North Carolina successfully repelled this assault.[8]

Following this action, Lane's Brigade was pulled out and sent to a less-active zone of the line (on the corps's right).[9] During the midafternoon hours, the First and Third Divisions, IX Corps assaulted a portion of the line to the left. Lane's Brigade advanced out from its prepared position in the main line, turned to the north (or left), and collapsed upon the flank of the attacking Federals (see Map 21, Appendix B). In this advance, the alignment of the regiments was as follows (west to east): 28th, 18th, 37th, 33rd, and 7th.[10] The North Carolinians initially suffered heavily from artillery fire (supporting the Federal attack). But they pushed onward, disrupting the enemy's advance, capturing several hundred prisoners, and temporarily overrunning a Union artillery battery. Thereafter, the men retired to the main line.

Lane's Brigade completed its participation at Spotsylvania with a brief encounter on May 21. Late on this day, Scales's and Lane's men conducted a reconnaissance of the enemy positions in front of Zion Church. Lane's Brigade was deployed to the left of Massaponax Church Road, with the 33rd, 28th, and 37th North Carolina Regiments arrayed in a front line and the 7th and 18th North Carolina Regiments posted in a supporting line.[11] The Confederates successfully advanced to and held a section of the Federal earthworks before being ordered to retire at dusk.

The North Carolinians marched to the North Anna on May 22. The command participated in the attack of Wilcox's Division upon the V Corps at Jericho Ford on May 23. Lane's Brigade was posted on the right of the divisional line in the following manner (from west to east): 28th, 33rd, 37th, and 18th North Carolina (the 7th North Carolina was initially left in the rear to cover a ford; see Map 26, Appendix B).[12] The brigade first advanced several hundred yards into some woods and drove in the enemy skirmishers. Upon reaching the opposing main line and encountering heavy enemy fire (from the First Division, V Corps), the 37th North Carolina broke and fled to the rear. This unit was rallied at the edge of woods near the start-off point. The entire brigade was withdrawn to this line and ordered to advance again. Upon encountering heavy enemy fire, the same regiment again broke to the rear. The remaining three units held their advanced position before being ordered to retire (see Map 27, Appendix B). Overall though, nothing was gained in this assault.

Lane's Brigade was present but lightly engaged at both Totopotomoy and Cold Harbor. On May 31, the command relieved Wofford's Brigade (of the First Corps) near Storr's (or Stowe's) Farm and Pole Green Church on Totopotomoy Creek.[13] In this position, they engaged in skirmishing and were subjected to artillery fire for much of the day. Most of the casualties sustained at this battle occurred on this day. On June 2, Wilcox's Division was moved to the southern end of the Confederate line at Cold Harbor, and the North Carolinians were posted on the division's left next to Breckinridge's command. General Lane was wounded during this action, and the command of the brigade fell to the ranking officer, Col. John D. Barry of the 18th North Carolina Regiment.[14] On the following day (June 3), the brigade easily repelled an assault upon its front by elements of the II Corps with little loss (see Map 38, Appendix B).

Despite having temporarily lost its commander and over 1,140 casualties (see Table 53, Appendix A), Lane's Brigade emerged from this campaign in a stable condition and with the largest brigade strength in the division. Most of its casualties occurred at the Wilderness and on May 12 at Spotsylvania. The latter included about 220 prisoners taken from the 18th and 28th Regiments by the II Corps at the Mule Shoe. These were likely included with the number of men captured in the successful assault upon Johnson's Division that day. General Lane returned to duty later in the year. His brigade continued to perform admirably during the siege of Petersburg.

The officially reported casualty figures for this brigade are among the most accurate of this study. The newspapers provided another patchwork of listings with some gaps.[15] The real assets are the official reports filed by General Lane in the fall of 1864.[16] He provided numerical tabulations of the losses for each regiment at each battle in these reports. Specific reports were filed for the Battles of the Wilderness, Spotsylvania (May 12, May 13–20, and May 21), North Anna (May 23), Totopotomoy or Storr's Farm (May 31), and Cold Harbor.

McGowan's Brigade

Like Lane's Brigade, this unit of five South Carolina regiments was one of the best in A. P. Hill's Light Division and then Wilcox's Division. The brigade achieved a splendid fighting record in every action, starting with the Seven Days' Battles outside Richmond in June 1862. It also experienced and persevered through a loss of commanders in two consecutive battles. First, Maxey Gregg, the original commander, was mortally wounded during the Battle of Fredericksburg. Then his successor, Samuel McGowan, was wounded during the Battle of Chancellorsville. The senior colonel, Abner Perrin of the 14th South Carolina Regiment, led the brigade so well at Gettysburg that when McGowan returned, Perrin was promoted to brigadier general and transferred to another brigade. At that battle on July 1, the South Carolinians decisively attacked and carried the final position of the I Corps northwest of Gettysburg. The total number of reported casualties for the brigade in 1863 was 1,048 men.[1]

Over the winter of 1863–64, McGowan's Brigade recovered much of its strength from returning personnel and new enlistments. At the start of the Overland Campaign, the brigade fielded about 2,230 men in five regiments: the 1st (Provisional), 12th, 13th, and 14th Infantry and the 1st (Orr's) Rifles. These units were raised primarily from the interior Uplands region of South Carolina.

McGowan's Brigade was heavily engaged on both days at the Wilderness. During the middle of the afternoon on May 5, it was dispatched to assist Heth's Division and deployed in relief of Cooke and Kirkland's Brigades astride Orange Plank Road (see Map 3, Appendix B). This area was the relative center of the battlefield and was the focus of numerous assaults by the Federals. McGowan's Brigade had to fight desperately throughout the remainder of the day to hold this position. The 1st South Carolina, 12th South Carolina, and 1st Rifles, in particular, lost heavily in this battle.[2] Overnight, the South Carolinians were shifted slightly and positioned entirely north of and adjacent to the road (see Map 5, Appendix B). The early morning Federal assault on May 6 likely caught much of this brigade in an unprepared state. With the collapse of Scales's and part of Lane's Brigades (to the east), McGowan's Brigade was quickly driven from its position.[3] There is a report that during this wholesale retirement, General Lee himself questioned McGowan regarding the performance of his men.[4] Afterward, the brigade was rallied and posted with Wilcox's Division for the remainder of the battle.

McGowan's Brigade arrived at Spotsylvania on May 9 and was deployed on the right of the corps's line.[5] The command remained relatively inactive in this position for several days. This changed dramatically on May 12. In the early morning hours of this day, the II Corps had overrun Johnson's Division at the Mule Shoe and, as a result, torn a huge gap in the main Confederate line. Ramseur's Brigade and Gordon's improvised division of the Second Corps had successfully restored the western and eastern edges of the break, yet there still remained a wide opening in the center of Johnson's original front. In order to plug this opening and regain the lost ground, Lee committed three brigades from the Third Corps. They arrived in succession.

Arriving last, McGowan's Brigade formed in the rear of the Confederate line and moved rapidly northward toward the original line of breastworks (see Map 20, Appendix B). The alignment of the brigade's regiments, from west to east, was: the 14th, 1st Rifles, 13th, 1st, and 12th. During this advance, the South Carolinians were subjected to very heavy enemy fire from the front and its open right flank. The 12th South Carolina, in particular, suffered severely. Additionally, Gen. Samuel McGowan and three regimental colonels fell during this assault. In spite of these command losses, the brigade successfully drove the Union forces out of the original line of breastworks; the enemy troops rallied and massed on the opposite side.[6] The left of the brigade linked up with men of Harris's Brigade (which had earlier advanced and cleared the portion of the works to the immediate west). The original line at the juncture of these two units formed a slight bend at an obtuse angle. For the remainder of the day, this sector was a focal point of continuous fighting over the breastworks by troops of Harris's and McGowan's Brigades against elements of the II and VI Corps.[7] This bend in the line was henceforth known as the Bloody Angle.

At darkness, the Confederate forces manning the salient of breastworks (known also as the Mule Shoe) were withdrawn to a new line in the rear. McGowan's Brigade, now led by Col. Joseph N. Brown of the 14th South Carolina Regiment, was sent farther back to rest.[8] The day-long battle on

May 12 had been one of the worst ordeals of the war, and all of the brigade's regiments had lost heavily. Most of the dead and many of the seriously wounded of the command were found by the Federals partially buried in the mud along the breastworks the following morning. For the remainder of the battle, McGowan's Brigade was posted with the Third Corps along the army's right and saw no further serious action.[9]

McGowan's Brigade, still commanded by Colonel Brown, next participated in the attack of Wilcox's Division upon the V Corps on May 23 at Jericho Mill (at the North Anna). The South Carolinians were deployed between Thomas's Brigade (to the left) and Lane's Brigade (on the right; see Map 26, Appendix B). The alignment of its regiments was, from west to east, as follows: the 12th, 1st, 1st Rifles, 14th, and 13th. Along with Lane's Brigade, these units advanced into dense woods; the three easternmost units kept their alignment with Lane's command. The Confederates encountered similar stiff resistance and were unable to advance any farther. The two westernmost units (12th and 1st Regiments) drifted to the west and lost contact with the rest of the brigade. They experienced initial success along with Thomas's and Scales's Brigades and routed most of the opposing Third Division, V Corps. The South Carolinians were halted by enemy artillery fire and then were struck in the right flank by three veteran regiments of the First Division, executing a counterattack (see Map 27, Appendix B). Both regiments were quickly forced to retreat.[10] In addition, Colonel Brown was captured. For the third consecutive battle, the brigade had lost heavily.

With the loss of Brown, the command of the brigade devolved upon Lt. Col. Isaac F. Hunt of the 13th South Carolina Regiment.[11] As a testament to the losses sustained by the South Carolinians on May 5, 6, 12, and 23, Hunt was the highest-ranking officer left in the brigade at this time. McGowan's Brigade was present at Totopotomoy and Cold Harbor but saw no further significant action. At the latter battle, the South Carolinians held the extreme southern (right) end of the Confederate line from June 2.[12]

A review of the unit rosters and the subsequent battle record indicates that McGowan's Brigade recovered quickly from this campaign. Many of the men slightly wounded at the Wilderness and Spotsylvania returned to the ranks at Cold Harbor or later in June. James Conner, a native South Carolinian, was promoted to brigadier general and placed temporarily in command of the brigade.[13] During the subsequent siege of Petersburg, the brigade was frequently called upon for offensive actions and performed every time with distinction.

General McGowan reported that his brigade sustained a total of 481 casualties at the Wilderness.[14] This is somewhat less than the total compiled for this study. The brigade was well covered by the South Carolina newspapers, but there are several gaps in the listings.[15] No listing for the 1st (Orr's) South Carolina Rifles was found for the Battle of Spotsylvania, and no listings were found for three of the units at North Anna. Regardless, the casualty figures are judged as being relatively accurate (see Table 54, Appendix A) and compare favorably or are close to figures provided in J. F. J. Caldwell's 1866 book on this brigade.[16]

Scales's Brigade

William Dorsey Pender, one of the bright young officers in the Army of Northern Virginia, was the original commander of this brigade. Under his leadership, it achieved a solid fighting reputation as part of A. P. Hill's Light Division. In the spring of 1863, Pender's Brigade was considered by many to be an identical, albeit somewhat smaller, copy of Lane's fellow North Carolinian brigade. With the promotion of Pender to command Hill's Division in the new Third Corps, Alfred M. Scales of the 13th North Carolina Regiment, the senior colonel, was promoted to lead the brigade. The other regiments in the command were the 16th, 22nd, 34th, and 38th North Carolina. Their personnel were raised principally from the mountainous western, north-central, and southeastern parts of the state. But the positive view of this brigade at higher headquarters began to diminish in mid-1863 after this change in leadership and some unfortunate events during the Gettysburg Campaign.

Scales's Brigade was committed on the first day at Gettysburg and lost heavily in an assault on the I Corps at Seminary Ridge (northwest of town). Two days later, the North Carolinians were selected to support the attack of the divisions of Pickett and Pettigrew (Heth) upon the center of the Union line posted on Cemetery Ridge. During the assault, Scales's Brigade again suffered very heavily. Chief among this loss was the brigade commander and all but one of the field officers.[1] The reported number of casualties for the battle was 535, though more-recent compilations have placed the actual total at 704. In any event, this number was proportionally the highest in the division. During the subsequent retreat from Gettysburg, close to 200 men were also lost at Falling Waters. Combining the figures for the other battles, these North Carolinians sustained a reported total loss of 1,477 men for the year. A more modern compilation indicates that this total loss may have been 1,646 men.[2]

The most important element to this discussion is that once Lee's army returned to Virginia, a significant number of men in Scales's Brigade deserted.[3] The Army of Northern Virginia had always experienced desertions from the ranks, but these were isolated or individual occurrences. This, however, was the first major incident in any unit during the war. In retrospect, one could conclude that Scales's Brigade had been overused at Gettysburg. According to the available historical record, during the planning for Pickett's and Pettigrew's assault on the night of July 2–3, General Lee himself requested the deployment of Scales and Lane to support Pettigrew. He probably was unaware of the condition of Scales's men after July 1 (Lane's command had only been lightly engaged against Federal cavalry on this day and was comparatively fresh). If anything, this was a testament to the reputation of these two North Carolinian brigades. Unfortunately, no commander or staff officer aware of the North Carolinians' situation spoke up at that time. In defense of Lee, there is a report that as the units formed for the charge on July 3, he observed that many soldiers slightly wounded two days earlier (likely in Scales's and Pettigrew's units) had been treated with bandages and returned to the ranks. He spoke up and questioned why such men were in the ranks and not kept in field hospitals in the rear.[4]

The pertinent fact to modern historians is that other brigades in the Third Corps did not see significant action at Gettysburg on any of the three days, namely the units of Mahone and Posey (Harris) in Anderson's Division and Thomas in Pender's own command. In the aftermath of the battle and subsequent retreat, it is likely that the men of Scales's Brigade were well aware of this. The losses from Gettysburg and Falling Waters combined with the later desertions left the brigade with only about 500 men.

Over the winter of 1863–64, the leadership of Scales's Brigade apparently worked diligently to improve issues of morale and unit strength. An examination of the regimental rosters reveals that they largely succeeded. A sizeable number of the wounded from 1862 and 1863 (including General Scales) and the deserters returned, and a large number of new recruits were added to the rolls. At the start of the Overland Campaign, the strength of the brigade had been rebuilt to a level (more than 1,700 men) close to that of the previous year.

Scales's Brigade was heavily engaged at the Battle of the Wilderness. On May 5, it was one of the first two brigades sent to support Heth's position astride Orange Plank Road. The North Carolinians were dispatched to the right of the line to relieve Walker's Brigade in the early evening hours (see

Map 3, Appendix B). The brigade initially garnered some success against elements of the II Corps, however, it began to lose its position and line as more units of this enemy command were committed. The arrival of Lane's North Carolinians near dusk staved off a potential disaster.[5] On May 6, Scales's Brigade was posted on the right of the corps's front line and was reportedly unprepared for the early morning Federal attack (see Map 5, Appendix B). Available reports reveal that most of the command quickly broke and retreated. This uncovered the units to the left and Lane's Brigade in the immediate rear and precipitated much of the wholesale retreat of the Third Corps.[6] Following the relief by the First Corps, Scales's men rallied in the rear and then were posted with Wilcox's Division next to the Second Corps.

As with the other units in Wilcox's Division, Scales's Brigade was largely inactive during the first several days of the Battle of Spotsylvania. The North Carolinians were committed to assist Lane's Brigade during the morning of May 12 (see Map 19, Appendix B).[7] Unlike the other units in Wilcox's Division, they actually saw limited action on this day. The brigade then returned to its original position near the court house, facing northeast, and remained inactive until the close of the battle. During the late hours of May 21, Scales's Brigade (along with Lane's command) was chosen to conduct a reconnaissance of the enemy line astride Massaponax Church Road. Scales's men were deployed south of this road. They advanced and reached (and temporarily held) the Union line of breastworks before being recalled.[8] Judging by the reported casualty returns, the brigade sustained most of its losses at Spotsylvania on this day. The majority of these occurred in the 13th and 38th North Carolina Regiments.

Scales's Brigade was one of the principal participants at Jericho Mill (North Anna) on May 23. Col. William L. J. Lowrance of the 34th North Carolina Regiment temporarily led the brigade at this battle. The North Carolinians were posted on the left (western) end of the division (see Map 26, Appendix B).[9] The alignment of the regiments in this action was reportedly as follows (from east to west): the 13th, 22nd, 34th, 38th, and 16th. During their initial attack, they routed the opposing Federal infantry. With the North Anna River at their backs, the situation for the V Corps appeared to be almost desperate. A further all-out advance was halted by enemy artillery, but Lowrance's men began to inch their way closer toward the guns. At this critical point, three reserve regiments of the V Corps struck first McGowan's Brigade and then Thomas's Brigade to the right. McGowan's two regiments and Thomas's full command fell back, uncovering the North Carolinians, who also had to retire, in the process, losing many captured (see Map 27, Appendix B). The 22nd North Carolina Regiment sustained over half of the loss in the brigade. The 16th North Carolina Regiment escaped by running out a ravine toward the river, then circling back to the west to reach the main line.[10]

During the remainder of the campaign, Scales's Brigade was lightly engaged. The regiments engaged in only light skirmishing at Totopotomoy in late May. They moved to Cold Harbor on June 2 and were posted next to Lane's Brigade on the right of the overall army line.[11] The North Carolinians assisted in repulsing the attack of the Union army on June 3. Overall, the battle loss on this day was light and concentrated in two units (13th and 22nd Regiments). One unit, the 38th Regiment, reported no losses for the battle.

At the close of the campaign, Scales's Brigade emerged intact but comparatively smaller in strength. The command would continue to see some action during the siege of Petersburg, though not to the same degree as Lane's and McGowan's Brigades. One could conclude that the high command considered the brigade to be less reliable than these other units in the division, especially in an offensive capacity.

The casualties for Scales's Brigade during the campaign are provided in Table 55, Appendix A. Based on the rosters of the five regiments, it is possible to provide the following daily breakdown for the casualties of the brigade at Spotsylvania: 15 for May 10 and May 12; 8 for May 13–20; and 86 on May 21. A similar breakdown for the losses at the Wilderness was not found. The casualties for the overall campaign may be slightly low. There are significant gaps in the newspapers, and nearly all of them failed to provide breakdowns for the various battles.[12] This observation particularly applies to the records for the 34th North Carolina Regiment; no complete casualty listings were found for this unit.

Thomas's Brigade

This brigade of four Georgia regiments had one distinction rarely found in the Army of Northern Virginia. The initial commander, Joseph R. Anderson, was wounded in June 1862 during the Seven Days' Battles around Richmond. The leadership of the brigade then devolved upon Col. Edward L. Thomas of the 35th Georgia Regiment. For nearly three years, Thomas continuously commanded the brigade until its surrender at Appomattox Court House.

The 14th, 35th, 45th, and 49th Georgia Regiments comprised this command and were recruited from the middle to western portions of the state.

During 1862 and the first part of 1863, Thomas's Brigade was one of the established units in A. P. Hill's Light Division. A review of its battle record during this period reveals that it sustained consistent but comparatively lower casualties that the other units. It was a somewhat smaller brigade (with only four regiments) but also seemed to have some luck. On July 1 at Gettysburg, the division commander, William Pender, initially placed the Georgians in reserve. As a result, the brigade escaped the fate of McGowan's and especially Scales's Brigades. For the following two days of the battle, Thomas's men engaged in active skirmishing and avoiding long-range artillery fire. For the year 1863, the total number of reported battle casualties was only 443.[1] This figure was significantly below the numbers for the other three brigades in the division and a fraction of that of Lane's or Scales's Brigades. At the start of the Overland Campaign, the strength of the brigade was about 1,600 men.

At the Battle of the Wilderness, Thomas's Brigade was dispatched to the relief of Heth's Division during the early evening hours of May 5. The Georgians arrived just in time to buttress and relieve Davis's Brigade on the left (northern) end of the line (see Map 3, Appendix B).[2] They successfully held this position for the remaining hours of daylight.[3] Overnight, the brigade was shifted to the southern side of Orange Plank Road (see Map 5, Appendix B).[4] On May 6, Thomas's Brigade was, along with the other units in the Third Corps, driven from the field in the first hour of fighting.[5] Although there are few reports regarding the experiences of the Georgians during this Federal attack, most of the brigade tried to hold the position. A compilation of the casualties reveals that the command lost about 25 percent of its men at the Wilderness, with most of the losses occurred on May 6. The 45th and 49th Georgia Regiments were especially hard hit. The brigade was rallied after the arrival of the First Corps and thereafter posted on the division's right in a quiet zone next to Heth's Division.

Like the other units in Wilcox's Division, Thomas's Brigade arrived at Spotsylvania on May 9 and saw little combat until May 12. During the morning of this day, the brigade was moved to the assistance of Lane's Brigade in the right-hand portion of the Mule Shoe salient (see Map 19, Appendix B). Two of the units, the 14th and 35th Georgia Regiments, additionally joined elements of Evans's fellow Georgia brigade (from the Second Corps) in the effort to clear the eastern portion of this area of enemy forces.[6] Like

Evans's units, these regiments apparently advanced beyond the original line of breastworks and were caught in a difficult situation, forcing the survivors to pull back.[7] At the end of this day, the entire brigade was returned to the original position of their division (near the court house and Fredericksburg Road) and saw no further serious action at this battle.

Thomas's Brigade next participated at Jericho Mill (North Anna) on May 23. The Georgians were initially successful, along with Scales's Brigade, in routing elements of the Fourth Division, V Corps (see Map 26, Appendix B).[8] Only a line of Federal artillery barred the men from successfully driving the enemy troops into the North Anna River. At this critical point, the Union command committed three reserve regiments. These units struck the right flank of the Confederate units closing upon the guns. First, two regiments of McGowan's Brigade were driven back, which then exposed the right flank of Thomas's Brigade. For the most part, the entire brigade broke to the rear, thereby exposing Scales to the same fate (see Map 27, Appendix B). The 35th and 45th Georgia Regiments lost heavily in this action. The alignment of the regiments during this attack was as follows (from west to east): 14th, 45th, 35th, and 49th.[9]

For the balance of the campaign, Thomas's Brigade was lightly engaged and sustained no further significant casualties at either Totopotomoy or Cold Harbor. For the record, the brigade was posted between Scales's and McGowan's commands at Cold Harbor on June 2. It is possible from the rolls to offer a daily breakdown of the losses sustained by the Georgians at Spotsylvania. On May 12, the brigade lost 167 men; the remaining 17 casualties occurred on May 10, 14, and 18–21. A similar breakdown of the daily casualties sustained by the brigade at the Wilderness was not found.

At the close of this campaign, Thomas's Brigade emerged intact but with significantly fewer numbers in the ranks. The battle losses at Spotsylvania and North Anna had not been overly high, but taken together with those at the Wilderness, the total was significant. Total casualties for the campaign represented about 47–48 percent of the original strength of the brigade. From this point thereafter in 1864, Thomas's Brigade seemed to be nearly forgotten. The Georgians were kept in the trenches and were rarely committed to offensive excursions during the summer and fall at Petersburg.

This brigade was overall poorly covered in the Georgia newspapers.[10] No listings were found for the 14th and 35th Georgia Regiments as well as for the 49th Georgia Regiment for battles after May 12. An article published in the postwar magazine *The Sunny South* (regarding the 35th Georgia) helped fill this void.[11] Additional beneficial information regarding casualties was obtained from Lillian Henderson's rosters.[12] Judging by the sum of all the available records and these additional sources, it is possible that the battle losses sustained by Thomas's Brigade during the Overland Campaign could have been slightly higher than shown in Table 56, Appendix A.

ANDERSON'S/MAHONE'S DIVISION

During 1862 and the first five months of 1863, the division of Maj. Gen. Richard H. Anderson was part of Longstreet's First Corps. With the death of Thomas J. "Stonewall" Jackson after the Battle of Chancellorsville and the resulting changes in the organization of the Confederate army, the division was transferred to A. P. Hill's new Third Corps. During the Overland Campaign (and much of the war), the organization was composed of the brigades of Mahone, Perrin, Wright, Harris, and Perry. Mahone's regiments were from Virginia, but the remaining organizations were from the Deep South states of Alabama, Georgia, Mississippi, and Florida. Three of these brigades were badly bloodied at Gettysburg; the remaining two emerged comparatively unscathed. Over the winter, the strength of Anderson's Division was restored with returning veterans and some new enlistees. At this stage of the war, the command was a veteran and reliable force.

As the campaign started, Anderson's Division was initially left in the rear to cover the Rapidan River crossings.[1] Once contact was made with the main enemy force in the Wilderness, it was released from this assignment and ordered to rejoin the main army. At the start of the campaign, Longstreet's First Corps had encamped in and around Gordonsville and had the greatest distance to march to the Wilderness. Due to a delay in discerning Federal intentions and getting the order out, Anderson's Division got started later in the morning and actually fell in behind Longstreet's corps on the march.

Anderson's Division arrived at the Wilderness battlefield at about eight in the morning on May 6. By this hour, the two divisions of the First Corps had completed the relief of Heth's and Wilcox's Divisions and restored most of the Confederate front to the north and south of Orange Plank Road. For the most part, the crisis resulting from the early morning rout of A. P. Hill's two divisions had ended. Upon arrival, Anderson's Division was temporarily attached by General Lee to Longstreet's Corps and placed in reserve.[2]

For the balance of the battle, this division was committed into battle on a piecemeal basis. Some brigades participated in the series of attacks upon the II Corps in the areas of Orange Plank and Brock Roads (see Map 8, Appendix B). Most of its remaining elements were posted in dense woods north of Orange Plank Road or kept in reserve. They subsequently confronted troops from the IX Corps and engaged in some desperate fighting in this area of the battlefield. General Longstreet was wounded by friendly fire during the first phase of these engagements. The ranking officer in this area was Major General Anderson, who was promptly assigned command of the First Corps by Lee.[3] William Mahone, the ranking brigadier under Anderson, then assumed command of the division.

Mahone's men led the march of the Third Corps to Spotsylvania on May 8.[4] The command followed in the wake of Ewell's Second Corps. As ordered by General Early (temporarily commanding the Third Corps; A. P. Hill was sick), the division turned north on Carpathian Road and headed for Todd's Tavern. The rear guard for the II Corps (First Division) was positioned at this location. During the late afternoon and early evening, elements of the division, assisted by elements of Hampton's cavalry division, sparred with this Federal force. Anderson's Division then proceeded to Spotsylvania Court House and the eastern part of this battlefield using a different (more-southern) route.

On May 9, General Early moved Mahone's command back to the western end of the Confederate line to cover the left flank of the First Corps.[5] This proved to be a fortuitous move, for the division was in an excellent position to cover Block House Road and Bridge (over the Po River; see Map 14, Appendix B). Perrin's and Harris's Brigades led this march to the Po; Perry's and Wright's Brigades brought up the rear. Later that day, elements of the II Corps crossed the river and probed this area for a possible weakness in the Confederate line. The following day (May 10), this Union force was pulled back. Following the Union withdrawal, the division, for the most part, was shifted back to the right of the line near the court house on May 11 and 12.[6]

During the fighting of May 12, Anderson's Division was again committed piecemeal to the various parts of the battlefield. Two brigades were sent to the Mule Shoe and Bloody Angle, fighting there for most of the day. A third element supported Lane's Brigade (of Wilcox's Division) in its counterattack against an assaulting force of the IX Corps. This action occurred during the afternoon. The remaining units were either lightly engaged or covered a quiet sector and saw no combat.

After being stalemated at the Mule Shoe on May 12, the Union army began shifting to its left. On May 14, elements of the V and VI Corps crossed the Ni River and drove Confederate cavalry pickets from an elevated feature (named Myers Hill) located about one and one-half miles in front of the main line. General Early reacted to this by sending two of Mahone's brigades to regain the hill (see Map 23, Appendix B).[7] This small operation was properly executed, and the Federal outpost was driven back across the Ni. Later in the evening, Generals Early and Mahone decided to recall these units and abandon this advanced position. The division subsequently saw little further action at the Spotsylvania.

Mahone's Division (now identified by that name) brought up the rear of the Third Corps march to North Anna on May 21–22. As a result of this positioning and insufficient direction from corps headquarters, the organization missed the action at Jericho Ford (May 23). The division was posted on May 23 on the right of the corps's line from the North Anna River toward Anderson's Tavern (see Maps 28 and 29, Appendix B). This section was positioned on a bluff overlooking the North Anna River and covered a crossing at Ox Ford. The brigades were positioned, from west to east, in the following manner: Mahone's (led by Weisiger), Sanders's (formerly Perrin's), Harris's, Wright's, and Perry's (led by Lang).[8] On May 24, elements of the First Division, IX Corps managed to cross the river upstream and conduct a feeble assault upon the portion of the line held by Harris's and Sanders's Brigades, which was easily repulsed.[9] For the remainder of this battle, the division participated in skirmishing and was subjected to some artillery shelling. The overall loss was comparatively light.

The Third Corps brought up the rear of the army's march from North Anna to Totopotomoy. Mahone's Division was deployed on the right end of the Third Corps's line, covering a portion of the southern bank of Totopotomoy Creek (see Map 31, Appendix B). The command engaged in only skirmishing during this battle and lost very lightly. At this point in the campaign, Finegan's Brigade joined the division and was merged with Perry's Brigade, with General Finegan assuming command of the consolidated unit from Colonel Lang.[10] On June 2, the division moved quickly from the Confederate left (at Totopotomoy Creek) to the right at Cold Harbor and Turkey Hill. The brigades were placed in reserve behind Hoke's Division in the following manner (from north to south): Mahone's (under Weisiger), Sanders's, Harris's, Wright's, and Finegan's.[11]

The following morning, June 3, the Federals attacked along the entire southern portion of the Confederate line at Cold Harbor. The only success in this disastrous and otherwise regrettable assault occurred at a section of line held by units of Breckinridge's Division, located to the south of Hoke's section (see Map 38, Appendix B). The closest units in reserve were the 2nd Maryland Battalion and Finegan's Brigade. Both rushed into the breach and restored the line.[12] For the remainder of this day and the following four to six days, Mahone's Division relieved Breckinridge's and Hoke's Divisions in the main line.[13] This was one of the hottest sectors of the battlefield, and the division sustained casualties from continuous sniping and some ill-planned forays beyond the breastworks.

For the most part, Anderson's/Mahone's Division emerged from this campaign in a substantially better condition than Heth's and Wilcox's Divisions. Only Perry's and Harris's Brigades had sustained proportionally heavy casualties. The addition of Finegan's three regiments to Perry's Brigade corrected the only glaring weakness in the organization. With the exception of Harris, all of the brigades could still, after Cold Harbor, put more than 1,000 men in the field. Until May 1864, General Mahone had been a reliable but generally average brigade commander. As a division commander, he blossomed with the additional responsibility and quickly became one of the ablest leaders in Lee's army at this level. His division was continually committed during the siege of Petersburg and frequently used as a strike force to counter Federal advances and excursions outside their earthworks.

Perrin's/Sanders's Brigade

The original commander of this brigade was Cadmus M. Wilcox. During the period of his leadership (1862–63), it was the largest and perhaps best brigade in Anderson's Division. The unit was composed of five veteran regiments from Alabama. In 1863 Wilcox's Brigade performed well at both Chancellorsville and Gettysburg, though the reported number of battle losses for this year, at 1,323 men, was the highest in the division.[1] When Wilcox was promoted to divisional command, the brigade was given to Abner Perrin of South Carolina. He had previously shown promise as a commander, temporarily leading McGowan's Brigade at Gettysburg. Over the winter, the brigade regained much of its former strength as many of the wounded from the battles in 1863 and earlier returned to their units. At the start of this campaign, Perrin's Brigade fielded about 1,635 men in five regiments (the 8th, 9th, 10th, 11th, and 14th Alabama). The personnel were raised from nearly half of the counties in the state, ranging from Mobile in the southwest to Decatur and Scottsboro in the north.

On May 6 at the Battle of the Wilderness, Perrin's Brigade was first placed in reserve supporting Field's Division of the First Corps.[2] In the late morning, it assisted this command in an assault upon the II and V Corps posted on the northern side of Orange Plank Road (see Map 7, Appendix B).[3] This advance coincided with the flanking movement engineered by General Longstreet against the Union troops deployed on the southern side of the road. This combined counterattack forced a retirement of the opposing troops. In the afternoon, the Alabamians were shifted to the left (northwest) to assist in repulsing an attack by elements of the IX Corps upon Law's Brigade (Field's Division) and Perry's Brigade of Anderson's command (see Map 8, Appendix B).[4] This fighting occurred in dense woods and was typical of most of the action in this battle.

At Spotsylvania, Perrin's Brigade first participated in skirmishing along the Po River at the Block House Bridge on May 10. During the morning of May 12, the brigade was dispatched from this position to the Mule Shoe and ordered to retake a portion of the lost earthworks of Johnson's Division while covering the eastern flank of Rodes's Division (see Map 20, Appendix B). During this advance, General Perrin was killed and much of the brigade was thrown into disorder. Col. J. Horace King of the 9th Alabama Regiment rallied elements of his unit and the 8th Alabama Regiment on the left, while Col. John C. C. Sanders reformed the 10th, 11th, and 14th Alabama Regiments on the right. These two components managed to reach and regain a section of the lost works to the immediate right of Ramseur's Brigade (Rodes's Division).[5] Harris's Brigade (see the next section) followed Perrin's Brigade in this movement. The two commands become intermingled and fought this way for the remainder of the day to hold this line against elements of the II and then VI Corps.

With the death of General Perrin, Colonel Sanders of the 11th Alabama Regiment assumed command of the brigade.[6] During the night of May 12–13, the unit was moved back to the eastern portion of the army's line (near Spotsylvania Court House). For the remainder of this battle, the Alabamians saw little action. On May 24 at North Anna, Sanders's Brigade (newly renamed) helped repel an attack by the First Division, IX Corps near Ox Ford (see

Map 28, Appendix B). For the following two days, the command skirmished with elements of the V Corps.[7]

Sanders's Brigade was present at both Totopotomoy (Bethesda Church) and Cold Harbor. The Alabamians were very lightly engaged at both battles. Most of the limited casualties at Totopotomoy occurred in one regiment (14th Alabama). From June 2 through June 8, the brigade was held in reserve at Cold Harbor behind Hoke's Division (see Map 38, Appendix B). On June 8, they relieved Hoke's command in the front line.[8] Most of the casualties in the brigade occurred from sniping and skirmishing while at this position.

Sanders's Brigade emerged from the campaign in a somewhat reduced but still satisfactory condition. The command would continue to see considerable action during the siege of Petersburg in June through August. Colonel Sanders was promoted to brigadier general but was killed in action on August 21. The command of the brigade then devolved upon Col. William H. Forney of the 14th Alabama Regiment.

The records for this brigade were found to be very comprehensive (see Table 57, Appendix A). Listings of casualties were found in Alabama and Richmond newspapers for all the regiments.[9] Many of these newspapers provided lists for individual battles. The only missing information was for the 11th Alabama Regiment at Cold Harbor.

Mahone's Brigade

William Mahone's brigade was composed of five regiments (the 6th, 12th, 16th, 41st, and 61st Virginia) from the Richmond, Petersburg, and Tidewater areas of southeastern Virginia. These units were present at every major battle of the army in 1862 and 1863 and seemed to frequently experience a bit of good fortune. In 1862, the reported number of casualties for Mahone's Brigade never exceeded 435 men at any one battle and typically was among the lowest in the division. At Gettysburg, the brigade was kept primarily in reserve and engaged in only limited skirmishing; its reported loss was only 102 men. Additionally, the reported total number of casualties for the year 1863 was 411 men.[1] This was proportionally the lowest total in the division and paled in comparison to those of Wilcox's and Wright's Brigades. During the winter of 1863–64, Mahone's Brigade received a substantial number of recruits and the strength of the command increased to about 1,805 men, making it the largest unit in the division.

During the Battle of the Wilderness, Mahone's Brigade on May 6 was again initially placed in reserve. In the late morning, the Virginians were selected to participate in Longstreet's flanking movement along the trail of the unfinished railroad and his subsequent assault upon the Federal army's left flank. The brigade was placed in the center of the first line between Wofford's and Anderson's Brigades (see Map 8, Appendix B).[2] The attack was more than successful, wresting the initiative from the Federals and forcing their retirement in this sector of the battlefield. Unfortunately, the Virginians obtained a negative distinction at this time. The friendly small-arms fire that struck General Longstreet and other officers reportedly came from the 12th Virginia Regiment of this brigade, though there has been some historic dispute regarding the particular unit associated with this unfortunate action.[3]

When Richard H. Anderson assumed leadership of the First Corps, William Mahone was assigned to command the division. Leadership of his Virginia brigade then devolved upon Col. David A. Weisiger of the 12th Virginia Regiment.[4] The Confederate army took several hours to reorganize and, in the late afternoon, assaulted the entire Federal front along Brock Road. Mahone's Brigade participated in this attack and was positioned in the center of the Confederate line astride Orange Plank Road (see Map 8, Appendix B).[5] The Federals were able to withstand this assault. The Confederates fell back to their entrenchments, ending the fighting in this portion of the battlefield.

During the march to Spotsylvania and the late hours of May 8, General Mahone committed his former command against the rear of the enemy column traveling on Carpathian Road west of Todd's Tavern.[6] The Virginians were assisted in this action by two brigades of Hampton's cavalry division. They managed to capture several supply wagons and engage elements of the First Division, II Corps. Darkness brought an end to an otherwise inconclusive fight. The action did have an influence upon the Union high command and caused a delay in the march of the II Corps to Spotsylvania.

On May 9, Mahone's Brigade was temporarily attached to Heth's Division. In response to a Federal move, this unit was shifted from the right of the army line to the left on May 10 (see Map 14, Appendix B). That afternoon, Heth's Division assaulted elements of the First Division, II Corps that had crossed the Po River upstream and west of the Block House Bridge. Weisiger's men supported this attack.[7] Thereafter, the Virginians were shifted back to the right portion of the Confederate line (near Spotsylvania Court House). During the afternoon of May 12, the brigade supported a counterattack by Lane's

Brigade upon elements of the IX Corps then assaulting a section of the main Confederate line (see Map 21, Appendix B).[8] Lane's North Carolinians were very successful in this movement and rolled up the Federals' southern flank. Both Lane's and Weisiger's commands, however, suffered heavily from enemy artillery fire.

There was one additional incident during this action. Lane's Brigade had collected several hundred prisoners and a couple of Union battle flags in their assault. These men and trophies were ushered to the rear and into the grasp of Weisiger's supporting lines.[9] The Virginians naturally claimed them as their prizes. In the aftermath, there were considerable discussions and accusations regarding the accuracy of the battle claims and trophies by both commands. The brigade thereafter conducted a minor but fruitless reconnaissance in force upon the entrenchments of the IX Corps before being recalled.[10] Weisiger's troops saw little further action at Spotsylvania.

Mahone's Brigade was next in action at North Anna on May 24. The Virginians assisted in the successful repulse of an attack by the First Division, IX Corps (see Map 28, Appendix B).[11] The brigade was present at Totopotomoy in late May but sustained no reported casualties. It joined the rest of Mahone's Division at Cold Harbor and, on June 2, was posted on the division's left in support of Hoke's Division (see Map 38, Appendix B). Over the next several days, the brigade relieved the units in the front line of breastworks and sustained considerable casualties from sniping and skirmishing.

Like Perrin's or Sanders's Brigade, Weisiger's command emerged from the campaign with a somewhat reduced but otherwise stable condition. The Virginians were still a reliable and capable fighting force. They would see considerable action in battles in and around Petersburg in June through October. In these actions, they would finally experience very heavy casualties.

The casualties for Mahone's Brigade during the campaign are provided in Table 58, Appendix A. The newspaper listings for this brigade provide a patchwork of records regarding casualties.[12] Several of these accounts provided combined listings for the Wilderness and Spotsylvania, with no distinctions between these battles. No listings were found for the 41st Virginia Regiment for the battles after the Wilderness, and no listings were found for the 6th and 12th Virginia Regiments at Cold Harbor. The respective books from the Virginia Regimental Histories Series were included in the research for this brigade.[13] In his report on the Wilderness, General Mahone indicated that the casualties in his brigade were 153 men (20 killed, 126 wounded, and

7 missing).[14] This is surprisingly very close to the total number of 156 found in this study. In addition, it is possible from the gathered information to provide reasonable estimates for the daily casualties for the brigade at Spotsylvania. They are as follows: 40 on May 8; 16 on May 10–11; 206 on May 12; and 3 on May 14.

Harris's Brigade

Nathaniel H. Harris was the newest brigadier general in the division, promoted in the fall of 1863 to replace Carnot Posey, who had died of wounds sustained at Bristoe Station in October. The brigade was composed of four veteran Mississippi regiments (the 12th, 16th, 19th, and 48th) raised from counties located along the lower Mississippi River and in the northern part of the state. During most of the battles in 1862, the brigade sustained heavy casualties. But this organization, like Mahone's Brigade, experienced good fortune at Gettysburg, where they were involved only in skirmishing and artillery shelling on the second and third days. The total number of reported casualties for 1863 was only 406 men, the smallest in the division.[1] Despite this recent fortune in battle, the strength of this Mississippi brigade was beginning to fall. By this stage in the war, it was becoming very difficult for units from the western states of the Confederacy serving in the eastern theater to obtain recruits and retain or recover all their furloughed men. On May 5, the strength of Harris's Brigade was only about 1,395 men.

After arriving at the Wilderness on May 6, Harris's Brigade was kept in reserve for much of the day. In the afternoon, elements of the IX Corps assaulted several Confederate brigades posted north of Orange Plank Road. This area was heavily wooded and bisected by several ravines. Initially, the Confederate units (Law's Brigade of Field's Division and Perry's Brigade of Anderson's Division) received the worst of this action. Harris's Brigade was dispatched to this area and assisted in stabilizing the Confederate line (see Map 8, Appendix B).[2]

At the Battle of Spotsylvania, Harris's Brigade initially moved in tandem with Perrin's Brigade. On May 9, the Mississippians were sent with Perrin's Alabamians to hold the sector of the line at the Block House Bridge and Po River.[3] In the morning of May 12, they followed Perrin's command in the march to the Mule Shoe (see Map 20, Appendix B). After Perrin formed and began his advance toward the Federal troops, Harris formed his brigade slightly to the east and similarly moved forward. In this counterattack, the 12th and 48th Mississippi Regiments were placed on the left and the 16th and 19th Mississippi Regiments were deployed on the right. The two latter units were subjected to very heavy enemy fire from the right and lost heavily. Nevertheless, the Mississippians successfully cleared the sector of the original earthworks in their front.[4] McGowan's Brigade shortly thereafter came forward and covered Harris's open right flank. These two units (with Perrin's and Ramseur's commands) subsequently held this line for the remainder of the day. The Federals massed at the opposite side of the fortifications and kept up a continuous heavy volume of fire. This fighting at this line was some of the most desperate of the campaign.

After darkness, the Confederates in the Mule Shoe slipped away to a new line of entrenchments in the rear. Harris's Brigade was sent back to Mahone's Division and posted in a section of the line near Spotsylvania Court House, facing east. On May 14, the Federal army began moving to Lee's right in an effort to move around the line of Confederate earthworks. Late on this day, Harris's Brigade supported Wright's command in an assault upon the lead elements of the Union forces conducting this operation (see Map 23, Appendix B).[5] After successfully driving back the opposing forces, the brigade was recalled and retired to the main line.

Harris's Brigade was next in action on May 24 at North Anna. Here, the Mississippians held a section of the Confederate line to the immediate southeast of Ox Ford and were assaulted on the twenty-fourth by elements of the First Division, IX Corps (see Map 28, Appendix B).[6] The attack was easily repulsed, and the command sustained very light casualties. Harris's Brigade was present at the remaining battles of the campaign. It apparently participated in some skirmishing at Totopotomoy on May 30 and 31 and then, with the other units in Mahone's Division, moved to Cold Harbor on June 2. At the latter battle, the Mississippians were placed in the center of the division in the rear of Hoke's Division (see Map 38, Appendix B). Beginning on June 8 and for the following several days, they relieved the troops in the front line of earthworks and sustained some casualties from sniping, artillery fire, and skirmishing.[7]

Harris's Brigade had fought well during this campaign and was commended for its service. The unit, however, sustained proportionally the highest casualties in Mahone's Division. As a result, its strength and effectiveness was diminished. The Mississippians saw considerable action during the Petersburg siege. Their small command was particularly badly cut up on August 21 at Globe Tavern.

The casualties sustained by Harris's Brigade during the campaign are provided in Table 59, Appendix A. The May 31 issue of the *Richmond Examiner* provides a listing of casualties for the entire brigade for the Wilderness (May 6) but for only May 12 at Spotsylvania.[8] This listing unfortunately did not differentiate between the two battles, and it is possible that some of the losses assigned to the Wilderness may have occurred at Spotsylvania (and vice versa). The majority of the losses sustained by Harris's Brigade at Spotsylvania occurred on May 12. It is also apparent that this newspaper listing did not include some slightly wounded men. Inspection reports were found for several of the companies in the 12th and 16th Mississippi Regiments in the CSRs. These list the number of casualties sustained by the unit for each battle. In many cases, the numbers slightly exceeded the tallies of names in the newspaper. Although the identities of the additional men are not known, the revised figures were incorporated into the total casualty numbers in Table 59. As for casualties for the brigade after May 12, only one list for the 48th Mississippi Regiment was found.[9] This tally covered combat losses incurred at North Anna and Cold Harbor. Dunbar Rowland's book was also checked for the study of this brigade.[10]

Wright's Brigade

This veteran all-Georgia brigade was one of the main components of Anderson's Division during the first two years of the war. Brig. Gen. Ambrose R. Wright was its only commander. With the promotion of William Mahone at the Wilderness, Wright became the senior brigadier general in the division. In 1863, Wright's Brigade performed admirably at the Battles of Chancellorsville, Gettysburg, and Manassas Gap; the latter action occurred on July 23 against two divisions of the III Corps and a cavalry brigade. The cost for these battles was high, and the brigade reported a combined 1,160 casualties for the year 1863.[1]

At this stage of the war, Wright's Brigade consisted of the 3rd, 22nd, and 48th Regiments and the small 2nd Battalion. The battles losses from 1863 reduced these units to only 800–900 men. Over the winter of 1863–64, many veterans returned from wounded furlough. The overall strength of the command increased significantly with the assignment of the 10th Georgia

Battalion. With this addition, the brigade started the campaign with about 1,685 men, which rivaled in size Mahone's and Perrin's Brigades and nearly matched the level the brigade had fielded before Gettysburg. The personnel in these five units were raised primarily from the central part of Georgia.

For the most part, Wright's Brigade experienced a run of good fortune during the Overland Campaign. During the Battle of the Wilderness, the Georgians were never seriously engaged. Initially, the command was placed in reserve. In the late morning and afternoon of May 6, it supported elements of Kershaw's Division (of the First Corps) in an assault upon Federal units positioned just south of Orange Plank Road (see Map 7, Appendix B).[2] This pattern of limited combat continued through the first several days of Spotsylvania. Wright's Brigade was shifted as a part of Mahone's Division to the Block House Bridge on May 9. When other brigades of the division were dispatched to other sectors of the battlefield on May 12, the Georgians remained in this position to cover the army's left.[3] Although somewhat isolated from the rest of Lee's forces, Wright's Brigade was ignored by the enemy and saw no action on this day.

Wright's command was finally committed into action on May 14. Early on this day, the brigade was reunited with Mahone's Division on the army's right. The Union army was beginning to move units across the Confederate front toward the open right flank, and Wright's Brigade was selected to counter this move and determine the enemy intentions. After about a week of limited activity, it appears that the Georgians were spoiling for a fight. With support from Harris's Brigade and elements of Chambliss's cavalry brigade, they performed this operation in a spirited manner, capturing a local high point (Myers Hill) and inflicting significantly higher casualties upon opposing forces of the V and VI Corps (see Map 23, Appendix B).[4] Having satisfied the intentions of Confederate commanders, these units were recalled at the end of the day.

Wright's Brigade was present at the remaining three battles of the campaign but again experienced little action. At North Anna, the brigade was posted along the river just east of Ox Ford (see Map 28, Appendix B).[5] This defensive position was subjected only to some heavy artillery shelling on May 24 and 25. At Totopotomoy, the Georgians engaged only in limited skirmishing in front of the main line of earthworks. At Cold Harbor, the command was moved to the army's right on June 2, in reserve between Harris's and Finegan's Brigades in support of Hoke's Division (see Map 38, Appendix B).

During June 3 and following several days, the Georgians relieved the latter command on the front line.

Wright's Brigade experienced one significant distinction in this campaign. The command sustained both overall and proportionally the lowest number of casualties of all of the infantry brigades in Lee's army. This applies to the units that were present at all of the battles. In view of its limited action, Wright's Brigade clearly emerged from the campaign with the highest strength in the division. The Georgians' stroke of fortune ran out at Petersburg, though. The brigade was continuously committed to battles in June, July, and August. The gradual attrition from these actions raised their total number of battle casualties to a level similar to those of the other brigades in Mahone's Division for the year.

General Wright took a leave of absence in the summer and, as requested by Gov. Joseph Brown of Georgia, was eventually transferred to duty in his home state. Command of the brigade was then given to Victor J. B. Girardey, a promising young brigade staff officer. He was unfortunately killed in action in August. The command was then assigned to a second staff officer, G. Moxley Sorrel (from the First Corps). He was wounded in February 1865.[6]

The casualties incurred by Wright's Brigade during the campaign are shown in Table 60, Appendix A. The availability of casualty lists for the units of this brigade ranged widely. The *Macon Daily Telegraph* published two listings for the casualties in the 10th Georgia Battalion by day for the entire campaign.[7] The *Augusta Daily Chronicle and Sentinel* provided a listing of casualties for the entire brigade for the period May 6–18.[8] Unfortunately, this listing is not differentiated by battle or day. Augusta's *Daily Constitutionalist* provided a list of the battle losses in the 22nd Georgia Regiment for the period May 6–June 30.[9] This list is similarly undifferentiated. Some additional information was obtained from Lillian Henderson's rosters.[10]

Perry's/Finegan's Brigade

Edward A. Perry's brigade (also known as the Florida Brigade) was the smallest infantry brigade in the Army of Northern Virginia. The Confederate government had directed that infantry and cavalry brigades in the field armies should be composed of units from the same state or, when not possible, from adjacent states. Perry's Brigade was a result of this directive. It consisted of three regiments from Florida, all the infantry from that state in Lee's army.

The men were recruited from the western Panhandle and northeastern portions of the state. At the start of this campaign, two of the regiments, the 2nd and 8th Florida, were severely understrength and could field a combined total only slightly more than the third unit, the 5th Florida. The condition of this brigade was mainly due to its service and battle losses in 1863. Perry's Brigade was heavily engaged on the second and third days at Gettysburg and lost nearly 60 percent of its field strength in this battle; much of this loss occurred supporting Pickett's/Pettigrew's/Trimble's Charge on July 3. Overall, total casualties for this command in 1863 was 588.[1] Over the winter, its strength rose from about 300 to 610 men, still making it the smallest brigade in the army. The increase stemmed primarily from the return of men wounded at Gettysburg, for very few recruits were added to this command during this period.

As with most of Anderson's Division, Perry's Brigade was initially placed in reserve in the morning hours of May 6 at the Wilderness. During the afternoon, the command was deployed in a heavily wooded area north of Orange Plank Road. Elements of Law's (led by Col. William Perry) Alabamian brigade (of Field's Division) observed an enemy force advancing from the north upon the flank and rear of the main Confederate line facing eastward toward Brock Road. Perry's Brigade was ordered to join the Alabamians and repel the Union advance. The larger enemy force, consisting of the Second and Third Divisions of the IX Corps, nearly overwhelmed the Floridians and Alabamians (see Map 8, Appendix B).[2] The Florida Brigade sustained a loss of more than 240 men (or almost 40 percent of its initial strength; see Table 61, Appendix A). In addition, Edward Perry was severely wounded at this time and lost for the remainder of the war. The command of the brigade then devolved upon Col. David Lang of the 8th Florida Regiment.[3] The timely arrival of reinforcements from Field's and Anderson's Divisions saved the two Confederate brigades and restored the line.

Perry's Brigade, still commanded by Lang, was not engaged at Spotsylvania to any real degree. It marched and countermarched with Mahone's Division between the eastern and western sides of the battlefield on May 9 and 12. For the remainder of this battle, the brigade held a portion of the main of breastworks southeast of Spotsylvania Court House, a relatively quiet sector outside the areas assaulted by the Federal army (see Map 21, Appendix B). At North Anna, Perry's Brigade was posted on the right of Mahone's Division, covering a section of the river east of Ox Ford (see Map 28, Appendix B). The

Floridians were subjected to some sniping and artillery shelling and sustained some casualties.[4]

The composition of the small Florida Brigade changed when Lee's army reached Totopotomoy (outside Richmond) during the last week of May. The War Department ordered four battalions plus four independent companies of infantry to move from their assignment in Florida and join the Army of Northern Virginia. These miscellaneous units were grouped into one brigade and placed under the local district commander, Brig. Gen. Joseph Finegan. Finegan's unit reached Richmond on May 25 and was assigned to Mahone's Division on May 28–29.[5] Considering that Perry's Brigade could field only about 350 men and was commanded by a colonel at this time, it was absorbed into Finegan's newly arrived brigade. The combined strength of the merged command was now in excess of 1,600 men.

Finegan's Brigade was present at Totopotomoy but sustained no recorded casualties. The command moved to Cold Harbor on June 2 and was posted on the right of the division in support of Hoke's and Breckinridge's Divisions (see Map 38, Appendix B).[6] During the early hours of June 3, the opposing Federal forces assaulted the southern portion of the Confederate line. For the most part, the attacks were easily repulsed, with severe losses to the Union forces and minimal casualties to the Confederate defenders. Elements of the II Corps, however, achieved a breakthrough in a portion of the line held by Breckinridge's Division. The closest troops in reserve were the 2nd Maryland Battalion and Finegan's Brigade. These units rushed into the advancing Union troops, halted their further advance, and ultimately recaptured the lost section of line.[7]

In order to avoid a repetition of this enemy success, a new line of breastworks was quickly constructed in the rear, manned by Finegan's Brigade. This position was thereafter subjected to continuous sniping from the Federals. On two occasions, General Finegan ordered troops to move out into the zone between the two main lines and clear out the snipers. The order amounted to a death sentence for the men given this assignment and served only to increase the casualties for this battle.[8] The few survivors who made it back to the lines were usually wounded.

At the close of the Overland Campaign, the strength of the augmented Florida Brigade was more in line with those of the other commands in Mahone's Division. Finegan's Brigade subsequently saw considerable action during the siege of Petersburg. During the months of June and July, the new units experienced significant losses in personnel due to sickness more so than combat. The four battalions and four independent companies were organized on June 8 to create the 9th, 10th, and 11th Florida Regiments. For purposes of reference, the compositions of these units were as follows: the 9th Regiment, formed from the 6th Battalion and three independent companies; the 10th Regiment, formed from the 1st Battalion and part of the 2nd Battalion; and the 11th Regiment, formed from the 4th Battalion, part of the 2nd Battalion, and one independent company.

Only one casualty listing was found in the newspapers for the Florida Brigade. The *Savannah Republican* printed the losses for the entire brigade at the Wilderness.[9] Without this list, the casualties for this command would not be known. Many of the men wounded on May 6 were actually returnees from wounded furlough after Gettysburg. Judging by the individual unit rolls in the CSRs, it appears that these men had not returned in the early spring and were never present at the Wilderness. The list was provided to a newspaper correspondent after the battle by the brigade's assistant adjutant general, Capt. Charles Seaton Fleming. When the two Florida brigades merged under Finegan, Fleming returned to his parent unit, the 2nd Florida Regiment. He was among the men needlessly killed on June 3.[10]

Newspaper listings of the losses for the 9th, 10th, and 11th Florida Regiments at Cold Harbor have not been found and may have never been published. Recent research has located several diaries from men in these units. These reported the following: on June 3, the 1st Florida Battalion lost 75–80 men, the 2nd Florida Battalion lost 85–90 men, and the 6th Florida Battalion lost 105 men. No mention was made of the 4th Florida Battalion or the four independent companies. Judging by these figures, it is safe to state that Finegan's new units lost at least 275 men at Cold Harbor.[11] The actual loss could have been higher (see Table 61).

ARTILLERY

The Third Corps fielded the largest infantry force in Lee's army and similarly contained the highest number of batteries. The corps artillery, commanded by Col. R. Lindsay Walker, consisted of twenty batteries in five battalions. Lt. Col. William T. Poague's battalion contained the batteries of Richards (Mississippi, Madison), Williams (C, 1st North Carolina or Charlotte), Wyatt (Virginia, Albemarle), and Utterback (Virginia, Warrenton). Lt. Col. William J.

Pegram's battalion consisted of the batteries of Zimmerman (South Carolina, Pee Dee), Ellet (Virginia, Richmond), Marye (Virginia, Fredericksburg), Brander (Virginia, Richmond), and Cayce (Virginia, Richmond). Lt. Col. David G. McIntosh commanded the batteries of Hurt (Alabama), Price (Virginia, Danville), Donald (Virginia, Rockbridge), and Clutter (Virginia, Jackson Flying). Lt. Col. Charles Richardson's battalion consisted of the batteries of Landry (Louisiana, Donaldsonville), Moore (Virginia, Norfolk), Penick (Virginia, Pittsylvania), and Grandy (Virginia, Norfolk Light Blues). Col. Allen S. Cutts commanded the Georgia batteries of Ross, Patterson, and Wingfield; this organization was also known as the 11th Georgia Battalion.

Several batteries of Poague's Battalion (Richards, Williams, and probably Utterback) were engaged at the Wilderness.[1] They were posted on the morning of May 6 on the western side of the Widow Tapp Field in the rear of Heth's and Wilcox's Divisions (see Map 5, Appendix B). When these infantry units were driven from their positions, these batteries covered their retirement and confronted much of the pursuing Union force. They held this position with little infantry support until relieved and rescued by the arrival of Longstreet's First Corps (see Map 6, Appendix B). Surprisingly, the battalion reported only fifteen casualties at this battle. McIntosh's, Pegram's, and Richardson's Battalions also reported one or two casualties at the Wilderness. It is not clear how this occurred since these commands were likely parked in the rear of the main battle area.

Each of the artillery battalions of the Third Corps was committed to action at the Battle of Spotsylvania. Three battalions were posted along the main line of breastworks on the Confederate right. Poague's Battalion was deployed at the "Heth" salient in support of this division. Pegram's Battalion was posted astride Fredericksburg Road near the court house, and Cutts's Battalion was deployed on the far right end opposite Massaponax Church Road.[2] Each of these commands engaged in long-range duels with Federal artillery. The first two commands were additionally in action on May 12 and 18 against elements of the IX Corps.[3] On May 10, McIntosh's and Richardson's Battalions supported Mahone's and Heth's Divisions (respectively) in their battle with the First Division, II Corps near the Block House Bridge and Po River.[4] After this action, these two artillery commands returned to the Third Corps sector on the right of the line and were held in reserve for the remainder of the battle.

Four of the five battalions were engaged at North Anna. Poague's and Pegram's commands supported Wilcox's failed attack upon the V Corps at Jericho Mill on May 23.[5] Their batteries in part dueled with the enemy corps's artillery and reportedly received the worst of the action (see Map 27, Appendix B). When the Third Corps formed and entrenched at a new line between Anderson's Station and Ox Ford on May 24, McIntosh's and Cutts's Battalions were posted on a bluff overlooking the ford and Chesterfield Bridge to the east (see Map 28, Appendix B).[6] They were subjected to considerable Federal artillery fire for several days. This was the first real action for Cutts's Battalion. The colonel himself was absent at this time, and in his place, Maj. John Lane led the battalion. Poague's and Pegram's Battalions were deployed to the southwest in support of Heth's and Wilcox's Divisions. Richardson's command was posted in the rear of these units.

During the limited engagement at Totopotomoy, the Third Corps covered the western portion of the Confederate line. The deployment of the corps artillery at this time is not well documented. All of the units were lightly engaged, with Cutts's and McIntosh's Battalions reporting minor losses. Mahone's and Wilcox's Divisions moved to Cold Harbor on June 2, accompanied by Pegram's, McIntosh's, Richardson's, and Cutts's (Lane's) Battalions. Pegram was placed on the left of the corps's line with Wilcox's Division, while the remaining three battalions were held in reserve with Mahone's Division in a second line behind Hoke's and Breckinridge's Divisions. Pegram's Battalion, followed by the other three commands, was heavily engaged on June 3 and contributed to the defeat of the massive Federal assault in the early morning hours.[7] McIntosh's, Richardson's, and Cutts's Battalions were deployed north of Pegram in the area of the earlier Federal breakthrough. For the next several days, all four battalions were subjected to continuous small-arms fire from enemy snipers.[8]

Heth's Division remained at Bethesda Church and covered the extreme left of the Confederate line. Poague's Battalion was attached with this division and was heavily engaged on June 2 and 3 (see Map 41, Appendix B).[9] Wyatt's and Richards's Batteries together sustained over fifty casualties in this battle, by far the heaviest loss in the corps artillery during the Overland Campaign. Judging by their loss, it appears that these batteries were deployed in a vulnerable position on these days.

The records for the Third Corps artillery are relatively complete (see Table 62, Appendix A). With the exception of Zimmerman's Battery (of Pegram's Battalion), the muster rolls are all present or nearly so. As with the artillery units in the First and Second Corps, casualty lists were found in the newspapers covering the major battles for nearly all the batteries. The only major omissions were listings for four Virginia batteries of Pegram's Battalion and Landry's, Penick's, and Grandy's Batteries of Richardson's Battalion. The respective books of the Virginia Regimental Histories Series and the first volume of the series on North Carolina troops were included in the research for these artillery commands.[10]

CHAPTER 7

Cavalry Corps

The cavalry of Maj. Gen. James E. B. "Jeb" Stuart was historically regarded as the elite arm of the Army of Northern Virginia. During the first two years of the war, Stuart's cavalry literally rode circles around opposing Union armies and bested the Federal cavalry in almost every engagement. This level of superiority began to change in 1863. In the spring of that year, Maj. Gen. Joseph Hooker reorganized the cavalry of the Army of the Potomac and grouped the arm in one command. Prior to this point in the war, cavalry units were parceled out to the various infantry corps and used at the discretion of the respective infantry leaders. Efforts were also made by the high command to rearm and increase the size of their cavalry and to find younger, more-aggressive leaders. These measures began to yield positive results by the late spring and summer. When Lt. Gen. Ulysses Grant came east in early 1864 to take over command of all the Union armies and the personal oversight of the Army of the Potomac, he brought Maj. Gen. Philip Sheridan with him to lead the cavalry corps. Under Sheridan, the competency and level of activity of Federal cavalry in Virginia continued to increase.

With the reorganization and expansion of the Federal cavalry, the Confederate command similarly increased the strength of Stuart's cavalry. For most of 1862, this mounted arm consisted of a division of two or three brigades. During the Gettysburg campaign, Stuart's cavalry was augmented by the attachment of several brigades from western Virginia. Over the winter of 1863–64, the command was reorganized as a corps of six brigades in three divisions, each brigade consisting of three or four units. The creation of additional commands was dictated by the increase in assigned units plus the availability of qualified leaders. Unlike the infantry, the cavalry in Lee's army experienced few battle casualties among the leadership during the first two years of the war. By 1864, there was actually a surplus of experienced, competent leaders available.

During the winter of 1863–64, the various cavalry brigades were dispatched to inactive areas of Virginia to procure forage for the horses and additional mounts. In the early spring, the ranks of the parent units swelled with the return of sick and wounded men and the addition of new recruits. By the first week of May, the strength of the corps was about 8,800 men (in twenty units). The average strength of a full regiment was about 475 men, which was considerably higher than that of a corresponding infantry regiment as this stage of the war. During the Overland Campaign, the Cavalry Corps was further reinforced with nine new units. Three comprised one full brigade, four others were assigned to existing brigades, and the remaining two new units were temporarily attached and later assigned to an independent cavalry brigade with the Richmond garrison. These nine units were, for the most part, new organizations with full ranks. Together, they increased the total strength of the corps by about 50 percent.

Stuart's cavalry historically performed missions of scouting, screening, and flank protection for Lee's army. For much of the war, its record in these capacities was unmatched by its Federal counterparts. The competency of the Confederate cavalry in these missions continued during the Overland Campaign. Stuart's brigades, in particular, rendered excellent service in the opening phases of the Battles of the Wilderness and Spotsylvania. As the campaign progressed, however, the level of service of the cavalry at times noticeably declined. This was apparently due, in part, to heavy personnel casualties and losses in mounts in some of the veteran units and, in part, to the employment of the new, inexperienced units.

The occurrence of casualties in the Confederate cavalry during this campaign was gathered primarily from Southern newspapers; the muster rolls seldom mention battle casualties. In fact, the muster rolls and records of the cavalry in the CSRs are among the worst in Lee's army. The May–June 1864 roll is missing in nearly all of the individual units. In most of the rolls for the year 1864, it appears that the most important issue with respect to the ranks is the possession of a horse. A large percentage of men are listed on the subsequent August or October 1864 rolls as being on furlough (to his home state or local area) to procure a new mount. Considering the fact that Southern soldiers had to furnish their own horses, this was clearly an increasing problem for the army.

The utilization of the Cavalry Corps during the campaign generally consisted of a period of movement and/or battle followed by a period of rest.

The latter was done more for the horses than for the men. As a result, brigades or regiments were apparently rotated in and out of active roles. For the most part, the cavalry avoided battle with infantry and engaged only Federal horsemen. As described in the preceding chapters, the actions involving the infantry of the opposing armies can be grouped into five battles. The actions of the cavalry, however, were considerably more numerous and involved many small actions and skirmishes during the movements to and on the periphery of these major battles. At a minimum, there were fifteen separate actions involving Confederate cavalry. In most instances, units were committed or deployed as individual brigades. One division of two brigades was primarily engaged as a complete, independent command in most of these engagements. This variation in employment throughout the campaign has been taken into consideration in the following discussions of the respective units.

FITZHUGH LEE'S DIVISION

This division was composed of two brigades: Brig. Gen. Williams C. Wickham led the 1st, 2nd, 3rd, and 4th Virginia Cavalry Regiments; Brig. Gen. Lunsford L. Lomax commanded the 5th, 6th, and 15th Virginia Cavalry Regiments. These seven units were originally raised from most of the counties in the Commonwealth and had served with Robert E. Lee or "Stonewall" Jackson since the spring of 1862. Their ranks included many of the best-educated, wealthy, and otherwise privileged men from Virginia. Wickham's Brigade was a fixture in the corps since early 1862; Lomax's Brigade was formed over the winter by the transfer of one regiment from each of the other three existing Virginia brigades in the Cavalry Corps. At the start of the Overland Campaign, the ranks of most of these seven regiments were full. Wickham's Brigade, in particular, was very large and fielded almost the twice the number of Lomax's Brigade. The division commander, Maj. Gen. Fitzhugh Lee, was a nephew of the Army of Northern Virginia's commander. He had earned his rank and position through competent service and not through any measure of nepotism.

During most of the campaign, the brigades of Wickham and Lomax were deployed and committed to battle together as a division. For that reason, the following discussion of their roles in the campaign is presented under the heading of their division. In early May, Fitzhugh Lee's Division was deployed near Fredericksburg, far to the east of the main Confederate army.[1] The cavalrymen covered the lower crossings of the Rappahannock River in this position as well as procured forage for the upcoming campaign. On May 4, the division began moving west in an effort to link up with the main Confederate army and detect the advance of the Federal army moving through the Wilderness. On May 5, the lead elements of the division collided with elements of the Union Second Division, Cavalry Corps near Todd's Tavern. While the main armies engaged in desperate fighting in the Wilderness (to the immediate west) on May 5 and 6, these opposing cavalry units lightly skirmished (see Map 4, Appendix B).[2]

At the conclusion of fighting on May 6, the Union high command elected to abandon the Wilderness and move around Lee's right to Spotsylvania Court House. The capture of the road intersection at this location would place the Army of the Potomac between the Army of Northern Virginia and Richmond. The ultimate goal of this move was to draw Lee out of the heavily wooded Wilderness and force him to fight a battle in the open landscape surrounding the court house. The main route for this movement was Brock Road, which led from Wilderness Tavern in the rear of the Federal army directly to Spotsylvania. About four and one-half miles northwest of the court house, this road intersected with Carpathian Road at Todd's Tavern. In positioning his division to cover the right flank of the Confederate army on May 5, Fitzhugh Lee now found his command squarely in the path of this planned Federal move.

On May 7, the Grant ordered General Sheridan to clear Brock Road of opposing Confederate forces. Sheridan committed elements of his First and Second Cavalry Divisions to the task. Fitzhugh Lee committed all of his forces to resisting him. Generally, Wickham was deployed to the right of the road and Lomax to the left (see Map 10, Appendix B). Both sides dismounted their personnel and fought primarily on foot.[3] The Virginians constructed improvised barricades with fence rails and fallen timber and yielded ground grudgingly. By the end of the day, the superior Union force had gained about two miles but had not cleared the way to the court house. At dusk, Sheridan recalled his forces and foolishly relinquished about one mile of their hard-fought gains.[4] With the retirement of the Union horsemen, the Confederates moved back to some of their earlier-constructed barricades. They worked through the night to improve their position by felling trees across the road and constructing more obstacles.

The following morning, Sheridan found the Confederates still blocking the road. When the Federal cavalry resumed the advance against Fitzhugh Lee's Division on May 8, they again met with stern resistance. By this time, the blockage of the road was becoming critical for Federal plans. The infantry of the V Corps was lined up on the road running north from Todd's Tavern and waiting to march. After a somewhat heated discussion with Sheridan, Grant decided to clear the road using the infantry of the V Corps. The commitment of this overwhelming force proved to be successful; however, Fitzhugh Lee's Virginians delayed their advance for several hours.[5] This delay permitted the advance portion of Lee's main army (the First Corps) to reach Brock Road north of the court house, relieve the cavalry, and construct a defensive line astride the road at Laurel Ridge.

While Fitzhugh Lee's command was battling along Brock Road, elements of Brig. Gen. James H. Wilson's Third Cavalry Division circled to the north and east and reached Spotsylvania Court House. Wickham dispatched the 3rd Virginia Cavalry Regiment to this point to cover his rear.[6] This force was driven from the court house before being reinforced by elements of Kershaw's Division (of the First Corps). Wilson retired in the face of the approaching infantry toward Fredericksburg (to the north). The success of the Confederates in holding Spotsylvania Court House and the Laurel Ridge position to the northwest contributed greatly to their overall success with the coming battle.

During the morning of May 9, Fitzhugh Lee's forces patrolled Fredericksburg Road north of the court house. The IX Corps reached the Spotsylvania battlefield using this route. Its lead elements sparred with portions of Wickham's Brigade for several hours.[7] Elements of the Third Corps arrived at midday and relieved the Virginians. At this time, Confederate scouts observed that Sheridan had collected the bulk of his command and headed south toward Richmond. Stuart decided to counter this Federal excursion with three brigades, slightly more than half of his forces. The remaining three brigades were left at Spotsylvania. Wickham's and Lomax's commands were among the units sent to follow Sheridan.[8]

Initially, Fitzhugh Lee's Division pursued and harassed the rear of Sheridan's column. Elements of Wickham's Brigade skirmished with the Federal rearguard at Jerrell's Mill and at Mitchell's Shop on this same day (May 9). One company of the 3rd Virginia Cavalry Regiment, in particular, got roughed up a bit at the latter engagement.[9] Wickham's command again skirmished with rear elements of the Union forces near Beaver Dam Station on May 10.[10] The following day, Stuart decided to move Lee's Division to Richmond ahead of Sheridan. The Virginians rode all night and reached Yellow Tavern on Telegraph Road (about six miles north of Richmond) before Sheridan's column on the morning of May 11.[11]

Stuart had Lee deploy his forces on a slight rise north of Yellow Tavern astride Telegraph Road. Wickham was posted to the right (or west) and Lomax to the left (or east).[12] As Sheridan's forces arrived, they deployed as skirmishers and advanced upon the Confederate position (see Map 17, Appendix B). Lee's men easily repulsed this first advance, but Sheridan brought up more troops (elements of the First and Third Divisions) and attacked the entire line. In a short time, this superior force overwhelmed the Confederates and drove them from the position.[13] General Stuart was mortally wounded during this battle and taken from the field.[14] Lomax's Brigade was particularly hard hit and lost heavily. The division retreated to the northern side of the Chickahominy River and then turned southward toward Richmond.[15] Sheridan consolidated his forces and moved to within a mile of the outer line of the capital's defenses.

Overnight, Fitzhugh Lee saw an opportunity to trap Sheridan's entire command. The Union cavalry was massed north of the outer line of the Richmond defenses between the Chickahominy River and Brook Road. The Richmond garrison blocked the Federals on the south. Gordon's Brigade, of North Carolinian cavalry, which had been trailing the Federals during much of the raid, moved to block them on the north and west. Lee then moved his division to the Meadow Bridge on the east (see Map 22, Appendix B). Military Road crossed the Chickahominy at this point, but Lee had his men tear up the planking over the highway bridge. On May 12, elements of the Richmond garrison and Gordon's Brigade began applying pressure on Sheridan (see the discussions for Gordon's Brigade, Hunton's Brigade, and Gracie's Brigades/Richmond Garrison below). The Union general recognized the situation and moved to escape the trap. Gregg's Second and Wilson's Third Divisions covered the rear while elements of Merritt's First Division established a bridgehead on the northern side of the river. Merritt's men first repaired the bridge and then attacked Lee's position. This assault was well conducted, and the Confederates were again driven from the field.[16] Sheridan's cavalry then crossed the river and rode southward to the James River opposite Bermuda Hundred. At this location, they obtained needed supplies and forage from Butler's Army of the James.

From May 17 to May 20, Fitzhugh Lee moved his command to Hanover Court House (Atlee Station) to rest, recuperate, and watch for Sheridan's next move.[17] While there was a moderate pause in the campaign, the War Department in Richmond sent the cavalry general a request. Bowing to public pressure and their personal feelings, President Davis and his senior advisor, Gen. Braxton Bragg, ordered him to take some of his men and destroy a Federal fort at Wilson's Wharf (Kennon's Landing) on the northern bank of the James River.[18] This post, one of several points established by General Butler earlier in the month to cover his supply line, was located about twenty miles downriver of Richmond and posed no real threat to the capital. The main point of interest was that the garrison consisted mainly of U.S.C.T. (U.S. Colored Troops) forces.

Fitzhugh Lee's force reached the outskirts of Wilson's Wharf on May 24. Following an initial reconnaissance of the ground and a demand for the garrison to surrender (which was rejected), the Confederates advanced upon the fort. The assault was easily repulsed, with considerable loss to the attacking troops. In retrospect, many men in ranks confessed that the entire operation was a useless employment of veteran cavalry and horses.[19]

Following this action, Fitzhugh Lee's Division returned to Hanover Court House and took up a position screening the right of Lee's army at the North Anna River.[20] On May 27 and 28, the Federal army left this battlefield, moved southeast toward Richmond, and crossed the Pamunkey River. The cavalry on both sides screened the movements of their respective main (infantry) force and skirmished frequently during these days in an effort to gain knowledge regarding the location and movement of the opposing army. These encounters led to a major engagement on Atlee Station Road at Haw's Shop (northeast of Richmond) on May 28.[21] Each army committed elements of five cavalry brigades to this battle. Maj. Gen. Wade Hampton commanded the Confederate forces; Sheridan was present to direct the Union cavalry. Wickham's Brigade was heavily engaged, while Lomax's Brigade was left at Hanover Court House (see Map 30, Appendix B). Most of the fighting was done on foot. Near the end of the day, Hampton elected to withdraw, which nearly turned into a rout.

During the following several days, the opposing armies took up fortified positions centering on Totopotomoy Creek. Fitzhugh Lee's Division screened the right flank of the Confederate army. On May 31, he moved his command to a key road intersection at Old Cold Harbor (on the northern bank of the Chickahominy River only about seven miles east of Richmond) and began constructing a defensive line.[22] Lomax was deployed to the left (north) and Wickham to the right (south; see Map 33, Appendix B). Clingman's Brigade (from Hoke's Division) arrived soon thereafter, and the infantry took position on the left of Lomax's Brigade. Sheridan arrived in the afternoon with his First Division and began probing the defensive line. In midafternoon, the Federals assaulted the Confederates. A combined flanking and frontal attack upon Clingman and Lomax was particularly successful, and the entire Confederate force was driven back almost a mile to New Cold Harbor.[23] Darkness ended the Federal success.

On June 1, Fitzhugh Lee reformed his division and held this new line until relieved by more infantry of Hoke's Division, Anderson's First Corps, and on June 2, Hill's Third Corps. The latter extended the main line to the northern bank of the Chickahominy. During most of the Battle of Cold Harbor, Fitzhugh Lee's Division screened the army's right and remained in reserve.[24] On June 7, Sheridan's cavalry set out on a second major raid. The main target of this expedition was the Virginia Central Railroad east and west of Gordonsville. A second goal was to try and link up with Maj. Gen. David Hunter's Union force (from the Department of West Virginia), at that time advancing upon either Charlottesville or Lynchburg. Hampton was dispatched with Fitzhugh Lee's and Butler's (formerly Hampton's) Divisions to counter this Federal effort.

The opposing cavalry forces collided at Trevilian Station (west of Louisa Court House) on June 11 and 12.[25] The first day's fight was a mostly mounted, back-and-forth affair. Fitzhugh Lee's Division arrived at the battlefield fortuitously somewhat late and captured Brig. Gen. George Custer's wagon train and, for a time, had his entire command isolated and trapped. Custer had got the best of Lee's Division at Yellow Tavern and Meadow Bridge, and to many Confederates it was a bit of wartime payback. The fighting on the second day was more intense and fought mainly by dismounted troops. Hampton took up a position along the railroad and deployed several artillery batteries. Sheridan selectively assaulted this position, was repulsed, and then broke off the battle. In this latter action, the brigades of Lee's Division were split. Wickham moved to and covered the left of the Confederate line (next to Butler's Division), while Lomax remained on the Confederate right.

It is clear that Fitzhugh Lee's Virginians saw more than their share of fighting during the Overland Campaign. The period of May 7–12 was especially hard on the personnel and their mounts. The total reported losses represented about one-third of the starting strength of each of his brigades. Prior to this period of the war, such casualty figures were unheard of in the Cavalry Corps. It should also be mentioned that five of the seven regimental commanders in the division became casualties during this campaign; they were lost at Todd's Tavern (May 7), Yellow Tavern (May 11), Meadow Bridge (May 12), and Cold Harbor (May 31). In addition to the personnel losses, many men lost their mounts and were sent home to procure a replacement. Combined with the actual casualties, it is not unreasonable to assume that by mid-June the strength of Lee's Division was reduced to less than 2,000 men, or nearly one-half of its starting strength of 3,500–3,700 men. In August, the division was sent to the Shenandoah Valley to assist Lt. Gen. Jubal Early in his defense of this vital portion of the Commonwealth. The strength of the division would continue to wane during that campaign.

The compiled casualties for the two brigades of Fitzhugh Lee's Division are shown in Tables 63 (Wickham's) and 64 (Lomax's) in Appendix A. The Virginia newspapers covered Wickham's Brigade fully. Casualty lists were printed for all the battles of the campaign.[26] The initially published lists covered the period of May 5–12 but failed to provide a daily breakdown. Accordingly, it is possible that individual compiled losses for the Wilderness, Todd's Tavern, and Spotsylvania (May 6–8) could be slightly in error. The combined total loss for these battles, however, is accurate. After May 13, the newspapers provided daily losses for this brigade.

Lomax's Brigade was similarly covered in the newspapers through May 13.[27] The casualties in the brigade apparently went unreported after this point in the campaign. They may have been slightly higher. For example, more-modern research cites that the losses for Fitzhugh Lee's Division at Cold Harbor on May 31 were about 80 men. This number is approximately 23 men higher than the total compiled from the incomplete rolls and newspapers.[28] Most of these appear to have occurred in Lomax's Brigade. If that is the case, then the total loss for this brigade may have been about 460–480 men. The respective books of the Virginia Regimental Histories Series were closely examined as a part of the research for this division.[29]

HAMPTON'S/BUTLER'S DIVISION

Wade Hampton was the senior divisional commander in the Cavalry Corps. A very wealthy planter and politician from South Carolina, Hampton had virtually no military experience before the war but was a natural leader and a quick learner.[1] Like Fitzhugh Lee, he was promoted to major general and given command of a cavalry division after Gettysburg. The South Carolinian had been wounded during that battle on July 3 but recovered and returned to his command in late 1863.

At the start of the campaign, Hampton's Division consisted of two brigades, Rosser's and Young's. The latter command fielded the only cavalry units in the army from the Deep South but was very small. The strength of the division was more than doubled in late May with the arrival of five new units. Two of these from Georgia were assigned to Young's Brigade; the remaining three came from South Carolina and formed a third brigade for the division.

Unlike Fitzhugh Lee's command, the three brigades of Hampton's Division were employed independently throughout most of the Overland Campaign. Their roles are accordingly presented separately. The three fought together as a division only at Trevilian Station at the end of this campaign. "Jeb" Stuart was mortally wounded on May 11 at Yellow Tavern, after which, initially, Gen. Robert E. Lee assumed direct command of the cavalry.[2] As the campaign progressed, however, Hampton gradually assumed command of the corps. For example, he directed the cavalry in the actions at Haw's Shop in late May and at Ashland in early June.[3] Trevilian Station, fought on June 11 and 12, was clearly his battle and triumph.[4] With the temporary promotion of Hampton, Brig. Gen. Thomas L. Rosser temporarily assumed command of the division in mid-May. In June, Brig. Gen. Matthew C. Butler was assigned by Hampton to take over the division.[5]

With the exception of Rosser's Brigade, the division remained with Lee's army for the rest of the year and played a prominent role in the successful defense of Petersburg. Rosser's Brigade was sent to the Shenandoah Valley to reinforce General Early in late August and served in that theater for the rest of the year.

Young's Brigade

At the start of the campaign, Brig. Gen. Pierce M. B. Young's brigade was the smallest in the Cavalry Corps. It consisted of three units, Cobb's and

Phillips's Georgia Legions and the Jeff Davis Legion, raised in Alabama and Mississippi. Together, these three commands fielded only twenty-four companies but were composed of veterans, having served in Hampton's Brigade for nearly two years.

For much of the campaign, the fortunes of battle seemed to be with Young's Brigade. During the Battle of the Wilderness, Hampton's Division covered the eastern flank of the Army of Northern Virginia. Hampton apparently held the brigade in reserve and used only Rosser during several cavalry actions on May 5 and 6. The next day, Hampton committed Young's Brigade against elements of David M. Gregg's Second Cavalry Division along Carpathian Road between Todd's Tavern and the Corbin Bridge over the Po River (see Map 10, Appendix B).[1] This engagement occurred following the initial success of Sheridan's forces against Fitzhugh Lee's Division on Brock Road to the east. In any event, a review of the reported casualties for the brigade reveals that it was lightly engaged on this day.

For the most part, Young's Brigade was again lightly engaged at Spotsylvania. On May 8, it covered the Po River and Shady Grove Church Road, the principal route for Lee's army to reach Spotsylvania. For the remainder of the battle, Hampton's Division covered the left (or western) flank of the Confederate army. Young's Brigade was engaged on May 9 and 10.[2] On the second of these days, it assisted Davis's Brigade (Heth's Division, Third Corps). These units repulsed an effort by the II Corps to advance from a bridgehead established south of the river.

As the opposing armies moved from Spotsylvania toward the North Anna River, Hampton moved his two brigades to Milford Station on May 21–22.[3] His forces joined Terry's and Corse's Brigades (of Pickett's Division) and quickly took up a defensive position against the II Corps.[4] These Confederate forces held this line and permitted Lee's army to march unopposed to the southern bank of the North Anna River. Late on May 23, Young's Brigade retired and took up a position covering the left (western) flank of the army (next to A. P. Hill's Third Corps).[5] During each of these actions, the brigade was again lightly engaged.

On May 26, the Union army again began moving southward around Lee's eastern flank. The opposing armies collided at Totopotomoy Creek (Bethesda Church). At this point of the campaign, General Young was temporarily assigned command of the North Carolina cavalry brigade in W. H. F. Lee's Division. This unit had lost their commander and one senior regimental colonel in battles on May 11–12. In the absence of Young, Col. Gideon J. Wright (of Cobb's Legion) assumed command of the brigade.[6] While the main armies prepared entrenched positions and skirmished at Totopotomoy Creek, Young's Brigade screened and covered the left (western) flank of the army near Hanover Court House. During May 27–31, the brigade engaged in several light skirmishes against Wilson's Third Cavalry Division.[7]

While the main armies were desperately engaged at Cold Harbor, Hampton concentrated his and W. H. F. Lee's Divisions against Wilson's division at Ashland (west of Hanover Court House) on June 1. The engagement resulted in a success for the Confederates.[8] Indeed, the Union cavalry was fortunate to escape a trap set by Hampton. Young's Brigade was present at this battle but was again lightly engaged. During the remainder of the first week of June, it covered the northern flank of the army.

On May 26–27, the 20th Georgia Battalion arrived in Richmond and was assigned to the brigade.[9] This unit had previously served in Georgia and South Carolina, patrolling the Atlantic coastline. Nevertheless, on May 28, Hampton temporarily attached the battalion to a new South Carolinian cavalry brigade (see "Butler's Brigade" below) and committed this ad-hoc command against Federal cavalry at Haw's Shop.[10] This encounter was a preliminary action to the Battle of Totopotomoy Creek and was a rather hotly contested engagement. The 20th Georgia Battalion was deployed on the Confederate southern (right) flank against veteran elements of the First and Second Cavalry Divisions.[10] As could be expected for men in their first real battle, the Georgians fared badly. Two days later (May 30), they participated in an action at Matadequin Creek (or Old Church) against many of the same veteran enemy units.[11] They arrived near the end of the battle and were swept away in the Confederate retreat.

In early June, the 20th Georgia Battalion officially joined Young's Brigade near Ashland. The brigade was additionally augmented by the arrival of the 7th Georgia Cavalry Regiment from Georgia.[12] These two units doubled the strength of the brigade. On June 7, Sheridan set out on a raid against the Virginia Central Railroad. Hampton responded by following with his division (under Butler) and Fitzhugh Lee's Division. The opposing cavalry forces collided at Trevilian Station (west of Louisa Court House) on June 11 and 12. Young's Brigade was heavily engaged on both days.[13] Most of the casualties again fell upon the two new units.

The search for casualties in this brigade proved to be very difficult. Casualty lists in Georgia newspapers were found for only one company in Cobb's Legion, all of Phillips's Legion, the entire 20th Georgia Battalion, and one company of the 7th Georgia Regiment.[14] The list for Phillips's Legion covered the period May 5–August 12 and appears to omit slightly wounded men. Nothing has ever been found for the Jeff Davis Legion. These sources and the rolls reveal a total of 100 casualties in the campaign for the three veteran units and 373 casualties in the two new units. Almost half of 373 men lost by the 7th Georgia Regiment and 20th Georgia Battalion were prisoners taken at Trevilian Station on June 11. These units were comparatively larger than the three veteran legions, but they were present for only about two weeks of the campaign. In view of these factors and the incomplete newspaper casualty lists, it appears that this brigade may have sustained more casualties in the campaign (see Table 65, Appendix A).

Rosser's Brigade

This brigade consisted of four Virginia cavalry units, the 7th, 11th, and 12th Regiments and the 35th Battalion. These units were recruited primarily from the Shenandoah Valley and surrounding counties. The organization was also recognized in the Cavalry Corps as the Laurel Brigade. Its commander was Brig. Gen. Thomas L. Rosser, a young and dashing Virginian. This command had, in part, served earlier in the war in the Valley and in western Virginia, officially becoming part of Lee's army during the summer of 1863. Rosser's Brigade spent the winter in Rockbridge County in the Shenandoah Valley. This proved to be very beneficial for the organization. In a postwar account, Rosser wrote that his mounts got fat from the abundant forage and that many sick and formerly wounded men returned to the ranks.[1] The Laurel Brigade left the Valley and reunited with Lee's army during the first days of May.

As the opposing Union and Confederate armies marched toward the Wilderness, Rosser's Brigade was committed early by General Hampton on May 5 to scout ahead of A. P. Hill's Third Corps and find the location of the enemy forces. Elements of the Laurel Brigade first encountered one brigade of Federal cavalry (from Wilson's Third Division) on Carpathian Road on the southern edge of what would soon become the Wilderness battlefield. With the assistance of a battery of horse artillery, Rosser's troops first repelled and then drove this enemy force toward the east and the second of Wilson's cavalry brigades posted in reserve at Robertson Run.[2] At the same time, Hill's corps advanced eastward along Orange Plank Road and effectively cut off the main escape route for Wilson's entire division (see Map 4, Appendix B).

For a short time, it appeared that this Union force would be totally encircled and captured by Rosser. Confederate forces blocked all the main roads, and the surrounding landscape consisted of dense woods. Wilson's men fortunately found a small wagon trail through the woods and used this track to reach Carpathian Road west of Todd's Tavern just ahead of Rosser's pursuing forces. The Union rear guard, however, had to fight its way out to safety.[3] Upon reaching this main road, Wilson's troops were aided in their retreat by elements of Gregg's Second Division. This Federal cavalry unit was posted along Carpathian Road and covered the left of the Union army. The withdrawal of Wilson's division represented a significant triumph for Rosser's Brigade that day.

Rosser continued to aggressively employ his brigade the following day (May 6). As the main armies were involved in a desperate battle in the dense woods to the north and northwest, Rosser advanced his command along a second wagon trail toward Brock Road north of Todd's Tavern. The Virginians collided with Custer's brigade of Torbert's First Division. At first, Rosser's lead unit, the 35th Virginia Cavalry Battalion, drove in the Federal cavalry's pickets. Custer responded by counterattacking with most of his command. Rosser then threw in the remainder of his brigade. Both sides also brought up and committed horse artillery to this engagement. By late morning, the Federals had forced the Virginians to withdraw with considerable loss.[4] Although Rosser had effectively tied down much of the Union cavalry for the day, his command had lost heavily. Subsequent newspaper accounts reported that the Laurel Brigade had lost nearly one-third of its strength on May 5 and 6. One member of the brigade called the second day's fight the "bloodiest day in the war."

Following two days of battle, Rosser's Brigade was sent to the rear to rest and recuperate. During the subsequent Battle of Spotsylvania, the brigade patrolled and covered the left (western) flank of the Confederate army. On May 14, Grant's army began showing signs of moving around Lee's right to the east-southeast. Hampton sent elements of the brigade in a raid to the Federal rear to confirm this move. Rosser's men came upon a Federal hospital and found numerous seriously wounded Confederate soldiers.[5] The bulk of these men were recaptured and taken back to the Southern line. On the following day (May 15), the brigade again raided the Federal rear.[6] The Virginians encountered some of the wagon train for Grant's army during this foray and sparred with the train guard. On May 19, Ewell's Second Corps similarly moved around the western flank of the Union army. This Confederate force collided with former heavy artillery units newly assigned to the Army of the Potomac at Harris Farm. The Laurel Brigade covered Ewell's northern flank during this action. On May 21, the opposing armies left the Spotsylvania battlefield. Rosser's Brigade was the last unit to leave.[7]

During the following five to six days, Rosser's Brigade was employed with Young's Brigade of Hampton's Division. The Virginians moved to Milford Station on May 22 and took up a defensive position against the II Corps for several days. This action covered the movement of Lee's army to the southern side of the North Anna River. On May 23, the brigade moved to a position covering the left (western) flank of the army south of the river. On May 28, the Virginians accompanied their division to Haw's Shop and became heavily engaged with Federal cavalry.[8] The Laurel Brigade was deployed on the left (northern) side of the Confederate line but surprisingly sustained light losses (see Map 30, Appendix B).

Following this action, Rosser's Brigade rejoined the cavalry forces located on Lee's left (near Hanover Court House). The Virginians were next engaged on June 1 at Ashland.[9] Confederate cavalry led by General Hampton nearly surrounded and trapped Wilson's Federal cavalry division during this battle. The Laurel Brigade attacked in concert with W. H. F. Lee's Division and again sustained only light losses. Wilson's forces sustained heavier casualties but again fortuitously escaped.

During the second week of June, Rosser's Brigade was part of the cavalry force sent to intercept Sheridan in his raid against the Virginia Central Railroad. The Virginians were present at the Battle of Trevilian Station and participated in the fighting on both June 11 and 12.[10] On the first of these days, the brigade gained some success against Custer's cavalry. Unfortunately, during this action, General Rosser was wounded, and command of the brigade devolved upon the senior-ranking colonel, Richard H. Dulany of the 7th Virginia Regiment. During the fighting of June 12, the Laurel Brigade occupied the right of Hampton's divisional front next to Lomax's Brigade. The brigade successfully repulsed several attacks made on its sector of the line. Following this battle, the brigade returned to the main army at Petersburg.

In August or September 1864, the Laurel Brigade was sent to the Shenandoah Valley to reinforce Jubal Early's forces.

A compilation of the losses identified for Rosser's Brigade during the Overland Campaign yielded about 332 casualties. Considering the degree of action for this brigade, this figure seems to be very low. The CSRs for all the units typically omit the May–June muster roll. A newspaper casualty list was found for only one unit from this brigade. Specifically, *The Sentinel* of Richmond listed 103 battle losses for the 11th Virginia Cavalry Regiment for the period May 5–June 3.[11] This tabulation appears to omit many of the slightly wounded men. The May 17 issue of the *Staunton Spectator & General Advertiser* also contained the names of about 20 men from the 12th Virginia Regiment who had been admitted to a local hospital with battle wounds.

Additional information regarding casualties was obtained from a number of outside sources—three diaries, two letters, two postwar books, and an inspection report for part of the 35th Virginia Battalion in the CSRs. The report indicates that Company A sustained 20 casualties between May 5 and May 12. This figure is proportionally greater than the numbers for the other companies in the 35th Battalion. One of the postwar books provides a nominal list of casualties in this unit for the entire campaign.[12] Many of the men in this list are not reported as casualties in the muster rolls. The second book and one of the diaries indicates that the brigade loss on May 5 (at the Wilderness) was 114 or 173 men.[13] A second diary reports that the brigade loss on May 6 was very heavy.[14] Similarly, the first diary states that the brigade loss on this day was very severe, especially in the 35th Battalion and the 11th and 12th Regiments. The writer additionally mentions that the loss was proportionally great in slightly wounded.[15] The respective books of the Virginia Regimental Histories Series were also checked, but these added only a few men to the casualty lists for the four units of this brigade.[16]

The additional sources provided figures regarding casualties primarily in the 11th Virginia Regiment. A third diary states that this unit lost 103 men on May 6, while a letter indicates that the total loss in killed and wounded for May 5 and 6 was 133.[17] A second letter mentions that the 11th Regiment lost between 120 and 150 men in battle between May 5 and 21 and that the entire brigade lost close to 600 men during the same period.[18] The actual truth may never be known, but judging by these additional sources, it may be reasonable to assume that the Laurel Brigade sustained at least 550 casualties during the campaign. Most of this number probably occurred during the Battle of the Wilderness.

The above-noted sources added the names of about 60 men as casualties, raising the confirmed total loss for the brigade to 392. Taken together, these sources reveal that the brigade losses were probably considerably more than this figure. For purposes of this study, a conservative estimate of the total casualties of Rosser's Brigade during the Overland Campaign is 522 men. This includes an additional 130 wounded at the Wilderness (2 in the 7th Regiment, 46 in the 11th Regiment, 51 in the 12th Regiment, and 31 in the 35th Battalion). The increase for the 11th Regiment matches the figure of 133 reported in the letter, while the increases in the 12th Regiment and 35th Battalion match the confirmed ratio of killed to wounded in the 11th Regiment and Company A, 35th Battalion. This raises the total loss for the brigade to the estimated total (see Table 66, Appendix A).

Butler's Brigade

Matthew C. Butler's brigade consisted of the 4th, 5th, and 6th South Carolina Cavalry Regiments. These units were organized in late 1862 and early 1863 from several existing battalions. Prior to the spring of 1864, these regiments served exclusively along the coastal areas of their home state and experienced little if any combat. The brigade was assigned to the Army of Northern Virginia in exchange for the 1st and 2nd South Carolina Cavalry Regiments, which had served in Hampton's Brigade for much of the war but had been sent home to recruit. Brigadier General Butler was a veteran officer of Hampton's Brigade who had been severely wounded the previous year at Brandy Station.

The three regiments of Butler's Brigade first congregated at the state capital, Columbia, where General Hampton reviewed them on April 20. All three units traveled the entire distance to Richmond (469 miles) on their mounts.[1] The 5th South Carolina Regiment apparently left immediately after this date and arrived in time to participate in the fighting at Swift Creek and Drewry's Bluff (with General Beauregard's forces) on May 10, 12, and 16. The 4th South Carolina Regiment left Columbia on April 29 and arrived in Richmond on May 23. During the journey, several days were allotted for rest and reshoeing the horses. The 6th South Carolina Regiment apparently departed last and reached Richmond on May 29. The march demonstrated the strategic mobility of cavalry, but it placed a severe hardship upon the horses. For example, when the 4th South Carolina was first sent into action on May 28, there were only about 400 serviceable mounts available.[2] This number of horses represented less than half of the available men. There was another problem in getting the troops ready for battle. In order to lighten the loads on the horses for this long trek, the rifles and carbines of the men were collected and shipped by rail. Difficulties and delays occurred in locating the arms at the railroad depot and getting them to the regiments.

As noted above, the 5th South Carolina Regiment participated in the fighting near Richmond against Butler's Army of the James. Elements of this unit were also temporarily attached to Fitzhugh Lee's Division and participated in the ill-advised attack against the Federal post at Wilson's Wharf on May 24. The reported total loss in these engagements for the regiment was fifty-one men. Following this action, General Hampton placed the 5th South Carolina in a temporary brigade with newly arrived 4th South Carolina Regiment and the 20th Georgia Battalion and committed them to action at Haw's Shop on May 28 (see Map 30, Appendix B). General Butler had not yet arrived from South Carolina, and in his absence, Col. Benjamin H. Rutledge of the 4th South Carolina assumed command of this makeshift organization.[3] Rutledge's cavalry reinforced Wickham's Brigade in the southern portion of the Confederate line. The personnel fought well but sustained heavy losses. In the end, Hampton elected to retire, and the Federals forces won the day.

Matthew Butler arrived in Richmond on May 29. The following day, the general was assigned the task of determining if Grant was moving the Federal army toward Cold Harbor. Butler left the newly arrived 6th South Carolina Regiment near Richmond and proceeded with the three units of Rutledge's ad-hoc command. The bulk of the 7th South Carolina Cavalry Regiment from the Richmond garrison was given to Butler for this operation. These units collided with Custer's Federal cavalry brigade at Matadequin Creek (or Old Church). In this engagement, the 4th and 5th South Carolina Regiments fought well for a time but, in the end, were driven from the field in a rather ignominious manner.[4]

Butler's Brigade then reunited in three units and for several days covered the right of Lee's army at Cold Harbor. Several days later, the command officially joined Hampton's Division near Ashland. The division was part of the forces employed to counter Sheridan's raid against the Virginia Central

Railroad near Gordonsville. The two forces met in a two-day battle at Trevilian Station on June 11 and 12. The South Carolinians were heavily engaged on both days.[5] Butler's Brigade lost heavily in personnel as well as their rear wagon train on June 11. The next day, the command fought mainly dismounted in a defensive position along the western side of the railroad. The South Carolinians were posted to the right of Young's (Wright's) Brigade on the divisional left. The opposing Union forces probed and unsuccessfully attacked this position for several hours before breaking off the battle. During this latter action, Hampton placed Butler in command of his division, and Colonel Rutledge again assumed leadership of the brigade. This change in command became permanent later in the year.

Although the muster rolls for this brigade for the year 1864 are weak, the casualty totals are among the most reliable in the Cavalry Corps (see Table 67, Appendix A). The brigade was well covered in the South Carolina newspapers, and there are nominal casualty lists for all of the units at every engagement during this campaign.[6] The brigade also lost two regimental commanders. Col. John Dunovant of the 5th South Carolina was slightly wounded at Haw's Shop on May 28. He returned to action in July. Col. Hugh K. Aiken of the 6th South Carolina was severely wounded at Trevilian's Station on June 11. He appeared to return to duty in October.

W. H. F. LEE'S DIVISION

William H. F. "Rooney" Lee was the second son of Robert E. Lee and a veteran cavalry leader in the Army of Northern Virginia. He was wounded at Brandy Station in June 1863 and captured shortly thereafter.[1] Lee was exchanged and returned to the army in the spring of 1864. His presence created a small dilemma for "Jeb" Stuart, the Cavalry Corps commander. The senior colonel in his former brigade, John R. Chambliss Jr., had been promoted to brigadier general in Lee's absence, and there was no opening in the army for a new cavalry brigade leader. Stuart and the army command resolved this problem by promoting Rooney Lee to major general and creating a third cavalry division. This new organization consisted of the brigades of Chambliss and Brig. Gen. James B. Gordon, which were withdrawn from Fitzhugh Lee's and Hampton's Divisions, respectively.

For the first part and much of the Overland Campaign, the brigades of Rooney Lee's Division operated independently. They were reunited and committed as a division only during the last part of May and in June. For this reason, descriptions of the actions for this division are presented with the brigades. As for the general himself, he figured prominently in one of the Confederate setbacks during the campaign. His men were screening the approach of the Union army to the North Anna River on May 23. After observing enemy forces cross the river at Jericho Mill, he is reported to have personally informed Cadmus Wilcox, one of the division commanders in Hill's Third Corps, that these troops were either cavalry or only two or three brigades of infantry and could be easily routed.[2] In actuality, the approaching column was the entire V Corps. As urged by Rooney Lee and the army command, Wilcox assaulted this force and was repulsed with considerable loss. Following this campaign, Rooney Lee's Division remained with the main body of the army and contributed valuable service during the siege of Petersburg.

Chambliss's Brigade

The brigade of John R. Chambliss consisted of the 9th, 10th, and 13th Virginia Cavalry Regiments. The 9th and 13th Regiments were recruited from the counties in the eastern and southeastern portions of the Commonwealth. The companies of the 10th Regiment were recruited on a wider basis. The men were veterans, their units having been organized in 1862 and having served in the Army of Northern Virginia at most of the campaigns and battles in 1862 and 1863. As with many of the commands in Stuart's Cavalry Corps, Chambliss's Brigade benefited from a period of inactivity over the winter of 1863–64. Many personnel procured a new mount and returned to the ranks. For example, on May 1, the 9th Virginia Regiment had about 600 officers and men present with the unit and another 100 men detached as couriers, scouts, or other duties.[1]

During the first three weeks of the Overland Campaign, Chambliss's Brigade was present but managed to avoid the worst of the conflicts. The Virginians covered the left (western) flank of Lee's army during the Battle of the Wilderness and were not engaged. On May 7, Chambliss was instructed to scout the rear area of the Union army in an effort to determine Grant's strategic intentions. The general took most of his forces, rode around this flank of Grant's army, and reached the Federals' winter encampment at Culpepper Court House. This site was found to be fully abandoned, indicating that Grant would likely, in the near future, not be returning and would be moving toward the east-southeast.[2] True to these observations and a subsequent report furnished by Chambliss, the Federal army began marching toward Spotsylvania Court House the following day.

Chambliss's Brigade was one of the three cavalry commands that stayed with Lee's army during the Battle of Spotsylvania. Initially, the Virginians were deployed on the left of the army. Elements of the brigade assisted Davis's Brigade (Heth's Division) and Young's Brigade in repelling a Federal move near the Po River on May 10.[3] Chambliss's Brigade was shifted to the right (eastern) flank of the army on May 11. For several days, the Virginians patrolled along the southern bank of the Po and Ni Rivers east of the main battlefield and protected the army's main supply line from the south.[4]

Elements of Chambliss's Brigade were posted on Myers Hill on May 14. Federal infantry belonging to the V and VI Corps approached this position during midday.[5] They were the vanguard of a major effort by Grant to move around Lee's right flank. Chambliss committed most of his command to this action but let infantry reinforcements from the Third Corps do the serious fighting (see Map 23, Appendix B). In the end, the Confederates blunted this attempted flanking movement. In the battle, the Confederates briefly captured Myers Hill from a brigade of the VI Corps before pulling back to the main line of earthworks near dusk. Despite being engaged for much of this action, Chambliss's Brigade reported light casualties. The following day (May 15), the Virginians sparred with two Federal cavalry regiments along Telegraph Road east of the battlefield.[6]

During the movement of opposing armies from Spotsylvania to the North Anna River, Chambliss's Brigade screened the southern side of the Po River as far as Guinea Bridge/Station and effectively kept the Federals from gathering intelligence regarding the movement of the main Confederate army.[7] As a part of this mission, portions of the brigade engaged with lead elements of Union cavalry and the V Corps at Guinea on May 21, at the Littleton Flippo farm on May 22, and along Telegraph Road on May 23.[8] Once enemy forces reached the North Anna River on May 23, the Virginians pulled back and covered the rear of Lee's army. During the subsequent Battle of North Anna, the brigade screened the army's flanks.

After North Anna, the opposing armies moved southeastward toward Richmond. On May 28, General Hampton, acting Cavalry Corps commander, decided to reconnoiter the movement of the Federal army in an area south of the Pamunkey River. Chambliss had initially concentrated his brigade near Hanover Court House. Rooney Lee, Chambliss's immediate senior, directed him to report to Hampton. The Confederate cavalry soon collided with Sheridan's Federal cavalry at a crossroads named Haw's Shop.[9] The opposing forces fought an intense, mostly dismounted battle for several hours. In the end, Hampton pulled his forces back, and Sheridan gained the battlefield. Chambliss's Brigade was deployed on the extreme left (northern) flank of the Confederate line (see Map 30, Appendix B). This must have been a relatively inactive sector of the battlefield because no casualties were found in the records for the brigade for this engagement. A recent publication on this battle and the campaign estimates that the Virginians sustained at least twenty-five casualties at Haw's Shop.[10]

Afterward, Rooney Lee's Division was moved and posted on the left flank of Lee's army near Hanover Court House.[11] The Virginians were lightly engaged near the court house on May 31 and more moderately engaged on June 1 at Ashland.[12] Their opponent in both of these cavalry actions was Wilson's Third Division. The latter engagement resulted in a Confederate triumph. The brigade also skirmished on June 10. Following the Battle of Cold Harbor, Chambliss's Brigade remained with Lee's army and saw considerable combat and activity during the remainder of the year at Petersburg. General Chambliss was killed in battle on August 16. Col. Richard L. T. Beale of the 9th Virginia then assumed command of the brigade.

Casualty figures for this brigade for the full campaign are provided in Table 68 in Appendix A. They reveal that the battle losses for this command were the lowest of the seven brigades in the corps. This was due, in large part, to the particular assignments and fortunes of war experienced by the brigade during the campaign. Yet difficulties were encountered in researching this brigade. The muster rolls for May and June 1864 are missing or were filed months later, for they appear to reflect the condition of the personnel at a later time and not at the end of June.

A nominal list for the 9th Virginia Regiment was found in a Richmond newspaper.[13] This provides a dated listing of the casualties for the unit during the period May 12–September 1, naming more than half of the confirmed losses in the brigade for this campaign. There are two published nominal lists for the 10th Virginia Regiment. The first provides battle losses up to June 5 but appears to be incomplete. A second, more detailed list gives the casualties for the unit between May 1 and October 1.[14] The individual casualties in these two newspapers are, unfortunately, not dated. No newspaper lists were ever found for the 13th Virginia Regiment. Few additional casualties were found in the various books of the Virginia Regimental Histories Series.[15]

In view of the gaps in the newspapers, it is likely that the battle losses for the brigade during the entire Overland Campaign were slightly higher than the compiled total shown in Table 68. The same source that estimated higher casualties for the brigade at Haw's Shop also estimated about 50 casualties at Ashland.[16] These two increases would place the total loss for Chambliss's Brigade during the campaign at about 150–155 men.

Gordon's Brigade

This brigade was formed after Gettysburg by the transfer of four North Carolina regiments from other brigades in Stuart's Cavalry Corps. Two of the regiments were veteran units. Specifically, the 1st Regiment had served in Hampton's Brigade, while the 2nd Regiment had been assigned to Rooney Lee's (later Chambliss's) Brigade. The 4th and 5th Regiments were relatively new to the army, having served with the army only during the Gettysburg Campaign. Their brigade commander, Brig. Gen. Beverly Robertson, had, in the opinions of General Stuart and the army commander, performed without distinction; he was reassigned to South Carolina for the duration of the war. The command of this new brigade was initially given to Col. Lawrence S. Baker of the 1st Regiment, but he was seriously wounded and placed on medical leave. The leadership then fell to James B. Gordon, also of the 1st Regiment.[1] He was promoted to brigadier general.

During the winter of 1863–64, Gordon's Brigade was somewhat diminished by the transfer of the 4th North Carolina Regiment to the Richmond garrison. The strengths of the remaining three regiments increased during the early spring by the return of personnel from wounded and sick leave and furlough to retrieve new mounts. This pattern applied to most of the brigades in Stuart's corps. During the Overland Campaign, the brigade was reinforced by the addition of the 3rd North Carolina Regiment.

In early May, Gordon's Brigade was assigned the mission of patrolling the Rapidan River in front of the main army. Gordon's men on picket observed the first crossing of the Union army on May 4.[2] During the Battle of the Wilderness, the North Carolinians covered the left flank of Lee's army. On May 7, the brigade was relocated to the right flank of the army. Gordon supported Young's Brigade in an action against Gregg's Second Cavalry Division along

Carpathian Road west of Todd's Tavern (see Map 10, Appendix B).[3] The 5th North Carolina Regiment, in particular, sustained some casualties during this engagement.

As a part of Rooney Lee's Division, Gordon's Brigade was positioned during the first two days of the Battle of Spotsylvania on the army's left flank. On May 9, the brigade was detached from the division and placed under Stuart's direct command.[4] This assignment was in response to a raid by Philip Sheridan against Richmond. The Federal cavalry commander departed the Spotsylvania battlefield on May 9 with nearly all of his corps. Gordon's Brigade followed in pursuit, elements of which caught up and skirmished with Sheridan's rear guard at Beaver Dam Station and the North Anna River on May 10.[5]

The North Carolinians continued to pressure the rear guard of Sheridan's columns on May 11. While the main body of the Federal cavalry confronted Stuart and Fitzhugh Lee's Division at Yellow Tavern, Gordon's men engaged elements of Gregg's Second Division at Goodall's Tavern or Ground Squirrel Bridge (over the South Anna River) about ten miles to the northwest.[6] The North Carolinians got the best of this fight and forced the Federals to continue their withdrawal. Unfortunately, Col. William H. Cheek of the 1st North Carolina was wounded at this action and lost for several months.

The fortunes of Gordon's Brigade changed the following day, May 12. Following the victory of Sheridan over Stuart at Yellow Tavern, the Federal commander decided to probe the outer defenses of Richmond. The War Department responded by seeking to trap Sheridan. While Fitzhugh Lee rallied his division on the eastern side of the Chickahominy River and blocked an escape route to the east, Gordon moved his brigade south from Yellow Tavern and took up a position east of Brook Church, blocking any escape to the west and north.[7] After being reinforced by elements of Hunton's infantry brigade, Gordon advanced upon the opposing Union cavalry (see Map 22, Appendix B). The opposing force, again Gregg's division, was ready this time. The Federal commander arrayed his entire division in an excellent defensive position. The Confederate forces were repulsed with considerable loss, and Gordon himself was badly wounded. He died of complications from the wound on May 18.[8]

In addition to this setback, Sheridan escaped the planned trap with his entire command later in the day to the east through Fitzhugh Lee's Division. The command of Gordon's Brigade temporarily devolved upon Col. Clinton

M. Andrews of the 2nd North Carolina.[9] The North Carolinians linked up with Fitzhugh Lee's Division and participated in the failed assault upon the Federal supply post at Wilson's Wharf (Kennon's Landing) on May 24.[10] The brigade rejoined the Army of Northern Virginia on May 25–26. Reinforcements in the form of the 3rd North Carolina Regiment arrived from eastern North Carolina that same day. The commander of this unit, Col. John A. Baker, was the ranking officer and thus assumed command of the brigade.[11]

On May 27, Baker's unit participated in a small battle at Hanovertown (Pollard's Farm). The North Carolinians were committed in concert with the 1st Maryland Cavalry Battalion against Custer's cavalry brigade. This battle went badly for the Southerners. The Marylanders were driven from the field, which forced the North Carolinians to hastily retire to avoid being encircled.[12] This was Baker's first battle, and he appeared to handle his brigade roughly. His former unit, the 3rd North Carolina Regiment, sustained the highest casualties in the brigade in this engagement. The following day, elements of Baker's command were included in the forces gathered by General Hampton to advance toward the Pamunkey River and determine the position and intentions of the Federal army.[13] Hampton's forces collided with Sheridan's cavalry at Haw's Shop and engaged in a desperate battle for most of the day. For the most part, the North Carolinians were kept in reserve and did not participate.

Following these actions, Baker rejoined Chambliss's Brigade, and Rooney Lee's Division, now united, was posted on the left of the army at Hanover Court House.[14] Brig. Gen. Pierce Young (from Hampton's Division) was temporarily placed in command of the North Carolinians. On May 31, Wilson's Third Division attacked Rooney Lee's Division at this location. The North Carolinians sustained most of the fighting and were driven from their position before darkness ended the Federal advance.[15] The 3rd North Carolina again experienced the heaviest casualties in the brigade in this battle.

The following day, June 1, Wilson advanced his division to Ashland and the South Anna River to destroy a railroad bridge. Hampton responded by bringing up a superior force of four brigades to trap the Federals. As a part of the Confederate effort, Young's (Gordon's) Brigade attacked the Union force at Ashland from the east-southeast. The opposing Federal troops (from McIntosh's brigade) were nearly surrounded but particularly resisted the assaults of the North Carolinians. General Young was wounded at this time, and command of the brigade again fell to Colonel Baker.[16] Wilson's second brigade (led by Chapman) broke through the Confederate forces on the north and rescued McIntosh's command. In the end, however, Wilson had to withdraw and lost heavily in this battle. A tabulation of the individual unit rosters reveals that the brigade sustained sixty-six casualties at Ashland. A more current study, however, places the total loss at about one hundred men.[17] The 5th North Carolina Regiment sustained nearly 50 percent of this loss.

While the opposing cavalry clashed at Hanover Court House and Ashland, the Union army moved and concentrated most of its forces at Cold Harbor (to the south). In concert with this strategic move, Wilson pulled his cavalry division back to the east during the evening of June 2 to cover the right (northern) flank of Grant's army. Rooney Lee moved his division eastward in pursuit on June 3. The lead elements, the 2nd and 5th North Carolina Regiments, collided with Wilson's troops at the earlier Haw's Shop battlefield. Baker's two regiments garnered some initial success, driving in the Federal pickets, and then withdrew to a wooded area on the southwestern side of the battlefield.[18] After an engagement of several hours in the woods, Wilson committed a superior force and Rooney Lee elected to pull back. The casualties for both sides in this mainly dismounted action were surprisingly light.

For the remainder of the year, Baker's men remained with Lee's main force. The North Carolinians played an active role during the siege of Petersburg. Colonel Andrews of the 2nd Regiment was killed on June 23. The command of the brigade changed one more time during 1864. Lt. Col. Rufus Barringer of the 1st Regiment was promoted to brigadier general and assigned to lead the brigade in June; his rank was backdated to June 1.[19] Barringer had acquired an excellent combat record and proved to be a worthy selection.

The muster rolls for this North Carolina cavalry brigade show a limited number of battle losses during the Overland Campaign. These casualties were well covered in the Richmond and North Carolina newspapers. The *Sentinel* of Richmond as well as the *Raleigh North Carolina Standard* provided nominal lists of the casualties for the entire brigade at Goodall's Tavern and at Brook Church (May 11 and 12).[20] A second Richmond newspaper, the *Daily Enquirer,* printed a second list in June covering the battle losses in the entire brigade between May 5 and June 1.[21] The first volume of the series on North Carolina Confederate Troops was also checked but failed to produce any significant information for this study.[22] Additional separate lists were also found for the 1st and 3rd Regiments for the periods of their activity during the campaign. These yield a total of 315 casualties for the brigade during the campaign. This total may, as hinted above, may be somewhat low. The two primary lists do not distinguish the casualties by date or by battle. The figures for the individual actions were estimated based upon the newspapers and other available information. These individual figures may, accordingly, be slightly in error. The total as shown in Table 69 in Appendix A, however, appears to be generally accurate.

HORSE ARTILLERY (BREATHED'S BATTALION)

Maj. R. Preston Chew directed the artillery for Stuart's Cavalry Corps. In a somewhat unique and layered command arrangement, this organization consisted of one battalion led by Maj. James Breathed. Breathed's Battalion consisted of the following five batteries: Hart's Washington (South Carolina) Light Artillery, Thomson's Ashby (Virginia) Light Artillery, Johnston's 1st Stuart (Virginia) Artillery, McGregor's 2nd Stuart (Virginia) Artillery, and Shoemaker's Lynchburg (Virginia) Beauregard Rifles. Each was a veteran unit with considerable service with the corps.

The batteries of the Horse Artillery were attached to the various commands of the Cavalry Corps as strategic and tactical situations of the campaign arose. For example, Thomson's Battery was attached to Rosser's Brigade on May 5 and participated in the fighting on that day against Wilson's Third Cavalry Division and its own attached light artillery.[1] On the following day, Shoemaker's Battery was additionally attached to Rosser's command.[2] Both this unit and Thomson's Battery were heavily engaged against Merritt's First Cavalry Division and its accompanying artillery. Shoemaker's Battery, in particular, took some casualties during this battle.

Johnston's Battery was attached to Fitzhugh Lee's Division and played a prominent role in delaying the advance of Union cavalry and the V Corps to Spotsylvania on May 8.[3] During one point in this action, the battery's guns were nearly captured by the advancing Federals. Captain Johnston was wounded getting three of the cannons away, while Major Breathed himself saved the fourth cannon. On May 9, Stuart attached Hart's and Johnston's Batteries to Fitzhugh Lee's Division and sent them toward Richmond.[4] The remaining three batteries (Shoemaker's, McGregor's, and Thomson's) stayed with Hampton at the Spotsylvania battlefield. Thomason's Battery sparred with artillery of the II Corps on the Po River on May 9 and accompanied Rosser's Brigade to Harris Farm on May 19.[5] McGregor's Battery supported

Chambliss's Brigade in the fighting at Myers's Hill on May 14 and in a skirmish at Guinea Station on May 21.[6] Hart's and Johnston's Batteries were present at Yellow Tavern on May 11 but were not heavily engaged. The 2nd Maryland (Baltimore Light) Artillery provided most of the artillery support for Stuart's cavalry during the battle.[7] This unit had previously been part of the Horse Artillery and was temporarily attached during Sheridan's raid against Richmond.

Johnston's, McGregor's, and Shoemaker's Batteries were committed to the Confederate effort at Haw's Shop on May 28.[8] They were deployed in a clearing at the northern end of the battlefield next to Rosser's Brigade. Surprisingly, the losses from this battle were light in each of the units. Thereafter, McGregor's Battery supported Young's Brigade during the engagement at Hanover Court House on May 31.[9] This unit also nearly lost its four cannons during this action, but they were withdrawn in a timely manner. During the Battle of Cold Harbor, Johnston's and Shoemaker's Batteries were lightly engaged supporting Fitzhugh Lee's Division from May 31 to June 3.[10] Lastly, Hart's Battery was heavily engaged while with Hampton's Division at Ashland on June 1.[11]

Hampton took four of the five Horse Artillery batteries to Louisa Court House and Gordonsville during the second week of June to counter Sheridan's raid upon the Virginia Central Railroad. The opposing cavalry forces clashed at Trevilian Station on June 11 and 12. Hart's, Shoemaker's, and Thomson's Batteries were heavily engaged and sustained some casualties.[12] These batteries especially helped repulse Federal assaults against Hampton's Division on June 12. Johnston's Battery was also present but reported little loss. The casualties for the Horse Artillery during the Overland Campaign are provided in Table 70, Appendix A.

For the most part, the casualties sustained by the Horse Artillery were not well documented. The muster rolls appear to have been filed months later, for the most part, and do not accurately report the status of the personnel and units in May and June. As for the newspapers, nominal lists of casualties were found for only Shoemaker's and Hart's Batteries.[13] As a supplement, several diaries were located for Thomson's and Shoemaker's Batteries.[14] The respective books from the Virginia Regimental Series were also checked.[15] Based on these sources, additional casualties were found. It is likely that the actual number of total casualties sustained by the artillery were slightly larger than the figures shown in Table 70. Most of the estimated increases likely occurred in McGregor's, Johnston's, and Thomson's Batteries.

CHAPTER 8

Separate Commands

HOKE'S DIVISION

This division was formed at Bermuda Hundred in late May 1864 from the brigades of Clingman, Colquitt, Hagood, and Martin. These units were part of Gen. Pierre G. T. Beauregard's forces opposing Butler's Army of the James outside Richmond. During the first part of the war, these brigades mostly served at various points along the Atlantic Seaboard. Due to limited combat in these areas in 1862 and 1863, the ranks of each of these commands were very full. While the Battles of the Wilderness and Spotsylvania were being contested to the north, these brigades were engaged to various degrees in several actions against Butler's army. At this time, they were actually serving in three separate divisions in Beauregard's command.[1] The four were gathered as a new division following the return of Pickett's Division and Hoke's Brigade (under Colonel Lewis) to the Army of Northern Virginia during the third week of May.

Maj. Gen. Robert F. Hoke was relatively new to this level of command. He formerly led a brigade from his home state of North Carolina in Early's Division of Lee's army and was wounded during the Battle of Chancellorsville in May 1863.[2] Following a wounded furlough, Hoke directed an attack upon a Federal garrison at Plymouth in eastern North Carolina in April 1864. His forces successfully captured this seaport and the entire garrison.[3] It was one of the few occasions in the war when Confederates were able to recaptured a lost strategic point. As a result of this success, Hoke was promoted to major general and given command of a division in Beauregard's new army.

On May 30, Hoke's Division was ordered by the War Department to reinforce Lee's army.[4] This directive was in response to the continued movement of Grant's Army of the Potomac toward Richmond and the dispatch of the XVIII Corps from Butler's army to Grant. At this stage of the campaign, Federal cavalry was sparring with Confederate cavalry in the area of Old Cold Harbor. Several key roads intersected at this point, and the crossroads was located several miles beyond the right end of the main Confederate line. The actions of the cavalry and the reinforcement of the XVIII Corps drew the interest of General Lee to this crossroads, and on May 31, he instructed Hoke to move his command to this point and provide support for the cavalry.[5]

In the afternoon of May 31, elements of the First Division of the Federal Cavalry Corps began pressuring Fitzhugh Lee's Division at Old Cold Harbor. The lead elements of Hoke's Division, three regiments of Clingman's Brigade, arrived and were posted to the left of Lee's dismounted troopers (see Map 33, Appendix B). The Federal attack was well planned and conducted, and the entire Confederate force was driven through and beyond the crossroads.[6] At dark, the remaining regiment of Clingman's Brigade along with Colquitt's Brigade arrived to assist in the formation of a new line about one mile to the west.

During the early hours of the following day, the rest of the division reached the battlefield, and the entire command constructed a line of breastworks. The front covered Cold Harbor Road and spanned from Boatswain Creek on the south to Bloody Run on the north. Clingman's Brigade was posted on the left next to Bloody Run; Colquitt's and Martin's Brigade extended the line to Boatswain Creek; and Hagood's Brigade, arriving last, was posted in reserve (see Map 34, Appendix B).[7] In response to the loss of Old Cold Harbor, Lee reinforced Hoke with Anderson's First Corps. Kershaw's Division and later Pickett's Division were positioned on the left of Hoke's Division, which was, at this time, temporarily attached to Anderson's corps. Hagood's Brigade was subsequently shifted to the left of the divisional front and posted slightly in front of the main line astride Bloody Run. This moved facilitated a linkup of Hoke's front with Kershaw's line (directly to the north).

During the late morning and afternoon of June 1, infantry from the VI and XVIII Corps arrived and began deploying across the fronts of Hoke's and Kershaw's Divisions. General Hoke apparently became concerned about his open right (southern) flank and decided to shift Hagood's Brigade from its position astride Bloody Run on the left to the opposite end of his line. He apparently failed to notify either Anderson or Kershaw of this change, which became a major problem when the Federal infantry assaulted Kershaw's and Hoke's lines in the evening.[8] The attacks upon the manned portions of the line were easily repulsed, but the gap created by shifting Hagood's Brigade was exploited by elements of the Second and Third Divisions, VI Corps and the Third Division, XVIII Corps (see Map 35, Appendix B). These Federal units advanced mostly unopposed through the ravine of Bloody Run and then moved upon the flanks and rear of the open ends of Kershaw's and Hoke's Divisions. The troops holding this end of the line were heavily punished at this time.[9] The line was ultimately regained, and the Federals repulsed with the arrival of reinforcements from other sections of the divisional line and the onset of darkness.

Overnight, Clingman's line was shifted slightly to the west, improving the division's entire line of breastworks. The division's alignment also was slightly changed. Hagood's Brigade was shifted from the far right and posted between Clingman's and Colquitt's Brigades. Martin's Brigade remained on the right next to Colquitt's command but was shifted to the south of Boatswain Creek.[10] As fate would have it, this portion of the Confederate line was the main focus of a massive Union assault during the early hours of June 3 by elements of the II and VI Corps (see Maps 38 and 39, Appendix B). Hoke's units experienced little difficulty in repulsing these attacks, inflicting severe casualties upon the enemy with very little loss to their own ranks.[11] For the remainder of the battle, this portion of the Confederate front was subjected to constant sniping and artillery fire.

Following Cold Harbor, Richmond newspapers published several articles addressing the performance and status of this "new" division in Lee's army. These articles contained numerous laudatory comments regarding the men's performance in this battle. Very little, if anything, was mentioned regarding the command failure on June 1. Hoke's Division sustained almost 3,000 casualties overall in May and early June but could still, at the close of the campaign, field nearly 5,900 men. These unusually high numbers were due to the fact that the component brigades had, as noted above, full ranks at the start of May.

Following the departure of Grant's army from Cold Harbor, Hoke's Division was moved back to Bermuda Hundred. From this point on June 15, it was rushed to Petersburg and returned to Beauregard's command. The division played a major role in the defense of that city and saw considerable action for the remaining months of 1864, defending both Richmond and Petersburg.

Clingman's Brigade

William L. Clingman's brigade consisted of four regiments from North Carolina that had served entirely in the defense of the Atlantic Seaboard. Their greatest notoriety to this point in the war had been participation in the successful defense of Charleston in the summer of 1863. The 31st and 51st North Carolina Regiments were part of the garrison of Battery Wagner during that campaign.[1] Two of the units, the 8th and 31st North Carolina Regiments, were captured on Roanoke Island in 1861 and had been exchanged later that year.[2] These four units were raised almost exclusively from the eastern portion of the state. During the short campaign against Butler's army, Clingman's Brigade was assigned to Hoke's Division. As a part of this organization, the North Carolinians were engaged at Drewry's Bluff on May 14–16 and at Bermuda Hundred on May 18–21.

When Clingman's Brigade was ordered to join Lee's army on May 30, the 61st North Carolina Regiment initially took over the entire front of the brigade in the early morning hours of May 31. Thus, it arrived at Cold Harbor later on this day. The remaining three regiments, the 8th, 31st, and 51st North Carolina, arrived in time to take part in the action against Federal cavalry at Old Cold Harbor (see Map 33, Appendix B). These units were arrayed with the 51st on the left, the 8th in the center, and the 31st on the right. During this action, the 51st North Carolina and some cavalry were forced to withdraw due to heavy pressure on their front and open flank. This precipitated the overall retreat of the Confederate forces from Old Cold Harbor.[3]

Clingman's Brigade was realigned on June 1, with the 8th North Carolina posted on the left (next to the ravine of Bloody Run). The 51st, 31st, and newly arriving 61st North Carolina continued the line to the south in that order.[4] The evening assault by the VI and XVIII Corps upon the fronts of Hoke's and Kershaw's Divisions was nearly disastrous to Clingman's Brigade (see Map 35, Appendix B). Elements of the Third Division advanced through the open ravine and enveloped the flank and rear of the 8th and 51st North Carolina Regiments. Unlike Wofford's Brigade of Kershaw's Division at the opposite side of this Federal success, these units did not break and flee to the rear in mass—they hung on and battled the superior enemy force. With the onset of darkness, the fighting deteriorated into a desperate close-order melee. Soon after the break in the line, the 31st North Carolina shifted most of its personnel to the left and joined in the melee.[5] All three of these regiments sustained heavy casualties and lost collectively almost 400 men in prisoners. The 61st North Carolina, in contrast, stayed in position and dealt only with the enemy troops in its front. This unit experienced light losses. The Confederate position in this portion of the battlefield was saved by the timely arrival of reinforcements from Colquitt's adjacent brigade and, ultimately, the onset of darkness.

Clingman's Brigade was next engaged on June 3 (see Map 39, Appendix B). During the massive Federal assault upon the Confederate line in this sector, the North Carolinians were initially placed in divisional reserve. At midday, the brigade relieved other units in a section of the front line.[6] The North Carolinians sustained few casualties on this day and during the remainder of this battle.

The brigade was sadly reduced in strength as a result of the fighting in May and the first week of June. The 8th, 31st, and 51st North Carolina Regiments, in particular, could field only a fraction of their original strengths. Overall, the brigade sustained 714 casualties at Cold Harbor, the highest brigade loss in Lee's army at this battle. In addition, the command reported about 460 casualties at Drewry's Bluff and Bermuda Hundred; the actual loss may have been somewhat higher. Clingman's Brigade saw considerable action in June through September during the siege of Petersburg and Richmond. The North Carolinians were especially hard hit at Fort Harrison in late September. After this action, only about 300–350 men were left in the ranks.

The records for this brigade are relatively poor. Many of the muster rolls for the year 1864 are missing. But North Carolina newspapers provided casualty lists for all the units for Drewry's Bluff. Following that battle, however, they must have lost interest in this command for only one list was found for Cold Harbor, which provided the casualties for the 31st North Carolina Regiment on May 31.[7] No similar records were found for the other regiments of the brigade for the battles on June 1 and 3. The respective volumes of Manarin and Jordan on North Carolina troops were also researched.[8] These books provided some beneficial results. In view of the deficiencies in the newspapers, it is entirely possible that the losses of this brigade at Cold Harbor were slightly higher. The compiled casualties for this brigade during the Drewry's Bluff Campaign and at Cold Harbor are provided in Table 71, Appendix A.

Hagood's Brigade

Johnson Hagood's brigade had a battle history very similar to that of Clingman's Brigade. The command was composed of four regiments and one battalion from South Carolina that, prior to 1864, had never left their home state. Most of these units played an active role in the defense of Charleston in the summer of 1863 and sustained some casualties during this operation. The men were recruited from the counties along the coast (especially Charleston) and the eastern portion of the state. As a consequence, the various units had little difficulty recruiting personnel, and by this stage of the war, the ranks of Hagood's Brigade were very full. For example, the 7th South Carolina Battalion fielded about 520 men in eight companies. The strengths of the four regiments (the 11th, 21st, 25th, and 27th South Carolina) ranged between 475 and 530 men. The number of men in the brigade would have been even higher except that three companies were left behind (temporarily) in South Carolina.

Hagood's Brigade was one of the first commands to arrive in Richmond from South Carolina. It was assigned (with Clingman's Brigade) to Hoke's Division. The South Carolinians saw considerable action against Butler's army. Their first action occurred on May 7 at Port Walthall Junction.[1] This encounter was followed by an action on May 7–9 at Swift Creek.[2] The brigade then took part in the larger battles of Drewry's Bluff on May 14–16 and Bermuda Hundred on May 18–21.[3] Hagood's command sustained a reported total of 911 casualties at these four battles. The loss amounted to about 40 percent of its original strength.

When Hoke's reorganized division moved to Cold Harbor, Hagood's Brigade brought up the rear. The South Carolinians missed most of the worst fighting on June 1. When Hoke's Division assumed a new line on June 2, the brigade was shifted to the left of the divisional front between Clingman's and Colquitt's Brigades. Its right was roughly anchored on Cold Harbor Road. Hagood's Brigade was attacked during the early morning hours of June 3 by elements of the VI Corps (see Map 39, Appendix B).[4] The South Carolinians easily repelled this assault with light loss. For the next six to eight days, the brigade was subjected to considerable sniping and artillery fire. This limited action appeared to cause more casualties than the major assault of June 3.

Hagood's Brigade sustained a reported 145 casualties at Cold Harbor. Added to the losses accumulated in May against the Army of the James, the total number of casualties exceeded 1,050 men. The field strength of the command was increased by the arrival of the aforementioned three companies (one each to the 11th, 21st, and 27th South Carolina Regiments). This added a total of about 250 men to the brigade. In addition, some who had sustained light wounds in May returned to the ranks. As a result, the strength of the command was again the highest in the division. Hagood's Brigade continued to see considerable combat during the remainder of 1864. A review of the rolls and newspaper lists reveals that the command sustained at least 1,200 more casualties during the months of June through September. In particular, its ranks were severely reduced at Globe Tavern (near Petersburg) on August 21.

The newspaper listings for this brigade are among the best found in this study.[5] The Charleston newspapers, in particular, provided comprehensive lists of the casualties sustained by all the units in each of the above-noted battles. In view of these findings, the numbers for Hagood's Brigade are considered very accurate. The compiled casualties for this brigade during the Drewry's Bluff Campaign and at Cold Harbor are provided in Table 72 in Appendix A.

Colquitt's Brigade

The Georgia brigade of Alfred H. Colquitt was an exception in Hoke's Division. The command was an integral part of D. H. Hill's (Rodes's) Division in Lee's army during much of 1862 and 1863. It had especially distinguished itself during the Peninsula Campaign and at the Battle of Antietam. In the aftermath of the Battle of Chancellorsville in May 1863, however, questions arose regarding the performance of the brigade and especially its commander. Specifically, the Georgians sat idly during the critical phase of the battle. The perceived problem was not with the personnel but with the leadership of General Colquitt.[1] Richmond authorities elected to resolve the issue by exchanging the general and his men for Daniels's large but relatively inexperienced brigade from North Carolina.[2]

After leaving Lee's army, Colquitt's Brigade was assigned to the forces defending Charleston. In early 1864, it was sent to counter a Federal excursion into northern Florida, a campaign culminating in a Confederate victory at Olustee in February.[3] Colquitt's Brigade played a major role in this victory and received considerable acclaim. The Georgians sustained almost 500 casualties in these two campaigns, but being assigned closer to home, were able to fill some of their depleted ranks with new recruits. The brigade was composed of five regiments (the 6th, 19th, 23rd, 27th, and 28th Georgia) recruited from the central to the northwestern parts of the state.

Colquitt's Brigade joined Beauregard's army in early May in an incremental fashion. The command was assigned to a small two-brigade division led by General Colquitt and participated in the Battle of Drewry's Bluff. Three of the five units of the brigade were principally engaged.[4] One regiment, the 6th Georgia, sustained heavy casualties in this battle. A second regiment, the 28th Georgia, was lightly involved. Another, the 27th Georgia, arrived in Virginia after the end of this battle.

The brigade reached the Cold Harbor battlefield on May 31 (see Maps 34 and 35, Appendix B). It was posted in the center of the division between Clingman's and Martin's Brigades. The Georgians remained in this position through the evening of June 1, when the Federals assaulted the entire divisional front. The attacks were easily repelled, though an enemy breakthrough to the left of Clingman's adjacent brigade caught the Georgians' attention. General Colquitt reacted quickly and sent about one-third of his brigade (the 28th Georgia, five companies of the 27th Georgia, and at least one company of the 23rd Georgia) to the assistance of Clingman's embattled command. These detached elements slammed into the Federal forces enveloping Clingman.[5] The impetus of their counterattack halted the advance and ultimately forced the enemy troops to retire.

On June 2, Colquitt's Brigade took over the portion of the divisional front between Cold Harbor Road and Boatswain Creek. This position was assaulted in the early morning hours of June 3 by elements of the II and VI Corps (see Maps 38 and 39, Appendix B).[6] The Georgians experienced little difficulty in repulsing this attack. For the remainder of the battle, they were subjected to constant sniping and artillery shelling.

Compared to Clingman's and Hagood's ill-fated organizations, Colquitt's Brigade emerged from the campaign in relatively good condition. The recorded number of casualties for the battles in May and early June amounted to only 350 men. The highest casualties occurred in the 6th Georgia Regiment at Drewry's Bluff and, as could be expected, in the 27th and 28th Regiments at Cold Harbor. The brigade continued to see considerable action during the siege of Petersburg and Richmond for the remainder of 1864.

The muster rolls for the five units comprising this brigade are generally poor. One, the 19th Georgia Regiment, has no rolls for all of 1864. The newspaper casualty listings are somewhat more informative. These were found for four of the five units (all but the 19th Georgia) for Cold Harbor.[7] But the newspaper listings for Drewry's Bluff appear to be less complete, and it is possible that the losses at this battle may have been somewhat higher. The casualties for Colquitt's Brigade during both the Drewry's Bluff Campaign and at Cold Harbor are provided in Table 73, Appendix A.

Martin's Brigade

The North Carolina regiments comprising this brigade as well as its commander, Brig. Gen. James G. Martin, had very little battle experience. One, the 17th North Carolina, had lost a portion of its personnel at Roanoke Island in 1861.[1] The three regiments comprising this brigade (the 17th, 42nd, and 66th North Carolina) otherwise spent the first two to three years of the war guarding the North Carolina coast and the Weldon Railroad. They were raised from counties around Kinston, along the headwaters of Albemarle Sound, and around Salisbury. Due to their prior service and lack of combat experience, the ranks of all three regiments were very full.

Once Martin's Brigade was sent into battle, the command seemed to continuously find good fortune. It was assigned to Whiting's Division in early May and, due to a leadership failure by this general, missed the Battle at Drewry's Bluff.[2] The North Carolinians were subsequently engaged at Bermuda Hundred on May 18–21 and overall sustained only about 235 casualties.[3] They arrived at the Cold Harbor battlefield with Hoke's Division on May 31 but were not seriously engaged on this day (see Map 34, Appendix B). On June 1–3, Martin's Brigade covered the right end of Hoke's line of breastworks. They were strongly attacked on June 1 and 3 but had little difficulty defending their sector on both occasions with little loss (see Maps 35 and 38, Appendix B).[4] The brigade suffered about 200 casualties at Cold Harbor, though almost a third of this number consisted of prisoners taken on June 3. Presumably, these men were on the picket line and were overrun in the early morning hours as the Federals advanced.

At the conclusion of the Battle of Cold Harbor, Martin's Brigade could field the second-highest strength in Hoke's Division. Like many new units assigned to Lee's army, this organization did experience a high rate of sickness in June. Unlike Hagood's and Clingman's ill-fated commands, the North Carolinians continued to find good fortune in the battles around Petersburg and Richmond throughout the summer and autumn months of 1864.

The records for Martin's Brigade were found to be quite limited. Casualty listings were located for all three regiments for the actions at Bermuda Hundred, but only one newspaper casualty list was found for Cold Harbor. Salisbury's *Carolina Watchman* of June 27, 1864, provides a complete list of the losses for the 42nd North Carolina Regiment between June 1 and 15.[5] Similar records for the 17th and 66th North Carolina Regiments have not been found. The losses for these two units at Cold Harbor could have been slightly higher (see Table 74, Appendix A).

Read's Artillery Battalion

In late May 1864, the artillery battalion of Maj. John P. W. Read was attached to Hoke's Division.[1] This unit, sometimes referred to as the 38th Virginia Artillery Battalion, consisted of the Virginia light-artillery batteries of Marshall, Macon, Caskie, and Blount. These individual commands were also known, respectively, as the Fauquier, Richmond Fayette, Richmond Hampden, and Lynchburg Artilleries. In the fall of 1862, these units absorbed several other Virginia light-artillery batteries. Arthur. L Rodgers's Loudoun Artillery was merged into the Fauquier Artillery. Edwin J. Anderson's Richmond Thomas Artillery was similarly assigned to the Hampden Artillery, and the Lynchburg Artillery absorbed most of John R. Johnson's Bedford Artillery. During the previous year of the war, this battalion had been assigned to Pickett's Division and was led by Maj. James Dearing. Over the winter of 1863–64, Dearing was promoted and transferred to the cavalry, making way for Read to command this battalion.

During the Battle of Cold Harbor, the four batteries were posted along the main line and breastworks of Hoke's Division. There is little reason to doubt that they played a major role in the repulse of the Federal assaults on June 1 and 3.[2] Read's Battalion also exchanged fire with Union batteries on June 1. Following the massive Federal attack on June 3, they were subjected to more enemy artillery shelling and continuous small-arms fire and sniping. The battalion sustained a total of thirty-five casualties during this battle (see Table 75, Appendix A). The losses in Read's Battalion were well covered in the local newspapers and the respective book for the Virginia Regimental Histories Series. An issue of the *Daily Richmond Enquirer* listed the casualties for all four batteries for the period May 16–June 8 (Drewry's Bluff and Cold Harbor).[3]

BRECKINRIDGE'S DIVISION

The division of John C. Breckinridge was detached to Lee's army from the Department of Western Virginia. In the spring of 1864, Breckinridge was also the commander of this department. A native of Kentucky, he was a very well-known figure and general in the Confederacy. Prior to the war, Breckinridge had served as vice president in the administration of James Buchanan and had been one of the unsuccessful candidates for the presidency in 1860 (losing to Abraham Lincoln). During the first part of the war, he served as a division commander in the Army of Tennessee.

Breckinridge's Division consisted of the following units: John Echols's brigade (the 22nd Virginia Regiment and the 23rd and 26th Virginia Battalions) and Gabriel C. Wharton's brigade (the 51st and 62nd Virginia Regiments and the 30th Virginia Sharpshooters Battalion). The 45th Virginia Regiment was normally part of Wharton's Brigade, but it had been detached and left in the Shenandoah Valley. The 62nd Virginia, a mounted-infantry regiment in John D. Imboden's cavalry brigade, had been temporarily dismounted and substituted in its place. These units were all part of the Confederate force that successfully defeated the Union army of Maj. Gen. Franz Sigel at New Market on May 15 in the Valley.[1] They received much acclaim from the Southern press and Lee's veterans for this victory. The men of these units were from the mountainous area of southwestern Virginia and the southern portion of modern-day West Virginia.

Following the retreat of Sigel's force to Winchester, Breckinridge's Division was ordered to join the Army of Northern Virginia.[2] This command moved by rail from the Shenandoah Valley, arriving at Hanover Junction on May 21.[3] The Virginians held this critical point until joined by Ewell's Second Corps and, subsequently, the remainder of Lee's army. The division was first held in reserve during the Battle of North Anna and then, on May 24–25, deployed on the right of the army adjacent to Ewell's corps (see Map 29, Appendix B).[4] The Virginians engaged in only light skirmishing on these days and sustained very few casualties.

Breckinridge's Division led Anderson's First Corps in the march from the North Anna battlefield to Totopotomoy Creek on May 27–28.[5] The small command moved forward along Atlee Station Road and took up a position along the southern side of this stream astride this road. Breckinridge's men quickly dug in and constructed earthworks along this line.[6] Units of the

Third Corps were deployed on their left along Totopotomoy Creek. Ewell's Second Corps was posted on their right, its line turning toward the south and spanning Shady Grove Road. On May 29, the VI and II Corps arrived and began probing Breckinridge's line. For the next three days, the two sides engaged in active skirmishing and artillery shelling (see Map 31, Appendix B). The Virginians successfully held their ground and inflicted considerable casualties upon the II Corps.[7] They did sustain some loss, though, principally in the 26th Virginia Battalion.

The division moved from its position along Totopotomoy Creek to Mechanicsville (west of Cold Harbor) during the night of June 1–2. It then moved to the Cold Harbor line during the afternoon and was placed on the right of Hoke's Division. Wharton's Brigade led the march.[8] General Echols became ill at this time, and command of his brigade devolved upon Col. George S. Patton of the 22nd Virginia Regiment. The brigade took up position on the right of Martin's Brigade (of Hoke's Division). Wharton's Brigade extended the line farther to the south. The six Virginia units of the division were aligned (from north to south) as follows: 26th Battalion, 22nd Regiment, 23rd Battalion, 30th Battalion, 51st Regiment, and 62nd Regiment (see Map 38, Appendix B).[9]

There was a significant flaw to this position. The sector covered by the 26th Battalion and one company of the 22nd Regiment formed a salient.[10] The ground in its front contained a patch of dense woods and a deep draw. The opposing elements of the II Corps were able to sustain a steady volume of rifle fire from the woods and, more importantly, mass a considerable body of troops in the draw safely out of the Confederates' line of fire. During the evening of June 2, skirmishers from the 26th Battalion were unable to clear this ground.

In the early morning hours of June 3, Grant's army attacked the southern portion of the entire Confederate line. For the most part, these assaults were easily repulsed, with heavy losses to the Federal forces and very light losses to the defenders. In the area of the salient, though, elements of the First Division, II Corps took advantage of the favorable ground, reached the Confederate line, and poured over the breastworks.[11] Some of the men of the 26th Virginia Battalion fled to the rear. Others tried to hold their position but were overwhelmed by the superior numbers. The breakthrough spilled over toward a reserve line held by the 2nd Maryland Battalion. This unit held its position and was soon joined by Finegan's Brigade (Mahone's Division), which had been posted in reserve. Together they counterattacked and drove the Federal forces back to the section of broken line.[12] The 22nd Virginia Regiment re-fused its left flank and contained the limit of the breakthrough on the southern side.[13] The 66th North Carolina Regiment of Martin's Brigade performed a similar action on the northern side. With their failure to widen and exploit the breakthrough, the Federals were ultimately forced to withdraw with considerable loss.

The Confederates constructed a new defensive line in the rear of the salient, and Breckinridge's Division was relieved by elements of Mahone's Division. General Breckinridge was injured from a fall from his horse during the battle; General Echols returned from sickness and took over command of the division.[14] For the next several days, the Virginians were rotated in and out of this portion of the main line. At the conclusion of the Battle of Cold Harbor, they were dispatched along with the Second Corps to Lynchburg. David Hunter had succeeded Sigel in the command of Federal forces in the Shenandoah. His force had marched largely unopposed through the Valley and was threatening this city. From this point through to the end of the war, Breckinridge's Division fought in and around the Valley.

Breckinridge's little division sustained over 400 casualties in this campaign (see Table 76, Appendix A). The actual loss was likely somewhat higher. Most of the muster rolls for the six units comprising this command are missing, and the newspapers covered only portions of the battles. The June 9 issue of the *Richmond Daily Examiner* provided the casualties for the 26th Virginia Battalion for May 31 and June 3.[15] The same day's issue of Richmond's *The Sentinel* provided the losses for Wharton's Brigade through June 3.[16] No casualty lists for this same period were found for the 22nd Regiment or 23rd Battalion in Echols's Brigade, and none were found for any unit in the division after June 3. A check of the respective books of the Virginia Regimental Histories Series was included in the research for this command.[17]

McLaughlin's Artillery Battalion

The artillery component accompanying Breckinridge's Division consisted of a battalion with Chapman's and Jackson's Virginia Batteries. The former was raised in Monroe County; the latter was actually a horse-artillery battery and was formed by transfers from the Virginia State Line and, principally, the 8th Virginia Cavalry Regiment. Both units had served in southwestern Virginia for most of the war. Maj. William McLaughlin commanded the battalion.

McLaughlin's Battalion was primarily engaged at Totopotomoy Creek on May 30 and 31. Jackson's Battery, in particular, participated in a long-range artillery duel with Federal batteries and fired upon infantry skirmishers on these days. The activity of this battery together with the strength of Breckinridge's position apparently deterred Union forces from attacking. Chapman's Battery was lightly engaged at Cold Harbor on June 3. Following the conclusion of that battle, McLaughlin's Battalion accompanied Breckinridge's Division to Lynchburg and subsequently the Shenandoah Valley.

The muster rolls for these two batteries contain gaps. Fortunately, a casualty list for Jackson's Battery was found in the Richmond newspapers.[1] This list provides the losses for this unit at Totopotomoy Creek on May 30–31. No similar list was found for Chapman's Battery. The compiled casualties are provided in Table 76, Appendix A.

MARYLAND LINE

This unusual organization consisted of one infantry battalion, one cavalry battalion, and three light-artillery batteries, commanded by Col. Bradley T. Johnson. These units comprised all the troops from the border state of Maryland in the Confederate army in northern Virginia. At the start of the campaign, the command was posted at Hanover Junction in the rear of Lee's army.[1] The infantry unit, the 2nd Maryland Battalion, consisted of eight veteran companies and had served with Steuart's Brigade at Gettysburg. The cavalry unit, the 1st Maryland Cavalry Battalion, consisted of five companies and had a shorter history. The artillery arm consisted of the 1st, 2nd, and 4th Maryland Light Artillery Batteries. These units periodically served with Lee's army earlier during the war. The men of the Maryland Line hailed primarily from counties in the eastern part of the state.

As the Federal army moved closer to Richmond, the various units of the Maryland Line were sent into action. The first to be committed was the 1st Maryland Cavalry Battalion. In response to Sheridan's cavalry raid toward Richmond, this unit left Hanover Junction on May 9 and joined with elements of Stuart's cavalry. On this and the following day (May 10), elements of this Maryland unit skirmished with Sheridan's troopers near Beaver Dam Station.[2] After the tenth, the 1st Maryland was attached to Fitzhugh Lee's Division of the Cavalry Corps. It was next lightly engaged on May 24–25 on the Pamunkey River in King William County.[3]

On May 27, Fitzhugh Lee committed the battalion to action at Pollard Farm (Hanovertown) on the road to Haw's Shop. The Marylanders were assigned the task of flanking Union cavalry facing Baker's (Gordon's) Brigade on a parallel road to the north. The opposing Federal force was Custer's brigade. The Federal general brought up about half of his command and drove the 1st Maryland from the field with considerable loss. Baker's command then had to rapidly retreat to avoid encirclement from Custer's pursuit of the Marylanders. In the aftermath of this engagement, both Confederate parties harbored ill feelings toward each other's respective command.[4]

On June 1, the battalion was deployed as part of the Confederate cavalry covering the northern flank of Lee's army (at Bethesda Church and Cold Harbor). The Marylanders were posted along the road from Hanover Court House westward to the Richmond, Fredericksburg, and Potomac Railroad. They sparred with elements of Wilson's cavalry division along this road and subsequently along the railroad north of Ashland. This Southern unit again received the worst of the exchange and was forced to withdraw. Lt. Col. Ridgely Brown, the commander of the unit, was killed in this action, having just returned to command after suffering a saber cut at Pollard's Farm on May 27.[5] In all fairness to the Marylanders, their strength was considerably reduced from the previous actions, and they were facing a superior Union force. Following the death of Brown, Colonel Johnson personally took over command of the cavalry.

The artillery component of the Maryland Line consisted of the 1st, 2nd, and 4th Maryland Light Artillery Batteries. These units were also known as the Maryland Flying Artillery, Baltimore Light Artillery, and Chesapeake Artillery, respectively. The 1st Maryland and 4th Maryland Batteries saw limited action during the Overland Campaign. They were attached to McIntosh's Battalion of the Third Corps's artillery in late May and were engaged only at Cold Harbor. For the remainder of the year, both units continued to serve with the battalion during the siege of Petersburg.

The 2nd Maryland Artillery Battery was assigned to Stuart's Cavalry Corps on May 9. It was heavily engaged at Yellow Tavern on May 11 and suffered severely (see Map 17, Appendix B).[6] Following this action, the battery was attached to the 1st Maryland Cavalry Battalion.[7] The artillery was present with the cavalry during the period of late May through early June but was kept in the rear and not seriously engaged at Pollard's Farm or Ashland on May 27 and June 1. Following the Battle of Cold Harbor, the 2nd Battery was transferred to the Second Corps. The Marylanders thereafter took part in the Valley Campaign.

The 2nd Maryland Infantry Battalion officially joined Lee's army at North Anna and was attached to Breckinridge's Division.[8] This unit first participated in minor skirmishing at Totopotomoy Creek on May 30 and 31. When the Third Corps moved to Cold Harbor on June 2, the Marylanders were placed in reserve behind Breckinridge's command.[9] The following morning, the Union army assaulted the entire southern portion of the Confederate line, and elements of the First Division, II Corps achieved a limited breakthrough in the sector held by Breckinridge. The 2nd Maryland Battalion (together with Finegan's Brigade of Mahone's Division) rushed into the breach, halted the enemy advance, and restored the line (see Map 38, Appendix B).[10] This was the only significant action for the unit during the campaign and cost the ranks more than forty casualties. Following the battle, the 2nd Maryland Battalion was assigned to Fry's Brigade (Heth's Division).

For the most part, the casualties in the five units forming the Maryland Line are well documented (see Table 77, Appendix A). The Richmond newspapers provided casualties lists for the 1st Cavalry Battalion at Beaver Dam Station and Pollard's Farm, for the 2nd Maryland Battery at Yellow Tavern, and for the 2nd Infantry Battalion and 1st Maryland Battery at Cold Harbor.[11] Noticeably absent, however, was a casualty list for the 1st Cavalry at Ashland (June 1). According to the muster rolls, the unit lost three men that day, including Lieutenant Colonel Brown. A more modern estimate places the battle loss of the unit on June 1 at about twenty men. If this is the case, the cavalry battalion sustained almost eighty-five casualties during the campaign. W. W. Goldsborough's book on the Maryland Line also proved to be a reliable and beneficial source for this study.[12]

MISCELLANEOUS UNITS

Army Provost Guard

The provost guard consisted of the 1st Virginia Infantry and the 39th Virginia Cavalry Battalions. The 1st Virginia Infantry consisted of about 215 men in five companies. The 39th Virginia Cavalry fielded a similar number of men in four companies. The men of this latter unit also served as couriers, scouts, and guides. For the most part, these units served at the army headquarters and were not engaged in any of the battles. Three men of the 39th Virginia

Cavalry were captured during the Overland Campaign, two on May 9 in Caroline County and one on May 31 near Cold Harbor. They were apparently serving as scouts at the time.

Richmond Garrison

During this campaign, the Richmond garrison consisted of four heavy artillery battalions, several battalions of light artillery, and one infantry battalion. Following his victory at Yellow Tavern on May 11, Sheridan decided to advance upon the capital and probe the outer defenses guarding the city. On May 12, his forces sparred with two regiments of Hunton's Brigade and elements of the permanent Richmond garrison at Brook Church (see Map 22, Appendix B). The result of this engagement was inconclusive since Sheridan was disinclined to get involved in a desperate battle against entrenched Confederate units far from his base. The following units of the Richmond garrison were engaged in this action: several companies of the 25th Virginia (Richmond City) Infantry Battalion; Company C, 20th Virginia Heavy Artillery Battalion; and Thornton's Virginia (Caroline) Light Artillery Battery (of Lightfoot's Battalion).[1] The infantry unit sustained twenty-seven casualties; the two artillery units together lost six men. As could be expected, the losses of these three units were provided in the Richmond newspapers.[2]

The 42nd Virginia Cavalry Battalion was attached to Hunton's Brigade in May and, accordingly, was also considered part of the Richmond garrison. This unit was attached to the Cavalry Corps in late May and was present at several of the actions against Federal cavalry near Cold Harbor. It was principally engaged at Matadequin Creek (Old Church) on May 30 (with Butler's Brigade) and lightly engaged at Hanovertown and Hanover Court House on May 27 and May 31, respectively.[3] The battalion sustained twenty-six reported casualties during the campaign. On June 8, this unit absorbed two companies of the 8th Confederate Cavalry and was redesignated the 24th Virginia Cavalry Regiment.

The 7th South Carolina Cavalry Regiment was a relatively inexperienced unit having been formed in 1863. It served with General Beauregard's forces in the battles east of Richmond in early and middle May. It was subsequently assigned to the Richmond garrison. Eight companies of the regiment were attached to Butler's Brigade in late May and participated in the cavalry battle at Matadequin Creek (Old Church) on May 30. For most of the engagement, the regiment was held in reserve. As the Federals began to drive the Confederates from the battlefield, the 7th South Carolina was ordered to charge the advancing enemy.[4] The attack of this unit enabled the other Confederate forces to successfully withdraw, though the charge cost the unit heavily in officers and men.

The compiled casualties for all of these miscellaneous units (including Gracie's Brigade, addressed below) are provided in Table 78, Appendix A.

Gracie's Brigade

The infantry brigade of Archibald Gracie Jr. was not part of the Army of Northern Virginia. It arrived in Richmond from East Tennessee in early May and was assigned to a newly forming Confederate army led by General Beauregard, who was responsible for defending Richmond against Benjamin Butler's Army of the James.[1] During the first eight days of May, Butler's army landed at Bermuda Hundred and began moving on the Richmond defenses at Drewry's Bluff and the railroad between Richmond and Petersburg (to the south). Gracie's Brigade was initially posted in the defensive lines outside Richmond.

Gracie's command consisted of the 41st, 43rd, 59th, and 60th Alabama Regiments and the 23rd Alabama Battalion. These were veteran units, having served with the Army of Tennessee and in East Tennessee earlier in the war. In response to the threat to Richmond from the north by Sheridan's cavalry, Gracie's Brigade was dispatched from Beauregard's command to the forces manning the outer ring of defenses north of the city on May 12 (see Map 22, Appendix B). The move took the troops through the center of the capital to the cheers of the residents.[2]

Once arriving at the defenses, Gracie deployed his brigade outside the earthworks astride Meadow Bridge Road (near Brook Church) and began advancing northward.[3] The 43rd Alabama Regiment was deployed in front of the brigade in a picket line and soon encountered dismounted troops of Sheridan's Third Cavalry Division buttressed by two batteries of horse artillery. These enemy forces halted Gracie's advance and forced a quick retirement. Sheridan withdrew his command later in the day, and Gracie's Brigade was returned to Beauregard. The Alabamians were then temporarily assigned to the division of Robert Ransom (in Beauregard's forces) and played a major role in the successful Battle of Drewry's Bluff on May 16.

The casualties for Gracie's Brigade at Brook Church on May 12 were provided in the May 30 issue of the *Daily Advertiser* of Montgomery.[4] The battle losses for this command on May 16 were also included in this issue and show that the brigade lost heavily in May (378 casualties reported).

Summary and Conclusions

Several conclusions can be drawn from studying the strengths and casualties of the Army of Northern Virginia during the Overland Campaign. First, it is apparent that Lee's army was stronger than has previously been believed. Its strength at the start of the campaign was about 66,000 men, or 4,000 higher than the traditional figure of 62,000. If one includes the units temporarily serving with Beauregard, the overall strength of the army is close to the estimated 75,000 men at Gettysburg. This illustrates that Lee's command had, for the most part, recovered over the winter. As described above, most of the individual brigades and battalions were combat ready and ably led. According to variable sources, morale at this point in the war ranged from guarded to high, and despite considerable logistical shortcomings, the condition of the army was good.

Second, the Army of Northern Virginia was reinforced substantially during the campaign, the total of additional men exceeding 30,000. The combined figure of 96,000 represents the maximum number of men available to Lee. This is a considerable figure and far exceeds the historic 78,000 men offered by Major Taylor of Lee's staff. It represents the greatest number of men the Confederate War Department ever concentrated at one point in the war and even exceeds the number collected for the Seven Days' Battles outside Richmond in 1862. Countering factors included battle casualties, substantial losses due to sickness, and a reduction in strength of the cavalry owing to the loss of mounts during the campaign.

A comparison of Lee's and Grant's strengths and losses is instructive. As documented in the *Official Records,* the Army of the Potomac started the campaign with an effective strength of about 118,000 men, from which, if we are to compare the like with like, should be deducted the 3,400 men of the provost guard and engineers. Based upon other figures provided in the same source, Grant's army received about 48,000 reinforcements during the Overland Campaign.[1] These principally consisted of units drawn from the Washington defenses, others returning from furlough, and new recruits. According to the report of Maj. Gen. William F. Smith, he brought about 16,000 men in the XVIII Corps to Grant at Cold Harbor. At the same time, it should be recognized that the army lost about 20,000 men whose terms of enlistment expired. This represented a serious loss, for these were all veteran soldiers. Grant's net increase is then about 44,000 men, or a maximum total of 162,000 men. The initial disparity in numbers between the Federal and Confederate armies decreased as the campaign progressed, especially in June.

The casualty figures for Lee's army are certainly larger than any previously reported. The compiled total loss of about 33,500 men in this campaign was greater than anything previously experienced by the army. Furthermore, when one considers only the battles of the first fifteen days (the Wilderness, Spotsylvania, and Sheridan's Richmond Raid) and the original size of Lee's army, the percentage loss sustained during this period (about 24,000 of 66,000) exceeds even the campaigns of Gettysburg and the Seven Days' Battles. In each of these earlier campaigns, the Army of Northern Virginia sustained more than 20,000 casualties but from a larger force. As a side thought, it should be mentioned that this researcher spent some effort compiling the Confederate losses at Gettysburg using available new sources together with personal research. Generally accepted sources place the total Confederate loss at this battle between a low of 20,451 to a high of 27,000. The latter figure likely covers the entire campaign and includes many stragglers and deserters captured after the battle. According to this author's research, the actual total for the Confederate losses at Gettysburg appears to be about 23,500 men. So the losses for the army during the Overland Campaign do appear to exceed those of Gettysburg.

Further insight regarding Confederate losses for the Overland Campaign can be obtained by comparing these numbers with those of the opposing Union forces. The four infantry corps in the Army of the Potomac sustained losses of about 42–48 percent of their original strength during the overall campaign. The highest loss occurred in the II Corps (Hancock); the lowest in the IX Corps (Burnside). The V Corps (Warren) and VI Corps (Sedgwick/Wright) fell closer to the percentage of the II Corps at 46 percent each. If one includes the additional reinforcements and their losses in the overall totals, these numbers are reduced to a range of 39–42 percent. The corresponding figures for the Confederate corps are 45 percent for Longstreet's First Corps,

67 percent for Ewell's Second Corps, and 42 percent for Hill's Third Corps. Like the Federal army, these percentages are reduced to some extent by the inclusion of the new personnel assigned to these commands during May and the first part of June. In comparison, Pickett's Division of the First Corps, which served with Beauregard during the first two weeks of May, lost about 29 percent of its starting strength (1,981 of 6,860) during same period.

The casualty figures are particularly high among the eight infantry divisions that entered the Wilderness and sustained the fighting at Spotsylvania. These units, which formed the backbone of Lee's army, were Kershaw's and Field's Divisions of the First Corps and the three each of the Second and Third Corps. As related earlier, their infantry strength had dwindled to a low of about 31,500 men at this point in the campaign (on May 20, at the close of the Battle of Spotsylvania). A review of Lee's dispatches and correspondence with Pres. Jefferson Davis and the War Department in Richmond during this period reveals his concern with his low infantry strength and the overall strategic situation. The arrival of Pickett's Division, Lewis's reinforced brigade (Hoke's), and Breckinridge's Division, followed by the commands of Hoke and Finegan, compensated for much of the losses at the first two battles and raised the confidence of Lee and the War Department at this critical point in the campaign.

One can draw further conclusions regarding the conditions of the individual corps at the end of the Overland Campaign by examining the casualties in their various divisions. The infantry of the Second Corps lost at least 12,240 men of an estimated maximum number of 21,150, a rate of almost 60 percent. This loss is appalling, considering that this organization received reinforcements of about 3,500 men and that the bulk of the compiled casualties (11,915) fell upon the initial force of about 17,655 men (yielding the aforementioned 67 percent). Johnson's Division, which was largely destroyed at Spotsylvania on May 12, leads all divisions with a loss of almost 84 percent. The respective losses for Rodes's and Early's Divisions for the entire campaign were about 57 and 44 percent, respectively. If the losses from the original compositions and strengths of these divisions are examined, then the respective rates rise to about 61 and 57 percent. Clearly, these commands saw more than their fair share of fighting during the campaign.

On top of its personnel losses, the Second Corps also lost one of three divisional commanders, nine of thirteen brigade commanders, and the majority of its field and line officers. In the view of many historians, this unit was never the same for the remainder of the war. Yet despite its terrible losses, this corps continued to function in the summer and fall of 1864, contending against very heavy odds against Sheridan in the Shenandoah Valley. At this stage in the war, it must have had a fundamentally strong organization, discipline, and spirit. After the Third Battle of Winchester (September 19, 1864), however, one could view the performance of this corps as failing to live up to previous standards.

Because the divisions of the First and Third Corps sustained fewer casualties, a case can be offered that they emerged from the campaign with their organizations and fighting capabilities relatively intact. Yet a close examination of the unit rosters reveals that these commands (and all the infantry for that matter) lost very heavily in line officers, noncommissioned officers, and many of their best men.

As for the cavalry and artillery, their battle losses were not nearly high as the infantry, though overall losses of over 800 in the artillery and between 2,500 and 3,300 in the cavalry were unheard of in the Civil War to this point. Due to its heavy losses in personnel and guns, Page's Artillery Battalion was later consolidated with Cutshaw's Artillery Battalion of the Second Corps. The battle losses of 3,300 men in the Cavalry Corps for the entire campaign represent about 25 percent of this arm's total strength. The original six brigades lost about 23 percent of their starting strength. As a comparison, Sheridan's Cavalry Corps lost about 26 percent of its strength over the same period. Like the infantry, the battle losses in Stuart's Cavalry Corps were not evenly distributed. The majority of casualties fell upon the Virginia brigades of Wickham, Lomax, and Rosser. For the cavalry, there was the additional issue of losses in mounts. If these are taken into account, the Overland Campaign may have cost this arm at least 50 percent of its effective strength.

The compilation of the unit casualties also provides some figures for the daily battle losses during Spotsylvania. The numbers reveal that on May 10, the total loss was in the magnitude of 1,486 men, with 780 of these taken as prisoners. On May 12, the action at the Mule Shoe or Bloody Angle cost the army close to 7,200 casualties. This excludes the actions involving the First and Third Corps at Laurel Ridge and outside the "Heth Salient" to the west and southeast. These local actions cost Lee's army an additional 500–700 men on this day.

As for the principal fighting in and around the Mule Shoe on May 12, the number of prisoners captured by Union forces for the entire day reached

4,046 unwounded and 296 wounded men. Of the latter figures, Johnson's Division lost 2,628 unwounded and 92 wounded prisoners. The batteries of Page's and Cutshaw's Battalions contributed another 185 unwounded and 19 wounded prisoners. Lane's Brigade, which was posted to the immediate right of Johnson's Division, similarly lost 250 prisoners, of whom 25 were wounded. Gordon's (Early's) and Rodes's Divisions contributed another 604 unwounded and 87 wounded prisoners. Lastly, the brigades of the Third Corps sent to this area of the battlefield lost 302 prisoners, of whom 61 were wounded. Thus, the position offered by the Federal side regarding this historical point of contention appears to hold the most validity. The commanding officer of the Second Corps, Richard Ewell, appears to have understated his loss in prisoners. In a similar manner, the compiled losses for the Second Corps during the actions on May 18 and 19 are 49 and 962, respectively. With respect to the action at Harris Farm in May 19, General Ewell reported that his loss was about 900 men. Again, it appears that he understated his losses.

It is possible that some of the casualties incurred throughout the campaign may be attributed to the incorrect dates or even battles. This particularly applies to losses actually sustained at the Wilderness and on the individual dates at Spotsylvania. For personnel wounded in action and not documented in a newspaper listing, the dates of their individual occurrences were frequently determined based upon the date of admission to a hospital and the typical time required to transport a man from the battlefield to the specific location. The documents in the CSRs reveal that the ambulances moved with some degree of immediacy and typically took a certain number of days to reach a specific hospital. In some cases, extenuating circumstances may have caused some delays in this process, thereby accounting for errors in this modern-day research in determining the actual date of the battle. On this basis, the totals for casualties at North Anna, Cold Harbor, and at the latter action of May 19 at Spotsylvania may have been very slightly inflated at the expense of the Wilderness and the initial days at Spotsylvania.

As mentioned briefly in the preceding unit discussions, it is possible, if not likely, that the actual Confederate casualties during the Overland Campaign were higher than those offered by this study. The available sources for a select number of units were limited, and as related earlier, only conservative estimates could be offered for these commands. This particularly applies to the Virginia and Louisiana units in the Johnson's Division and several regiments in Battle's Brigade of the Second Corps, three regiments in Kirkland's

Brigade, parts of Harris's and Finegan's Brigades in the Third Corps, and most of the Cavalry Corps. Based on an overall appraisal of the complied data, it is possible that the actual casualties for Lee's army during the entire campaign were 200–300 more than the compiled total.

The Army of Northern Virginia in the years 1862–63 was a splendid weapon of war, capable of both strategic and tactical offensive operations. The army, collectively and individually, was highly motivated and accustomed to achieving success. Furthermore, success was the accepted standard. Much of this probably had its basis with Robert E. Lee's personal sense of duty, and there is reason to assume that the officers and men were imbued with this as well. Yet there was more to the success and motivation of the army. The men were clearly fighting to protect their homes from an invading adversary. The personal diaries and letters examined for this study reveal an underlying concern for fellow soldiers. In other words, the individual men were fighting to protect and maintain the lives of their fellow soldiers. For anyone who has served in combat, this is not surprising.

The sources also reveal that the men in the ranks were well aware of the achievements of their particular unit in previous battles of the war. This was clearly a point of significant pride. Given that most of the infantry and cavalry brigades were formed of units from the same state, this pride in unit became attached to or associated with a greater pride for the home or representative state. This often led to the development of rivalries between the various brigades within a higher headquarters (division or corps) and likely proved to be a further motivating factor and a major advantage in battle. By comparison, organizations that establish consistency and stability are often more successful in present-day business and sports.

Compare this to the organization of the opposing Union armies. The typical Federal infantry or cavalry brigade was purposefully composed of regiments from two or more states. The composition of each brigade often changed with the addition of newly recruited units and transfers. In early 1863, the commander of the Army of the Potomac, Maj. Gen. Joseph Hooker, attempted to address this problem of unit pride with the introduction of distinctive corps and divisional patches, but less than one year later, the succeeding army commander, Maj. Gen. George G. Meade, broke up two of the original five infantry corps and merged their units into the other three. This occurred before the commencement of the Overland Campaign and was not necessitated by battle losses. In an article written by veteran

Alexander W. Webb and published as part of *Battles and Leaders of the Civil War,* Webb argues that this consolidation caused great dissatisfaction and much confusion in the execution of orders and handling of troops during the Battle of the Wilderness.[2] Compared to Lee's army, there was clearly less continuity and stability.

The many listings of battle casualties in the newspapers throughout the Confederacy reveal that the people back home knew the identities of the organizations (mainly regiments and brigades) from their home state in Lee's army. It is clear also that they were aware of the history and battle achievements of these units. To them, they were more than just the military organization in which their family member(s) or friends were serving. This interaction with home likely reinforced the attitude and motivation of the soldier in the ranks.

By the close of the Battle of Cold Harbor in mid-June 1864, it is apparent that the condition of the army was changing. Fractures started forming in the standards of success and unit pride. The addition of numerous conscripts to fill the ranks was likely part of the problem. These men were typically assigned on a random basis to established units to satisfy manpower needs. This was in marked contrast to the method for enlisted or volunteer personnel, who could join a unit of their choice, generally one from their home area or county (with family and friends already in the ranks). In most cases, conscripts lacked the sense of comradeship and connection with the particular unit. As a result of this and other factors, desertions increased in many commands. The consolidation of units, which began over the previous winter and were necessitated in May by heavy battle losses, also led to a decline in performance.

By mid-June, the Army of Northern Virginia was no longer able to operate at its earlier level of proficiency nor could it pose a major offensive threat to the Federal war effort. This was due partly to the fact that Lee's forces were tied down by the immediate need to defend Richmond. This alone limited the general's options and ensured that Grant would continue to hold the initiative. But even without the perceived need to defend Richmond, the attrition in officers, noncommissioned officers, and veteran soldiers suffered by Lee's army during the Overland Campaign ensured that the previously held high standards of motivation and success in the ranks was diminishing.

There were local Confederate successes in the fighting around Petersburg and Richmond in June–September 1864. Most of these were in the nature of counterattacks, and their success was due in large part to Federal blunders and mismanagement rather than Confederate skill. If the campaign of Gettysburg in 1863 caused the beginning of the decline in the overall offensive capability and condition of the Army of Northern Virginia, the Overland Campaign marked the completion of this process. After the close of this campaign, the condition of Lee's army had markedly declined, and the march to Appomattox Court House had begun.

There is one more point to be addressed. It is the hope of this writer that this book will generate a renewed interest throughout the states of the Confederacy and in the descendants of former Confederate soldiers to locate and make public additional sources of casualties in Lee's army during the last year of the war. This would include additional newspapers (such as the aforementioned *Charlottesville Chronicle* and *Rockingham Register & Virginia Advertiser*), diaries, and individual document collections. Such additional resources could be of assistance in filling the gaps noted herein. There is still a need for significant research regarding the Confederate armies in 1864 and 1865, foremost being the Petersburg and the Shenandoah Valley Campaigns in the eastern theater and the Atlanta Campaign in the western theater.

Appendix A

TABLES

TABLE 1. Army of Northern Virginia Strength, April 20, 1864

Army HQ	
Provost Guard (principally the 1st Bn. Va. Inf.)	320
Escort, couriers, etc. (& 39th Bn Va. Cav.)	230
Total	*550*
Second Corps (Ewell)	
Corps Staff	16
Early's Division (less Hoke's Brigade)	4,575
Johnson's Division	5,450
Rodes's Division (less 12th Ga. & 43rd N.C. Inf. Rgts.)	7,188
Total	*17,229*
Third Corps (Hill)	
Corps Staff	16
Anderson's Division	6,992
Heth's Division	7,506
Wilcox's Division	7,830
Total	*22,344*
Cavalry Corps (Stuart)	
Corps Staff	13
Hampton's Division (two brigades)	3,235
F. Lee's Division (three brigades)	5,309
Total	*8,557*
Artillery	
First Corps (Cabell's Bn. only)	427
Second Corps (five battalions)	1,690
Third Corps (five battalions & Haskell's Bn., First Corps)	2,315
Cavalry Corps	422
Total	*4,854*
Maryland Line (at Hanover Junction)	810
Grand Total	*54,344*

TABLE 2. Army of Northern Virginia Units in East Tennessee Strength, March 31, 1864

First Corps (Longstreet)	
Corps Staff	17
Kershaw's Division	4,934
Field's Division (less Law's Brigade)	4,224
Law's Brigade (temp. att'd to Buckner's Division)	1,270*
Artillery (Huger's Bn.)	459
Total	*10,904*

*Estimate provided in Thomas L. Livermore, *Numbers & Losses in the Civil War in America; 1861–1865* (1900; reprint, Dayton, Ohio, 1986), 111.

TABLE 3. Army of Northern Virginia Strength, June 30, 1864

Army HQ		No Report
First Corps (Anderson)		
Corps Staff		17
Pickett's Division		4,917
Field's Division		4,797
Kershaw's Division		4,546
Total		*14,277*
Second Corps (Early)		
Absent—Serving in the Shenandoah Valley		
Third Corps (Hill)		
Corps Staff		16
Mahone's Division		5,334
Heth's Division		5,636
Wilcox's Division		4,677
Total		*15,663*
Dept. of N.C. & So. Va. (Beauregard)		
Dept. Staff		12
Hoke's Division		5,309
B. Johnson's Division		6,970
Total		*12,291*
Cavalry Corps (Hampton)		
Hampton's Division	No Report, est.	~ 3,100
F. Lee's Division		1,683
W. H. F. Lee's Division		2,867
Dearing's Brigade	No Report, est.	~ 1,800
Total		*4,550*
Artillery		
First Corps		1,609
Second Corps	(one bn., two bns. serving in the Valley)	640
Third Corps		2,223
Dept. of N.C. & So. Va.		1,072
Total		*5,544*
Grand Total		*52,325*
	(or about 57,225 men, including the unreported cavalry units)	

TABLE 4. Army of Northern Virginia Strength, May 5, 1864

First Corps	
Corps Staff	15
Kershaw's Division	5,180
Field's Division	6,090
Total	*11,285*
Second Corps	
Corps Staff	15
Early's Division	4,700
Johnson's Division	5,495
Rodes's Division (less two rgts. with Beauregard)	7,445
Total	*17,655*
Third Corps	
Corps Staff	15
Provost Guard (5th Ala. Bn.)	135
Anderson's Division	7,140
Heth's Division	7,460
Wilcox's Division	7,925
Total	*22,675*
Artillery	
First Corps	1,595
Second Corps	1,700
Third Corps	1,910
Total	*5,205*
Cavalry Corps	
Corps Staff	20
Hampton's Division	2,475
F. Lee's Division	3,450
W. Lee's Division	2,905
Horse Artillery	470
Total	*9,320*
Estimated Total Army Strength	*66,140*

TABLE 5. Army of Northern Virginia Reinforcements Received during the Campaign

First Corps Units	
Pickett's Division (rejoined at Milford Station, May 21)	5,370
Total	*5,370*
Second Corps Units (rejoined parent commands at the end of Spotsylvania)	
Hoke's Brigade (under Lewis)—to Ramseur's Division	1,360
From Rodes's Division (temporarily serving with Hoke's Brigade)—12th Ga. Rgt. (Doles's Brigade), 43rd N.C. Rgt. (Daniels's Brigade)	855
Total	*2,215*
Miscellaneous Units	
Maryland Line (primarily posted in the rear of the army until joining in late May)	
2nd Md. Inf. Bn. (eventually to Walker's Brigade, Heth's Division)	285
1st Md. Cav. Rgt. (later went with F. Lee's Division to the Shenandoah Valley)	375
1st (Dement), 2nd (Griffin), & 4th (Chew) Md. Batteries (eventually to Third Corps & Cavalry Corps)	240
Finegan's Brigade (joined in late May)—originally 1st, 2nd, 4th, & 6th Fla. Bns. & three indep. cos.; reorganized on June 8 to form 9th, 10th, & 11th Fla. Rgts. (to Anderson's/Mahone's Division)	1,270
20th S.C Rgt. (joined late May; to Henegan's Brigade)	850
12th Ga. Bn. & one indep. co. (to 38th Ga. Rgt.)—joined in late May (to Gordon's/Evans's Brigade)	450
Total	*3,470*
Separate Commands	
Breckinridge's Division (two brigades & two artillery batteries; joined at North Anna)	2,510
Hoke's Division—four brigades	
(all but three cos. joined at Cold Harbor in late May)	6,850
(remaining three cos. joined in early June during the Battle of Cold Harbor)	250
Read's (38th Va.) Artillery Bn. (formerly First Corps, attached to Hoke's Division)	375
Total	*9,985*
Additional Cavalry Units	
7th Ga. Rgt. & 20th Ga. Bn. (joined in late May; to Young's Brigade)	985
3rd N.C. Rgt. (joined third week of May; to Gordon's Brigade)	550
Butler's Brigade (joined in late May; to Hampton's Division)	1,990

(continued)

TABLE 5. Army of Northern Virginia Reinforcements Received during the Campaign (*continued*)

Miscellaneous Units (originally assigned to Beauregard & saw action in battles around Richmond in late May–early June)	
7th S.C. (8 cos.)	510
42nd Va. Bn.	420
Total	*4,455*
Estimated Total Reinforcements to Army of Northern Virginia in the form of additional units	*25,495*

TABLE 6. Increases in Infantry Brigade Strength, May 5 through mid-June 1864 (New and Returning Personnel)

	Average Increase per Brigade	*Number of Brigades*	*Total Increase*
First Corps			
Kershaw's Division	190	4	760
Field's Division	220	5	1,100
Pickett's Division	60	4	240
Second Corps			
Early's Division	65	4	260
Johnson's Division	35	4	140
Rodes's Division	90	5	450
Third Corps			
Anderson's Division	75	5	375
Heth's Division	155	4	620
Wilcox's Division	155	4	620
Total			*4,565*

TABLE 7. Casualties at the Wilderness, May 5–7, 1864*

	Killed	*Wounded*	*Wounded & Captured*	*Missing*	*Total*
First Corps					
Corps Staff	0	3	0	0	3
Kershaw's Division	195 (27)	891 (64)	13	39	1,138
Field's Division	274 (44)	1,451 (74)	38 (4)	155	1,918
Total	*469 (71)*	*2,345 (138)*	*51 (4)*	*194*	*3,059*
Second Corps					
Corps Staff	No Loss				0
Johnson's Division	164 (23)	660 (27)	32	369	1,225
Early's Division	112 (19)	465 (30)	31	134	742
Rodes's Division	126 (12)	451 (24)	13 (5)	135	725
Total	*402 (54)*	*1,576 (81)*	*76 (5)*	*638*	*2,692*
Third Corps					
Corps Staff	0	1	0	0	1
Heth's Division	246 (33)	1,705 (90)	36 (9)	305	2,292
Wilcox's Division	179 (28)	1,080 (86)	48 (9)	405	1,712
Anderson's Division	115 (18)	460 (21)	20 (1)	130	725
Total	*540 (79)*	*3,246 (197)*	*104 (19)*	*840*	*4,730*
Cavalry Corps	59 (5)	437 (15)	2	18	516
Corps Field & Horse Artillery	7(1)	29	0	0	36
Grand Total	*1,477 (210)*	*7,633 (431)*	*233 (28)*	*1,690*	*11,033*

*For an explanation of the numbers in parentheses in this and the following tables, see pages 19 and 27 of the text.

TABLE 8. Casualties at Spotsylvania, May 8–21, 1864

	Killed	*Wounded*	*Wounded & Captured*	*Missing*	*Total*
First Corps					
Corps Staff	No Loss				0
Kershaw's Division	94 (11)	313 (26)	8	74	489
Field's Division	76 (14)	328 (22)	2 (1)	25	431
Pickett's Division (w/Staff)	1	0	0	0	1
Total	*171 (25)*	*641 (48)*	*10 (1)*	*99*	*921*
Second Corps					
Corps Staff	0	2	0	0	2
Johnson's Division	127 (23)	305 (23)	99 (11)	2,731	3,262
Early's Division	203 (32)	576 (39)	68 (12)	586	1,433
Rodes's Division	398 (81)	1,363 (94)	143 (32)	1,468	3,372
Total	*728 (136)*	*2,246 (156)*	*310 (55)*	*4,785*	*8,069*
Third Corps					
Corps Staff	No Loss				0
Heth's Division	79 (16)	341 (22)	3 (1)	25	448
Wilcox's Division	211 (30)	558 (50)	69 (17)	443	1,281
Mahone's Division	199 (31)	662 (51)	36 (11)	136	1,033
Total	*489 (77)*	*1,561 (123)*	*108 (29)*	*604*	*2,762*
Cavalry Corps*	79 (10)	331 (17)	9	55	474
Corps Field & Horse Artillery	48 (6)	178 (10)	20 (8)	215	461
Grand Total	*1,515 (254)*	*4,957 (354)*	*457 (93)*	*5,758*	*12,687*

*Figures include the cavalry action at Todd's Tavern on May 7.

TABLE 9. Casualties during Sheridan's Richmond Raid, May 9–24, 1864

	Killed	*Wounded*	*Wounded & Captured*	*Missing*	*Total*
Cavalry Corps	54 (10)	244 (16)	7 (2)	161	466
Other Units					
Field & Horse Artillery	2 (1)	17	0	13	32
Infantry (Richmond Garrison)	16 (5)	54 (6)	0	1	71
Pickett's Division	6 (3)	38 (4)	1 (1)	1	46
Misc. Troops (Heth's Division)	0	0	0	1	1
Grand Total	*78 (19)*	*353 (26)*	*8 (3)*	*177*	*616*

TABLE 10. Casualties at Wilson's Wharf (Kennon's Landing), May 24, 1864

	Killed	*Wounded*	*Wounded & Captured*	*Missing*	*Total*
Cavalry Corps	24 (7)	62 (3)	1	2	89

TABLE 11. Casualties at the North Anna, May 20–26, 1864*

	Killed	*Wounded*	*Wounded & Captured*	*Missing*	*Total*
First Corps					
Kershaw's Division	8	53 (3)	1	63	125
Field's Division	10 (1)	43 (3)	0	28	81
Pickett's Division	3	25	3	78	109
Total	*21 (1)*	*121 (6)*	*4*	*169*	*315*
Second Corps					
Early's Division	0	9	0	61	70
Gordon's Division	0	2	0	8	10
Rodes's Division	10 (3)	51 (7)	1 (1)	24	86
Total	*10 (3)*	*62 (7)*	*1 (1)*	*93*	*166*
Third Corps					
Heth's Division	4 (1)	30 (2)	1	67	102
Wilcox's Division	56 (9)	348 (42)	10 (3)	317	731
Mahone's Division	22 (3)	75 (9)	0	52	149
Total	*82 (13)*	*453 (53)*	*11 (3)*	*436*	*982*
Breckinridge's Division (attached to Second Corps)	0	6	0	1	7
Cavalry Corps	6	17 (1)	2	24	49
Corps Field & Horse Artillery	5 (1)	27 (2)	0	1	33
Grand Total	*124 (18)*	*686 (69)*	*18 (4)*	*724*	*1,552*

*These figures include the actions at Guinea Station and Milford Station.

TABLE 12. Casualties at Totopotomoy (Bethesda Church), May 27–31, 1864*

	Killed	*Wounded*	*Wounded & Captured*	*Missing*	*Total*
First Corps					
Kershaw's Division	0	5	0	2	7
Field's Division	10 (2)	25	0	3	38
Pickett's Division	3 (1)	10	0	2	15
Total	*13 (3)*	*40*	*0*	*7*	*60*
Second Corps					
Ramseur's Division	60 (20)	139 (9)	30 (8)	72	301
Gordon's Division	2	14	0	5	21
Rodes's Division	41 (7)	186 (14)	3 (1)	48	278
Total	*103 (27)*	*339 (23)*	*33 (9)*	*125*	*600*
Third Corps					
Heth's Division	1 (1)	4	1	3	9
Wilcox's Division	7 (3)	21 (2)	0	9	37
Mahone's Division	5 (3)	11	0	9	25
Total	*13 (7)*	*36 (2)*	*1*	*21*	*71*
Unassigned Units					
Breckinridge's Division	7 (1)	28 (1)	1 (1)	37	73
Maryland Line	0	1	0	0	1
Total	*7 (1)*	*29 (1)*	*1 (1)*	*37*	*74*
Cavalry Corps	120 (35)	412 (37)	48 (17)	179	759
Corps Field & Horse Artillery	7	22	0	0	29
Grand Total	*263 (73)*	*878 (63)*	*83 (27)*	*369*	*1,593*

*Also includes several cavalry actions.

TABLE 13. Casualties at Cold Harbor, May 31–June 12, 1864

	Killed	Wounded	Wounded & Captured	Missing	Total
First Corps					
Kershaw's Division	99 (22)	353 (14)	11	235	698
Field's Division	68 (5)	178 (5)	0	9	255
Pickett's Division	36 (11)	239 (14)	3 (1)	31	309
Total	*203 (38)*	*770 (33)*	*14 (1)*	*275*	*1,262*
Second Corps					
Ramseur's Division	58 (9)	258 (18)	1	30	347
Gordon's Division	19 (7)	63 (2)	0	4	86
Rodes's Division	50 (10)	222 (19)	1 (1)	8	281
Total	*127 (26)*	*543 (39)*	*2 (1)*	*42*	*714*
Third Corps					
Heth's Division	87 (17)	417 (45)	6 (1)	53	563
Wilcox's Division	14 (7)	71 (10)	0	15	100
Mahone's Division	102 (12)	433 (38)	1	22	558
Total	*203 (36)*	*921 (93)*	*7 (1)*	*90*	*1,221*
Unassigned Units					
Hoke's Division	152 (23)	594 (49)	34 (6)	464	1,244
Breckinridge's Division	15 (3)	107 (6)	7	186	315
Maryland Line	6	37 (3)	0	0	43
Total	*173 (26)*	*738 (58)*	*41 (6)*	*650*	*1,602*
Cavalry Corps	34 (7)	163 (11)	2	54	253
Corps Field & Horse Artillery	48 (8)	175 (19)	0	12	235
Grand Total	*788 (141)*	*3,310 (253)*	*66 (9)*	*1,123*	*5,287*

TABLE 14. Casualties during Sheridan's Trevilian Raid, June 7–12, 1864

	Killed	*Wounded*	*Wounded & Captured*	*Missing*	*Total*
Cavalry Corps	80 (6)	362 (40)	1	318	761
Horse Artillery	3	22 (3)	0	0	25
Misc. Infantry (Heth's Division)	0	0	0	1	1
Grand Total	*83 (6)*	*384 (43)*	*1*	*319*	*787*

TABLE 15. Summary of Overland Campaign Casualties in the Army of Northern Virginia

	Killed	*Wounded*	*Wounded & Captured*	*Missing*	*Total*
First Corps					
Corps Staff	0	3	0	0	3
Kershaw's Division	396 (60)	1,615 (107)	33	413	2,457
Field's Division	438 (66)	2,025 (103)	40 (5)	220	2,723
Pickett's Division	49 (15)	312 (18)	7 (1)	112	480
Total	*883 (141)*	*3,955 (228)*	*80 (6)*	*745*	*5,663*
Second Corps					
Corps Staff	0	2	0	0	2
Johnson's/Gordon's Division	312 (53)	1,044 (52)	131 (11)	3,117	4,604
Early's/Ramseur's Division	433 (80)	1,447 (96)	130 (20)	883	2,893
Rodes's Division	625 (111)	2,273 (155)	161 (37)	1,683	4,742
Total	*1,370 (244)*	*4,766 (303)*	*422 (68)*	*5,683*	*12,241*
Third Corps					
Corps Staff	0	1	0	0	1
Heth's Division	417 (68)	2,497 (159)	47 (11)	455	3,416
Wilcox's Division	467 (77)	2,078 (190)	127 (29)	1,189	3,861
Anderson's/Mahone's Division	443 (67)	1,641 (119)	57 (12)	350	2,491
Total	*1,327 (212)*	*6,217 (468)*	*231 (52)*	*1,994*	*9,769*

Additional Infantry Units					
Hoke's Division	152 (23)	594 (49)	34 (6)	464	1,244
Breckinridge's Division	22 (4)	141 (7)	8 (1)	224	395
Md. Line & Rich. Garrison	22 (5)	92 (9)	0	1	115
Total	*196 (32)*	*827 (65)*	*42 (7)*	*689*	*1,754*
Cavalry Corps & Attached Units	352 (68)	1,604 (77)	70 (19)	491	2,517
Field & Horse Artillery	117 (17)	448 (31)	20 (8)	241	826
Grand Army Total 1	*4,245 (714)*	*17,817 (1,172)*	*865 (160)*	*9,843*	*32,770*
*Grand Army Total 2**	*4,352 (727)*	*18,263 (1,218)*	*867 (160)*	*10,164*	*33,646*

*These figures include the actions at Wilson's Wharf (Kenon's Landing) and Trevilian Station.

TABLE 16. Infantry Strength of the First Corps at Selected Points during the Campaign

	At Wild. 5/5	At Spot. 5/8	Aft. Spot. 5/21	At CH 5/31	Aft. CH 6/12
Kershaw's Division					
Kershaw's Brigade	1,590	1,365	1,310	2,100	1,955
Humphreys's Brigade	940	685	635	650	620
Wofford's Brigade	1,615	1,440	1,405	1,390	1,180
Bryan's Brigade	1,025	830	860	845	710
Total	*5,170*	*4,320*	*4,210*	*4,985*	*4,465*
Field's Division					
Gregg's Brigade	850	475	490	515	520
Jenkins's/Bratton's Brigade	1,590	1,240	1,265	1,285	1,325
Anderson's Brigade	1,390	1,120	1,110	1,110	1,105
Benning's Brigade	995	790	765	770	770
Law's Brigade	1,255	1,025	1,015	1,010	955
Total	*6,080*	*4,650*	*4,645*	*4,690*	*4,675*
Pickett's Division					
Kemper's Brigade			1,110	1,040	1,060
Hunton's Brigade			1,660	1,575	1,380
Barton's Brigade			1,210	1,210	1,260
Corse's Brigade			1,355	1,345	1,310
Total			*5,335*	*5,170*	*5,010*
Corps Total	*11,250*	*8,970*	*14,190*	*14,845*	*14,150*

TABLE 17. Infantry Strength of the Second Corps at Selected Points during the Campaign

	At Wild. 5/5	At Spot. 5/8	Aft. Spot. 5/21	At CH 5/31	Aft. CH 6/12
Johnson's/Gordon's Division					
Walker's (Stonewall) Brigade	1,320	1,075	285	300	300
Jones's Brigade	1,850	1,220	310	310	310
Steuart's Brigade	1,610	1,375	140	130	150
Stafford's Brigade	705	560	225	200	170
Total	*5,485*	*4,230*	*960*	*940*	*930*
Early's/Ramseur's Division					
Hays's Brigade	900	725	460	445	420
Gordon's/Evans's Brigade	2,270	1,975	1,290	1,700	1,510
Pegram's Brigade	1,520	1,350	875	600	575
Hoke's Brigade			1,360	1,310	1,170
Total	*4,690*	*4,050*	*3,985*	*4,055*	*3,675*
Rodes's Division					
Ramseur's Brigade	1,440	1,415	760	690	655
Daniel's/Grimes's Brigade	1,500	1,420	1,175	995	910
Doles's Brigade	1,365	1,105	735	705	660
Battle's Brigade	1,810	1,540	1,060	965	850
Johnston's Brigade	1,320	1,315	590	590	570
Total	*7,435*	*6,795*	*4,320*	*3,945*	*3,645*
Corps Total	*17,610*	*15,075*	*9,265*	*8,940*	*8,250*

TABLE 18. Infantry Strength of the Third Corps at Selected Points during the Campaign

	At Wild. 5/5	At Spot. 5/8	Aft. Spot. 5/21	At CH 5/31	Aft. CH 6/12
Heth's Division					
Cooke's Brigade	1,960	1,190	1,095	1,065	1,110
Kirkland's Brigade	2,150	1,695	1,605	1,605	1,470
Davis's Brigade	1,690	1,125	1,030	1,055	975
Walker's/Fry's Brigade					
Va. Units	895	750	725	700	665
Ala./Tenn. Units	755	535	490	460	450
Total	*7,450*	*5,295*	*4,945*	*4,885*	*4,670*
Wilcox's Division					
Lane's Brigade	2,350	1,960	1,430	1,265	1,235
McGowan's Brigade	2,230	1,775	1,380	1,180	1,230
Scales's Brigade	1,735	1,385	1,305	1,090	1,070
Thomas's Brigade	1,600	1,215	1,050	835	825
Total	*7,915*	*6,335*	*5,165*	*4,370*	*4,360*
Anderson's/Mahone's Division					
Perrin's/Sanders's Brigade	1,635	1,390	1,240	1,200	1,180
Mahone's Brigade	1,805	1,660	1,390	1,350	1,300
Harris's Brigade	1,395	1,350	970	955	895
Wright's Brigade	1,685	1,690	1,500	1,480	1,460
Perry's Brigade*	610	370	370	350	325
Finegan's Brigade				1,270	940
Total	*7,130*	*6,460*	*5,470*	*6,605*	*6,100*
Corps Total	*22,495*	*18,090*	*15,580*	*15,860*	*15,130*

*Merged with Finegan's Brigade in late May 1864.

TABLE 19. Infantry Strength of Miscellaneous Units at Selected Points during the Campaign

	At Wild. 5/5	At Spot. 5/8	Aft. Spot. 5/21	At CH 5/31	Aft. CH 6/12
Hoke's Division					
Clingman's Brigade				1,610	900
Hagood's Brigade				1,580	1,740
Colquitt's Brigade				1,720	1,545
Martin's Brigade				1,890	1,640
Total				*6,800*	*5,825*
Breckinridge's Division					
Echols's Brigade			1,345	1,280	970
Wharton's Brigade			1,040	1,030	960
Total			*2,385*	*2,310*	*1,930*
Army of Northern Virginia Total	*51,355*	*42,135*	*41,420**	*48,755*	*45,285*

*This figure includes Breckinridge's Division, Pickett's Division, and Lewis's Brigade (reinforced). Prior to their arrival, Lee's infantry strength had fallen to about 31,500 men.

TABLE 20. Humphreys's (Mississippi) Brigade*

	F&S	*13th Rgt.*	*17th Rgt.*	*18th Rgt.*	*21st Rgt.*	*Total*
Wilderness						
KIA		14 (3)	2 (1)	15 (4)	26 (2)	57 (10)
WIA	1	48 (5)	41	64 (10)	89 (6)	243 (21)
W&C		0	1	2	1	4
MIA		0	0	1	3	4
Total	*1*	*62*	*44*	*82*	*119*	*308*
Spotsylvania						
KIA	1	2	0	1	0	4
WIA		16 (1)	12 (1)	5	10 (1)	43 (3)
W&C		1	1	1	1	4
MIA		12	16	16	7	51
Total	*1*	*31*	*29*	*23*	*18*	*102*
North Anna						
KIA		0	1	0	0	1
WIA		0	1	1	0	2
W&C		0	0	0	0	0
MIA		1	2	0	0	3
Total		*1*	*4*	*1*	*0*	*6*
Totopotomoy						
KIA		0	0	0	0	0
WIA		0	0	1	0	1
W&C		0	0	0	0	0
MIA		0	0	0	0	0
Total		*0*	*0*	*1*	*0*	*1*
Cold Harbor						
KIA		5 (2)	3 (1)	3	6	17 (3)
WIA		11 (1)	12	10	9	42 (1)
W&C		0	0	0	0	0
MIA		1	0	0	0	1
Total		*17*	*15*	*13*	*15*	*60*
Campaign Total	*2*	*111 (108)*	*92*	*120*	*152 (150)*	*477 (472)*

*Abbreviations used in this and the following tables are as follows: KIA, killed in action; WIA, wounded in action; W&C, wounded and captured; MIA, missing in action. For an explanation of the numbers in parentheses in this and the following tables, see pages 19 and 27 of the text.

TABLE 21. Kershaw's (South Carolina) Brigade

	F&S	*2nd Rgt.*	*3rd Rgt.*	*7th Rgt.*	*8th Rgt.*	*15th Rgt.*	*3rd Bn.*	*20th Rgt.*	*Totals*
Wilderness									
KIA		11 (1)	18 (5)	20 (4)	0	11 (3)	6 (1)		66 (14)
WIA		39 (1)	56 (8)	54 (3)	1	58 (9)	26 (1)		234 (22)
W&C		0	2	1	0	1	0		4
MIA		2	5	3	0	1	0		11
Total		*52*	*81*	*78*	*1*	*71*	*32*		*315*
Spotsylvania									
KIA		8	5 (4)	6	6 (1)	10 (1)	12 (1)		47 (7)
WIA		18 (2)	21 (1)	24 (1)	8 (1)	34 (6)	26 (1)		131 (12)
W&C		0	0	0	0	3	0		3
MIA	1	0	0	0	6	2	1		10
Total	*1*	*26*	*26*	*30*	*20*	*49*	*39*		*191*
North Anna									
KIA		0	1	1	1	1	1		5
WIA		4 (1)	8	13 (1)	1	3	4		33 (2)
W&C		0	1	0	0	0	0		1
MIA		1	26	11	1	1	14		54
Total		*5*	*36*	*25*	*3*	*5*	*19*		*93*

(continued)

TABLE 21. Kershaw's (South Carolina) Brigade (*continued*)

	F&S	*2nd Rgt.*	*3rd Rgt.*	*7th Rgt.*	*8th Rgt.*	*15th Rgt.*	*3rd Bn.*	*20th Rgt.*	*Totals*
Totopotomoy									
KIA		0	0	0	0	0	0		0
WIA		0	0	0	0	0	0		0
W&C		0	0	0	0	0	0		0
MIA		0	0	0	2	0	0		2
Total		*0*	*0*	*0*	*2*	*0*	*0*		*2*
Cold Harbor									
KIA		8 (1)	6 (3)	10	3 (2)	2 (2)	2	16 (3)	47 (11)
WIA		26 (2)	20	20 (1)	9 (1)	21 (2)	8	62	166 (6)
W&C		1	0	0	0	0	0	0	1
MIA		1	0	1	0	1	0	2	5
Total		*36*	*26*	*31*	*12*	*24*	*10*	*80*	*219*
Campaign Total	*1*	*119 (118)*	*169 (164)*	*164 (163)*	*38*	*149 (146)*	*100 (98)*	*80*	*820 (808)*

TABLE 22. Wofford's (Georgia) Brigade

	F&S	*16th Rgt.*	*18th Rgt.*	*24th Rgt.*	*Cobb's Legion*	*Phillips's Legion*	*3rd Bn. SS*	*Total*
Wilderness								
KIA		12 (2)	8	13	5	6	0	44 (2)
WIA		46 (5)	30 (2)	44 (2)	33 (3)	39 (2)	19 (1)	211 (15)
W&C		1	1	0	0	1	0	3
MIA		6	1	1	4	0	1	13
Total		*65*	*40*	*58*	*42*	*46*	*20*	*271*
Spotsylvania								
KIA		10	6 (1)	6	4	8 (1)	3	37 (2)
WIA	1	17 (2)	16 (2)	29 (3)	17 (1)	20 (2)	15	115 (1)
W&C		0	0	0	0	0	0	0
MIA		1	6	1	1	0	2	11
Total	*1*	*28*	*28*	*36*	*22*	*28*	*20*	*163*
North Anna								
KIA		0	1	0	0	0	0	1
WIA		0	0	0	3	3	6	12
W&C		0	0	0	0	0	0	0
MIA		1	0	0	2	0	0	3
Total		*1*	*1*	*0*	*5*	*3*	*6*	*16*

(continued)

TABLE 22. Wofford's (Georgia) Brigade (*continued*)

	F&S	*16th Rgt.*	*18th Rgt.*	*24th Rgt.*	*Cobb's Legion*	*Phillips's Legion*	*3rd Bn. SS*	*Total*
Totopotomoy								
KIA		0	0	0	0	0	0	0
WIA		0	1	0	0	1	0	2
W&C		0	0	0	0	0	0	0
MIA		0	0	0	0	0	0	0
Total		*0*	*1*	*0*	*0*	*1*	*0*	*2*
Cold Harbor								
KIA		5 (2)	2	5 (1)	1	1	1	15 (3)
WIA		10 (2)	24 (1)	14 (2)	15 (1)	12	4	79 (6)
W&C		1	1	6	0	0	1	9
MIA		50	39	47	7	20	0	163
Total		*66*	*66*	*72*	*23*	*33*	*6*	*266*
Campaign Total	*1*	*160 (158)*	*136 (135)*	*166 (163)*	*92 (91)*	*111 (110)*	*52*	*718 (710)*

Table 23. Bryan's (Georgia) Brigade

	F&S	*10th Rgt.*	*50th Rgt.*	*51st Rgt.*	*53rd Rgt.*	*Total*
Wilderness						
KIA		6	4	3	15 (1)	28 (1)
WIA	1	67 (1)	37 (2)	33 (2)	63 (1)	201 (6)
W&C		2	1	0	0	3
MIA		5	3	1	2	11
Total	*1*	*80*	*45*	*37*	*80*	*243*
Spotsylvania						
KIA		4 (2)	1	0	1	6 (2)
WIA		7	6	4	7 (1)	24 (1)
W&C		0	0	0	1	1
MIA		0	0	0	2	2
Total		*11*	*7*	*4*	*11*	*33*
North Anna						
KIA		0	0	0	1	1
WIA		2	1	1 (1)	2	6 (1)
W&C		0	0	0	0	0
MIA		0	1	0	2	3
Total		*2*	*2*	*1*	*5*	*10*
Totopotomoy						
KIA		0	0	0	0	0
WIA		0	0	0	2	2
W&C		0	0	0	0	0
MIA		0	0	0	0	0
Total		*0*	*0*	*0*	*2*	*2*
Cold Harbor						
KIA		5 (2)	6 (1)	5	4 (2)	20 (5)
WIA		25	15	10	16 (1)	66 (1)
W&C		0	0	1	0	1
MIA		0	14	32	20	66
Total		*30*	*35*	*48*	*40*	*153*
Campaign Total	*1*	*123 (122)*	*89*	*90 (88)*	*138 (136)*	*441 (436)*

TABLE 24. Gregg's (Texas) Brigade

	F&S	3rd Ark. Rgt.	1st Tex. Rgt.	4th Tex. Rgt.	5th Tex. Rgt.	Total
Wilderness						
KIA	2	11 (2)	22 (1)	22 (2)	15 (2)	72 (7)
WIA	1	65 (4)	91 (5)	99 (4)	96 (1)	352 (14)
W&C		10 (3)	3	0	1	14 (3)
MIA		9	6	3	1	19
Total	*3*	*95*	*122*	*124*	*113*	*457*
Spotsylvania						
KIA		3 (2)	4 (1)	4	5	16 (3)
WIA		7 (1)	12	4	3	26 (1)
W&C		0	0	0	0	0
MIA		1	2	2	1	6
Total		*11*	*18*	*10*	*9*	*48*
North Anna						
KIA		0	0	0	0	0
WIA		0	1	0	0	1
W&C		0	0	0	0	0
MIA		1	0	1	1	3
Total		*1*	*1*	*1*	*1*	*4*
Totopotomoy						
KIA		0	0	0	1 (1)	1
WIA		0	0	0	0	0
W&C		0	0	0	0	0
MIA		0	0	0	0	0
Total		*0*	*0*	*0*	*1*	*1*
Cold Harbor						
KIA		1	0	2	5	8
WIA		4	4	7	14	29
W&C		0	0	0	0	0
MIA		0	0	1	0	1
Total		*5*	*4*	*10*	*19*	*38*
Campaign Total	*3*	*112 (110)*	*145*	*145*	*143 (140)*	*548 (543)*

TABLE 25. Jenkins's/Bratton's (South Carolina) Brigade

	F&S	*1st Rgt.*	*2nd Rifles*	*5th Rgt.*	*6th Rgt.*	*Palmetto SS*	*Total*
Wilderness							
KIA	1	18 (3)	9 (2)	16 (2)	8 (1)	8 (2)	60 (10)
WIA	1	87 (3)	76 (2)	86 (5)	63 (1)	65 (4)	378 (15)
W&C		0	1	5	0	0	6
MIA		1	0	14	0	1	16
Total	*2*	*106*	*86*	*121*	*71*	*74*	*460*
Spotsylvania							
KIA		2 (1)	4 (1)	0	4 (2)	3 (1)	13 (5)
WIA		18 (2)	20 (1)	11	21	31 (2)	101 (5)
W&C		0	0	0	0	0	0
MIA		0	0	1	0	0	1
Total		*20*	*24*	*12*	*25*	*34*	*115*
Milford Station							
MIA		1					1
North Anna							
KIA		0	1	0	2	1	4
WIA		2	4 (2)	3	0	3	12 (2)
W&C		0	0	0	0	0	0
MIA		0	2	2	2	0	6
Total		*2*	*7*	*5*	*4*	*4*	*22*
Totopotomoy							
KIA		0	0	1	0	2	3
WIA		0	2	0	3	5	10
W&C		0	0	0	0	0	0
MIA		0	0	0	0	0	0
Total		*0*	*2*	*1*	*3*	*7*	*13*
Cold Harbor							
KIA		0	3	2	1	3 (2)	9 (2)
WIA		1	2	1	2	8	14
W&C		0	0	0	0	0	0
MIA		0	2	0	0	3	5
Total		*1*	*7*	*3*	*3*	*14*	*28*
Campaign Total	*2*	*130 (129)*	*126*	*142 (138)*	*106 (105)*	*133 (130)*	*639 (630)*

TABLE 26. Benning's (Georgia) Brigade

	F&S	*2nd Rgt.*	*15th Rgt.*	*17th Rgt.*	*20th Rgt.*	*Total*
Wilderness						
KIA		13 (4)	9 (5)	13 (3)	10 (4)	45 (16)
WIA	1	57	45	61 (1)	73 (6)	237 (7)
W&C		2	0	0	0	2
MIA		0	2	0	2	4
Total	*1*	*72*	*56*	*74*	*85*	*288*
Spotsylvania						
KIA		1	3 (2)	2	3	9 (2)
WIA		5	26 (3)	10 (1)	25	66 (4)
W&C		0	0	0	0	0
MIA		0	3	0	1	4
Total		*6*	*32*	*12*	*29*	*79*
North Anna						
KIA		0	0	0	0	0
WIA		0	1	0	3	4
W&C		0	0	0	0	0
MIA		0	0	1	1	2
Total		*0*	*1*	*1*	*4*	*6*
Totopotomoy						
KIA		2	1 (1)	1	0	4 (1)
WIA		0	2	2 (1)	2	6 (1)
W&C		0	0	0	0	0
MIA		0	1	0	1	2
Total		*2*	*4*	*3*	*3*	*12*
Cold Harbor						
KIA		1	1 (1)	0	0	2 (1)
WIA		4	7 (2)	4	4	19 (2)
W&C		0	0	0	0	0
MIA		0	0	2	0	2
Total		*5*	*8*	*6*	*4*	*23*
Campaign Total	*1*	*85 (84)*	*101 (100)*	*96*	*125 (123)*	*408 (404)*

TABLE 27. Law's (Alabama) Brigade

	F&S	*4th Rgt.*	*15th Rgt.*	*44th Rgt.*	*47th Rgt.*	*48th Rgt.*	*Total*
Wilderness							
KIA		14 (1)	6 (1)	8	15 (2)	6 (1)	49 (5)
WIA		55 (5)	40 (3)	40 (3)	56 (8)	23 (3)	214 (22)
W&C		2	0	0	0	1	3
MIA		5	12	8	15	8	48
Total		*76*	*58*	*56*	*86*	*38*	*314*
Spotsylvania							
KIA		0	6 (1)	10	4 (2)	2	22 (3)
WIA		6	15	26 (3)	17 (2)	5	69 (5)
W&C		0	0	1 (1)	1	0	2 (1)
MIA		1	1	0	0	1	3
Total		*7*	*22*	*37*	*22*	*8*	*96*
North Anna							
KIA		0	1	0	2 (1)	0	3 (1)
WIA		6 (1)	2	5	0	4	17 (1)
W&C		0	0	0	0	0	0
MIA		0	1	3	2	1	7
Total		*6*	*4*	*8*	*4*	*5*	*27*
Totopotomoy							
KIA		0	0	0	0	0	0
WIA		0	2	0	1	1	4
W&C		0	0	0	0	0	0
MIA		0	0	0	0	0	0
Total		*0*	*2*	*0*	*1*	*1*	*4*
Cold Harbor							
KIA		4	6 (1)	7	5 (1)	3	25 (2)
WIA	1	14 (1)	14	24 (1)	6	6 (1)	65 (3)
W&C		0	0	0	0	0	0
MIA		0	0	0	0	0	0
Total	*1*	*18*	*20*	*31*	*11*	*9*	*90*
Campaign Total	*1*	*107 (106)*	*106 (105)*	*132 (131)*	*124*	*61*	*531 (528)*

TABLE 28. Anderson's (Georgia) Brigade

	F&S	7th Rgt.	8th Rgt.	9th Rgt.	11th Rgt.	59th Rgt.	Total
Wilderness							
KIA		8 (1)	9 (1)	19 (3)	9 (1)	3	48 (6)
WIA		57 (2)	46 (2)	66 (2)	55 (3)	46 (6)	270 (15)
W&C		0	3 (1)	6	2	2	13 (1)
MIA		5	17	12	25	9	68
Total		*70*	*75*	*103*	*91*	*60*	*399*
Spotsylvania							
KIA		3 (1)	1	2	1	9	16 (1)
WIA		10	11	11	9 (2)	25 (5)	66 (7)
W&C		0	0	0	0	0	0
MIA		1	2	3	1	4	11
Total		*14*	*14*	*16*	*11*	*38*	*93*
North Anna							
KIA		1	0	1	0	1	3
WIA		5	0	2	1	1	9
W&C		0	0	0	0	0	0
MIA		0	1	1	3	4	9
Total		*6*	*1*	*4*	*4*	*6*	*21*
Totopotomoy							
KIA		0	0	1	0	1	2
WIA		0	5	0	0	0	5
W&C		0	0	0	0	0	0
MIA		0	1	0	0	0	1
Total		*0*	*6*	*1*	*0*	*1*	*8*
Cold Harbor							
KIA		5	2	7	6	4	24
WIA	1	12	12	3	8	15	51
W&C		0	0	0	0	0	0
MIA		1	0	0	0	0	1
Total	*1*	*18*	*14*	*10*	*14*	*19*	*76*
Campaign Total	*1*	*108 (107)*	*110 (109)*	*134 (133)*	*120*	*124 (123)*	*597 (593)*

TABLE 29. Kemper's (Virginia) Brigade

	1st Rgt.	*3rd Rgt.*	*7th Rgt.*	*11th Rgt.*	*24th Rgt.*	*Total*
Milford Station						
KIA	0	0	2	0	0	2
WIA	0	0	7	13	0	20
W&C	0	0	0	3	0	3
MIA	0	0	26	42	0	68
Total	*0*	*0*	*35*	*58*	*0*	*93*
North Anna						
KIA	0	0	0	0	0	0
WIA	0	0	0	0	0	0
W&C	0	0	0	0	0	0
MIA	0	0	1	0	0	1
Total	*0*	*0*	*1*	*0*	*0*	*1*
Totopotomoy						
KIA	0	0	1	0	0	1
WIA	0	0	0	0	0	0
W&C	0	0	0	0	0	0
MIA	0	0	0	0	0	0
Total	*0*	*0*	*1*	*0*	*0*	*1*
Cold Harbor						
KIA	0	1	2	0	1	4
WIA	4	5	1	4 (1)	5	19 (1)
W&C	0	0	0	0	0	0
MIA	0	2	1	0	0	3
Total	*4*	*8*	*4*	*4*	*6*	*26*
Campaign Total	*4*	*8*	*41*	*62*	*6*	*121*
(Drewry's Bluff)						
KIA	10 (4)	0	4 (2)	29 (13)	42 (9)	85 (28)
WIA	17 (2)	1	40	91	106	255 (2)
W&C	0	0	0	0	1 (1)	1 (1)
MIA	4	0	2	0	6	12
Total	*31*	*1*	*46*	*120*	*155*	*353*

TABLE 30. Hunton's (Virginia) Brigade

	F&S	*8th Rgt.*	*18th Rgt.*	*19th Rgt.*	*28th Rgt.*	*32nd Rgt.*	*56th Rgt.*	*Total*
Brook Church (Sheridan's 1st Raid)								
KIA		0	w/Corse	2 (1)	0	4 (2)	0	6 (3)
WIA		0		19 (2)	0	19 (2)	0	38 (4)
W&C		0		0	0	1	0	1
MIA		0		0	0	1	0	1
Total		*0*		*21*	*0*	*25*	*0*	*46*
North Anna								
KIA		0	0	0	0	To Corse	1	1
WIA		0	0	0	3		0	3
W&C		0	0	0	0		0	0
MIA		0	1	0	1		0	2
Total		*0*	*1*	*0*	*4*		*1*	*6*
Totopotomoy								
KIA		0	0	1	1 (1)		0	2 (1)
WIA		0	0	0	7		0	7
W&C		0	0	0	0		0	0
MIA		0	0	0	0		0	0
Total		*0*	*0*	*1*	*8*		*0*	*9*

Cold Harbor								
KIA	1	2	2	6 (1)	5 (1)		2 (2)	18 (4)
WIA	1	11	13	44 (4)	46 (3)		44 (2)	159 (9)
W&C		0	0	0	0		1 (1)	1 (1)
MIA		1	2	0	1		0	4
Total	2	14	17	50	52		47	182
Campaign Total	*2*	*14*	*18*	*72*	*64*	*25*	*48*	*243*
(Drewry's Bluff)								
MIA				3		1	4	
Total			*32* (w/Corse)					

TABLE 31. Barton's (Virginia) Brigade

	9th Rgt.	*14th Rgt.*	*38th Rgt.*	*53rd Rgt.*	*57th Rgt.*	*Total*
Milford Station						
MIA	2					2
North Anna						
KIA	0	0	0	0	0	0
WIA	0	0	0	2	0	2
W&C	0	0	0	0	0	0
MIA	0	1	1	1	0	3
Total	*0*	*1*	*1*	*3*	*0*	*5*
Totopotomoy						
KIA	0	0	0	0	0	0
WIA	0	0	0	0	1	1
W&C	0	0	0	0	0	0
MIA	0	1	0	0	1	2
Total	*0*	*1*	*0*	*0*	*2*	*3*
Cold Harbor						
KIA	0	1 (1)	0	0	0	1 (1)
WIA	3	2	2	2	2	11
W&C	0	0	0	0	0	0
MIA	1	0	0	0	0	1
Total	*4*	*3*	*2*	*2*	*2*	*13*
Campaign Total	*6*	*5*	*3*	*5*	*4*	*23*
(Chester Station and Drewry's Bluff)						
KIA	21 (2)	30 (8)	26 (8)	11 (4)	13 (5)	101 (27)
WIA	84 (11)	132 (7)	124 (9)	67	74 (2)	481 (29)
W&C	0	0	1	1	0	2
MIA	1	15	8	4	3	31
Total	*106*	*177*	*159*	*83*	*90*	*615*

TABLE 32. Corse's (Virginia) Brigade

	F&S	*15th Rgt.*	*17th Rgt.*	*18th Rgt.*	*29th Rgt.*	*30th Rgt.*	*32nd Rgt.*	*Total*
Brook Church (Sheridan's 1st Raid)								
Total							*(25, w/Hunton)*	
Spotsylvania								
KIA			1					1
Total			*1*					*1*
Milford Station								
MIA				To Hunton		1		1
Total						*1*		*1*
North Anna								
KIA		0	0		0	0	0	0
WIA		0	0		0	0	0	0
W&C		0	0		0	0	0	0
MIA		0	0		1	0	0	1
Total		*0*	*0*		*1*	*0*	*0*	*1*
Totopotomoy								
KIA		0	0		0	0	0	0
WIA		0	0		2	0	0	2
W&C		0	0		0	0	0	0
MIA		0	0		0	0	0	0
Total		*0*	*0*		*2*	*0*	*0*	*2*

(continued)

TABLE 32. Corse's (Virginia) Brigade (*continued*)

	F&S	*15th Rgt.*	*17th Rgt.*	*18th Rgt.*	*29th Rgt.*	*30th Rgt.*	*32nd Rgt.*	*Total*
Cold Harbor								
KIA		1	4 (2)		2 (1)	1	5 (3)	13 (6)
WIA		8 (2)	4		21	13 (2)	4	50 (4)
W&C		0	0		2	0	0	2
MIA		1	0		21	1	0	23
Total		*10*	*8*		*46*	*15*	*9*	*88*
Campaign Total		*10*	*9*		*49*	*16*	*9*	*93*
(Drewry's Bluff)								
KIA		24 (5)	13 (6)	4 (1)	29 (4)	11 (1)		81 (19)
WIA	2	99 (9)	24 (3)	27 (6)	104 (5)	65 (1)		321 (24)
W&C		0	1	0	1	0		2
MIA	1	2	0	1	13	0		17
Total	*3*	*125*	*38*	*32*	*147*	*76*		*421*

TABLE 33. First Corps Artillery

1. CABELL'S BATTALION

	Manly's (N.C.) Btty.	*McCarthy's (Va.) Btty.*	*Carlton's (Ga.) Btty.*	*Callaway's (Ga.) Btty.*	*Bn. Total*
Wilderness					
	Not in Action, No Loss				
Spotsylvania					
KIA	1	0	2	0	3
WIA	4	5 (1)	7	0	16 (1)
MIA	0	0	0	0	0
Total	*5*	*5*	*9*	*0*	*19*
North Anna					
KIA	0	0	0	1 (1)	1 (1)
WIA	3	0	0	0	3
Total	*3*	*0*	*0*	*1*	*4*
Totopotomoy					
KIA	0	1	0	0	1
WIA	0	0	0	0	0
Total	*0*	*1*	*0*	*0*	*1*
Cold Harbor					
KIA	1	1	0	2 (1)	4 (1)
WIA	11 (1)	4	2	10 (2)	27 (3)
MIA	0	0	0	0	0
Total	*12*	*5*	*2*	*12*	*31*
Campaign Total	*20*	*11*	*11*	*13*	*55*

2. HASKELL'S BATTALION

	Garden's (S.C.) Btty.	*Ramsey's (N.C.) Btty.*	*Flanner's (N.C.) Btty.*	*Lamkin's (Va.) Btty.*	*Bn. Total*
Wilderness					
	Not in Action, No Loss				
Spotsylvania					
KIA	0	0	2	0	2
WIA	2 (2)	2	11	0	15 (2)
Total	*2*	*2*	*13*	*0*	*17*

(continued)

2. HASKELL'S BATTALION (*continued*)

	Garden's (S.C.) Btty.	*Ramsey's (N.C.) Btty.*	*Flanner's (N.C.) Btty.*	*Lamkin's (Va.) Btty.*	*Bn. Total*
North Anna					
KIA	0	0	0	0	0
WIA	0	2	0	2	4
Total	*0*	*2*	*0*	*2*	*4*
Totopotomoy					
	Not in Action, No Loss				
Cold Harbor					
KIA	0	0	0	0	0
WIA	4	1 (1)	1	1	7 (1)
MIA	0	0	0	0	0
Total	*4*	*1*	*1*	*1*	*7*
Campaign Total	*6*	*5*	*14*	*3*	*28*

3. HUGER'S BATTALION

	Moody's (La.) Btty.	*Fickling's (S.C.) Btty.*	*Woolfolk's (Va.) Btty.*	*Taylor's (Va.) Btty.*	*Parker's (Va.) Btty.*	*Smith's (Va.) Btty.*	*Total*
Wilderness							
	Not in Action, No Loss						
Spotsylvania							
KIA	2	2	1	0	0	0	5
WIA	6 (1)	6 (1)	2	3 (1)	6	3	26 (3)
MIA	0	0	0	0	0	0	0
Total	*8*	*8*	*3*	*3*	*6*	*3*	*31*
North Anna							
KIA	0	0	0	0	0	0	0
WIA	0	0	0	0	1	0	1
Total	*0*	*0*	*0*	*0*	*1*	*0*	*1*
Totopotomoy							
KIA	0	0	0	0	0	0	0
WIA	1	0	0	0	0	0	1
Total	*1*	*0*	*0*	*0*	*0*	*0*	*1*

3. HUGER'S BATTALION (*continued*)

	Moody's (La.) Btty.	*Fickling's (S.C.) Btty.*	*Woolfolk's (Va.) Btty.*	*Taylor's (Va.) Btty.*	*Parker's (Va.) Btty.*	*Smith's (Va.) Btty.*	*Total*
Cold Harbor							
KIA	0	0	0	2 (1)	0	0	2 (1)
WIA	1	1	0	1 (1)	0	0	3 (1)
MIA	0	0	0	0	0	0	0
Total	*1*	*1*	*0*	*3*	*0*	*0*	*5*
Campaign Total	*10*	*9*	*3*	*6*	*7*	*3*	*38*

FIRST CORPS ARTILLERY TOTAL

Wilderness	
Not in Action, No Loss	
Spotsylvania	
KIA	10
WIA	57 (6)
MIA	0
Total	*67*
North Anna	
KIA	1 (1)
WIA	8
MIA	0
Total	*9*
Totopotomoy	
KIA	1
WIA	1
Total	*2*
Cold Harbor	
KIA	6 (2)
WIA	37 (5)
MIA	0
Total	*43*
Campaign Total	*121*

TABLE 34. Walker's (Stonewall) Brigade

	F&S	*2nd Va. Rgt.*	*4th Va. Rgt.*	*5th Va. Rgt.*	*27th Va. Rgt.*	*33rd Va. Rgt.*	*Total*
Wilderness							
KIA		8	7 (2)	10 (4)	5 (3)	9 (1)	39 (10)
WIA		42 (2)	46	46 (1)	20	29	183 (3)
W&C		0	1	2	0	0	3
MIA		0	13	6	2	0	21
Total		*50*	*67*	*64*	*27*	*38*	*246*
Spotsylvania							
KIA		4	10	15 (3)	4 (1)	10	43 (4)
WIA	2	18 (2)	32 (1)	30 (7)	13	18	113 (10)
W&C		7 (2)	7	7	3	3	27 (2)
MIA		109	125	181	92	85	592
Total	*2*	*138*	*174*	*233*	*112*	*116*	*775*
North Anna							
KIA		0	0	0	0	0	0
WIA		0	0	1	0	0	1
W&C		0	0	0	0	0	0
MIA		3	1	0	1	0	5
Total		*3*	*1*	*1*	*1*	*0*	*6*

Totopotomoy (Bethesda Church)							
KIA		0	0	0	0	0	0
WIA		0	2	0	0	1	3
W&C		0	0	0	0	0	0
MIA		0	0	0	0	0	0
Total		*0*	*2*	*0*	*0*	*1*	*3*
Cold Harbor							
KIA		0	0	2	0	0	2
WIA		4	3	3	2	1	13
W&C		0	0	0	0	0	0
MIA		0	0	0	0	0	0
Total		*4*	*3*	*5*	*2*	*1*	*15*
Campaign Total	*2*	*195 (187)*	*247 (241)*	*303 (298)*	*142 (140)*	*156*	*1,045 (1,024)*

TABLE 35. Jones's (Virginia) Brigade

	F&S	*21st Rgt.*	*25th Rgt.*	*42nd Rgt.*	*44th Rgt.*	*48th Rgt.*	*50th Rgt.*	*Total*
Wilderness								
KIA	2	5	4 (2)	4	4	23 (4)	14 (3)	56 (9)
WIA	1	23 (2)	30 (2)	27 (1)	33 (2)	52	57 (1)	223 (8)
W&C		0	6	1	1	6	12	26
MIA		2	184	11	7	7	81	292
Total	*3*	*30*	*224*	*43*	*45*	*88*	*164*	*597*
Spotsylvania								
KIA		5 (2)	1	4 (1)	4 (2)	4 (2)	9 (2)	27 (9)
WIA		17 (2)	2	10 (2)	3 (1)	8	10	50 (5)
W&C		3	6	12 (2)	5 (1)	2	11 (3)	39 (6)
MIA	2	46	57	219	154	111	207	796
Total	*2*	*71*	*66*	*245*	*166*	*125*	*237*	*912*
North Anna								
KIA		0	0	0	0	0	0	0
WIA		0	0	1	0	0	0	1
W&C		0	0	0	0	0	0	0
MIA		0	0	0	0	0	0	0
Total		*0*	*0*	*1*	*0*	*0*	*0*	*1*

Totopotomoy (Bethesda Church)								
KIA		0	0	0	0	0	0	0
WIA		0	1	1	0	0	0	2
W&C		0	0	0	0	0	0	0
MIA		0	1	1	0	0	0	2
Total		*0*	*2*	*2*	*0*	*0*	*0*	*4*
Cold Harbor								
KIA		2	0	1 (1)	0	3 (1)	2 (2)	8 (4)
WIA		11	0	4	1	3	2	21
W&C		0	0	0	0	0	0	0
MIA		0	0	0	0	0	0	0
Total		*13*	*0*	*5*	*1*	*6*	*4*	*29*
Campaign Total	*5*	*114*	*292*	*296 (294)*	*212 (211)*	*219 (217)*	*405 (404)*	*1,543 (1,537)*

TABLE 36. Steuart's Brigade

	F&S	*1st N.C. Rgt.*	*3rd N.C. Rgt.*	*10th Va. Rgt.*	*23rd Va. Rgt.*	*37th Va. Rgt.*	*Total*
Wilderness							
KIA		14	7	10 (2)	9 (1)	3	43 (3)
WIA		49 (3)	53 (4)	37 (1)	35 (1)	7 (1)	181 (10)
W&C		0	0	0	0	0	0
MIA		0	1	2	0	4	7
Total		*63*	*61*	*49*	*44*	*14*	*231*
Spotsylvania							
KIA	1 (1)	11 (3)	2	4	6 (3)	9 (3)	33 (10)
WIA		23	29 (3)	11	21	12	96 (3)
W&C		3	1	1	5	7	17
MIA	2	334	242	171	148	192	1,089
Total	*3*	*371*	*274*	*187*	*180*	*220*	*1,235*
North Anna	Not in Action, No Loss						
Totopotomoy (Bethesda Church)							
KIA		1	0	0	0	0	1
WIA		6	0	0	0	0	6
W&C		0	0	0	0	0	0
MIA		2	1	0	0	0	3
Total		*9*	*1*	*0*	*0*	*0*	*10*

Cold Harbor							
KIA		1	1 (1)	0	0	2 (1)	4 (2)
WIA		4	2	2	1	4	13
W&C		0	0	0	0	0	0
MIA		0	0	0	0	0	0
Total		*5*	*3*	*2*	*1*	*6*	*17*
Campaign Total	*3*	*448 (447)*	*339 (334)*	*238 (236)*	*225 (224)*	*240 (238)*	*1,493 (1,482)*

TABLE 37. Stafford's (Louisiana) Brigade

	F&S	*1st Rgt.*	*2nd Rgt.*	*10th Rgt.*	*14th Rgt.*	*15th Rgt.*	*Total*
Wilderness							
KIA	1 (1)	4 (2)	12 (1)	3	3	3	26 (4)
WIA		8	20	19	14	11 (1)	72 (1)
W&C		0	0	1	1	1	3
MIA	2	14	4	9	12	8	49
Total	*3*	*26*	*36*	*32*	*30*	*23*	*150*
Spotsylvania							
KIA		6	6	4	3 (1)	5	24 (1)
WIA		12 (2)	9 (1)	8	10 (2)	7	46 (5)
W&C		2	3 (1)	2	7	2	16 (1)
MIA		35	59	58	57	43	252
Total		*55*	*77*	*72*	*77*	*57*	*338*
North Anna							
KIA		0	0	0	0	0	0
WIA		0	0	0	0	0	0
W&C		0	0	0	0	0	0
MIA		1	1	0	0	1	3
Total		*1*	*1*	*0*	*0*	*1*	*3*
Totopotomoy (Bethesda Church)							
KIA		0	0	0	1	0	1
WIA		0	2	0	1	0	3
W&C		0	0	0	0	0	0
MIA		0	0	0	0	0	0
Total		*0*	*2*	*0*	*2*	*0*	*4*
Cold Harbor							
KIA		2 (1)	2	0	0	1	5 (1)
WIA		3	2	3	3	5 (1)	16 (1)
W&C		0	0	0	0	0	0
MIA		2	1	1	0	0	4
Total		*7*	*5*	*4*	*3*	*6*	*25*
Campaign Total	*3*	*89*	*121 (120)*	*108 (104)*	*112 (111)*	*87 (86)*	*520 (513)*

TABLE 38. Hays's (Louisiana) Brigade

	F&S	*5th Rgt.*	*6th Rgt.*	*7th Rgt.*	*8th Rgt.*	*9th Rgt.*	*Total*
Wilderness							
KIA		12 (3)	5 (1)	4 (1)	6	9 (3)	36 (8)
WIA		20	10	13 (1)	19 (2)	30	92 (3)
W&C		17	3	2	1	0	23
MIA		13	75	10	3	2	103
Total		*62*	*93*	*29*	*29*	*41*	*254*
Spotsylvania							
KIA		2	2	6	7	6 (1)	23 (1)
WIA	1	11 (1)	9 (3)	12	14	19	66 (4)
W&C		3	1	7	1	1	13
MIA		21	18	71	42	13	165
Total	*1*	*37*	*30*	*96*	*64*	*39*	*267*
North Anna							
KIA		0	0	0	0	0	0
WIA		0	0	0	0	3	3
W&C		0	0	0	0	0	0
MIA		2	0	0	0	0	2
Total		*2*	*0*	*0*	*0*	*3*	*5*
Totopotomoy (Bethesda Church)							
KIA		0	0	0	0	0	0
WIA		0	0	0	0	1	1
W&C		0	0	0	0	0	0
MIA		0	1	0	0	0	1
Total		*0*	*1*	*0*	*0*	*1*	*2*
Cold Harbor							
KIA		2	0	0	2	2	6
WIA		3	5 (1)	4	9	6	27 (1)
W&C		0	0	0	0	0	0
MIA		1	0	0	3	0	4
Total		*6*	*5*	*4*	*14*	*8*	*37*
Campaign Total	*1*	*107*	*129*	*129*	*107 (106)*	*92 (91)*	*565 (563)*

TABLE 39. Gordon's/Evans's (Georgia) Brigade

	13th Rgt.	*26th Rgt.*	*31st Rgt.*	*38th Rgt.*	*60th Rgt.*	*61st Rgt.*	*12th Bn.*	*Total*
Wilderness								
KIA	10 (2)	7 (1)	13	5	7 (1)	6		48 (4)
WIA	59 (8)	24 (3)	48 (1)	37 (5)	29 (2)	40 (4)		237 (23)
W&C	1	4	1	2	0	0		8
MIA	1	7	1	9	4	4		26
Total	*71*	*42*	*63*	*53*	*40*	*50*		*319*
Spotsylvania								
KIA	27 (6)	33 (6)	9 (2)	16 (1)	14 (2)	6 (1)		105 (18)
WIA	68 (4)	64 (3)	33	37 (5)	39 (1)	18 (1)		259 (14)
W&C	19 (5)	6 (2)	5 (2)	4	4	3 (2)		41 (11)
MIA	34	25	55	63	33	75		285
Total	*148*	*128*	*102*	*120*	*90*	*102*		*690*
Milford Station								
MIA				5			5	
North Anna								
KIA	0	0	0	0	0	0	0	0
WIA	0	0	0	2	1	0	1	4
W&C	0	0	0	0	0	0	0	0
MIA	0	0	1	9	4	2	0	16
Total	*0*	*0*	*1*	*11*	*5*	*2*	*1*	*20*

Totopotomoy (Bethesda Church)								
KIA	0	0	0	1 (1)	0	0	0	1 (1)
WIA	1	2 (1)	1	0	1	0	1	6 (1)
W&C	0	0	0	0	0	0	0	0
MIA	0	0	0	0	0	0	0	0
Total	*1*	2	*1*	*1*	*1*	*0*	*1*	*7*
Cold Harbor								
KIA	3 (1)	6 (1)	2	8	2	4 (1)	8 (2)	33 (5)
WIA	24 (4)	11	6	23	16 (2)	9 (1)	52 (6)	141 (13)
W&C	0	0	0	1	0	0	0	1
MIA	0	2	0	4	5	0	1	12
Total	*27*	*19*	*8*	*36*	*23*	*13*	*61*	*187*
Campaign Total	*247 (242)*	*191*	*175*	*226*	*159 (157)*	*167 (166)*	*63*	*1,228 (1,220)*

TABLE 40. Pegram's (Virginia) Brigade

	F&S	*13th Rgt.*	*31st Rgt.*	*49th Rgt.*	*52nd Rgt.*	*58th Rgt.*	*Total*
Wilderness							
KIA		4 (1)	7 (1)	9 (1)	6 (3)	3 (1)	29 (7)
WIA	1	22 (2)	27	26 (1)	21	37 (1)	134 (4)
W&C		0	0	0	0	0	0
MIA		0	4	0	1	0	5
Total	*1*	*26*	*38*	*35*	*28*	*40*	*168*
Spotsylvania							
KIA		12 (2)	13 (3)	14 (2)	19 (8)	16 (3)	74 (18)
WIA	1	42 (3)	67 (9)	45 (1)	59 (1)	37 (2)	251 (16)
W&C		0	1	1 (1)	9 (1)	3	14 (2)
MIA		9	11	7	7	97	131
Total	*1*	*63*	*92*	*67*	*94*	*153*	*470*
North Anna							
KIA		0	0	0	0	0	0
WIA		0	0	0	1	0	1
W&C		0	0	0	0	0	0
MIA		2	2	0	3	6	13
Total		*2*	*2*	*0*	*4*	*6*	*14*

Totopotomoy (Bethesda Church)							
KIA	2	3 (2)	7 (4)	13 (5)	31 (6)	2 (1)	58 (18)
WIA		21 (1)	22 (2)	20 (1)	42 (2)	17 (1)	122 (7)
W&C		0	1 (1)	13 (3)	12 (4)	4 (1)	30 (9)
MIA		2	4	20	26	9	61
Total	*2*	*26*	*34*	*66*	*111*	*32*	*271*
Cold Harbor							
KIA		0	2 (1)	1	3 (1)	0	6 (2)
WIA		6	5	3	2	3	19
W&C		0	0	0	0	0	0
MIA		0	0	0	0	0	0
Total		*6*	*7*	*4*	*5*	*3*	*25*
Campaign Total	*4*	*123 (122)*	*173 (171)*	*172 (169)*	*242 (234)*	*234 (232)*	*948 (932)*

TABLE 41. Hoke's (North Carolina) Brigade

	F&S	*6th Rgt.*	*21st Rgt.*	*54th Rgt.*	*57th Rgt.*	*Total*
Milford Station						
MIA				1		1
Total				*1*		*1*
Spotsylvania						
MIA		0	3	2	0	5
Total		*0*	*3*	*2*	*0*	*5*
North Anna						
KIA		0	0	0	0	0
WIA		0	0	0	1	1
W&C		0	0	0	0	0
MIA		0	15	3	6	24
Total		*0*	*15*	*3*	*7*	*25*
Totopotomoy (Bethesda Church)						
KIA		1 (1)	0	0	0	1 (1)
WIA		6 (1)	2	0	2 (1)	10 (1)
W&C		0	0	0	0	0
MIA		9	1	0	0	10
Total		*16*	*3*	*0*	*2*	*21*
Cold Harbor						
KIA		6 (1)	4 (1)	2	1	13 (2)
WIA		18 (1)	26 (1)	20 (3)	7	71 (2)
W&C		0	0	0	0	0
MIA		5	5	1	3	14
Total		*29*	*35*	*23*	*11*	*98*
Campaign Total		*45*	*56*	*29*	*20*	*150*
Drewry's Bluff						
Total		*0*	*21*	*34*	*25*	*80*

TABLE 42. Ramseur's (North Carolina) Brigade

	F&S	*2nd Rgt.*	*4th Rgt.*	*14th Rgt.*	*30th Rgt.*	*Total*
Wilderness						
KIA		1	1	1	1	4
WIA		4	7	5	8	24
W&C		0	0	0	0	0
MIA		0	0	1	1	2
Total		*5*	*8*	*7*	*10*	*30*
Spotsylvania						
KIA		26 (5)	37 (6)	23 (4)	32 (5)	118 (20)
WIA		59 (4)	118 (6)	111 (5)	85 (7)	373 (22)
W&C		5 (1)	3 (3)	4 (2)	7 (2)	19 (8)
MIA		23	12	20	88	143
Total		*113*	*170*	*158*	*212*	*653*
North Anna						
KIA		0	0	1	0	1
WIA		3 (1)	4	7 (1)	0	14 (2)
W&C		0	0	0	0	0
MIA		1	0	2	2	5
Total		*4*	*4*	*10*	*2*	*20*
Totopotomoy (Bethesda Church)						
KIA		0	0	6	1	7
WIA		8 (1)	10 (2)	15	9 (2)	42 (5)
W&C		0	0	0	0	0
MIA		6	7	14	5	32
Total		*14*	*17*	*35*	*15*	*81*
Cold Harbor						
KIA		3	4	2 (1)	2 (1)	11 (2)
WIA		9	7	9 (2)	12	37 (2)
W&C		0	0	0	0	0
MIA		0	0	0	0	0
Total		*12*	*11*	*11*	*14*	*48*
Campaign Total		*148 (144)*	*210 (209)*	*221 (217)*	*253 (250)*	*832 (820)*

TABLE 43. Daniel's/Grimes's (North Carolina) Brigade

	F&S	*32nd Rgt.*	*43rd Rgt.*	*45th Rgt.*	*53rd Rgt.*	*2nd Bn.*	*Total*
Wilderness							
KIA		1	w/Hoke	10	3 (1)	1	15 (1)
WIA		7		39 (2)	18	8	72 (2)
W&C		0		0	0	0	0
MIA		2		1	6	1	10
Total		*10*		*50*	*27*	*10*	*97*
Spotsylvania							
KIA	2 (1)	24 (4)	0	22 (6)	17 (3)	5	70 (14)
WIA		44 (4)	0	111 (18)	61 (6)	32 (3)	248 (31)
W&C		16 (2)	0	8 (2)	5 (1)	1	30 (5)
MIA		218	4	149	29	24	424
Total	*2*	*302*	*4*	*290*	*112*	*62*	*772*
North Anna							
KIA		0	4 (1)	1	2	0	7 (1)
WIA		2	12 (1)	10 (3)	1 (1)	3	28 (5)
W&C		0	0	0	0	0	0
MIA		0	8	4	3	0	15
Total		*2*	*24*	*15*	*6*	*3*	*50*

Totopotomoy (Bethesda Church)							
KIA		0	14 (1)	3 (1)	2 (1)	0	19 (3)
WIA		7	53 (5)	12	12	6 (1)	90 (6)
W&C		0	3 (1)	0	0	0	3 (1)
MIA		0	3	2	0	1	6
Total		*7*	*73*	*17*	*14*	*7*	*118*
Cold Harbor							
KIA		0	5 (1)	3	1 (1)	0	9 (2)
WIA		7	33 (7)	11	8	3	62 (7)
W&C		0	0	0	0	1 (1)	1 (1)
MIA		1	2	2	0	0	5
Total		*8*	*40*	*16*	*9*	*4*	*77*
Campaign Total	*2*	*329 (328)*	*141*	*388 (384)*	*168*	*86 (85)*	*1,114 (1,108)*
Drewry's Bluff			84 (w/Hoke)				

TABLE 44. Doles's (Georgia) Brigade

	F&S	*4th Rgt.*	*12th Rgt.*	*21st Rgt.*	*44th Rgt.*	*Total*
Wilderness						
KIA	1	35 (2)	20 (3)	0	13 (2)	69 (7)
WIA		87 (3)	50 (3)	4	45 (2)	186 (8)
W&C		4 (3)	1	0	1 (1)	6 (4)
MIA		4	4	0	2	10
Total	*1*	*130*	*75*	*4*	*61*	*271*
Spotsylvania						
KIA		19 (3)	22 (7)	1	24 (5)	66 (15)
WIA		63 (1)	57 (8)	2	49 (5)	171 (14)
W&C		7	9	2	26 (4)	44 (4)
MIA		78	150	19	196	443
Total		*167*	*238*	*24*	*295*	*724*
North Anna						
KIA		1 (1)	0	0	0	1 (1)
WIA		1	2	2	0	5
W&C		0	0	0	0	0
MIA		0	0	1	0	1
Total		*2*	*2*	*3*	*0*	*7*
Totopotomoy (Bethesda Church)						
KIA		0	0	1	1 (1)	2 (1)
WIA		2	5 (1)	1	4	12 (1)
W&C		0	0	0	0	0
MIA		0	1	1	1	3
Total		*2*	*6*	*3*	*6*	*17*
Cold Harbor						
KIA	1	0	1	5 (1)	1 (1)	8 (2)
WIA		3 (1)	6	15 (1)	5	29 (2)
W&C		0	0	0	0	0
MIA		0	0	1	0	1
Total		*3*	*7*	*21*	*6*	*38*
Campaign Total	*2*	*304*	*328*	*55*	*368 (367)*	*1,057 (1,056)*
Drewry's Bluff				34	(w/Hoke)	

TABLE 45. Battle's (Alabama) Brigade

	3rd Rgt.	*5th Rgt.*	*6th Rgt.*	*12th Rgt.*	*61st Rgt.*	*Total*
Wilderness						
KIA	9	7 (1)	11 (3)	0	8	35 (4)
WIA	29 (1)	34 (5)	49 (2)	5	38 (5)	155 (13)
W&C	2	4 (1)	1	0	0	7 (1)
MIA	23	42	18	2	18	103
Total	*63*	*87*	*79*	*7*	*64*	*300*
Spotsylvania						
KIA	20 (5)	9 (1)	10	12 (1)	8 (1)	59 (8)
WIA	49 (4)	46 (1)	55	60 (1)	45 (4)	255 (10)
W&C	1	2	1	1	2 (1)	7 (1)
MIA	18	27	42	38	37	162
Total	*88*	*84*	*108*	*111*	*92*	*483*
North Anna						
KIA	1 (1)	0	0	0	0	1 (1)
WIA	1	1	0	0	2 (1)	4 (1)
W&C	0	0	0	0	1 (1)	1 (1)
MIA	1	1	0	0	1	3
Total	*3*	*2*	*0*	*0*	*4*	*9*
Totopotomoy (Bethesda Church)						
KIA	2	4 (1)	1	2	4 (2)	13 (3)
WIA	5 (1)	9	7	9 (1)	8	38 (2)
W&C	0	0	0	0	0	0
MIA	0	1	1	3	1	6
Total	*7*	*14*	*9*	*14*	*13*	*57*
Cold Harbor						
KIA	4	4	2	6 (3)	3 (1)	19 (4)
WIA	14 (1)	11 (1)	13 (3)	25	14 (2)	77 (7)
W&C	0	0	0	0	0	0
MIA	1	0	1	0	0	2
Total	*19*	*15*	*16*	*31*	*17*	*98*
Campaign Total	*180*	*202 (200)*	*212 (209)*	*163 (162)*	*190*	*947 (941)*

TABLE 46. Johnston's (North Carolina) Brigade

	F&S	*5th Rgt.*	*12th Rgt.*	*20th Rgt.*	*23rd Rgt.*	*Total*
Wilderness						
KIA		1 (1)	1	1	0	3 (1)
WIA		1	3	6 (1)	4 (1)	14 (2)
W&C		0	0	0	0	0
MIA		4	3	2	1	10
Total		*6*	*7*	*9*	*5*	*27*
Spotsylvania						
KIA		26 (10)	32 (7)	15 (7)	11	84 (24)
WIA	2	67 (1)	115 (12)	56	76 (4)	316 (17)
W&C		15 (6)	17 (4)	3 (2)	8 (2)	43 (14)
MIA		123	55	56	62	296
Total	2	*231*	*219*	*130*	*157*	*739*
North Anna		Not in Action, No Loss				
Totopotomoy (Bethesda Church)						
KIA		0	0	0	0	0
WIA		1	1	2 (1)	0	4 (1)
W&C		0	0	0	0	0
MIA		1	0	0	0	1
Total		*2*	*1*	*2*	*0*	*5*
Cold Harbor						
KIA		0	1	1	1	3
WIA		5 (1)	2	6	4 (1)	17 (2)
W&C		0	0	0	0	0
MIA		0	0	0	0	0
Total		*5*	*3*	*7*	*5*	*20*
Campaign Total	2	*244*	*230 (229)*	*148*	*167 (166)*	*791 (789)*

TABLE 47. Second Corps Artillery

1. NELSON'S BATTALION

	F&S Corps Art.	*Milledge's (Ga.) Btty.*	*Kirkpatrick's (Va.) Btty.*	*Massie's (Va.) Btty.*	*Bn. Total*
Wilderness					
KIA	1	0	0	0	0
WIA		2	0	0	2
MIA		0	0	0	0
Total	*1*	*2*	*0*	*0*	*2*
Spotsylvania					
KIA		1	0	0	1
WIA		2	3	2	7
MIA		0	0	0	0
Total		*3*	*3*	*2*	*8*
North Anna		Not in Action, No Loss			
Totopotomoy (Bethesda Church)					
KIA		0	0	1	1
WIA		1	0	2	3
MIA		0	0	0	0
Total		*1*	*0*	*3*	*4*
Cold Harbor					
KIA		1 (1)	4 (1)	2 (2)	7 (4)
WIA		5	25 (2)	1	31 (2)
MIA		0	0	0	0
Total		*6*	*29*	*3*	*38*
Campaign Total	*1*	*12*	*32*	*8*	*52*

(continued)

2. BRAXTON'S BATTALION

	Carpenter's (Va.) Btty.	*Hardwick's (Va.) Btty.*	*Cooper's (Va.) Btty.*	*Bn. Total*
Wilderness				
	Not in Action, No Loss			
Spotsylvania				
KIA	1	0	3 (1)	4 (1)
WIA	5	6	2	13
MIA	1	0	0	1
Total	*7*	*6*	*5*	*18*
North Anna				
	Not in Action, No Loss			
Totopotomoy (Bethesda Church)				
	Not in Action, No Loss			
Cold Harbor				
KIA	0	1	1	2
WIA	0	1	2	3
MIA	0	0	0	0
Total	*0*	*2*	*3*	*5*
Campaign Total	*7*	*8*	*8*	*23*

3. PAGE'S BATTALION

	Reese's (Ala.) Btty.	*Carter's (Va.) Btty.*	*Montgomery's (Va.) Btty.*	*Fry's (Va.) Btty.*	*Bn. Total*
Wilderness					
	Not in Action, No Loss				
Spotsylvania					
KIA	4	1	0	3	8
WIA	6	4	4	8	22
W&C	1	7 (3)	3 (1)	4 (3)	15 (7)
MIA	33	52	24	20	129
Total	*44*	*64*	*31*	*35*	*174*

3. PAGE'S BATTALION (*continued*)

	Reese's (Ala.) Btty.	*Carter's (Va.) Btty.*	*Montgomery's (Va.) Btty.*	*Fry's (Va.) Btty.*	*Bn. Total*
North Anna					
		Not in Action, No Loss			
Totopotomoy (Bethesda Church)					
		Not in Action, No Loss			
Cold Harbor					
KIA	1	0	1	0	2
WIA	0	0	0	0	0
MIA	0	0	0	0	0
Total	*1*	*0*	*1*	*0*	*2*
Campaign Total	*45*	*64*	*32*	*35*	*176*

4. CUTSHAW'S BATTALION

	Carrington's (Va.) Btty.	*Tanner's (Va.) Btty.*	*Garber's (Va.) Btty.*	*Bn. Total*
Wilderness				
KIA	0	0	0	0
WIA	0	0	1	1
MIA	0	0	0	0
Total	*0*	*0*	*1*	*1*
Spotsylvania				
KIA	7	2	2 (1)	11 (1)
WIA	5	2	11	18
W&C	4 (1)	0	0	4 (1)
MIA	33	23	0	56
Total	*49*	*27*	*13*	*89*
North Anna				
		Not in Action, No Loss		
Totopotomoy (Bethesda Church)				
KIA	0	0	0	0
WIA	1	0	0	1
Total	*1*	*0*	*0*	*1*

(*continued*)

4. CUTSHAW'S BATTALION (*continued*)

	Carrington's (Va.) Btty.	*Tanner's (Va.) Btty.*	*Garber's (Va.) Btty.*	*Bn. Total*
Cold Harbor				
KIA	0	0	0	0
WIA	0	0	1	1
MIA	0	0	0	0
Total	*0*	*0*	*1*	*1*
Campaign Total	*50*	*27*	*15*	*92*

5. HARDAWAY'S BATTALION

	F&S	*Jones's (Va.) Btty.*	*Smith's (Va.) Btty.*	*Graham's (Va.) Btty.*	*Dance's (Va.) Btty.*	*Griffin's (Va.) Btty.*	*Bn. Total*
Wilderness							
			Not in Action, No Loss				
Spotsylvania							
KIA	1 (1)	0	5 (2)	0	1	0	7 (3)
WIA	1	9	11 (1)	2	3	0	26 (1)
W&C		0	0	0	0	0	0
MIA		0	24	0	0	0	24
Total	*2*	*9*	*40*	*2*	*4*	*0*	*57*
North Anna							
MIA		0	0	1	0	0	1
Total		*0*	*0*	*1*	*0*	*0*	*1*
Totopotomoy (Bethesda Church)							
			Not in Action, No Loss				
Cold Harbor							
KIA		0	0	0	0	3	3
WIA		1	0	4	1	3 (2)	9 (2)
Total		*1*	*0*	*4*	*1*	*6*	*12*
Campaign Total	*2*	*10*	*40*	*7*	*5*	*6*	*70*

SECOND CORPS ARTILLERY TOTAL

Wilderness	
KIA	1
WIA	3
MIA	0
Total	*4*
Spotsylvania	
KIA	31 (5)
WIA	86 (1)
W&C	19 (8)
MIA	210
Total	*346*
North Anna	
KIA	0
WIA	0
MIA	1
Total	*1*
Totopotomoy (Bethesda Church)	
KIA	1
WIA	4
Total	*5*
Cold Harbor	
KIA	14 (4)
WIA	44 (4)
MIA	0
Total	*58*
Campaign Total	*414*

TABLE 48. Cooke's (North Carolina) Brigade

	F&S	*15th Rgt.*	*27th Rgt.*	*46th Rgt.*	*48th Rgt.*	*Total*
Wilderness						
KIA	1	9 (1)	15 (4)	42 (2)	13	80 (7)
WIA	1	134 (8)	168 (10)	249 (10)	168 (11)	720 (39)
W&C		1	0	3 (1)	1	5 (1)
MIA		7	0	5	2	14
Total	*2*	*151*	*183*	*299*	*184*	*819*
Spotsylvania						
KIA		3 (2)	2	7 (2)	3	15 (4)
WIA		21 (1)	25 (1)	31 (3)	24 (1)	101 (6)
W&C		0	1 (1)	0	0	1 (1)
MIA		0	0	0	2	2
Total		*24*	*28*	*38*	*29*	*119*
North Anna						
KIA		1 (1)	0	1	1	3 (1)
WIA		1	0	6	2 (1)	9 (1)
W&C		0	0	0	0	0
MIA		1	3	0	7	11
Total		*3*	*3*	*7*	*10*	*23*
Totopotomoy						
KIA		0	0	0	0	0
WIA		0	0	1	0	1
W&C		0	0	0	0	0
MIA		0	0	0	0	0
Total		*0*	*0*	*1*	*0*	*1*
Cold Harbor						
KIA		2 (2)	4 (1)	5	10 (2)	21 (5)
WIA	1	20 (4)	21 (3)	19 (1)	35 (2)	96 (10)
W&C		1	0	0	1	2
MIA		4	0	1	9	14
Total	*1*	*27*	*25*	*25*	*55*	*133*
Campaign Total	*3*	*205 (201)*	*239 (233)*	*370 (360)*	*278 (267)*	*1,095 (1,064)*

TABLE 49. Kirkland's (North Carolina) Brigade

	F&S	*11th Rgt.*	*26th Rgt.*	*44th Rgt.*	*47th Rgt.*	*52nd Rgt.*	*Total*
Wilderness							
KIA		4 (2)	16 (3)	12 (1)	12 (6)	0	44 (12)
WIA		47 (4)	139 (11)	73 (3)	88 (3)	10	357 (21)
W&C		0	4 (4)	0	2	0	6 (4)
MIA		4	31	1	4	49	89
Total		*55*	*190*	*86*	*106*	*59*	*496*
Spotsylvania							
KIA		4 (2)	1	6 (1)	3	3 (2)	17 (5)
WIA		21	18	23	19	14 (1)	95 (1)
W&C		0	1	0	1	0	2
MIA		2	6	2	1	1	12
Total		*27*	*26*	*31*	*24*	*18*	*126*
Milford Station							
MIA		0	0	0	0	1	1
Total		*0*	*0*	*0*	*0*	*1*	*1*
North Anna							
KIA		0	0	0	0	0	0
WIA		0	1	0	5	0	6
W&C		0	0	0	1	0	1
MIA		2	6	1	3	0	12
Total		*2*	*7*	*1*	*9*	*0*	*19*
Totopotomoy							
KIA		0	0	1 (1)	0	0	1 (1)
WIA		0	0	2	0	0	2
W&C		0	0	1	0	0	1
MIA		0	0	2	0	0	2
Total		*0*	*0*	*6*	*0*	*0*	*6*
Cold Harbor							
KIA		1	8 (2)	9 (4)	7 (2)	4	29 (8)
WIA	1	22	33 (3)	24 (3)	24 (4)	25 (2)	129 (12)
W&C		0	0	1	1	0	2
MIA		0	1	6	0	7	14
Total	*1*	*23*	*42*	*40*	*32*	*36*	*174*
Campaign Total	*1*	*107*	*265 (261)*	*164 (160)*	*171 (168)*	*114 (113)*	*822 (810)*

TABLE 50. Davis's Brigade

	F&S	*1st Conf. Bn.*	*2nd Miss. Rgt.*	*11th Miss. Rgt.*	*26th Miss. Rgt.*	*42nd Miss. Rgt.*	*55th N.C. Rgt.*	*Total*
Wilderness								
KIA	1	4	14 (4)	9	16 (1)	17 (5)	36 (4)	97 (14)
WIA		23	92 (4)	39 (2)	60 (4)	87 (8)	146 (12)	447 (30)
W&C		1	0	1	1 (1)	3 (1)	10	16 (2)
MIA		0	4	6	3	4	9	26
Total	*1*	*28*	*110*	*55*	*80*	*111*	*201*	*586*
Spotsylvania								
KIA		1	7	6 (2)	4 (1)	2	5 (3)	25 (6)
WIA		6	14	18 (2)	15	12 (1)	16	81 (3)
W&C		0	0	0	0	0	0	0
MIA		1	0	0	1	0	0	2
Total		*8*	*21*	*24*	*20*	*14*	*21*	*108*
North Anna								
KIA		0	0	0	1	0	0	1
WIA		0	0	1	0	1	3	5
W&C		0	0	0	0	0	0	0
MIA		0	0	1	1	5	0	7
Total		*0*	*0*	*2*	*2*	*6*	*3*	*13*

Totopotomoy								
KIA		0	0	0	0	0	0	0
WIA		0	1	0	0	0	0	1
W&C		0	0	0	0	0	0	0
MIA		0	0	1	0	0	0	1
Total		*0*	*1*	*1*	*0*	*0*	*0*	*2*
Cold Harbor								
KIA		4	2	6	4	7 (2)	1	24 (2)
WIA		25 (2)	21 (1)	33 (1)	38 (6)	15 (3)	8 (1)	140 (14)
W&C		0	0	1	0	0	0	1
MIA		0	1	2	2	2	0	7
Total		*29*	*24*	*42*	*44*	*24*	*9*	*172*
Campaign Total	*1*	*65*	*156 (152)*	*124 (121)*	*146 (135)*	*155 (149)*	*234 (233)*	*881 (856)*

TABLE 51. Walker's/Fry's (Archer's) Brigade

	13th Ala. Rgt.	*1st Tenn. (PA) Rgt.*	*7th Tenn. Rgt.*	*14th Tenn. Rgt.*	*5th Ala. Bn.*	*Total*
Wilderness						
KIA	2	6	4	4		16
WIA	39 (2)	24	15	15 (1)		93 (3)
W&C	3	0	0	0		3
MIA	48	24	11	28		111
Total	*92*	*54*	*30*	*47*		*223*
Spotsylvania						
KIA	2	4	3	2	0	11
WIA	10 (1)	7	8 (1)	5	1	31 (2)
W&C	0	0	0	0	0	0
MIA	1	3	3	1	0	8
Total	*13*	*14*	*14*	*8*	*1*	*50*
North Anna						
KIA	0	0	0	0		0
WIA	0	3	0	1		4
W&C	0	0	0	0		0
MIA	4	1	3	4		12
Total	*4*	*4*	*3*	*5*		*16*
Totopotomoy						
Total	*0*	*0*	*0*	*0*		*0*
Cold Harbor						
KIA	0	1	1 (1)	0		2 (1)
WIA	7 (1)	0	7 (1)	3 (2)		17 (4)
W&C	0	0	0	0		0
MIA	0	1	4	0		5
Total	*7*	*2*	*12*	*3*		*24*
Campaign Total	*116*	*74*	*59*	*63*	*1*	*313*

TABLE 52. Walker's/Fry's (Brockenbrough's) Brigade

	F&S	*40th Va. Rgt.*	*47th Va. Rgt.*	*55th Va. Rgt.*	*22nd Va. Bn.*	*Total*
Wilderness						
KIA		1	3	2	3	9
WIA		26 (2)	17 (1)	21 (1)	24 (3)	88 (7)
W&C		2 (2)	0	4	0	6 (2)
MIA		17	10	31	7	65
Total		*46*	*30*	*58*	*34*	*168*
Spotsylvania						
KIA		1	1	5	4 (1)	11 (1)
WIA	1	5 (1)	9 (1)	12	6	33 (2)
W&C		0	0	0	0	0
MIA		0	0	1	0	1
Total	*1*	*6*	*10*	*18*	*10*	*45*
Richmond Raid & Milford Station						
MIA		0	1	0	1 (des.)	2
Total		*0*	*1*	*0*	*1*	*2*
North Anna						
KIA		0	0	0	0	0
WIA		0	1	1	4 (1)	6 (1)
W&C		0	0	0	0	0
MIA		5	9	5	4	23
Total		*5*	*10*	*6*	*8*	*29*
Cold Harbor						
KIA		2	5	3 (1)	1	11 (1)
WIA	1	11 (1)	6 (1)	6	11 (1)	35 (3)
W&C		0	0	1 (1)	0	1 (1)
MIA		3	2	5	4	14
Total	*1*	*16*	*13*	*15*	*16*	*61*
Campaign Total	*2*	*73*	*64*	*97*	*69*	*305*

TABLE 53. Lane's (North Carolina) Brigade

	F&S	*7th Rgt.*	*18th Rgt.*	*28th Rgt.*	*33rd Rgt.*	*37th Rgt.*	*Total*
Wilderness							
KIA		6 (3)	7	18	14	1 (1)	46 (4)
WIA		56	38 (2)	58 (5)	61 (6)	23 (2)	236 (15)
W&C		6	1 (1)	7 (1)	2	1	17 (2)
MIA		38	16	7	39	35	135
Total		*106*	*62*	*90*	*116*	*60*	*434*
Spotsylvania							
KIA	1 (1)	13 (2)	1	12 (2)	2 (1)	26 (4)	55 (10)
WIA		34 (3)	18 (1)	26 (1)	28 (5)	46 (8)	152 (18)
W&C		3	5 (1)	11 (3)	3	12 (2)	34 (6)
MIA		5	137	92	28	29	291
Total	*1*	*55*	*161*	*141*	*61*	*113*	*532*
North Anna							
KIA		1 (1)	0	5 (1)	5 (1)	1	12 (3)
WIA		1 (1)	3	26 (3)	28	23 (5)	81 (9)
W&C		0	0	0	2	0	2
MIA		3	3	2	7	10	25
Total		*5*	*6*	*33*	*42*	*34*	*120*
Totopotomoy							
KIA		1 (1)	2 (1)	1 (1)	1	0	5 (3)
WIA		4	6 (1)	5 (1)	0	2	17 (2)
W&C		0	0	0	0	0	0
MIA		0	1	0	0	0	1
Total		*5*	*9*	*6*	*1*	*2*	*23*
Cold Harbor							
KIA		1 (1)	1 (1)	1 (1)	2 (2)	4 (2)	9 (7)
WIA	1	1	6 (1)	5	7 (1)	8 (1)	28 (3)
W&C		0	0	0	0	0	0
MIA		1	0	0	0	0	1
Total	*1*	*3*	*7*	*6*	*9*	*12*	*38*
Campaign Total	*2*	*174*	*245*	*276 (274)*	*229 (228)*	*221 (218)*	*1,147 (1,141)*

TABLE 54. McGowan's (South Carolina) Brigade

	F&S	*1st Prov.*	*1st Rifles*	*12th Rgt.*	*13th Rgt.*	*14th Rgt.*	*Total*
Wilderness							
KIA		12 (4)	14 (4)	16 (2)	5	10 (3)	57 (13)
WIA		123 (15)	85 (10)	68 (5)	53 (4)	66 (4)	395 (38)
W&C		3 (1)	0	1	0	1 (1)	5 (2)
MIA		8	1	21	5	8	43
Total		*146*	*100*	*106*	*63*	*85*	*500*
Spotsylvania							
KIA		18	20 (2)	26 (2)	21 (3)	11	96 (7)
WIA	1	51 (4)	40 (3)	47 (3)	56 (4)	47 (5)	242 (19)
W&C		5 (3)	5 (2)	7 (1)	4 (1)	1 (1)	22 (8)
MIA		9	27	47	5	13	101
Total	*1*	*83*	*92*	*127*	*86*	*72*	*461*
North Anna							
KIA		4	5 (1)	1	4	4	18 (1)
WIA		19 (1)	18 (3)	21 (4)	39 (8)	36 (2)	133 (18)
W&C		1	1 (1)	0	0	1 (1)	3 (2)
MIA		23	9	11	9	11	63
Total		*47*	*33*	*33*	*52*	*52*	*217*

(continued)

TABLE 54. McGowan's (South Carolina) Brigade (*continued*)

	F&S	*1st Prov.*	*1st Rifles*	*12th Rgt.*	*13th Rgt.*	*14th Rgt.*	*Total*
Totopotomoy							
KIA		0	0	1	0	0	1
WIA		0	0	0	0	0	0
MIA		0	0	0	0	0	0
Total		*0*	*0*	*1*	*0*	*0*	*1*
Cold Harbor							
KIA		0	0	0	0	0	0
WIA		2	1	1	2	3 (1)	9 (1)
W&C		0	0	0	0	0	0
MIA		0	0	0	0	0	0
Total		*2*	*1*	*1*	*2*	*3*	*9*
Campaign Total	*1*	*278 (269)*	*226 (224)*	*268 (266)*	*203 (200)*	*212 (207)*	*1,188 (1,167)*

TABLE 55. Scales's (North Carolina) Brigade

	13th Rgt.	*16th Rgt.*	*22nd Rgt.*	*34th Rgt.*	*38th Rgt.*	*Total*
Wilderness						
KIA	10 (3)	2	4	10 (1)	6 (2)	32 (6)
WIA	53 (6)	27 (1)	69 (2)	40 (2)	34 (6)	223 (17)
W&C	2 (1)	0	2	2 (2)	2	8 (3)
MIA	35	17	28	17	12	109
Total	*100*	*46*	*103*	*69*	*54*	*372*
Spotsylvania						
KIA	10 (4)	2	1	3	7 (3)	23 (7)
WIA	28 (2)	5	8	10	12 (1)	63 (3)
W&C	0	0	0	0	0	0
MIA	2	1	2	1	12	18
Total	*40*	*8*	*11*	*14*	*31*	*104*
North Anna						
KIA	1	4	0	2 (2)	0	7 (2)
WIA	6 (2)	12 (2)	15 (2)	5	6	44 (5)
W&C	0	2	1	0	0	3
MIA	14	29	86	33	24	186
Total	*21*	*47*	*102*	*40*	*30*	*240*
Totopotomoy						
KIA	0	1	0	0	0	1
WIA	0	2	0	0	1	3
W&C	0	0	0	0	0	0
MIA	0	1	5	0	1	7
Total	*0*	*4*	*5*	*0*	*2*	*11*
Cold Harbor						
KIA	3	0	0	0	0	3
WIA	9	0	7 (3)	3 (1)	0	19 (4)
W&C	0	0	0	0	0	0
MIA	2	1	8	1	0	12
Total	*14*	*1*	*15*	*4*	*0*	*34*
Campaign Total	*175 (172)*	*106*	*236 (230)*	*127*	*117 (116)*	*761 (751)*

TABLE 56. Thomas's (Georgia) Brigade

	F&S	14th Rgt.	35th Rgt.	45th Rgt.	49th Rgt.	Total
Wilderness						
KIA		7 (1)	5 (2)	9	23 (2)	44 (5)
WIA		33 (2)	21 (2)	102 (12)	70 (6)	226 (22)
W&C		1	0	4	13 (2)	18 (2)
MIA	1	33	23	30	31	118
Total	*1*	*74*	*49*	*145*	*137*	*406*
Spotsylvania						
KIA		18 (2)	9 (3)	6	4 (1)	37 (5)
WIA		24 (3)	37 (3)	22 (2)	18 (2)	101 (10)
W&C		10 (2)	1 (1)	1	1	13 (3)
MIA		16	13	3	1	33
Total		*68*	*60*	*32*	*24*	*184*
Milford Station						
MIA		1	0	0	0	1
Total		*1*	*0*	*0*	*0*	*1*
North Anna						
KIA		1 (1)	8 (1)	9 (1)	1	19 (3)
WIA		11 (1)	29 (1)	41 (6)	9 (2)	90 (10)
W&C		0	0	1 (1)	1	2 (1)
MIA	1	11	22	7	2	43
Total	*1*	*23*	*59*	*58*	*13*	*154*
Totopotomoy						
KIA		0	0	1	0	1
MIA		0	0	0	0	0
Total		*0*	*0*	*1*	*0*	*1*
Cold Harbor						
KIA		0	2	0	0	2
WIA		3 (1)	2	5	5 (1)	15 (2)
W&C		0	0	0	0	0
MIA		2	0	0	0	2
Total		*5*	*4*	*5*	*5*	*19*
Campaign Total	2	*171*	*172 (168)*	*241 (236)*	*179 (177)*	*765 (754)*

TABLE 57. Perrin's/Sanders's (Alabama) Brigade

	F&S	*8th Rgt.*	*9th Rgt.*	*10th Rgt.*	*11th Rgt.*	*14th Rgt.*	*Total*
Wilderness							
KIA		7	3 (2)	15	6	11 (2)	42 (4)
WIA		43 (2)	17 (1)	54 (4)	20 (2)	57 (3)	191 (12)
W&C		0	0	0	0	0	0
MIA		8	16	8	0	5	37
Total		*58*	*36*	*77*	*26*	*73*	*270*
Spotsylvania							
KIA	1	6	2	11	4	12	36
WIA	1	23 (2)	11	41 (3)	18 (1)	20 (4)	114 (10)
W&C		2	0	1	0	0	3
MIA		3	3	8	2	3	19
Total	*2*	*34*	*16*	*61*	*24*	*35*	*172*
North Anna							
KIA		2	0	3	0	2	7
WIA		6 (2)	0	12 (2)	5 (1)	6	29 (5)
W&C		0	0	0	0	0	0
MIA		3	4	2	0	13	22
Total		*11*	*4*	*17*	*5*	*21*	*58*
Totopotomoy							
KIA		1 (1)	0	0	0	1 (1)	2 (2)
WIA		0	0	0	0	6	6
W&C		0	0	0	0	0	0
MIA		0	0	0	0	6	6
Total		*1*	*0*	*0*	*0*	*13*	*14*
Cold Harbor							
KIA		6	0	6	1	1 (1)	14 (1)
WIA		14	11	19 (1)	11 (2)	7 (2)	62 (5)
W&C		0	0	0	0	0	0
MIA		0	0	0	0	1	1
Total		*20*	*11*	*25*	*12*	*9*	*77*
Campaign Total	*2*	*124 (121)*	*67 (65)*	*180 (179)*	*67*	*151*	*591 (585)*

TABLE 58. Mahone's (Virginia) Brigade

	F&S	*6th Rgt.*	*12th Rgt.*	*16th Rgt.*	*41st Rgt.*	*61st Rgt.*	*Total*
Wilderness							
KIA		4 (1)	7 (1)	3 (1)	8 (2)	4 (1)	26 (6)
WIA	1	34 (4)	43 (6)	13	23 (1)	12 (2)	126 (13)
W&C		1	0	0	0	0	1
MIA		0	0	2	0	1	3
Total	*1*	*39*	*50*	*18*	*31*	*17*	*156*
Spotsylvania							
KIA		3 (1)	20 (4)	5 (2)	7 (2)	13 (3)	48 (12)
WIA		38 (4)	49 (4)	31 (2)	24 (1)	46 (8)	188 (19)
W&C		9 (3)	1	0	0	0	10 (3)
MIA		12	5	0	2	0	19
Total		*62*	*75*	*36*	*33*	*59*	*265*
Milford Station							
MIA		0	0	0	1 (des.)	0	1
Total		*0*	*0*	*0*	*1*	*0*	*1*
North Anna							
KIA		0	3	0	4	0	7
WIA		1	5	1	2	3	12
W&C		0	0	0	0	0	0
MIA		1	0	1	8	1	11
Total		*2*	*8*	*2*	*14*	*4*	*30*
Totopotomoy							
			Not in Action, No Loss				
Cold Harbor							
KIA		1	1 (1)	4	2	2	10 (1)
WIA		13 (2)	8 (1)	5	12	5	43 (3)
W&C		0	0	0	0	1	1
MIA		5	4	0	2	5	16
Total		*19*	*13*	*9*	*16*	*13*	*70*
Campaign Total	*1*	*122*	*146 (145)*	*65 (64)*	*95*	*93 (91)*	*522 (518)*

TABLE 59. Harris's (Mississippi) Brigade

	12th Rgt.	*16th Rgt.*	*19th Rgt.*	*48th Rgt.*	*Total*
Wilderness					
KIA	1	5	2 (1)	3	11 (1)
WIA	4	19 (1)	11	4	38 (1)
W&C	0	0	0	0	0
MIA	2	0	0	0	2
Total	*7*	*24*	*13*	*7*	*51*
Spotsylvania					
KIA	13	39 (5)	19 (2)	13 (2)	84 (9)
WIA	33 (2)	77 (3)	45 (3)	29 (1)	184 (9)
W&C	2 (1)	8 (1)	8 (3)	5 (2)	23 (8)
MIA	8	22	42	20	92
Total	*56*	*146*	*114*	*67*	*383*
North Anna					
KIA	1	1	1	0	3
WIA	1	2	3 (1)	3	9 (1)
W&C	0	0	0	0	0
MIA	0	2	2	1	5
Total	*2*	*5*	*6*	*4*	*17*
Totopotomoy					
KIA	0	0	0	0	0
WIA	0	0	1	1 (1)	2 (1)
W&C	0	0	0	0	0
MIA	0	0	0	0	0
Total	*0*	*0*	*1*	*1*	*2*
Cold Harbor					
KIA	7 (1)	7 (1)	6	4	24 (2)
WIA	12 (4)	8	14	7	41 (14)
W&C	0	0	0	0	0
MIA	3	0	2	0	5
Total	*22*	*15*	*22*	*11*	*70*
Campaign Total	*87*	*190 (189)*	*156*	*90*	*523 (522)*

TABLE 60. Wright's (Georgia) Brigade

	3rd Rgt.	*22nd Rgt.*	*48th Rgt.*	*2nd Bn.*	*10th Bn.*	*Total*
Wilderness						
KIA	0	0	0	1 (1)	1	2 (1)
WIA	1	0	2	0	0	3
W&C	0	0	0	0	0	0
MIA	0	0	0	0	0	0
Total	*1*	*0*	*2*	*1*	*1*	*5*
Spotsylvania						
KIA	11 (4)	8 (3)	3	2	7 (3)	31 (10)
WIA	67 (8)	38 (2)	32 (1)	9 (1)	30 (1)	176 (13)
W&C	0	0	0	0	0	0
MIA	0	1	3	1	0	5
Total	*78*	*47*	*38*	*12*	*37*	*212*
North Anna						
KIA	0	0	0	0	3 (1)	3 (1)
WIA	2	3 (1)	1	2	10 (1)	18 (2)
W&C	0	0	0	0	0	0
MIA	1	1	1	3	0	6
Total	*3*	*4*	*2*	*5*	*13*	*27*
Totopotomoy						
			Not in Action, No Loss			
Cold Harbor						
KIA	2	0	2	0	1	5
WIA	7	5 (1)	6 (1)	0	7 (1)	25 (3)
W&C	0	0	0	0	0	0
MIA	0	0	0	0	0	0
Total	*9*	*5*	*8*	*0*	*8*	*30*
Campaign Total	*91*	*56*	*50 (49)*	*18*	*59*	*274 (273)*

TABLE 61. Perry's/Finegan's (Florida) Brigade

	F&S	*2nd Rgt.*	*5th Rgt.*	*8th Rgt.*	*9th Rgt.*	*10th Rgt.*	*11th Rgt.*	*Total*
Wilderness								
KIA		15 (2)	17 (4)	2				34 (6)
WIA	2	24	54 (3)	22 (2)				102 (5)
W&C		3	13 (1)	3				19 (1)
MIA		18	67	3				88
Total	*2*	*60*	*151*	*30*				*243*
Spotsylvania								
KIA		0	0	0				0
WIA		0	0	0				0
W&C		0	0	0				0
MIA		0	1	0				1
Total		*0*	*1*	*0*				*1*
North Anna								
KIA		0	0	2 (1)				2 (1)
WIA		3	2	2 (1)				7 (1)
W&C		0	0	0				0
MIA		1	0	7				8
Total		*4*	*2*	*11*				*17*

(continued)

TABLE 61. Perry's/Finegan's (Florida) Brigade (*continued*)

	F&S	*2nd Rgt.*	*5th Rgt.*	*8th Rgt.*	*9th Rgt.*	*10th Rgt.*	*11th Rgt.*	*Total*
Totopotomoy								
KIA		0	1 (1)	2				3 (1)
WIA		0	1	2				3
W&C		0	0	0				0
MIA		0	3	0				3
Total		*0*	*5*	*4*				*9*
Cold Harbor								
KIA		4	3 (1)	2	25 (4)	15 (3)	0	49 (8)
WIA	1	8 (1)	9 (1)	9 (1)	83 (10)	125 (9)	27 (3)	262 (25)
W&C		0	0	0	0	0	0	0
MIA		0	0	0	0	0	0	0
Total	*1*	*12*	*12*	*11*	*108*	*140*	*27*	*311*
Campaign Total	*3*	*76 (75)*	*171 (170)*	*56*	*108*	*140*	*27*	
							Perry	*305 (303)*
							Finegan	*276*
							Grand Total	*581 (579)*

TABLE 62. Third Corps Artillery

1. POAGUE'S BATTALION

	F&S	*Richards's (Miss.) Btty.*	*Williams's (N.C.) Btty.*	*Wyatt's (Va.) Btty.*	*Utterback's (Va.) Btty.*	*Bn. Total*
Wilderness						
KIA		2	1	0	1 (1)	4 (1)
WIA	1	6	4	0	0	11
MIA		0	0	0	0	0
Total	*1*	*8*	*5*	*0*	*1*	*15*
Spotsylvania						
KIA		0	2 (1)	0	0	2 (1)
WIA		1	1	1	0	3
MIA		0	0	0	0	0
Total		*1*	*3*	*1*	*0*	*5*
North Anna						
KIA	1	0	0	0	0	1
WIA		0	0	0	0	0
MIA		0	0	0	0	0
Total	*1*	*0*	*0*	*0*	*0*	*1*
Totopotomoy						
		Not in Action, No Loss				
Cold Harbor						
KIA		5 (1)	1	8	0	14 (1)
WIA	1	17 (1)	3 (1)	23 (5)	1	45 (7)
MIA		0	0	0	0	0
Total	*1*	*22*	*4*	*31*	*1*	*59*
Campaign Total	*2 (3)*	*31*	*12*	*32*	*2*	*80*

2. CUTTS'S (11TH GEORGIA) BATTALION

	F&S	*Ross's Btty.*	*Patterson's Btty.*	*Wingfield's Btty.*	*Bn. Total*
Wilderness					
		Not in Action, No Loss			

(continued)

2. CUTTS'S (11TH GEORGIA) BATTALION (*continued*)

	F&S	*Ross's Btty.*	*Patterson's Btty.*	*Wingfield's Btty.*	*Bn. Total*
Spotsylvania					
		Not in Action, No Loss			
North Anna					
KIA		0	0	0	0
WIA	2	2	4 (1)	3	11 (1)
MIA		0	0	0	0
Total	*2*	*2*	*4*	*3*	*11*
Totopotomoy					
KIA		1	0	0	1
WIA		3	0	0	3
MIA		0	0	0	0
Total		*4*	*0*	*0*	*4*
Cold Harbor					
KIA		0	1	0	1
WIA	1	2	5	0	8
MIA		0	0	0	0
Total	*1*	*2*	*6*	*0*	*9*
Campaign Total	*3*	*8*	*10*	*3*	*24*

3. MCINTOSH'S BATTALION

	Hurt's (Ala.) Btty.	*Price's (Va.) Btty.*	*Donald's (Va.) Btty.*	*Clutter's (Va.) Btty.*	*Bn. Total*
Wilderness					
KIA	0	0	0	0	0
WIA	0	0	1	0	1
Total	*0*	*0*	*1*	*0*	*1*
Spotsylvania					
KIA	0	1	0	0	1
WIA	0	2	0	8 (1)	10 (1)
MIA	0	0	0	0	0
Total	*0*	*3*	*0*	*8*	*11*

3. MCINTOSH'S BATTALION (*continued*)

	Hurt's (Ala.) Btty.	*Price's (Va.) Btty.*	*Donald's (Va.) Btty.*	*Clutter's (Va.) Btty.*	*Bn. Total*
North Anna					
KIA	0	0	0	1	1
WIA	0	1	0	0	1
Total	*0*	*1*	*0*	*1*	*2*
Totopotomoy					
KIA	0	0	0	1	1
WIA	0	0	0	1	1
Total	*0*	*0*	*0*	*2*	*2*
Cold Harbor					
KIA	1	3	0	0	4
WIA	0	9	1	0	10
MIA	0	0	0	0	0
Total	*1*	*12*	*1*	*0*	*14*
Campaign Total	*1*	*16*	*2*	*11*	*30*

4. RICHARDSON'S BATTALION

	Landry's (La.) Btty.	*Moore's (Va.) Btty.*	*Penick's (Va.) Btty.*	*Grandy's (Va.) Btty.*	*Bn. Total*
Wilderness					
KIA	0	0	0	0	0
WIA	0	0	1	0	1
Total	*0*	*0*	*1*	*0*	*1*
Spotsylvania					
KIA	0	1	0	0	1
WIA	0	5 (1)	0	2	7 (1)
MIA	0	0	0	0	0
Total	*0*	*6*	*0*	*2*	*8*
North Anna					
	Not in Action, No Loss				
Totopotomoy					
	Not in Action, No Loss				

(continued)

4. RICHARDSON'S BATTALION (*continued*)

	Landry's (La.) Btty.	*Moore's (Va.) Btty.*	*Penick's (Va.) Btty.*	*Grandy's (Va.) Btty.*	*Bn. Total*
Cold Harbor					
KIA	0	0	0	0	0
WIA	0	0	0	3 (1)	3 (1)
MIA	0	0	0	0	0
Total	*0*	*0*	*0*	*3*	*3*
Campaign Total	*0*	*6*	*1*	*5*	*12*

5. PEGRAM'S BATTALION

	F&S	*Zimmer's (S.C.) Btty.*	*Ellet's Va.) Btty.*	*Marye's (Va.) Btty.*	*Brander's (Va.) Btty.*	*Cayce's (Va.) Btty.*	*Bn. Total*
Wilderness							
KIA		0	0	0	0	1	1
WIA		0	1	0	0	0	1
Total		*0*	*1*	*0*	*0*	*1*	*2*
Spotsylvania							
KIA		0	0	0	0	0	0
WIA	1	0	7	0	1	2	11
MIA		0	0	2	0	1	3
Total	*1*	*0*	*7*	*2*	*1*	*3*	*14*
North Anna							
KIA		0	1	0	0	1	2
WIA		4	2 (1)	0	0	1	7 (1)
Total		*4*	*3*	*0*	*0*	*2*	*9*
Totopotomoy							
			Not in Action, No Loss				
Cold Harbor							
KIA		0	0	0	0	0	0
WIA		0	2	1	1	1	5
Total		*0*	*2*	*1*	*1*	*1*	*5*
Campaign Total	*1*	*4*	*13*	*3*	*2*	*7*	*30*

THIRD CORPS ARTILLERY TOTAL

Wilderness	
KIA	5 (1)
WIA	14
MIA	0
Total	*19*
Spotsylvania	
KIA	4 (1)
WIA	31 (2)
MIA	3
Total	*38*
North Anna	
KIA	4
WIA	19 (2)
MIA	0
Total	*23*
Totopotomoy	
KIA	2
WIA	4
MIA	0
Total	*6*
Cold Harbor	
KIA	19 (1)
WIA	71 (8)
MIA	0
Total	*90*
Campaign Total	*176*

TABLE 63. Wickham's (Virginia) Brigade

	1st Cav. Rgt.	*2nd Cav. Rgt.*	*3rd Cav. Rgt.*	*4th Cav. Rgt.*	*Total*
Wilderness					
KIA	0	1	1	0	2
WIA	0	2	4	1	7
MIA	0	1	0	0	1
Total	*0*	*4*	*5*	*1*	*10*
Todd's Tavern & Spotsylvania					
KIA	19 (3)	13 (1)	8	14	54 (4)
WIA	55 (3)	47 (1)	27 (1)	85 (3)	214 (8)
W&C	1	0	3	3	7
MIA	6	4	16	4	30
Total	*81*	*64*	*54*	*106*	*305*
Mitchell's Shop & Beaver Dam					
KIA		1	5 (1)	1	7 (1)
WIA		5	10	4	19
W&C		0	2	0	2
MIA		0	7	0	7
Total		*6*	*24*	*5*	*35*
Yellow Tavern					
KIA	0	7 (4)	3	4	14 (4)
WIA	13 (2)	38 (4)	16	19	86 (6)
W&C	2	0	0	0	2
MIA	0	6	3	0	9
Total	*15*	*51*	*22*	*23*	*111*
Wilson's Wharf					
KIA	4	5 (1)	2	6 (4)	17 (5)
WIA	12 (1)	12 (1)	5	12	41 (2)
W&C	0	0	0	1	1
MIA	0	1	0	0	1
Total	*16*	*18*	*7*	*19*	*60*
Hanovertown					
KIA		1			1
WIA		0			0
MIA		1			1
Total		*2*			*2*

TABLE 63. Wickham's (Virginia) Brigade (*continued*)

	1st Cav. Rgt.	*2nd Cav. Rgt.*	*3rd Cav. Rgt.*	*4th Cav. Rgt.*	*Total*
Haw's Shop					
KIA	4	4 (2)	6 (2)	2	16 (4)
WIA	10	14	29 (2)	11 (1)	64 (3)
W&C	0	2	0	0	2
MIA	1	5	0	1	7
Total	*15*	*25*	*35*	*14*	*89*
Cold Harbor					
KIA	0	0	0	0	0
WIA	4	9 (1)	4	1	18 (1)
MIA	3	0	1	1	5
Total	*7*	*9*	*5*	*2*	*23*
Trevilian Station					
KIA	0	1	4 (1)	1	6 (1)
WIA	1	14 (3)	25 (5)	23 (2)	63 (10)
MIA	0	0	0	3	3
Total	*1*	*15*	*29*	*27*	*72*
Campaign Total	*135 (134)*	*194 (193)*	*181 (179)*	*197 (195)*	*707 (701)*

TABLE 64. Lomax's (Virginia) Brigade

	F&S	*5th Cav. Rgt.*	*6th Cav. Rgt.*	*15th Cav. Rgt.*	*Total*
Wilderness					
KIA		1	2	1	4
WIA	1	3	9 (1)	16 (2)	29 (3)
MIA		0	2	1	3
Total	*1*	*4*	*13*	*18*	*36*
Todd's Tavern and Spotsylvania					
KIA		4 (1)	7 (2)	3 (1)	14 (4)
WIA		12	27 (2)	24 (2)	63 (4)
W&C		1	0	0	1
MIA		2	4	5	11
Total		*19*	*38*	*32*	*89*
Beaver Dam					
MIA		2			2
Total		*2*			*2*
Yellow Tavern					
KIA		8 (1)	5 (2)	2	15 (3)
WIA		24 (1)	21 (2)	22 (2)	67 (5)
W&C		1	0	0	1
MIA		62	33	28	123
Total		*95*	*59*	*52*	*206*
Miscellaneous Actions, King William County (May 10–24)					
MIA		3			3
Total		*3*			*3*
Haw's Shop					
KIA		0	0	0	0
WIA		1	0	2	3
MIA		1	0	0	1
Total		*2*	*0*	*2*	*4*
Cold Harbor					
KIA		1	3 (2)	2	6 (2)
WIA		7	15	3	25

TABLE 64. Lomax's (Virginia) Brigade (*continued*)

	F&S	*5th Cav. Rgt.*	*6th Cav. Rgt.*	*15th Cav. Rgt.*	*Total*
Cold Harbor (*continued*)					
W&C		0	1	0	1
MIA		12	10	3	25
Total		*20*	*29*	*8*	*57*
Trevilian Station					
KIA		0	1	1	2
WIA		6 (1)	11	0	17 (1)
MIA		12	8	1	21
Total		*18*	*20*	*2*	*40*
Campaign Total	*1*	*163*	*159*	*114*	*437*

TABLE 65. Young's Brigade

	F & S	*Davis (Ala.-Miss.) Legion*	*Cobbs's (Ga.) Legion*	*Phillips's (Ga.) Legion*	*20th Ga. Cav.Bn.*	*7th Ga. Cav. Rgt.*	*Total*
Wilderness							
KIA		0	1	0			1
WIA		2	5	0			7
MIA		0	0	4			4
Total		*2*	*6*	*4*			*12*
Spotsylvania							
KIA		2	0	2 (1)			4 (1)
WIA		1	4	1			6
W&C		1	2	0			3
Total		*4*	*6*	*3*			*13*
Miscellaneous Actions, King George County (May 15–16)							
MIA		0	8	1			9
Milford Station							
MIA		0	3	4			7
North Anna							
KIA		0	2	0			2
WIA		0	1	2			3
W&C		0	1	1			2
Total		*0*	*4*	*3*			*7*
Haw's Shop							
KIA					17 (10)		17 (10)
WIA					44 (7)		44 (7)
W&C					4 (1)		4 (1)
MIA					8		8
Total					*73*		*73*
Hanover Court House							
KIA		0	1	0			1
WIA		0	2	0			2
MIA		0	4	0			4
Total		*0*	*7*	*0*			*7*

TABLE 65. Young's Brigade (*continued*)

	F & S	*Davis (Ala.-Miss.) Legion*	*Cobbs's (Ga.) Legion*	*Phillips's (Ga.) Legion*	*20th Ga. Cav.Bn.*	*7th Ga. Cav. Rgt.*	*Total*
Matadequin Creek							
KIA					5 (1)		5 (1)
WIA					24 (1)		24 (1)
MIA					9		9
Total					*38*		*38*
Cold Harbor							
KIA		0	0	0	0	0	0
WIA		2	3	0	3	1	9
MIA		2	2	0	1	0	5
Total		*4*	*5*	*0*	*4*	*1*	*14*
Trevilian Station							
KIA		2	4	2	6	12 (1)	26 (1)
WIA		8	2	10 (1)	7 (2)	44 (9)	71 (12)
MIA	1	11	7	2	5	183	209
Total	*1*	*21*	*13*	*14*	*18*	*239*	*306*
Campaign Total	*1*	*31*	*52*	*29*	*133*	*240*	*486*

TABLE 66. Rosser's (Laurel) Brigade

	F&S	7th Va. Cav. Rgt.	11th Va. Cav. Rgt.	12th Va. Cav. Rgt.	35th Va. Cav. Bn.	Total
Wilderness						
KIA		10 (1)	13 (1)	20 (3)	7	50 (5)
WIA	2	53 (1)	120 (5)	134 (1)	69 (4)	378 (11)
W&C		0	0	1	1	2
MIA		0	1	2	2	5
Total	2	*63*	*134*	*157*	*79*	*435*
Spotsylvania						
KIA		2	1	0	2	5
WIA		4	7	2	5 (1)	18 (1)
W&C		0	1	0	0	1
MIA		2	0	0	0	2
Total		*8*	*9*	*2*	*7*	*26*
Milford Station						
MIA		1	2	1	0	4
Total		*1*	*2*	*1*	*0*	*4*
North Anna						
KIA		0	0	0	0	0
WIA		1	1	3	0	5
MIA		0	0	3	0	3
Total		*1*	*1*	*6*	*0*	*8*
Haw's Shop						
KIA		5 (3)	0	0	1	6 (3)
WIA		12	6 (2)	2 (1)	4	24 (3)
W&C		0	1	0	0	1
MIA		1	0	2	0	3
Total		*18*	*7*	*4*	*5*	*34*
Ashland						
KIA		0	1	3	0	4
WIA		6 (1)	3	1	2	12 (1)
MIA		0	0	0	1	1
Total		*6*	*4*	*4*	*3*	*17*

TABLE 66. Rosser's (Laurel) Brigade (*continued*)

	F&S	*7th Va. Cav. Rgt.*	*11th Va. Cav. Rgt.*	*12th Va. Cav. Rgt.*	*35th Va. Cav. Bn.*	*Total*
Trevilian Station						
KIA		0	0	0	1	1
WIA	1	13	1	5 (1)	4	24 (1)
MIA		0	0	0	0	0
Total	*1*	*13*	*1*	*5*	*5*	*25*
Campaign Total	*3*	*110*	*158 (157)*	*179*	*99*	*549 (548)*

TABLE 67. Butler's (South Carolina) Brigade

	F&S	4th Cav. Rgt.	5th Cav. Rgt.	6th Cav. Rgt.	Total
Drewry's Bluff Campaign					
KIA			3		3
WIA			39 (1)		39 (1)
MIA			2		2
Total			*44*		*44*
Charles County Court House (May 20)					
KIA			0		0
WIA			7		7
MIA			0		0
Total			*7*		*7*
Haw's Shop					
KIA		32 (8)	4 (1)		36 (9)
WIA	1 (1)	49 (7)	23 (3)		73 (11)
W&C		21 (7)	3 (3)		24 (10)
MIA		25	3		28
Total	*1 (1)*	*127*	*33*		*161*
Atlee Station					
KIA		0	0		0
WIA		3	1		4
MIA		0	0		0
Total		*3*	*1*		*4*
Matadequin Creek					
KIA		9 (2)	4 (1)		13 (3)
WIA		18 (2)	19 (2)		37 (4)
W&C		6 (3)	0		6 (3)
MIA		18	0		18
Total		*51*	*23*		*74*
Cold Harbor					
KIA		0	0	0	0
WIA		1 (1)	3	1	5 (1)
MIA		0	1	0	1
Total		*1*	*4*	*1*	*6*

TABLE 67. Butler's (South Carolina) Brigade (*continued*)

	F&S	*4th Cav. Rgt.*	*5th Cav. Rgt.*	*6th Cav. Rgt.*	*Total*
Trevilian Station					
KIA		18 (2)	8 (1)	19 (1)	45 (4)
WIA	1	37 (4)	49 (6)	100 (6)	187 (16)
W&C		0	0	1	1
MIA		53	8	24	85
Total	*1*	*108*	*65*	*144*	*318*
Campaign Total	*2*	*290 (289)*	*126*	*145*	*563 (562)*

TABLE 68. Chambliss's (Virginia) Brigade

	9th Cav. Rgt.	*10th Cav. Rgt.*	*13th Cav. Rgt.*	*Total*
Spotsylvania				
KIA	1	0	1	2
WIA	17 (2)	5 (1)	8 (1)	30 (4)
MIA	1	4	2	7
Total	*19*	*9*	*11*	*39*
Yellow Tavern				
MIA		1		1
Total		*1*		*1*
King George County (May 16)				
MIA			1	1
Total			*1*	*1*
Guinea Station				
KIA	2	0	0	2
WIA	4 (1)	2	0	6 (1)
W&C	1	1	0	2
MIA	1	0	0	1
Total	*8*	*3*	*0*	*11*
North Anna				
KIA	0	1	0	1
WIA	1	1	0	2
MIA	1	0	0	1
Total	*2*	*2*	*0*	*4*
Haw's Shop				
	No Reported Loss			
Hanover Court House				
KIA	1	0	1	2
WIA	7 (1)	3	5	15 (1)
MIA	0	0	0	0
Total	*8*	*3*	*6*	*17*

TABLE 68. Chambliss's (Virginia) Brigade (*continued*)

	9th Cav. Rgt.	*10th Cav. Rgt.*	*13th Cav. Rgt.*	*Total*
Ashland				
KIA	2	2	3	7
WIA	10 (2)	3	9 (1)	22 (3)
MIA	2	1	1	4
Total	*14*	*6*	*13*	*33*
Cold Harbor				
KIA	1	0	0	1
WIA	6	0	0	6
W&C	1	0	0	1
MIA	0	0	0	0
Total	*8*	*0*	*0*	*8*
Campaign Total	*59*	*24*	*31*	*114*

TABLE 69. Gordon's (North Carolina) Brigade

	F&S	1st Cav. Rgt.	2nd Cav. Rgt.	3rd Cav. Rgt.	5th Cav. Rgt.	Total
Wilderness						
KIA		0	1		1	2
WIA		2	0		14 (1)	16 (1)
MIA		1	1		3	5
Total		*3*	*2*		*18*	*23*
Spotsylvania						
MIA		1	1			2
Beaver Dam						
MIA		1				1
Ground Squirrel Bridge						
KIA		3	0		2	5
WIA		9 (2)	5		16 (1)	30 (3)
MIA		0	0		1	1
Total		*12*	*5*		*19*	*36*
Brook Church						
KIA	1 (1)	3 (1)	1		5	9 (2)
WIA		10 (1)	7 (1)		17	34 (2)
MIA		0	0		0	0
Total	*1*	*13*	*8*		*21*	*43*
Miscellaneous Action (May 20)						
WIA			1			1
MIA			1			1
Total			*2*			*2*
Wilson Wharf						
KIA		1	0		6 (2)	7 (2)
WIA		10 (1)	1		10	21 (1)
MIA		0	1		0	1
Total		*11*	*2*		*16*	*29*
Hanovertown						
KIA		0	0	2	0	2
WIA		0	0	11	2	13
MIA		3	4	23	1	31
Total		*3*	*4*	*36*	*3*	*46*

TABLE 69. Gordon's (North Carolina) Brigade (*continued*)

	F&S	*1st Cav. Rgt.*	*2nd Cav. Rgt.*	*3rd Cav. Rgt.*	*5th Cav. Rgt.*	*Total*
Haw's Shop						
W&C				1		1
MIA				2		2
Total				*3*		*3*
Hanover Court House						
KIA		0	0	3	0	3
WIA		4 (1)	4 (1)	16 (2)	0	24 (4)
MIA		1	1	5	8	15
Total		*5*	*5*	*24*	*8*	*42*
Ashland						
KIA		1	1 (1)	2	9 (3)	13 (4)
WIA	2	8 (1)	2	16 (1)	21 (2)	49 (4)
MIA		2	1	0	2	5
Total	*2*	*11*	*4*	*18*	*32*	*67*
Second Haw's Shop & Cold Harbor						
KIA		0	1	0	1	2
WIA		0	3 (1)	4	8 (1)	15 (2)
MIA		0	3	0	2	5
Total		*0*	*7*	*4*	*11*	*22*
Campaign Total	*3*	*60*	*40*	*85*	*128*	*316*

TABLE 70. Horse Artillery (Breathed's Battalion)

	F&S	*Hart's (S.C.) Btty.*	*Shoemkr's (Va.) Btty.*	*Johnston's (Va.) Btty.*	*McGregor's (Va.) Btty.*	*Thomson's (Va.) Btty.*	*Total*
Wilderness							
KIA		0	1	0	0	0	1
WIA		0	9	0	0	3	12
MIA		0	0	0	0	0	0
Total		*0*	*10*	*0*	*0*	*3*	*13*
Spotsylvania							
KIA		0	1	0	2	0	3
WIA		0	0	3 (1)	1	0	4 (1)
W&C		0	0	0	0	1	1
MIA		0	0	2	0	0	2
Total		*0*	*1*	*5*	*3*	*1*	*10*
Yellow Tavern							
KIA	1 (1)	0	0	0	0	0	1 (1)
WIA		1	0	0	0	0	1
MIA		3	0	1	0	0	4
Total	*1*	*4*	*0*	*1*	*0*	*0*	*6*
Haw's Shop							
KIA		0	1	0	0	0	1
WIA		0	2	1	0	0	3
MIA		0	0	0	0	0	0
Total		*0*	*3*	*1*	*0*	*0*	*4*
Hanover Court House							
KIA		0	0	0	1	0	1
WIA		0	0	0	0	0	0
MIA		0	0	0	0	0	0
Total		*0*	*0*	*0*	*1*	*0*	*1*
Cold Harbor							
KIA		0	0	0	0	0	0
WIA		0	0	1	2	0	3
MIA		0	0	0	0	0	0
Total		*0*	*0*	*1*	*2*	*0*	*3*

TABLE 70. Horse Artillery (Breathed's Battalion) (*continued*)

	F&S	*Hart's (S.C.) Btty.*	*Shoemkr's (Va.) Btty.*	*Johnston's (Va.) Btty.*	*McGregor's (Va.) Btty.*	*Thomson's (Va.) Btty.*	*Total*
Trevilian Station							
KIA		0	0	0	0	3	3
WIA		8 (2)	6	0	0	8	22 (2)
MIA		0	0	0	0	0	0
Total		*8*	*6*	*0*	*0*	*11*	*25*
Campaign Total	*1*	*12*	*20*	*8*	*6*	*15*	*62*

TABLE 71. Clingman's (North Carolina) Brigade

	F&S	*8th Rgt.*	*31st Rgt.*	*51st Rgt.*	*61st Rgt.*	*Total*
Drewry's Bluff Campaign						
KIA		20 (6)	17 (9)	47 (22)	15 (7)	99 (44)
WIA		67	85 (9)	113	60	325 (9)
W&C		1	2	7	0	10
MIA		2	3	19	0	24
Total		*90*	*107*	*186*	*75*	*458*
Cold Harbor						
KIA		10 (1)	17 (2)	21 (3)	9 (1)	57 (7)
WIA	2	23 (3)	88 (3)	77 (9)	39 (3)	229 (18)
W&C		8 (1)	6 (1)	18 (4)	0	32 (6)
MIA		193	86	116	1	396
Total	2	*224*	*197*	*232*	*49*	*714*

TABLE 72. Hagood's (South Carolina) Brigade

	7th Bn.	*11th Rgt.*	*21st Rgt.*	*25th Rgt.*	*27th Rgt.*	*Total*
Drewry's Bluff Campaign						
KIA	69 (25)	41 (19)	62 (25)	65 (26)	32 (3)	269 (98)
WIA	109	69	147	133	106 (1)	564 (1)
W&C	8	2	1	3	0	14
MIA	16	13	11	15	9	64
Total	*202*	*125*	*221*	*216*	*147*	*911*
Cold Harbor						
KIA	4 (2)	5 (1)	3 (1)	4	6 (1)	22 (5)
WIA	40 (2)	24 (2)	18 (4)	19 (2)	21 (1)	122 (11)
W&C	0	0	0	0	0	0
MIA	1	0	0	0	0	1
Total	*45*	*29*	*21*	*23*	*27*	*145*

TABLE 73. Colquitt's (Georgia) Brigade

	F&S	*6th Rgt.*	*19th Rgt.*	*23rd Rgt.*	*27th Rgt.*	*28th Rgt.*	*Total*
Drewry's Bluff Campaign							
KIA		10 (6)	4 (1)	4	0	4	22 (7)
WIA		75	32 (1)	25	0	8	140
W&C		0	0	0	0	0	0
MIA		0	0	1	0	0	1
Total		*85*	*36*	*30*	*0*	*12*	*163*
Cold Harbor							
KIA		6 (1)	1	9 (2)	16 (2)	8	40 (5)
WIA	1	12 (1)	11	18	62 (9)	38 (3)	142 (13)
W&C		0	0	0	1	0	1
MIA		0	1	0	3	0	4
Total	*1*	*18*	*13*	*27*	*82*	*46*	*187*

TABLE 74. Martin's (North Carolina) Brigade

	F&S	*17th Rgt.*	*42nd Rgt.*	*66th Rgt.*	*Total*
Drewry's Bluff Campaign					
KIA		17 (3)	11 (1)	10 (4)	38 (10)
WIA		73 (6)	91	33	197 (6)
W&C		0	0	0	0
MIA		1	0	0	1
Total		*91*	*102*	*43*	*236*
Cold Harbor					
KIA		10 (4)	13	10 (2)	33 (6)
WIA		26 (1)	42	33 (6)	101 (7)
W&C		0	1	0	1
MIA		0	58	5	63
Total		*36*	*114*	*48*	*198*

TABLE 75. Read's (38th Virginia) Artillery Battalion*

	F&S	*Marshall's Btty.*	*Macon's Btty.*	*Sullivan's Btty.*	*Blount's Btty.*	*Total*
Drewry's Bluff Campaign						
KIA		2	0	0	3	5
WIA		3	0	0	11	14
MIA		0	0	0	0	0
Total		*5*	*0*	*0*	*14*	*19*
Cold Harbor						
KIA		1	5 (1)	2	0	8 (1)
WIA	1	3	2	7 (1)	2 (1)	15 (2)
MIA		0	0	12	0	12
Total	*1*	*4*	*7*	*21*	*2*	*35*

*Hoke's Divisional Artillery Battalion.

TABLE 76. Breckinridge's Division

ECHOLS'S (VIRGINIA) BRIGADE

	22nd Rgt.	*23rd Bn.*	*26th Bn.*	*Total*	*McLaughlin's Artillery Bn.*
North Anna					
KIA	0	0	0	0	0
WIA	2	0	0	2	0
W&C	0	0	0	0	0
MIA	0	0	0	0	0
Total	*2*	*0*	*0*	*2*	*0*
Totopotomoy					
KIA	1	2 (1)	1	4 (1)	1
WIA	5	5	7 (1)	17 (1)	10
W&C	0	1	0	1	0
MIA	4	0	29	33	0
Total	*10*	*8*	*37*	*55*	*11*
Cold Harbor					
KIA	5	5 (1)	3	13 (1)	0
WIA	28 (1)	15 (1)	16 (1)	59 (3)	2
W&C	0	0	7	7	0
MIA	27	4	154	185	0
Total	*60*	*24*	*180*	*264*	*2*
Campaign Total	*72*	*32*	*217*	*321*	*13*

WHARTON'S (VIRGINIA) BRIGADE

	51st Rgt.	*62nd Rgt.*	*30th Bn.*	*Total*	*Division Total*
North Anna					
KIA	0	0	0	0	0
WIA	3	0	1	4	6
W&C	0	0	0	0	0
MIA	1	0	0	1	1
Total	*4*	*0*	*1*	*5*	*7*

WHARTON'S (VIRGINIA) BRIGADE (*continued*)

	51st Rgt.	*62nd Rgt.*	*30th Bn.*	*Total*	*Division Total*
Totopotomoy					
KIA	2	1	0	3	8 (1)
WIA	8	3	0	11	38 (1)
W&C	0	0	0	0	1
MIA	0	0	4	4	37
Total	*10*	*4*	*4*	*18*	*84*
Cold Harbor					
KIA	2 (2)	0	0	2 (2)	15 (3)
WIA	11	20 (2)	17 (1)	48 (3)	109 (6)
W&C	0	0	0	0	7
MIA	1	0	0	1	186
Total	*14*	*20*	*17*	*51*	*317*
Campaign Total	*28*	*24*	*22*	*74*	*408*

TABLE 77. Maryland Line

	1st Cav. Bn.	*2nd Inf. Bn.*	*1st Arty. Btty.*	*2nd Arty. Btty.*	*4th Arty Btty.*	*Total*
Beaver Dam and Yellow Tavern						
KIA	3				0	3
WIA	8				11	19
W&C	2 (2)				0	2 (2)
MIA	1				9	10
Total	*14*				*20*	*34*
Pamunkey River						
KIA	0					0
WIA	1					1
MIA	3					3
Total	*4*					*4*
Pollard's Farm and Totopotomoy						
KIA	4 (1)	0				4 (1)
WIA	11 (1)	1				12 (1)
W&C	2 (1)	0				2 (1)
MIA	29	0				29
Total	*46*	*1*				*47*
Ashland						
KIA	1					1
WIA	0					0
MIA	2					2
Total	*3*					*3*
Cold Harbor						
KIA		6	1	0		7
WIA		36 (3)	2	1		39 (3)
MIA		0	0	0		0
Total		*42*	*3*	*1*		*46*
Campaign Total	*67 (66)*	*43*	*3*	*1*	*20*	*134 (133)*

TABLE 78. Miscellaneous Units

GRACIE'S (ALABAMA) BRIGADE

	F&S	*41st Rgt.*	*43rd Rgt.*	*59th Rgt.*	*60th Rgt.*	*23rd Bn.*	*Total*
Brook Church							
KIA		2	4 (1)	1 (1)	0	0	7 (2)
WIA	1	1	26 (3)	5	4	0	37 (3)
MIA		0	1	0	0	0	1
Total	*1*	*3*	*31*	*6*	*4*	*0*	*45*

RICHMOND GARRISON

	7th S.C. Cav. Rgt.	*42nd Va. Cav. Bn.*	*25th Va. Inf. Bn.*	*20th Va. HA Bn.*	*Thornton's Va. Btty.*	*Total*
Drewry's Bluff Campaign						
KIA	1	0				1
WIA	2	3				5
MIA	2	9				11
Total	*5*	*12*				*17*
Brook Church						
KIA			9 (3)	0	1 (1)	10 (2)
WIA			18 (3)	2	3	23 (3)
MIA			0	0	0	0
Total			*27*	*2*	*4*	*33*
Hanovertown, Hanover Court House, and Haw's Shop						
KIA	0	0				0
WIA	1	1 (1)				2 (1)
MIA	4	2				6
Total	*5*	*3*				*8*
Matadequin Creek						
KIA	11 (3)	4				15 (3)
WIA	54 (1)	18 (2)				72 (3)
W&C	8 (2)	0				8 (2)
MIA	9	5				14
Total	*82*	*27*				*109*

(continued)

RICHMOND GARRISON (*continued*)

	7th S.C. Cav. Rgt.	*42nd Va. Cav. Bn.*	*25th Va. Inf. Bn.*	*20th Va. HA Bn.*	*Thornton's Va. Btty.*	*Total*
Hanover Court House and Cold Harbor						
KIA	0	0				0
WIA	2	1				3
Total	*2*	*4*				*6*
Campaign Total	*89*	*34*				*123*

ARMY ESCORT/HQ GUARD

	39th Va. Cav. Bn.
Miscellaneous Actions, Caroline County (May 9)	
MIA	2
Total	*2*
Hanover Court House	
MIA	1
Total	*1*
Campaign Total	*5*

Appendix B

MAPS

All maps are by George Skoch and were previously published in the following books by Gordon C. Rhea: *The Battle of the Wilderness, May 5–6, 1864* (1994); *The Battles for Spotsylvania Court House and the Road to Yellow Tavern, May 7–12, 1864* (1997); *To the North Anna River: Grant and Lee, May 13–25, 1864* (2000); and *Cold Harbor: Grant and Lee, May 26–June 3, 1864* (2002).

THE BATTLE OF THE WILDERNESS

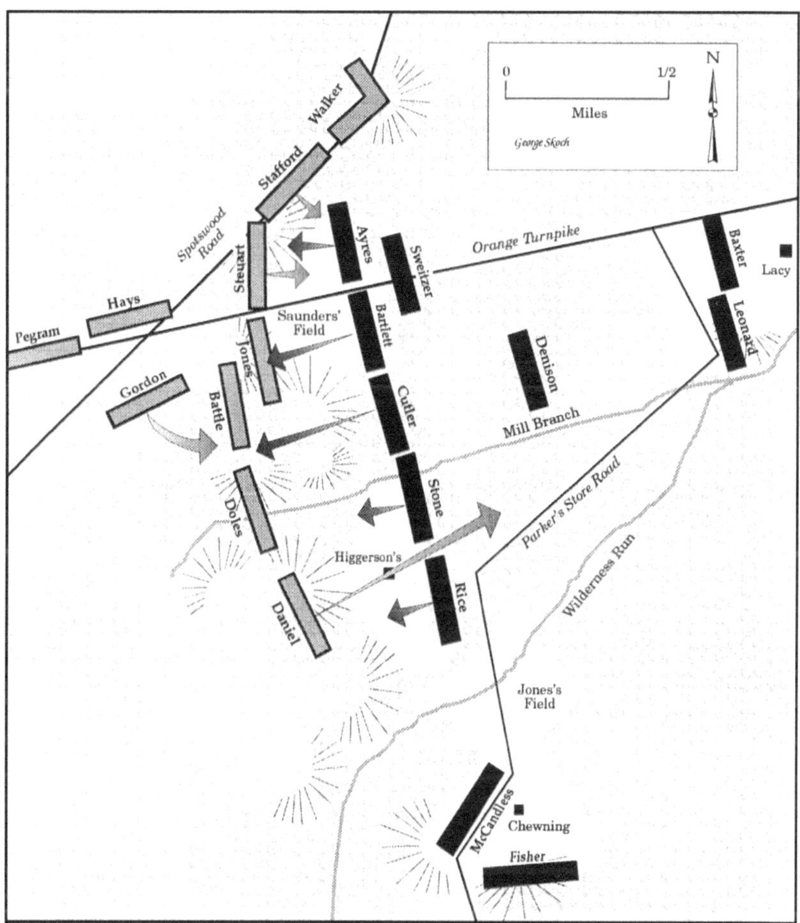

1. The turnpike front on May 5, 1 p.m.–3 p.m.

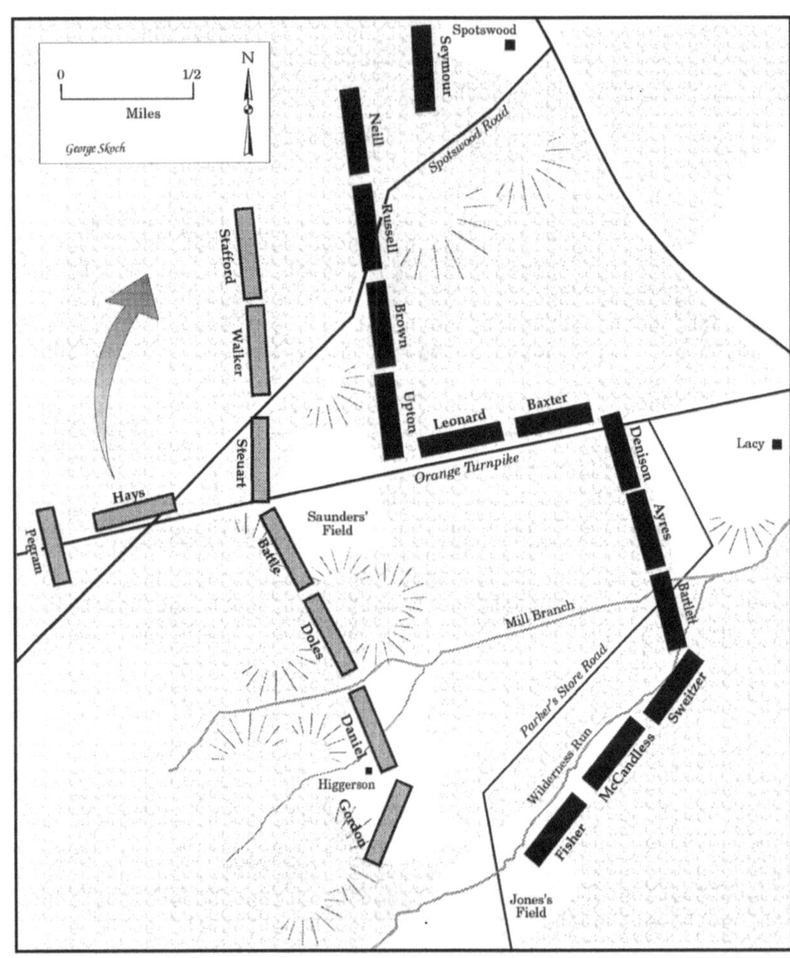

2. Sedgwick's assault on May 5, 3 p.m.–5 p.m.

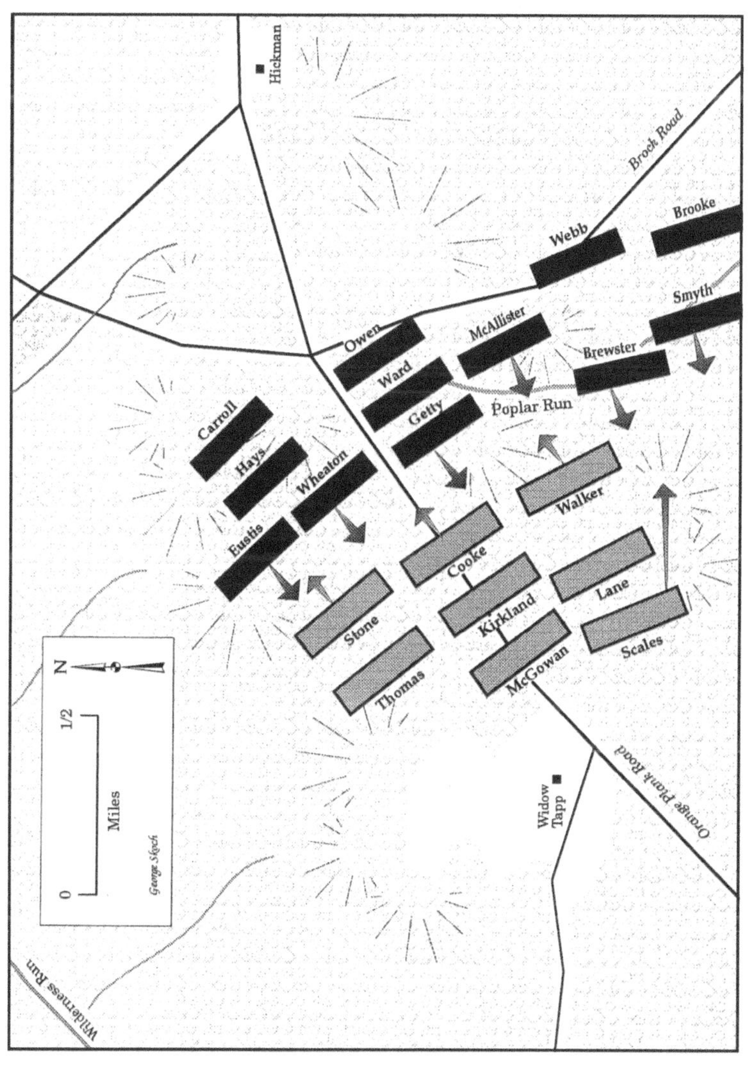

3. The Orange Plank Road front on May 5, 4:30 p.m.–9:00 p.m.

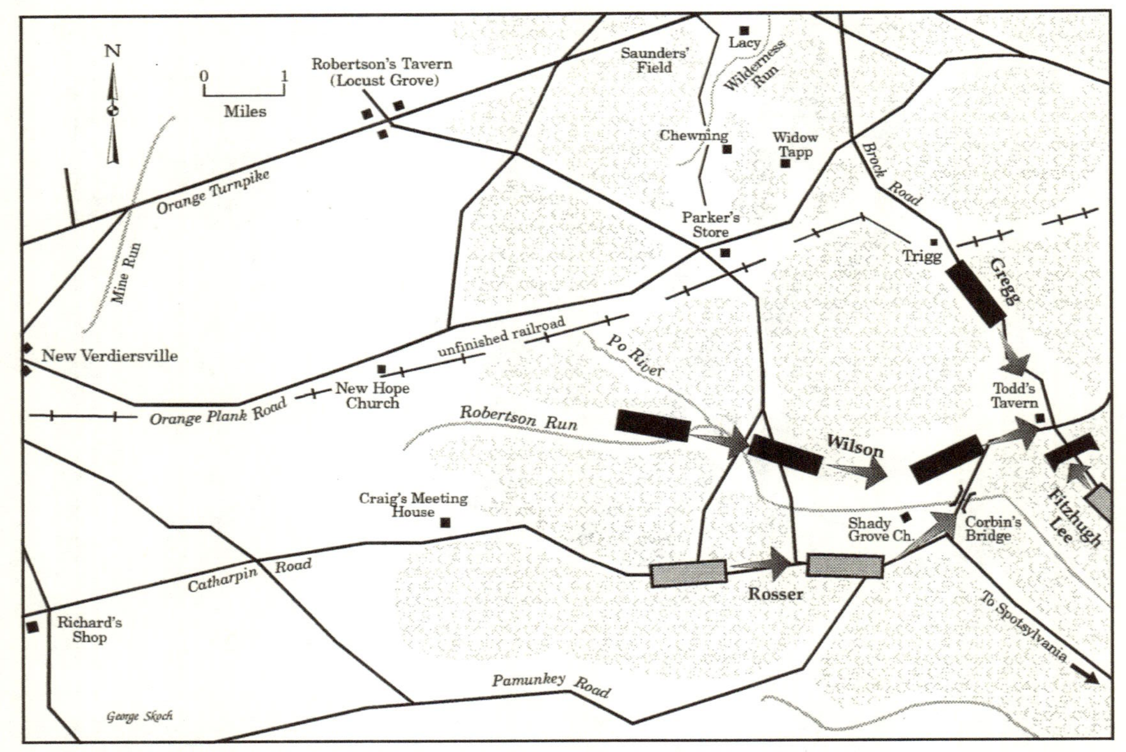

4. Cavalry maneuvers on the afternoon of May 5

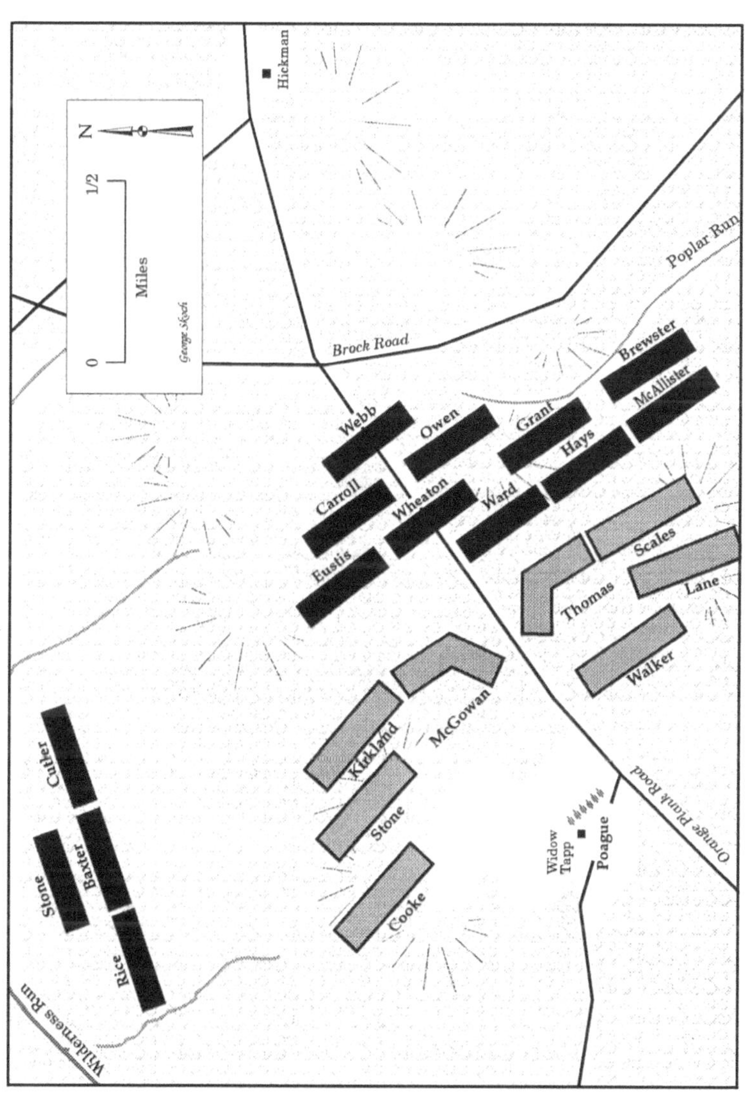

5. The Orange Plank Road front on May 6 at 5 a.m.

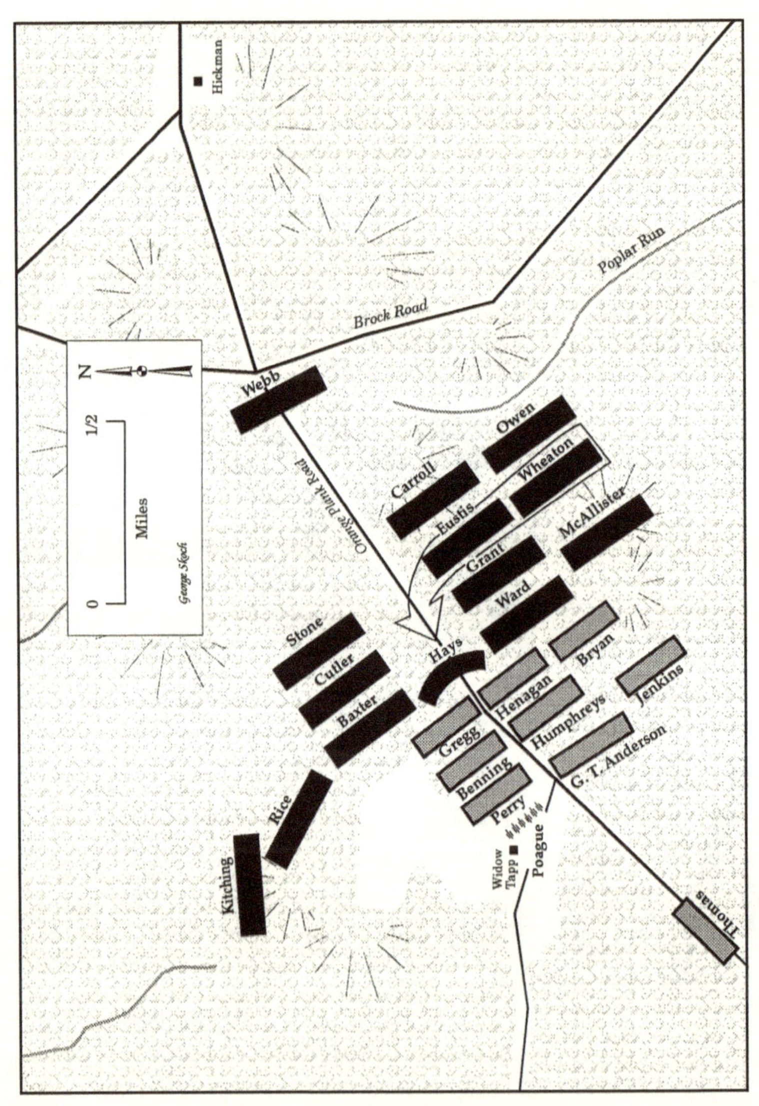

6. Longstreet's counterattack on May 6, 6 a.m.–10 a.m.

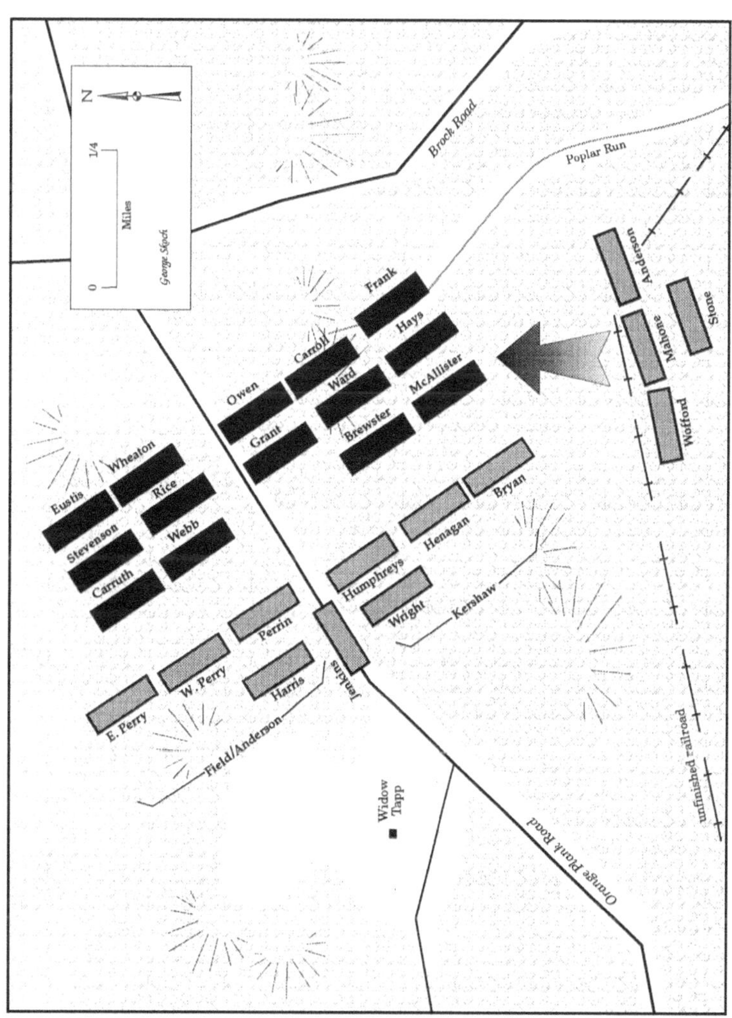

7. Longstreet's flank attack on May 6 at 11 a.m.

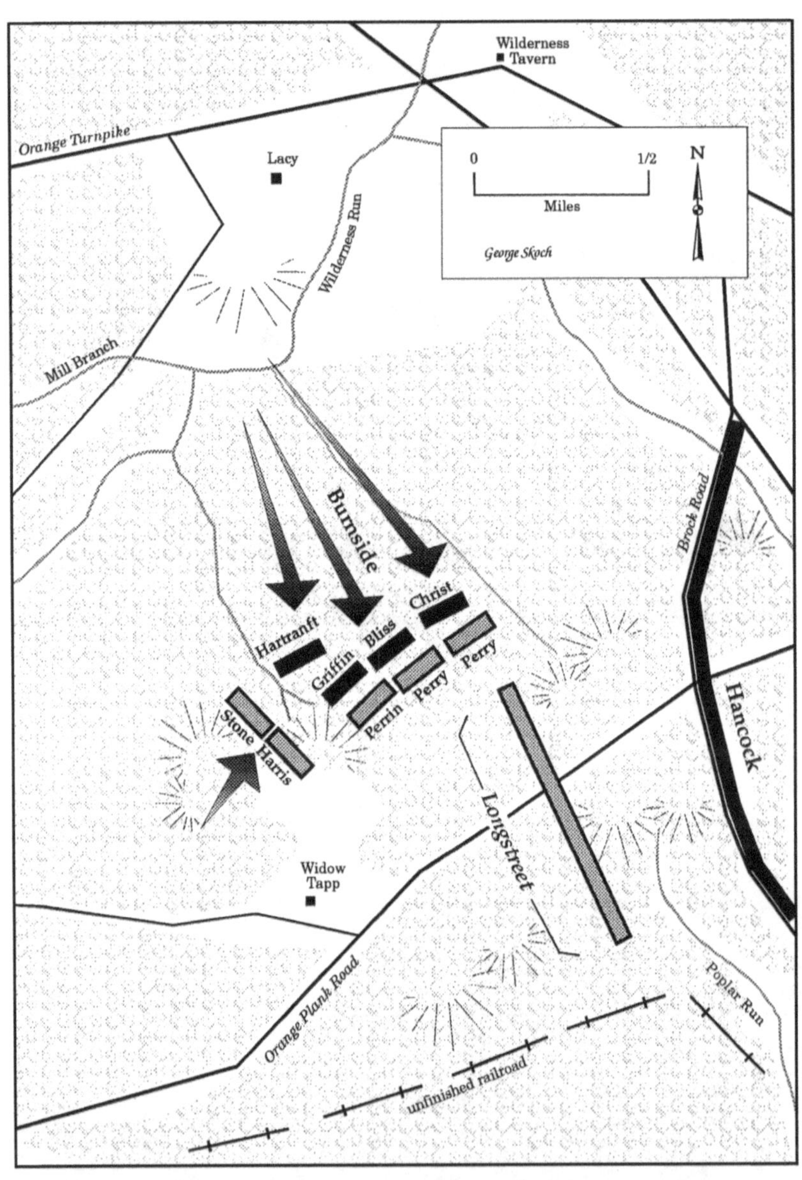

8. Burnside's assault on the afternoon of May 6

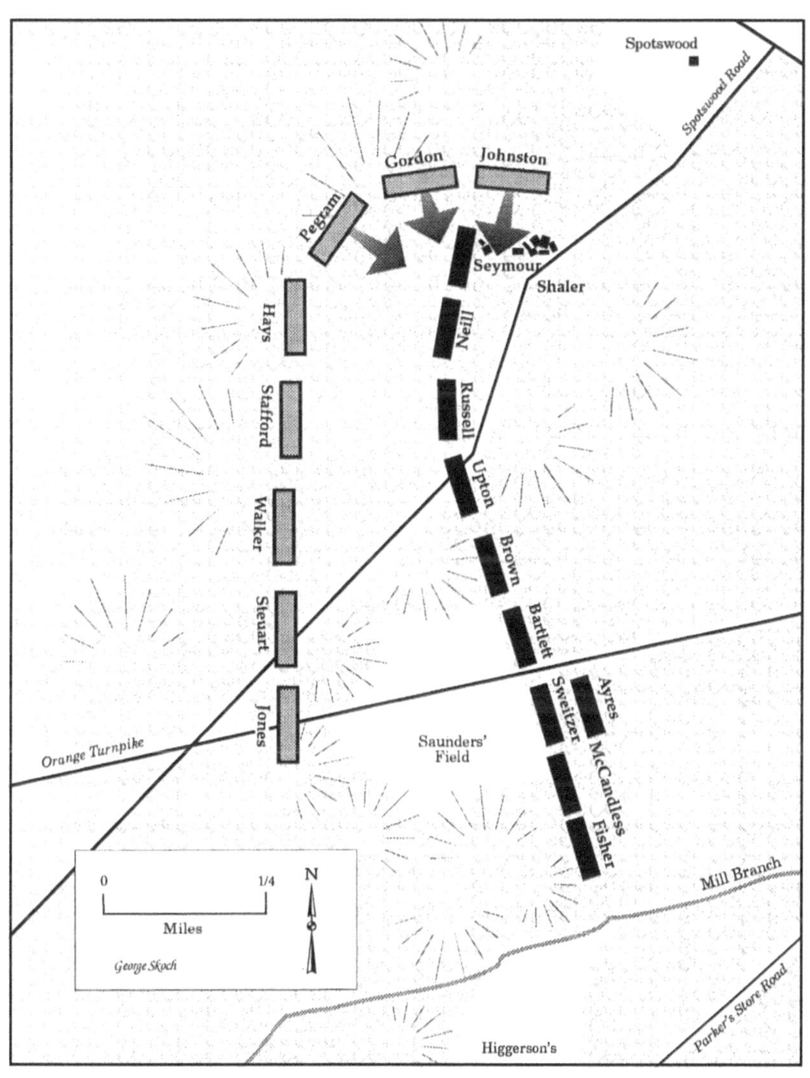

9. Gordon's attack on the evening of May 6

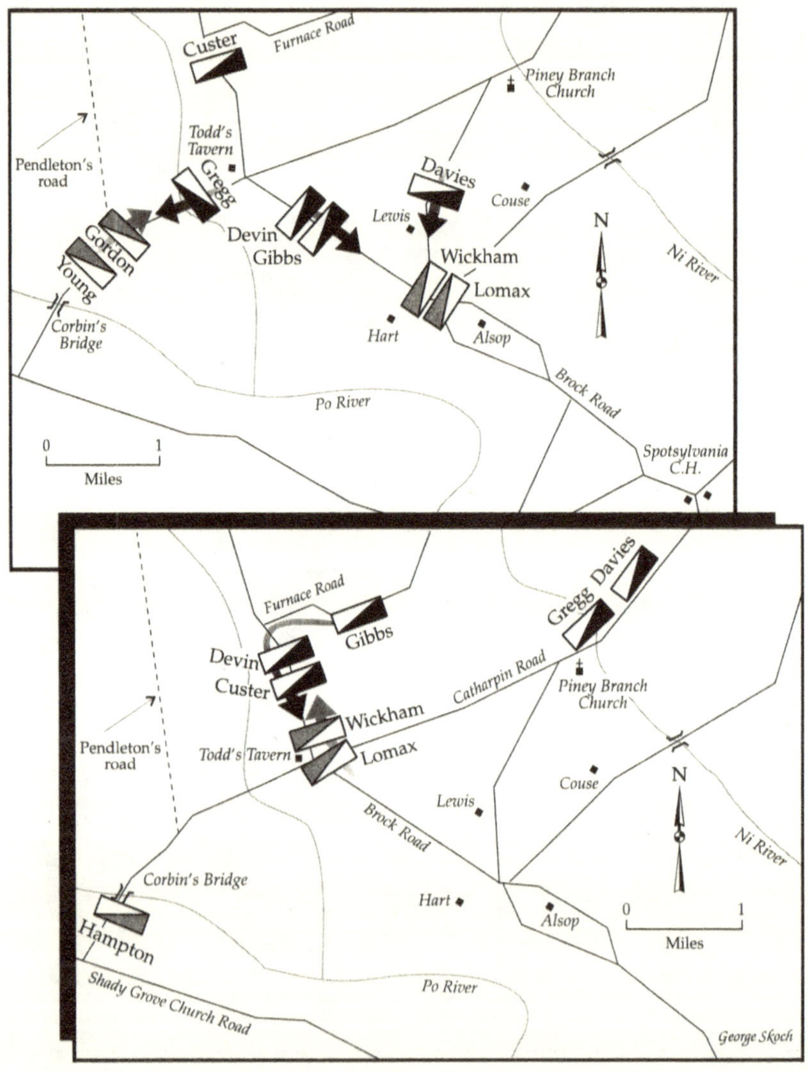

10. Cavalry engagements on May 7. Lower panel: action during morning and early afternoon; upper panel: action from 3 p.m. until dark.

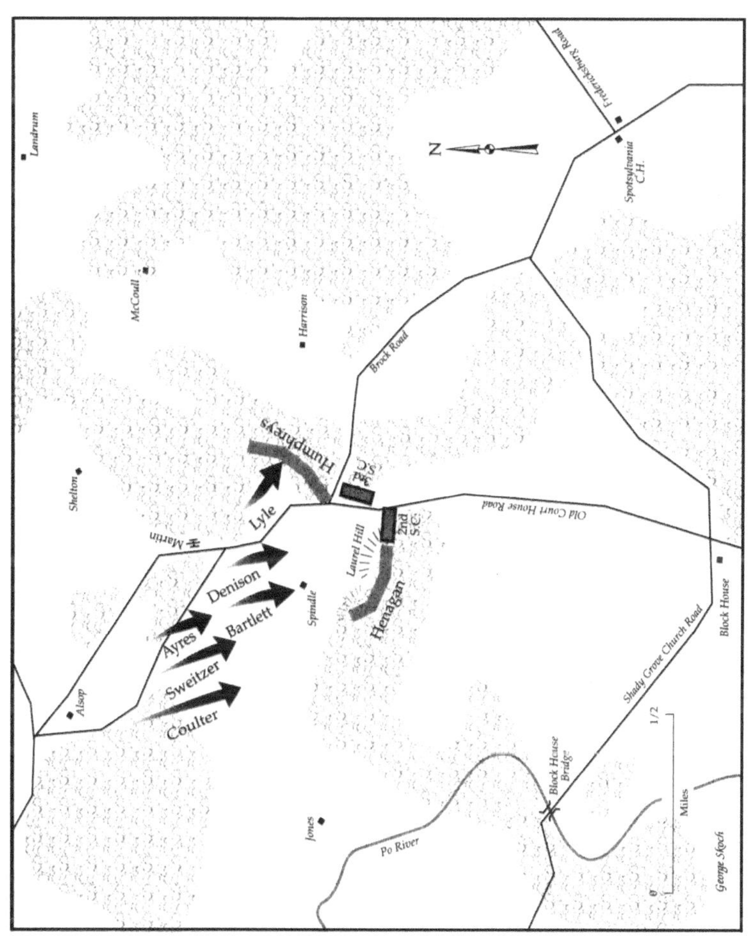

11. Warren's initial attack on Laurel Ridge, on May 8 at 8:30 a.m.

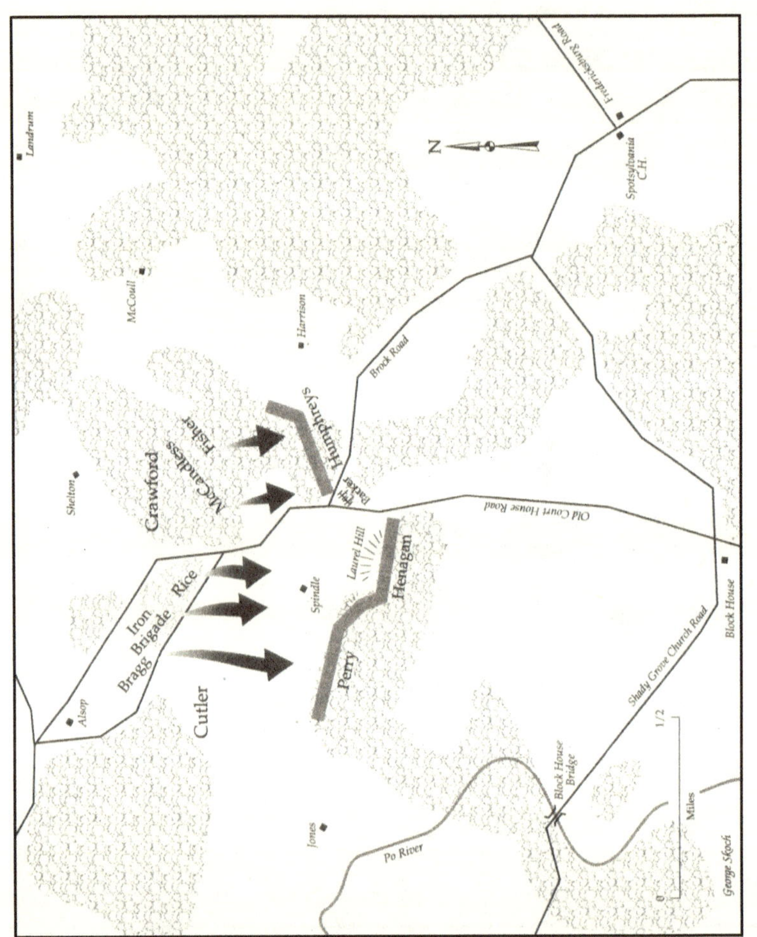

12. Warren's second attack on Laurel Ridge, on May 8, at 10:30 a.m.

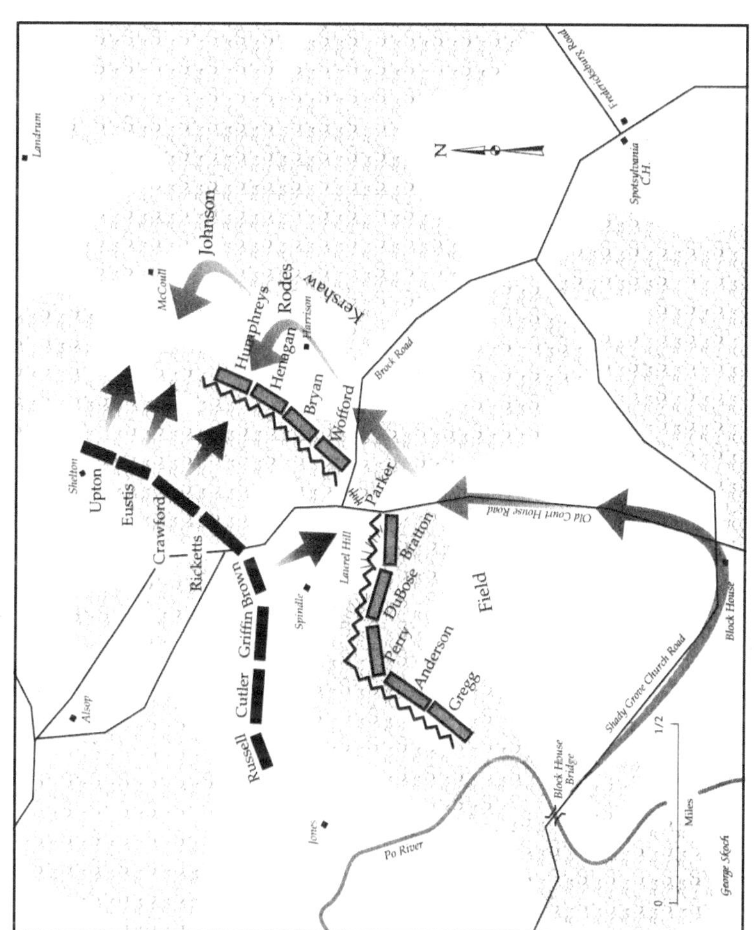

13. Meade's evening attack and Ewell's arrival on May 8 at 6:30 p.m.

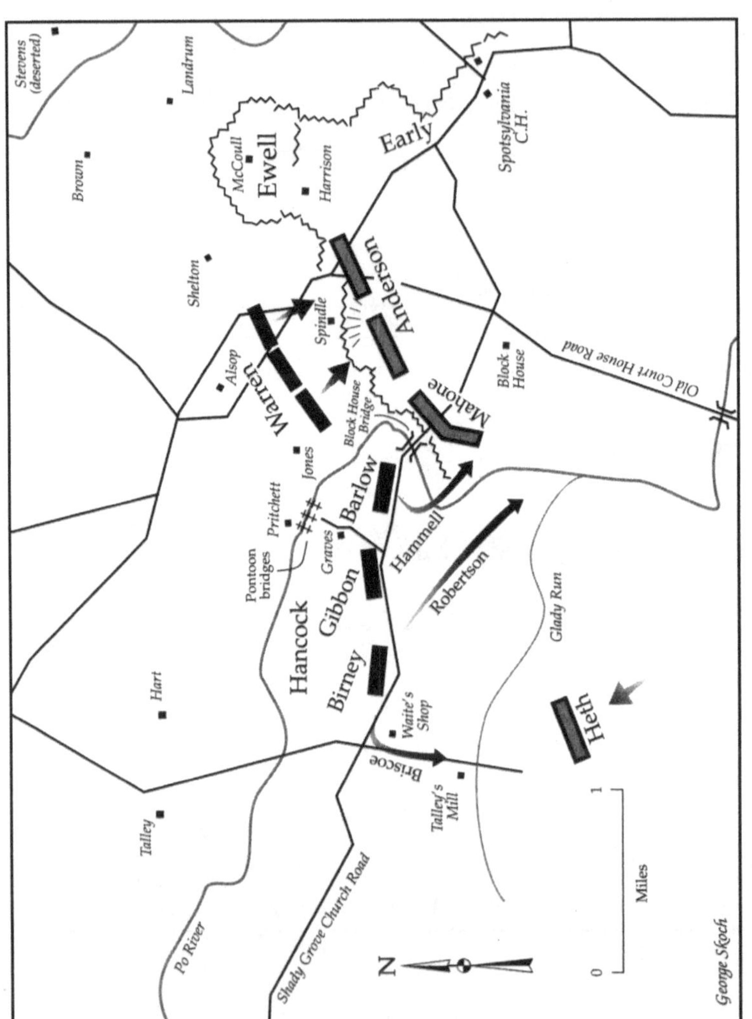

14. Union probes on the morning of May 10

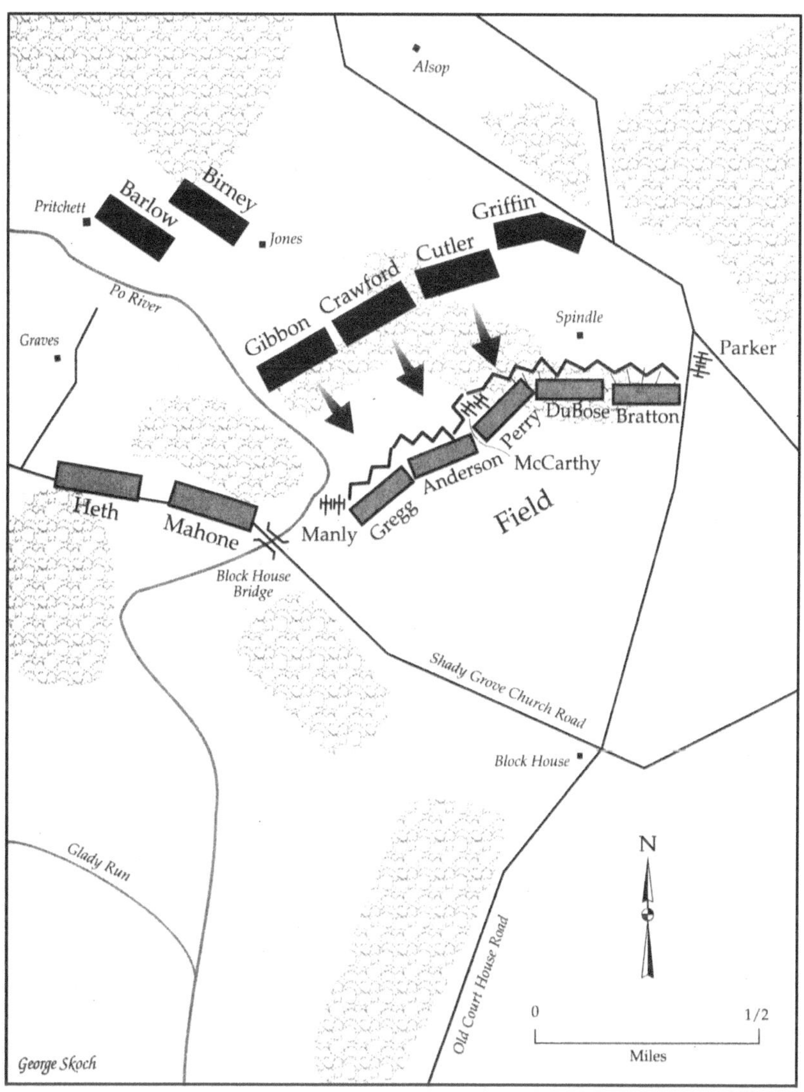

15. Warren's attack against Field on May 10 at 4 p.m.

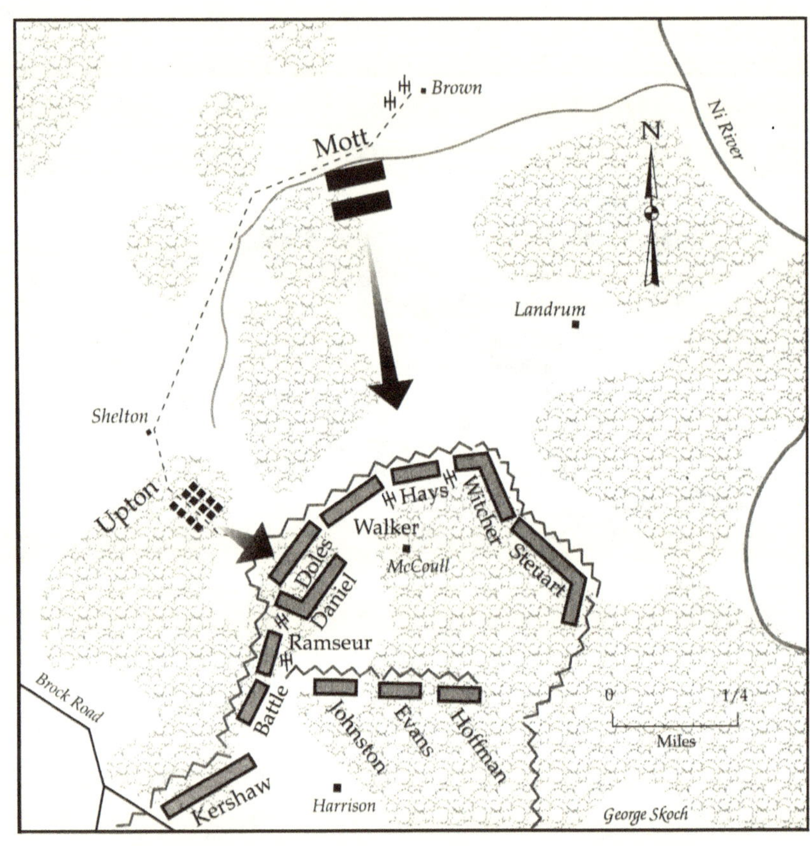

16. Upton's and Mott's attacks against Ewell on the evening of May 10

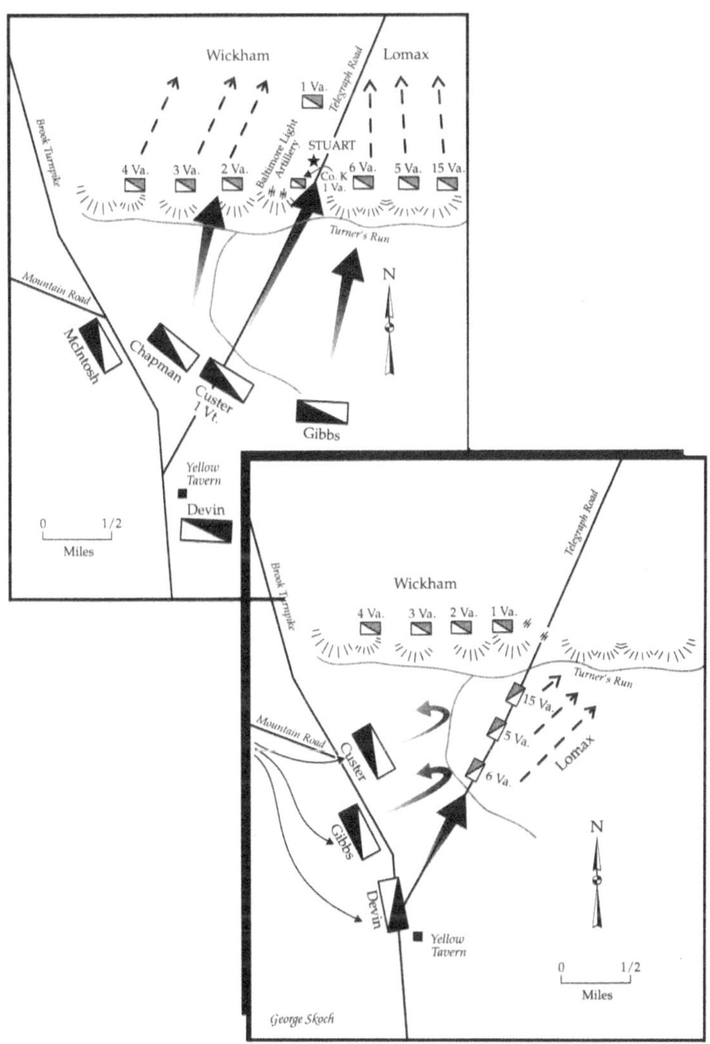

17. Sheridan's attack against Stuart at Yellow Tavern on May 11. Lower panel: morning action; upper panel, afternoon action.

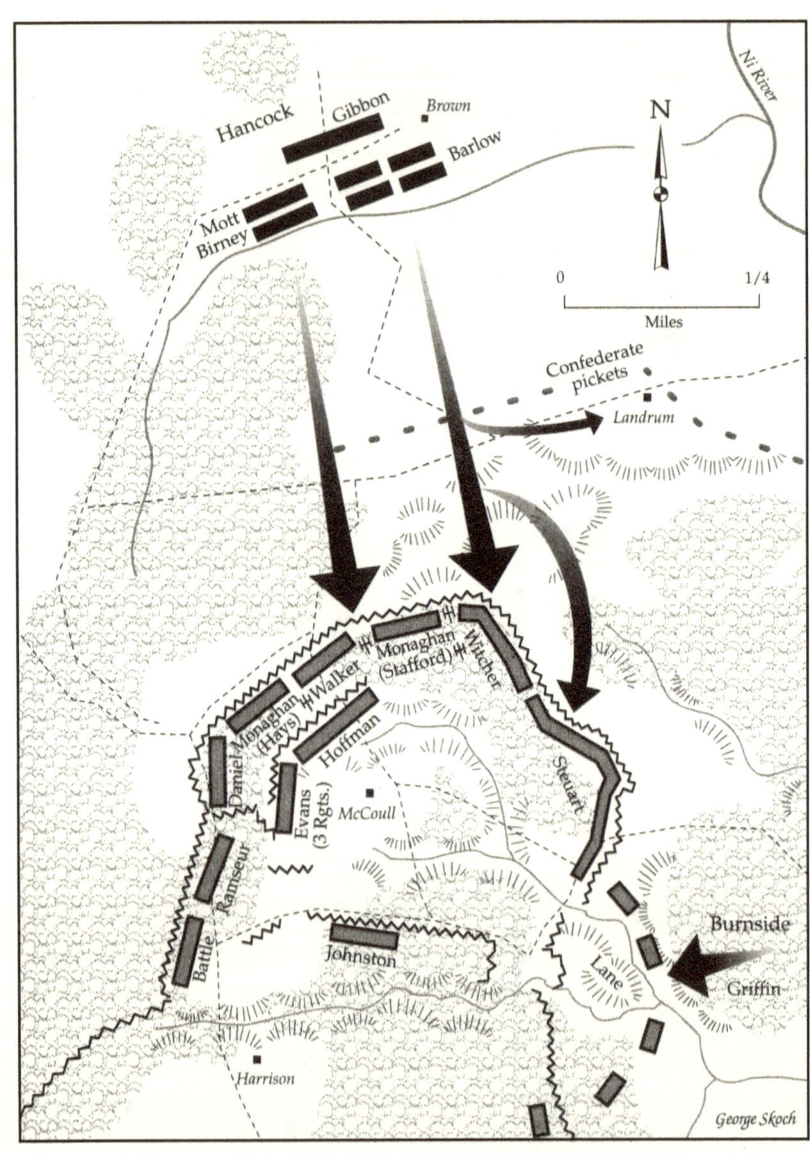

18. Hancock's and Burnside's attacks on May 12 at 4:30 a.m.

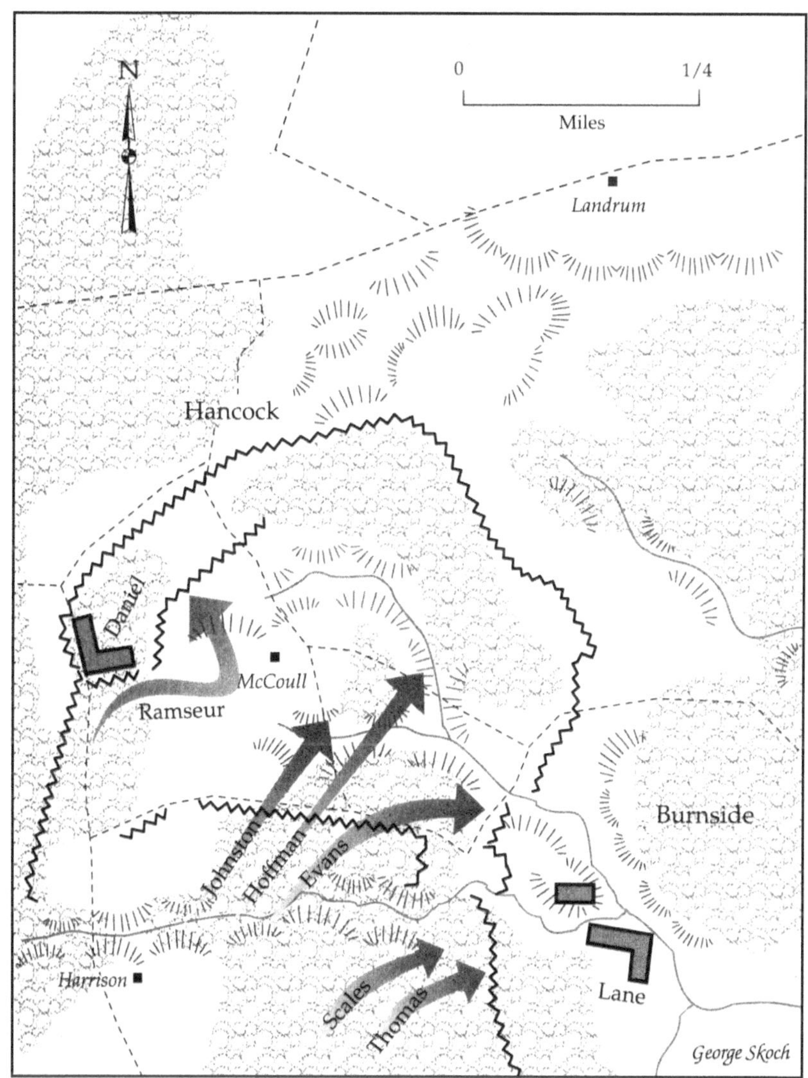

19. The Confederate response, by brigade, on May 12, 5 a.m.–6 a.m.

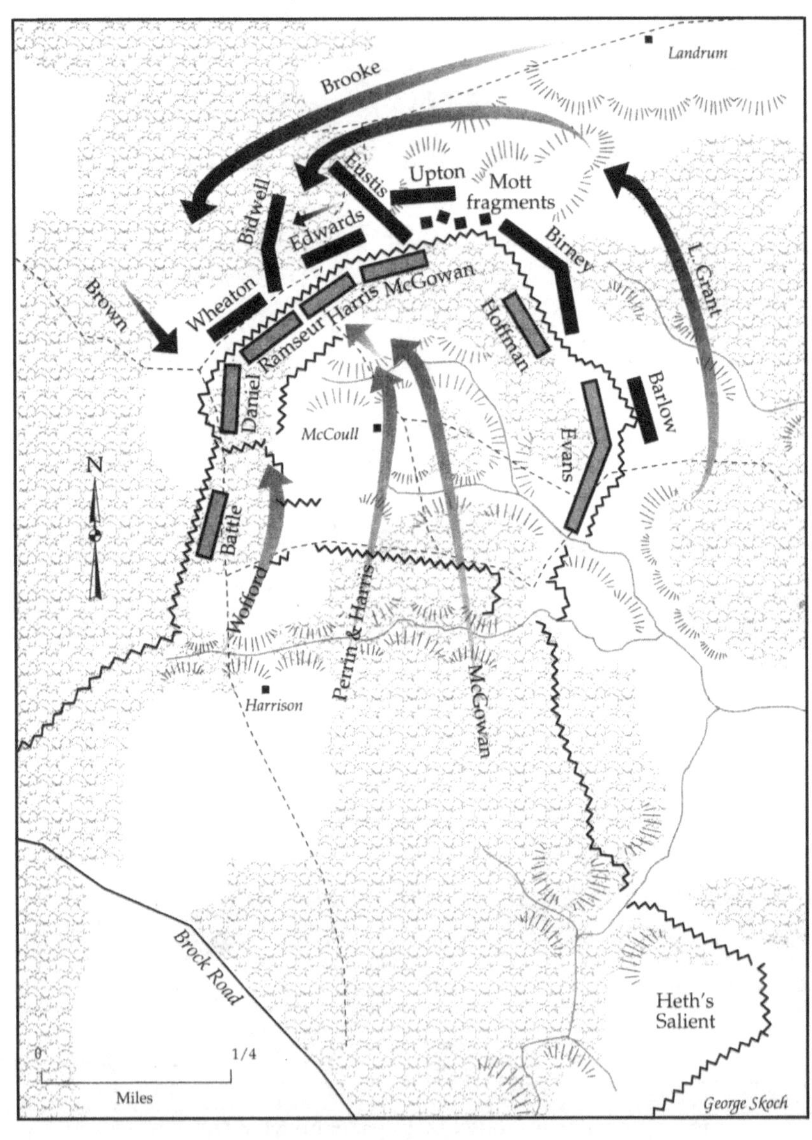

20. Grant and Lee reinforcing the Bloody Angle on May 12,
7:30 a.m.–10:00 a.m.

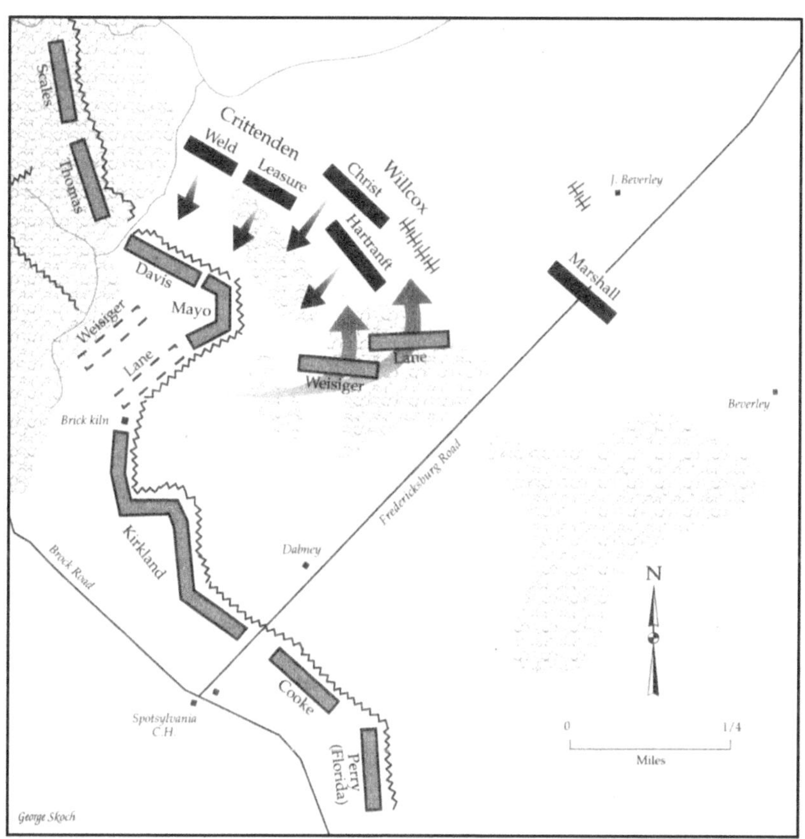

21. Fighting near Heth's Salient on May 12, 2 p.m.–3 p.m.

THE NORTH ANNA RIVER

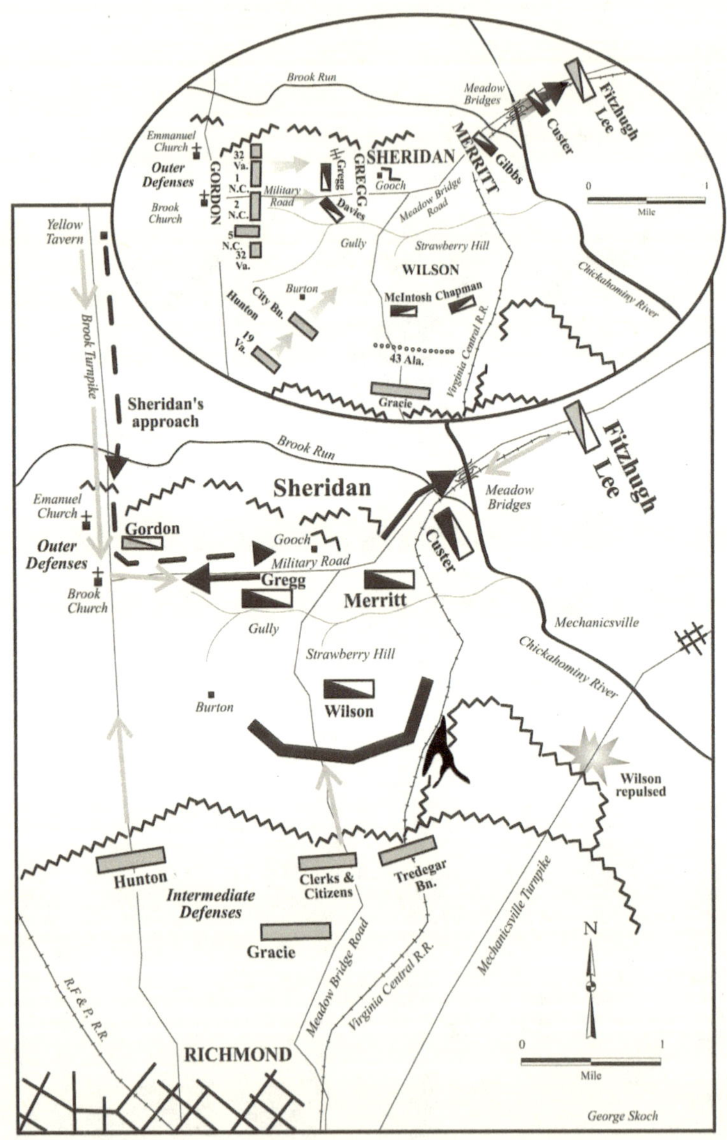

22. Battle of Meadow Bridge on May 12

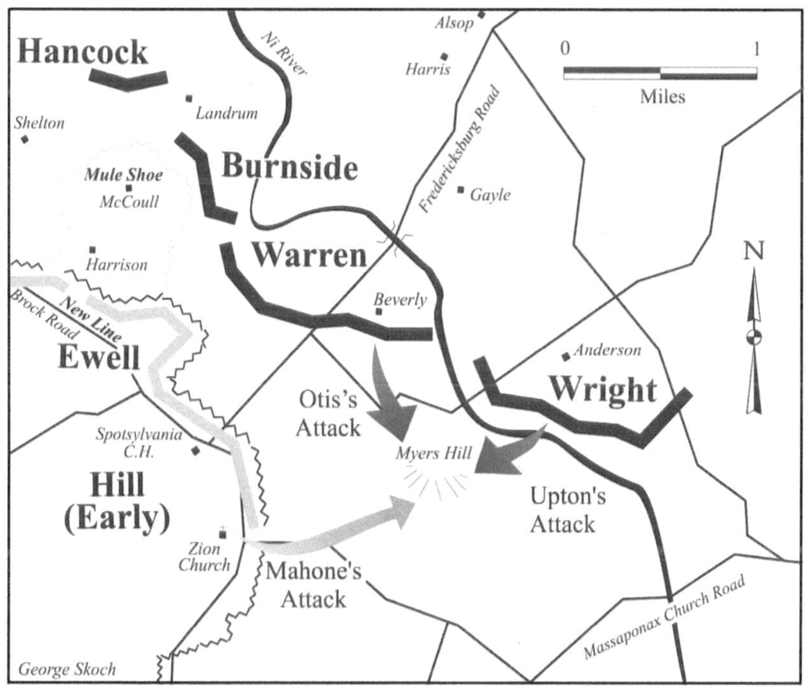

23. Operations at Myers Hill on May 14

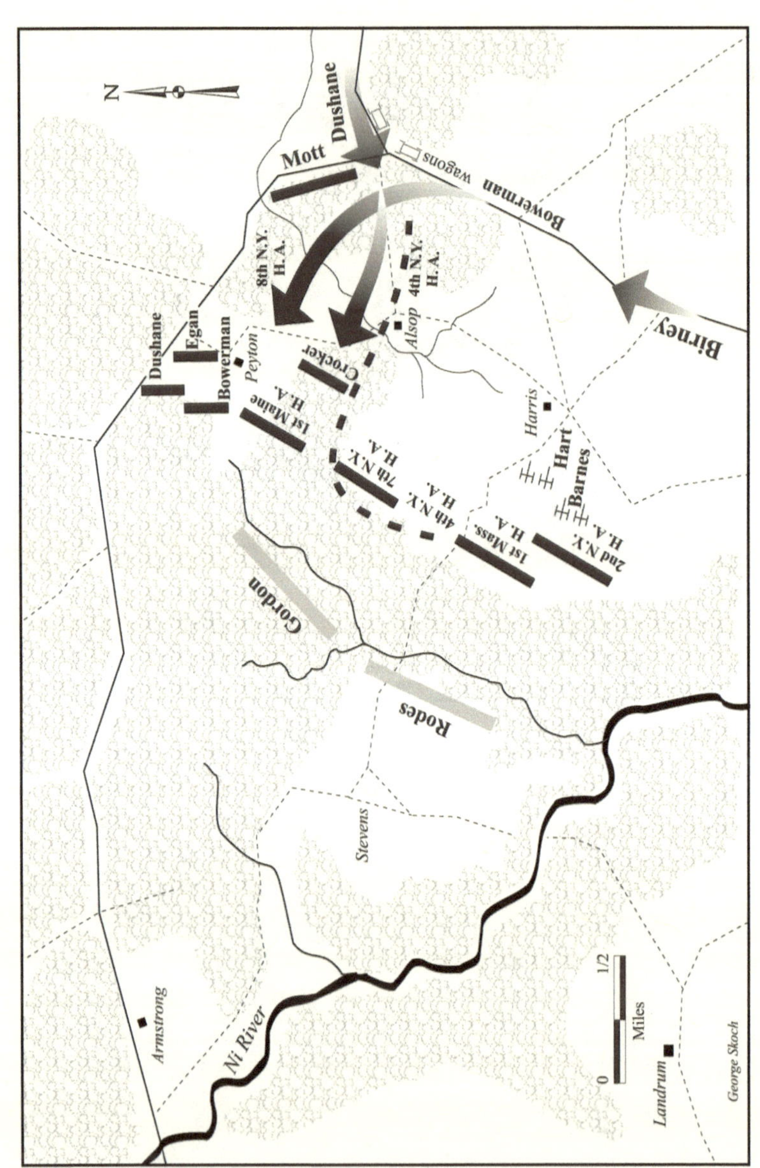

24. Battle of Harris Farm, second stage

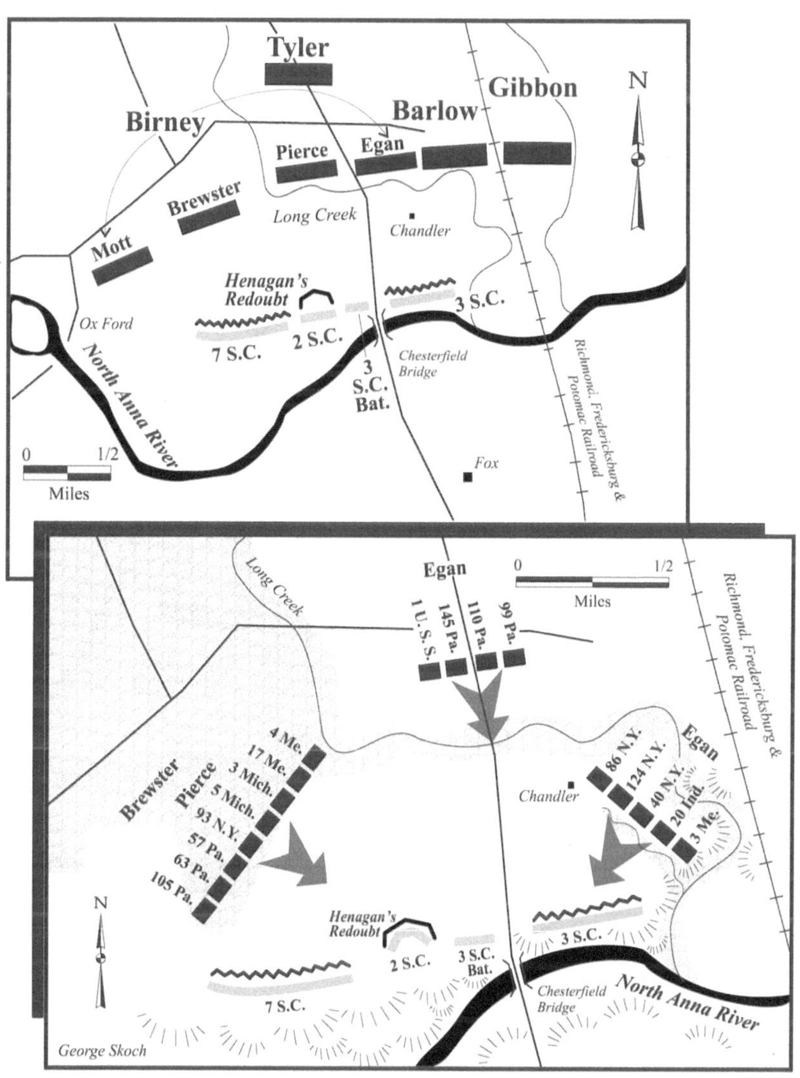

25. Hancock's attack at Henagan's Redoubt

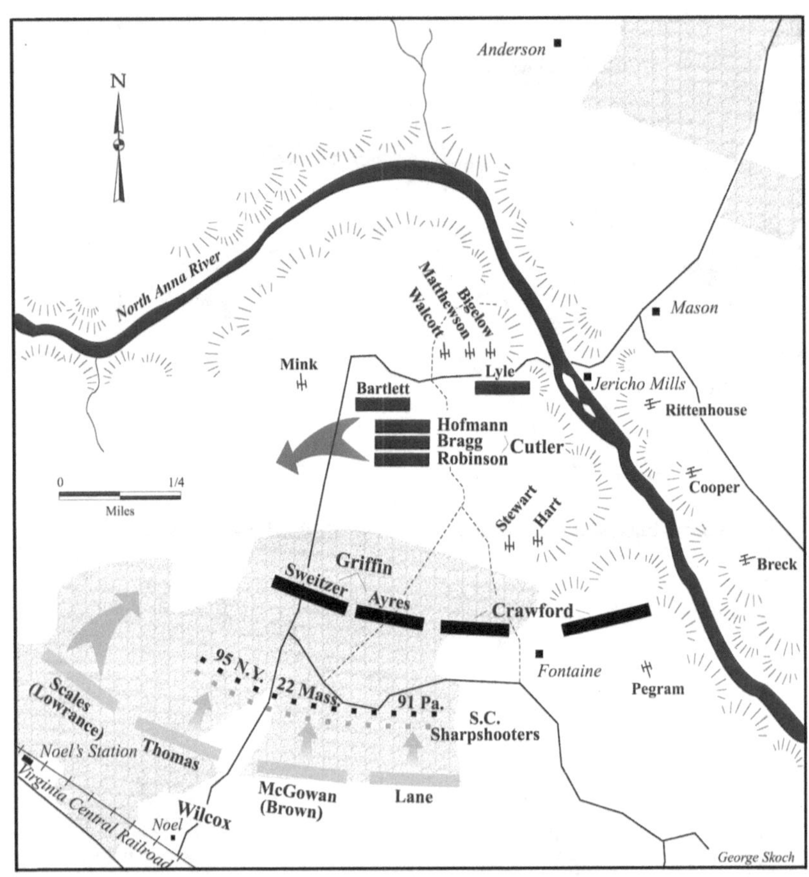

26. Battle of Jericho Mills, first stage

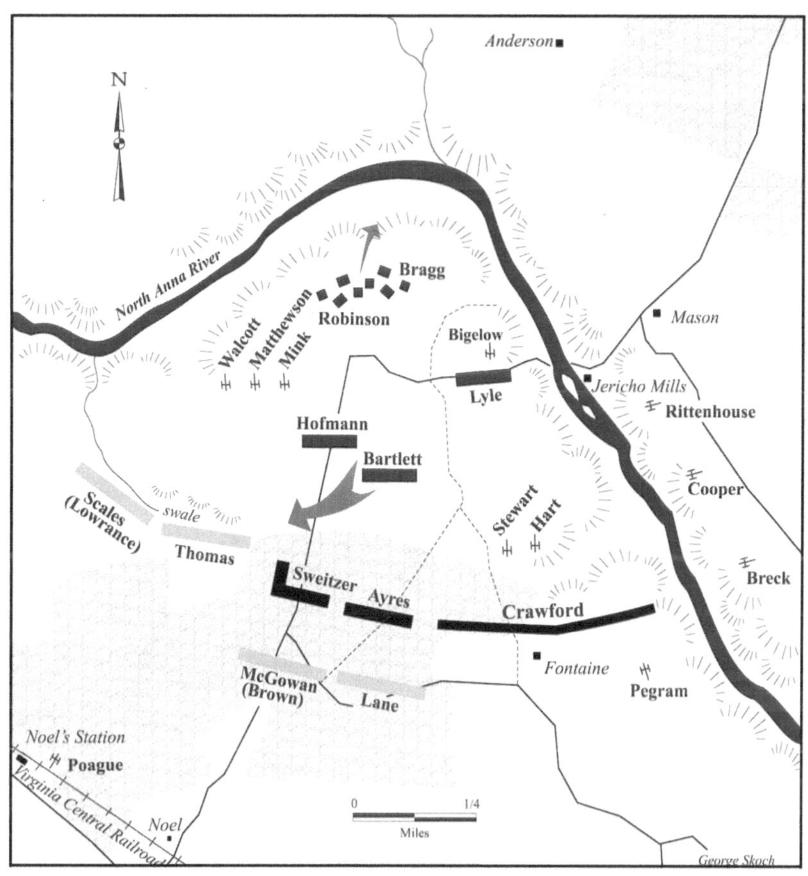

27. Battle of Jericho Mills, second stage

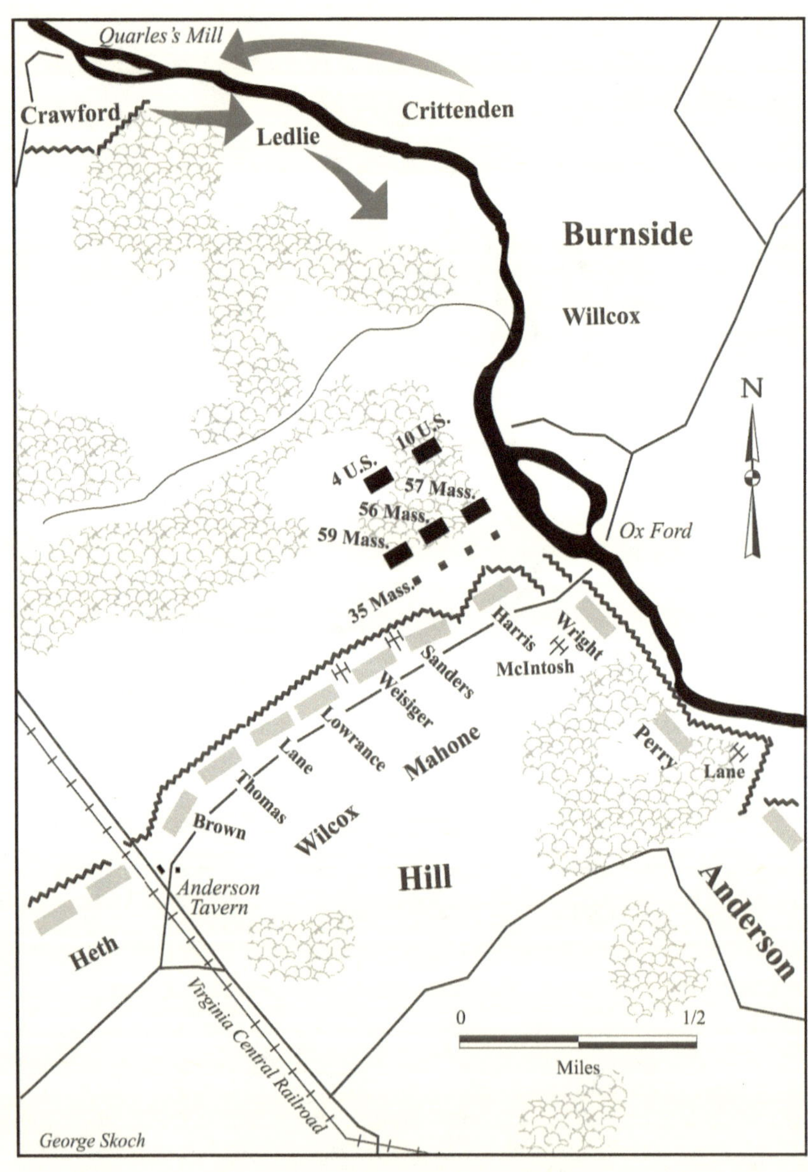

28. Battle of Ox Ford on May 24

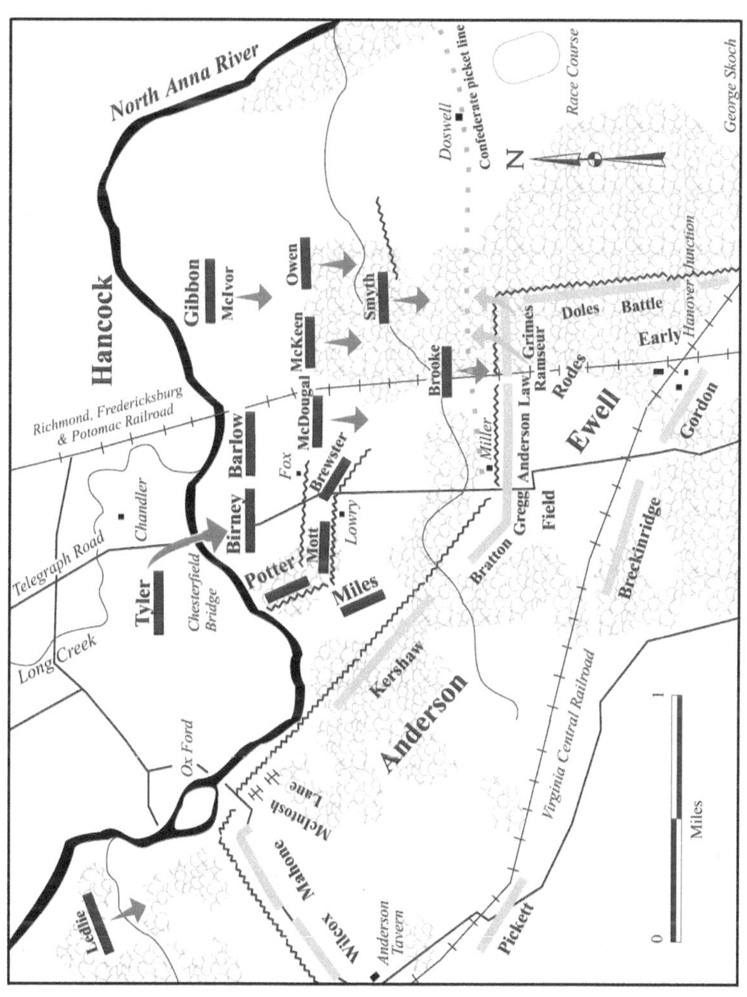

29. Fighting on Union and Confederate Second Corps fronts

COLD HARBOR

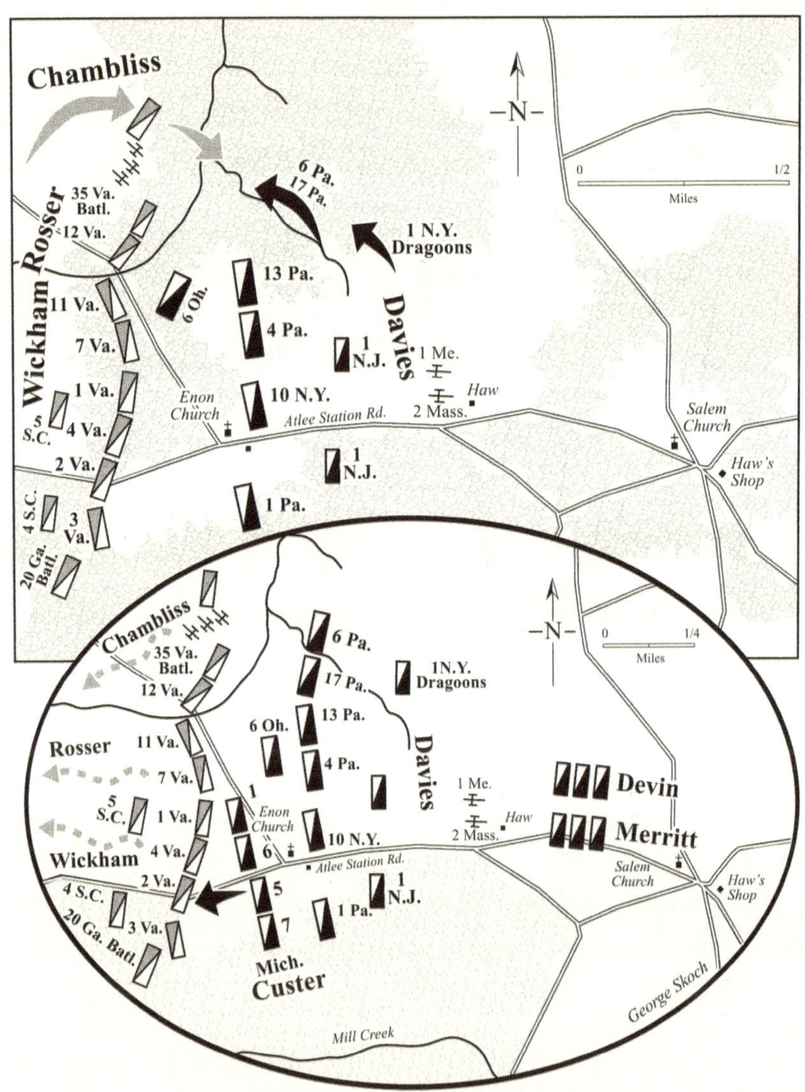

30. Battle of Haw's Shop, second stage

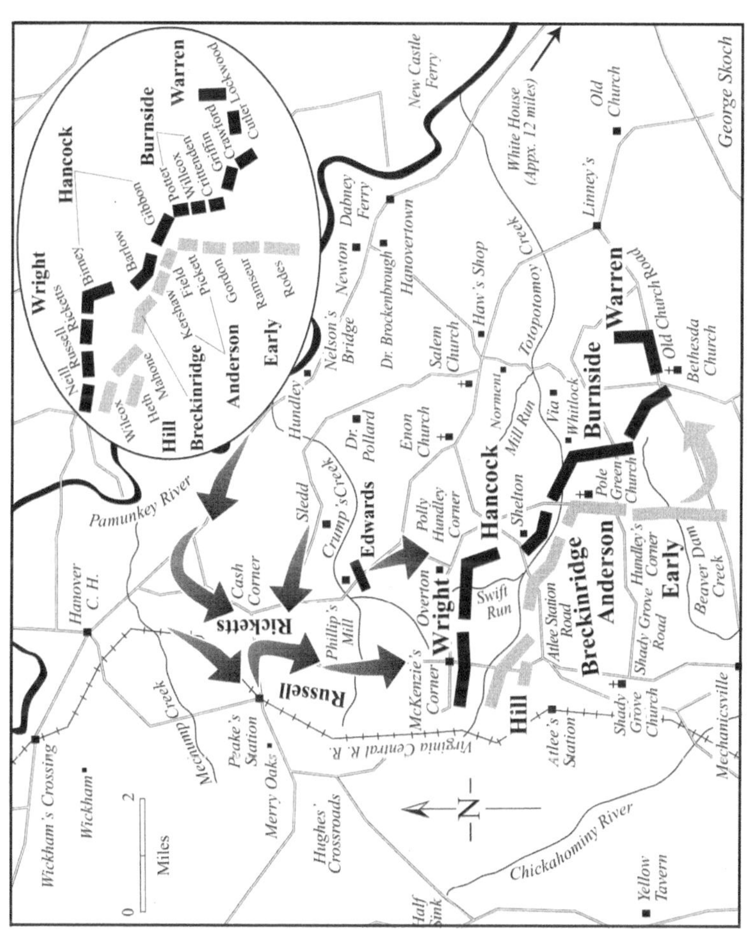

31. Union and Confederate infantry operations on May 30

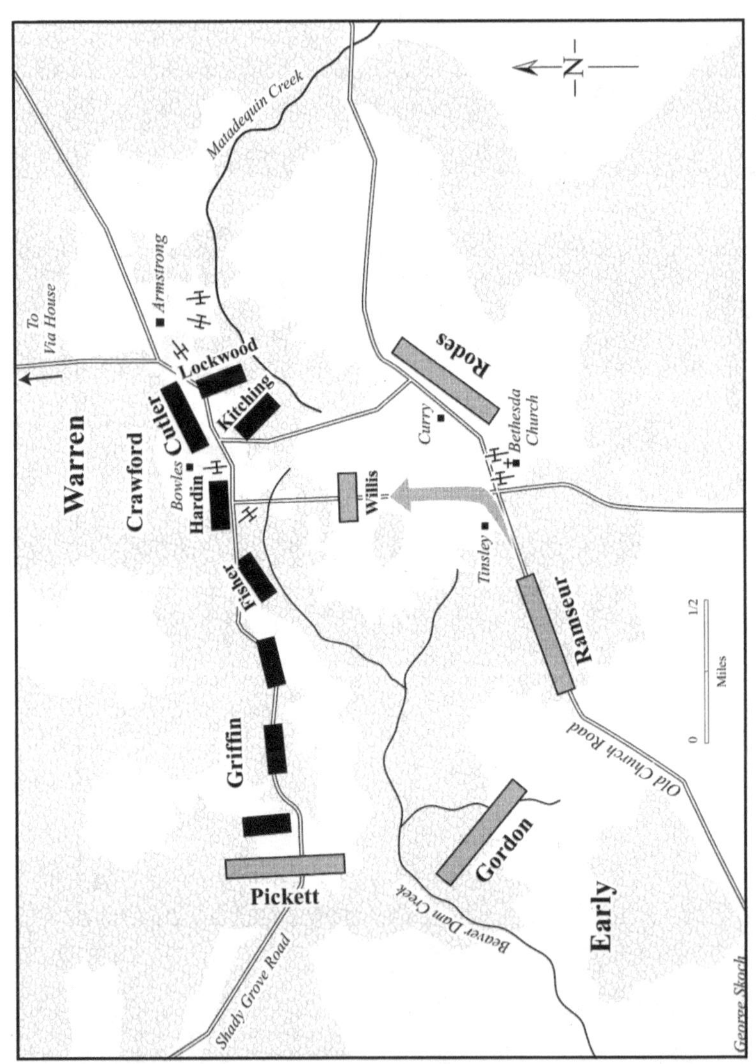

32. Battle of Bethesda Church, second stage

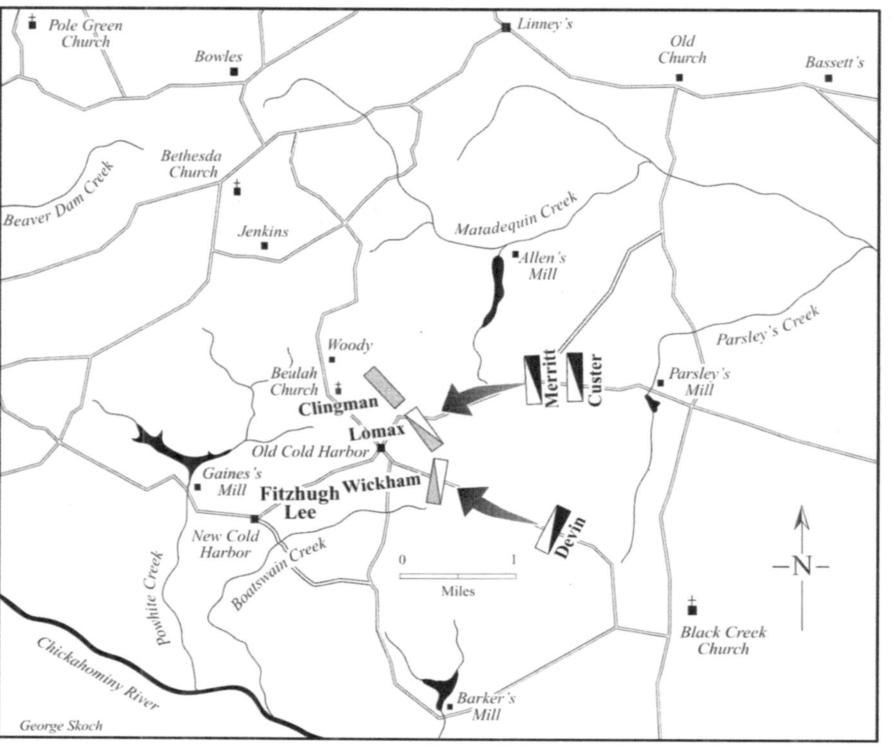

33. Sheridan's capture of Old Cold Harbor on May 31

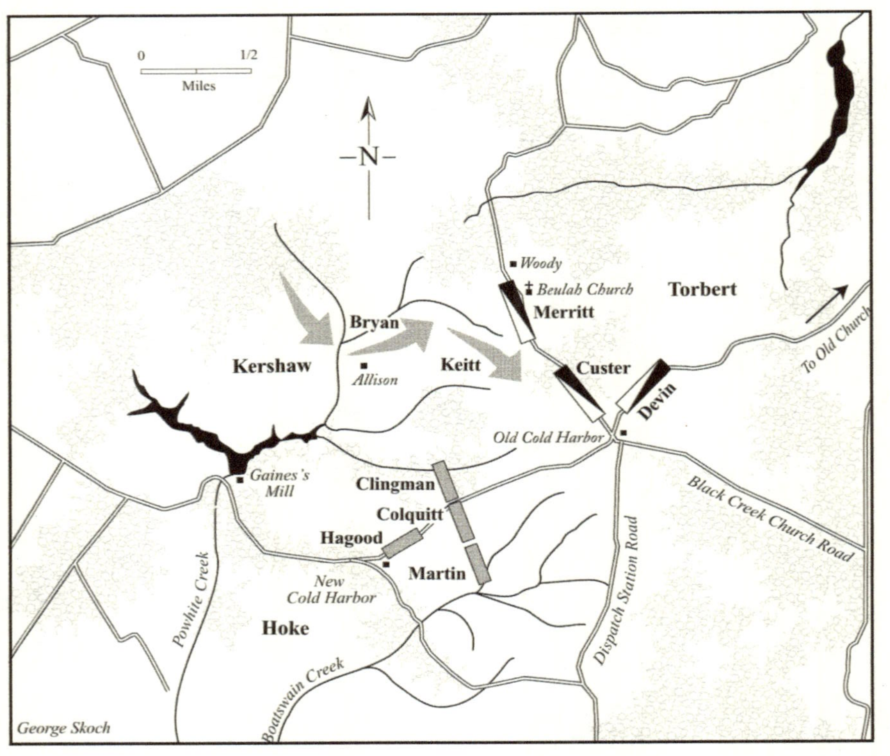

34. Keitt's attack against Torbert on morning of June 1

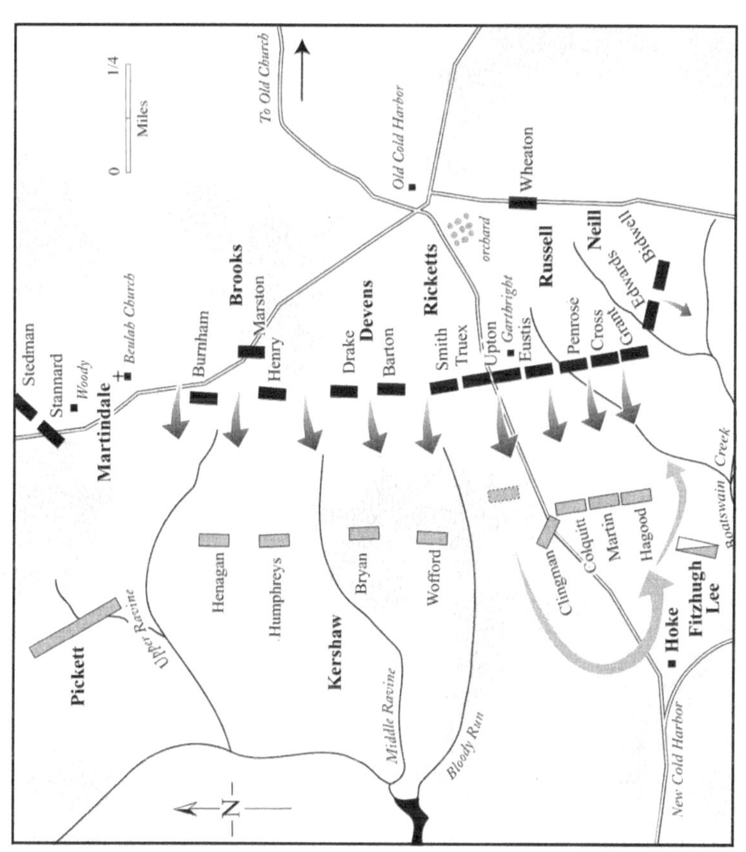

35. Cold Harbor attack on evening of June 1

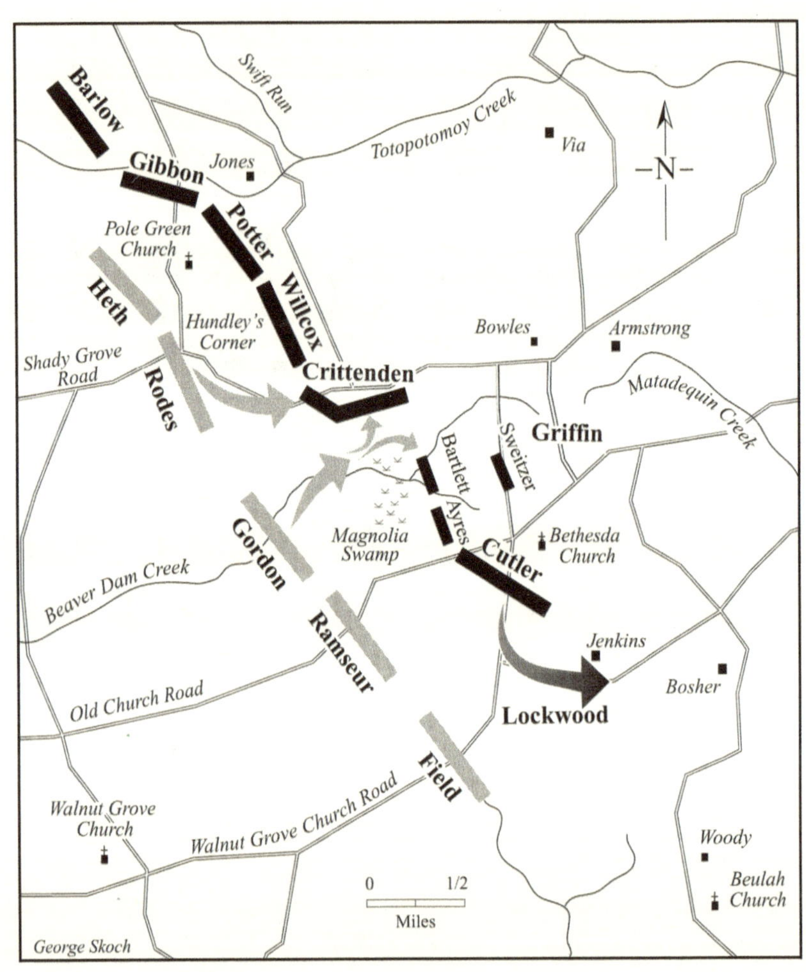

36. Bethesda Church attack on evening of June 1

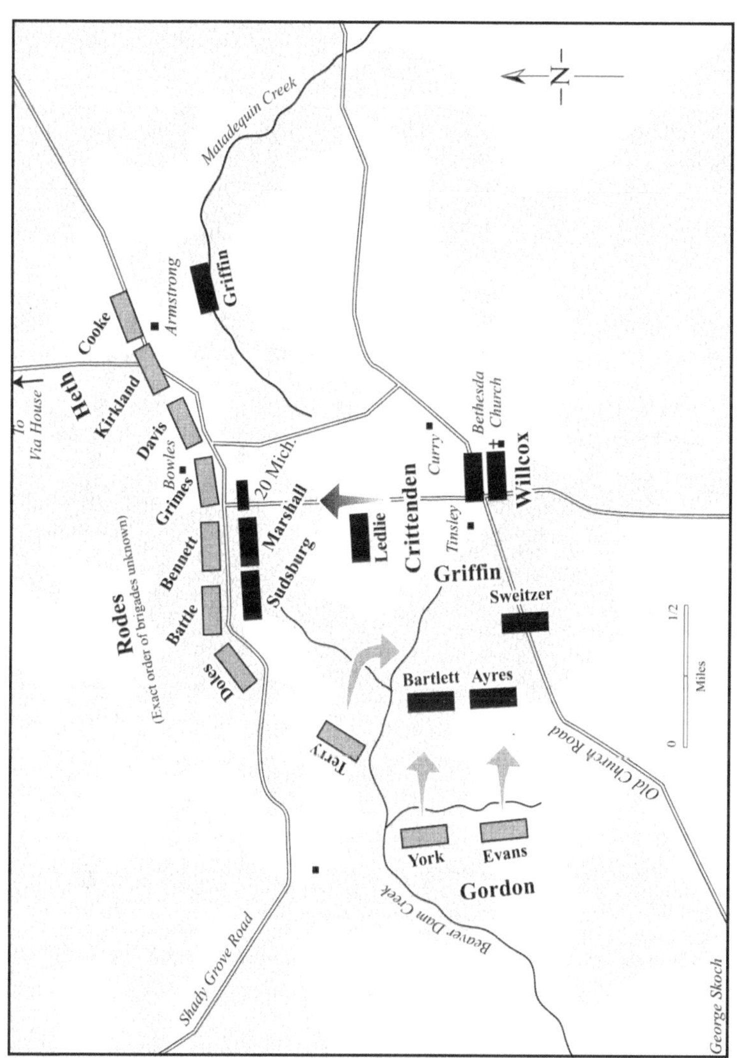

37. Bethesda Church sector on evening of June 2

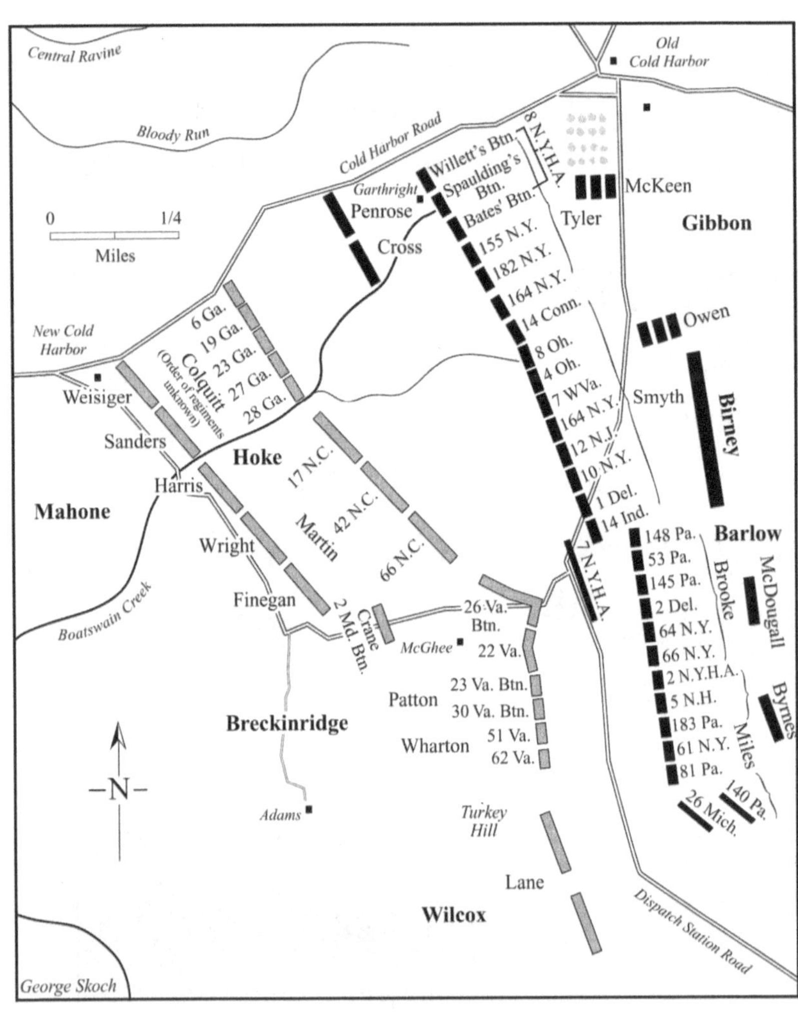

38. Hancock's attack formation on morning of June 3

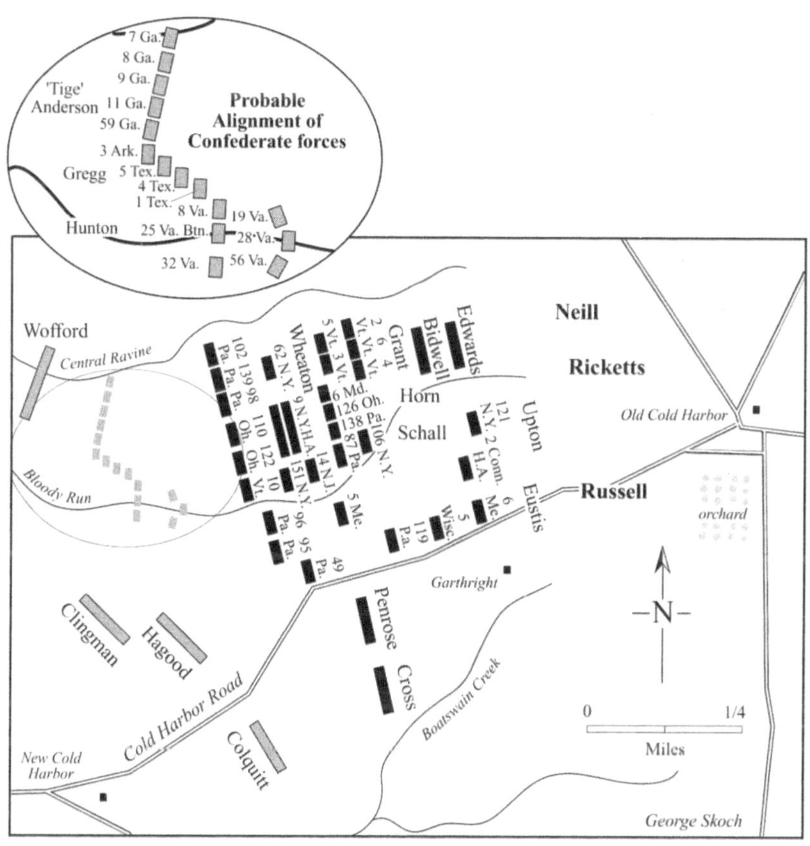

39. Wright's attack formation on morning of June 3

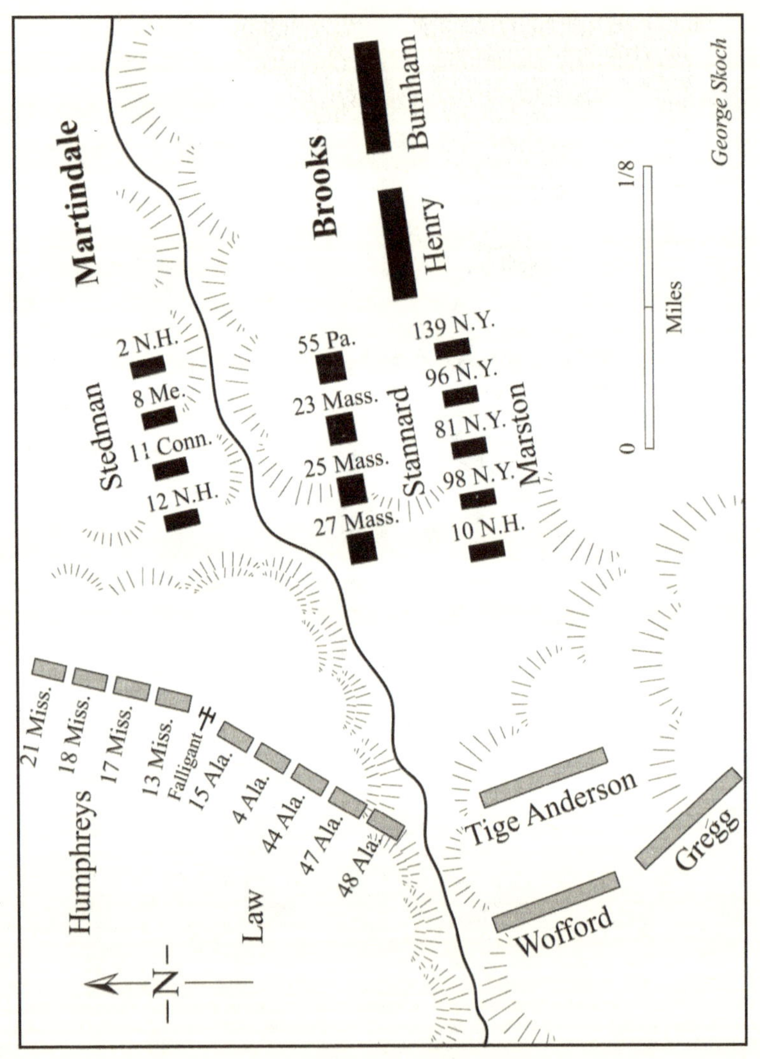

40. Smith's attack formation on morning of June 3

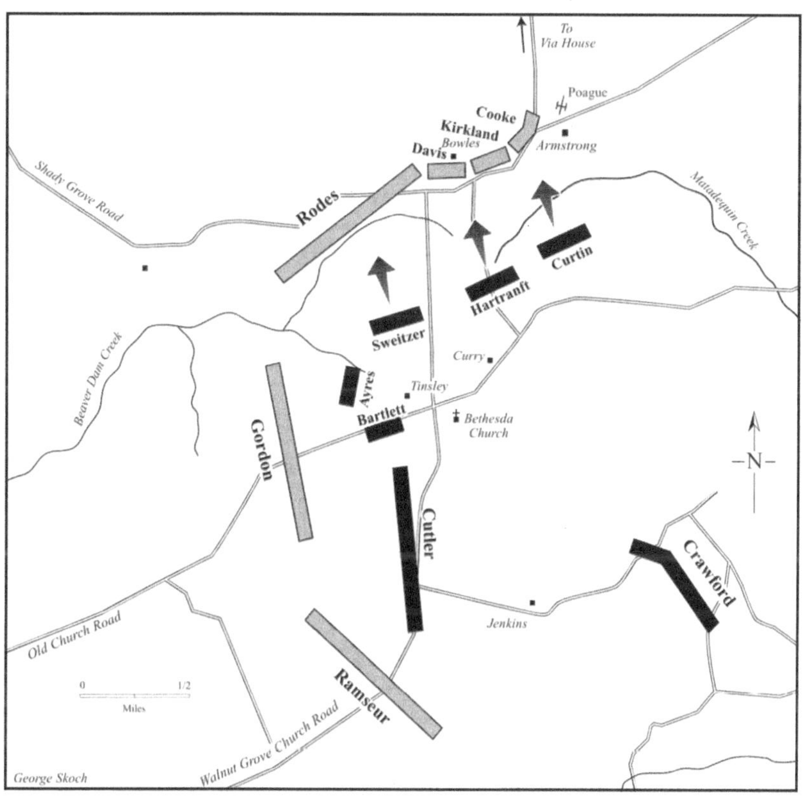

41. Burnside's and Warren's attacks on morning of June 3

Appendix C

ARMY OF NORTHERN VIRGINIA ORDER OF BATTLE DURING THE OVERLAND CAMPAIGN

FIRST CORPS

Kershaw's Division

Humphreys's Brigade
Kershaw's Brigade
Wofford's Brigade
Bryan's Brigade

Field's Division

Gregg's Brigade
Jenkins's/Bratton's Brigade
Benning's Brigade
Law's Brigade
Anderson's Brigade

Pickett's Division

Kemper's Brigade
Hunton's Brigade
Barton's Brigade
Corse's Brigade

Artillery

Cabell's Battalion
Huger's Battalion
Haskell's Battalion

SECOND CORPS

Johnson's/Gordon's Division

Walker's (Stonewall) Brigade*
Jones's Brigade*
Steuart's Brigade*
Stafford's Brigade†

Early's/Ramseur's Division

Hays's Brigade†
Gordon's/Evans's Brigade‡
Pegram's Brigade
Hoke's Brigade

Rodes's Division

Ramseur's Brigade
Daniel's/Grimes's Brigade
Doles's Brigade
Battle's Brigade
Johnston's Brigade§

Artillery

Hardaway's Battalion
Page's Battalion
Cutshaw's Battalion

* Surviving Virginia remnants formed Terry's Brigade after May 12, 1864. Remnants of two North Carolina units (Steuart's Brigade) transferred to Ramseur's Brigade that same date.

† Surviving remnants consolidated after the Wilderness and assigned to Johnson's Division, independent again at Spotsylvania, then afterward permanently consolidated in Gordon's Division.

‡ Transferred to Gordon's Division after May 12, 1864.

§ Transferred to Early's Division after May 6, 1864.

Braxton's Battalion
Nelson's Battalion

THIRD CORPS

Heth's Division

Cooke's Brigade
Kirkland's Brigade
Davis's Brigade
Walker's/Fry's Brigade

Wilcox's Division

Lane's Brigade
McGowan's Brigade
Scales's Brigade
Thomas's Brigade

Anderson's/Mahone's Division

Perrin's/Sanders's Brigade
Mahone's Brigade
Harris's Brigade
Wright's Brigade
Perry's/Finegan's Brigade

Third Corps Artillery

Poague's Battalion
Pegram's Battalion
McIntosh's Battalion
Richardson's Battalion
Cutts's Battalion

CAVALRY CORPS

Fitzhugh Lee's Division

Wickham's Brigade
Lomax's Brigade

Hampton's/Butler's Division

Young's Brigade
Rosser's Brigade
Butler's Brigade

W. H. F. Lee's Division

Chambliss's Brigade
Gordon's Brigade

Horse Artillery (Breathed's Battalion)

SEPARATE COMMANDS

Hoke's Division

Clingman's Brigade
Hagood's Brigade
Colquitt's Brigade
Martin's Brigade
Read's Artillery Battalion

Breckinridge's Division

Echols's Brigade
Wharton's Brigade
McLaughlin's Artillery Battalion

Maryland Line

Notes

INTRODUCTION

1. R. Ernest Dupuy and Trevor N. Dupuy, *The Compact History of the Civil War* (New York, 1960), 291; Calvin L. Collier, *They'll Do to Tie To: The Story of the 3rd Arkansas Regiment, C.S.A.* (Little Rock, 1959), 178.

2. William D. Matter, *If It Takes All Summer: The Battle of Spotsylvania* (Chapel Hill, N.C., 1988), 266.

3. Noah Andre Trudeau, *Bloody Roads South* (Boston, 1989), 302–307.

4. Martin T. McMahon, "Cold Harbor," *Battles and Leaders of the Civil War,* 4 vols. (New York, 1956), 4:213.

5. Margaret Leech, *Reveille in Washington, 1860–1865* (New York, 1941), 398.

6. Southern Memorial Association, "Confederate Hospitals in Lynchburg, Virginia," 2003–2011, Old City Cemetery of Lynchburg, Virginia, http://www.gravegarden.org/hospitals.htm.

7. Reports of Union Losses for the Overland Campaign, *War of the Rebellion: A Compilation of the Official Records of the Union and Confederate Armies,* 130 vols. (Washington, D.C., 1880–1901), ser. 1, 36(1):119–80. (Hereafter cited as *OR;* all references are to series 1 unless otherwise noted.)

8. Abstract from trimonthly return of the Army of the Potomac, Apr. 30, 1864, and abstract from return of the IX Corps for Apr. 1864, ibid., 36(1):1036, 1045.

9. "The Opposing Forces at Cold Harbor," *Battles and Leaders,* 4:185.

10. Dupuy and Dupuy, *Compact History of the Civil War,* 304.

11. "The Opposing Forces in Grant's Campaign against Richmond," *Battles and Leaders,* 4:184; Alexander S. Webb, "Through the Wilderness," ibid., 169.

1. THE INITIAL STRENGTH OF THE ARMY OF NORTHERN VIRGINIA

1. Abstract of returns for the Department of East Tennessee, Mar. 31, 1864, *OR,* 32(3):721.

2. Abstract of returns for the Army of Northern Virginia, June 30, 1864, ibid., 40:707.

3. Abstracts of returns for the Army of Northern Virginia, ibid., 33:1075, 1135, 1157, 1191, 1216, 1233–34, 1271.

4. Louis H. Manarin, Weymouth T. Jordan et al., *North Carolina Troops, 1861–1865: A Roster,* 17 vols. (Raleigh, N.C., 1961–[2009]), 4:400. (Hereafter cited as Manarin and Jordan, *N.C. Troops.*)

5. Report of Col. J. R. Hagood, *OR,* 36(1):1069.

3. CASUALTIES DURING THE OVERLAND CAMPAIGN: AN OVERVIEW

1. Reports of Col. J. W. Henagan, Brig. Gen. Goode Bryan, Brig. Gen. William Mahone, Brig. Gen. J. H. Lane, and Brig. Gen. Samuel McGowan, *OR,* 36(1):1060, 1062, 1064, 1091, 1094.

2. James H. Lane, "History of Lane's North Carolina Brigade [Report of General Lane]," *Southern Historical Society Papers* 9 (1882): 124–29, 146–53, 241–44.

3. See *OR,* 25(2):798.

4. FIRST CORPS

Kershaw's Division

1. Douglas Southall Freeman, *Lee's Lieutenants,* 3 vols. (New York, 1941), 3:299–302.

2. Ibid., 309.

3. Gordon. C. Rhea, *The Battle of the Wilderness, May 5–6, 1864* (Baton Rouge, La., 1994), 308–313; John Cannan, *The Wilderness Campaign, May 1864* (Conshohocken, Pa., 1993), 155.

4. Rhea, *Battle of the Wilderness,* 308–313; Cannan, *Wilderness Campaign,* 171–73.

5. Rhea, *Battle of the Wilderness,* 393.

6. Gordon C. Rhea, *The Battles for Spotsylvania Court House and the Road to Yellow Tavern, May 7–12, 1864* (Baton Rouge, La., 1997), 52; National Park Service, *Spotsylvania Court House Battle Maps,* 12 maps, Drawing NMP-F5 3026 (Washington, D.C.: National Park Service, 1950), map 1.

7. Matter, *If It Takes All Summer,* 59, 69.

8. Rhea, *Battles for Spotsylvania,* 82; National Park Service, *Spotsylvania Court House Battle Maps,* map 2.

9. Gordon C. Rhea, *To the North Anna River: Grant and Lee, May 13–25, 1864* (Baton Rouge, La., 2000), 115, 124; Matter, *If It Takes All Summer,* 295, 299; National Park Service, *Spotsylvania Court House Battle Maps,* maps 9–11.

10. J. Michael Miller, *The North Anna Campaign: "Even to Hell Itself," May 21–26, 1864* (Lynchburg, Va., 1989), 96.

11. Gordon C. Rhea, *Cold Harbor: Grant and Lee, May 26–June 3, 1864* (Baton Rouge, La., 2002), 123.

12. Ibid., 198–200.

13. Ibid., 206.

14. Ibid., 247–50, 254–55.

Humphreys's Brigade

1. Returns of casualties in Confederate forces, *OR,* 25(1):806, 27(2):338, 30(2):291, 31(1):475.

2. Rhea, *Battle of the Wilderness,* 309–11; Robert Garth Scott, *Into the Wilderness with the Army of the Potomac* (Bloomington, Ind., 1988), 119, 121.

3. Rhea, *Battles for Spotsylvania,* 57; Matter, *If It Takes All Summer,* 59, 62.

4. Rhea, *Battles for Spotsylvania,* 305; Matter, *If It Takes All Summer,* 256, 260.

5. Rhea, *Cold Harbor,* 232, 252, 253–54, 349, 352.

6. *Daily Richmond Enquirer,* June 14, 1864, pg. 3, col. 3 (21st Miss.); and July 18, 1864, pg. 1, col. 6 (18th Miss.).

Kershaw's Brigade

1. Returns of casualties in Confederate forces, *OR,* 25(1):806, 27(2):338, 30(2):291, 31(1):475; Robert K. Krick, *The Gettysburg Death Roster* (Dayton, Ohio, 1981), 6.

2. Rhea, *To the North Anna River,* 288, 296, 300–303; Miller, *North Anna Campaign,* 59–60.

3. Rhea, *Cold Harbor,* 198–200.

4. Ibid.; James Alex Milling, "Jim Milling and the War, 1862–1865," n.d., Laurens County Library, Laurens, S.C., 9.

5. Rhea, *Cold Harbor,* 254–55.

6. *(Columbia) Daily South Carolinian,* May 25, 1864, pg. 2, cols. 3–4 (entire brigade); June 8, 1864, pg. 3, col. 1 (20th S.C.); and June 18, 1864, pg. and col. nos. unknown (3rd S.C.); *Camden (S.C.) Weekly Confederate,* May 18, June 8, 1864, pg. and col. nos. unknown (2nd S.C.); *Charleston Mercury,* June 9, 1864, pg. 1, col. 2 (8th S.C.); July 19, 1864, pg. 1, col. 5 (2nd S.C.).

7. Report of Col. John W. Henagan for the Wilderness, *OR,* 36(1):1062.

Wofford's Brigade

1. Returns of casualties in Confederate forces, *OR,* 25(1):806, 27(2):338, 31(1):475.

2. Rhea, *Battle of the Wilderness,* 357, 368.

3. Ibid., 393.

4. Matter, *If It Takes All Summer,* 59.

5. Rhea, *Battles for Spotsylvania,* 266.

6. Rhea, *Cold Harbor,* 232.

7. Ibid., 247–50.

8. *(Atlanta) Daily Intelligencer,* June 4, 1864, pg. 1, cols. 3–5 (entire brigade).

9. *Athens (Ga.) Southern Watchman,* June 1, 1864, pg. 2, col. 5 (24th Ga.); *Daily Richmond Enquirer,* June 8, 1864, pg. 2, col. 4 (24th Ga.); *Macon (Ga.) Daily Telegraph,* June 6, 1864, pg. 2, col. 5 (18th Ga.); and July 6, 1864, pg. 2, col. 2 (Co. A, Phillips's Legion).

10. Lillian Henderson, ed., *Roster of the Confederate Soldiers of Georgia, 1861–1865,* 7 vols. (Hapeville, Ga., 1955–58; reprint, 1994).

Bryan's Brigade

1. Returns of casualties in Confederate forces, *OR,* 25(1):806, 27(2):338, 31(1):475; Krick, *Gettysburg Death Roster,* 6.

2. Rhea, *Battle of the Wilderness,* 312.

3. Rhea, *Battles for Spotsylvania,* 90.

4. Rhea, *Cold Harbor,* 250, 254.

5. *Augusta (Ga.) Daily Chronicle & Sentinel,* May 19, 1864, pg. 4, col. 2 (10th, 53rd Ga.); *(Atlanta) Daily Intelligencer,* May 29, 1864, pg. 2, col. 2 (53rd Ga.); *Savannah Republican,* June 3, 1864, pg. 1, col. 4 (50th Ga.); and Aug. 19, 1864, pg. 1, col. 3 (50th Ga.); *Macon (Ga.) Daily Telegraph,* June 21, 1864, pg. 2, col. 2 (51st Ga.); and *Daily Richmond Enquirer,* June 28, 1864, pg. 2, col. 2 (10th Ga.).

6. Lillian Henderson, ed., *Roster of the Confederate Soldiers of Georgia, 1861–1865.*

7. Report of Brig. Gen. Goode Bryan, *OR,* 36(1):1064.

Field's Division

1. Freeman, *Lee's Lieutenants,* 2:xxxviii.

2. "The Opposing Forces at Knoxville, Tennessee," *Battles and Leaders,* 3:752.

3. Freeman, *Lee's Lieutenants,* 3:304–305.

4. Ibid., 310–12.

5. Rhea, *Battle of the Wilderness,* 283–91.

6. Ibid., 291–94.

7. Ibid., 351–55.

8. Ibid., 370–73, 399–400.

9. Ibid., 383–86.

10. Ibid., 389–96.

11. Rhea, *Battles for Spotsylvania,* 82; National Park Service, *Spotsylvania Court House Battle Maps,* 12 maps, Drawing NMP-F5 3026 (Washington, D.C.: National Park Service, 1950), maps 2–3.

12. National Park Service, *Spotsylvania Court House Battle Maps,* maps 9–11.

13. Rhea, *To the North Anna River,* 347; Miller, *North Anna Campaign,* 109.

14. Rhea, *To the North Anna River,* 346.

15. Rhea, *Cold Harbor,* 108, 125.

16. Ibid., 232, 264.

17. See *OR,* 36(1):1064.

18. "Confederate States Army Casualties: Lists and Narrative Reports, 1861–65," Records of the Adjutant and Inspector General's Department, Record Group 109, War Department Collection of Confederate Records, National Archives, Washington, D.C. [hereafter cited as RG 109, NA], microfilm M836.

Gregg's Brigade

1. Freeman, *Lee's Lieutenants,* 3:285, 301, 303.

2. Ibid., 343.

3. Returns of casualties in Confederate forces, *OR,* 27(2):339, 30(2):291, 31(1):235, 475; Krick, *Gettysburg Death Roster,* 8.

4. Col. Harold B. Simpson, *Hood's Texas Brigade: A Compendium* (Hillsboro, Tex., 1977); CSRs, Gregg's Brigade, Records of Confederate Military Organizations, 1861–65, RG 109, NA, microfilm M317 (Ark.) and M227 (Tex.).

5. Scott, *Into the Wilderness,* 123–25; Rhea, *Battle of the Wilderness,* 299–301; Evander M. Law, "From the Wilderness to Cold Harbor," *Battles and Leaders,* 4:125.

6. Scott, *Into the Wilderness,* 125; Rhea, *Battle of the Wilderness,* 302–303; Evander M. Law, "From the Wilderness to Cold Harbor," *Battles and Leaders,* 4:125.

7. Collier, *They'll Do to Tie To,* 178–81.

8. Matter, *If It Takes All Summer,* 154–55.

9. Rhea, *Cold Harbor,* 264.

10. Ibid., 346.

11. *Daily Richmond Examiner,* May 27, 1864, pg. 1, cols. 5–6 (5th Tex.); *Richmond Enquirer,* June 4, 1864, pg. 2, cols. 4–5 (1st Tex.).

12. Simpson, *Hood's Texas Brigade,* 535; *Petersburg Daily Express,* June 29, 1864, pg. 1, col. 6 (3rd Ark.).

Jenkins's/Bratton's Brigade

1. Ulysses S. Grant, "Chattanooga" (and editors' note), *Battles and Leaders,* 3:690.

2. Returns of casualties in Confederate forces, *OR,* 31(2):233, 475.

3. Rhea, *Battle of the Wilderness,* 368–73.

4. Ibid., 393–97.

5. Rhea, *Battles for Spotsylvania,* 84; Matter, *If It Takes All Summer,* 91.

6. Rhea, *Battles for Spotsylvania,* 305.

7. *Charleston Mercury,* May 25, 1864, pg. 2., col. 3 (Palmetto SS); *(Columbia) Daily South Carolinian,* May 27, 1864, pg. 2, col. 2 (2nd S.C.); May 25, 1864, pg. 2, col. 5 (5th S.C.); June 16, 1864, pg. 3, col. 2 (5th S.C.); May 26, 1864, pg. 3, col. 3 (6th S.C.); May 26, 1864, pg. 3, col. 1 (Palmetto SS); and May 29, 1864, pg. 2, col. 2 (Palmetto SS).

Benning's Brigade

1. Freeman, *Lee's Lieutenants,* 2:219n.

2. Returns of casualties in Confederate forces, *OR,* 27(2):340, 30(2):291, 31(1):475; Krick, *Gettysburg Death Roster,* 8.

3. Rhea, *Battle of the Wilderness,* 303–304.

4. Joseph P. Fuller Diary (Co. B, 20th Ga.), May 4–June 13, 1864, no. 2218, Southern Historical Papers Collection, University of North Carolina, Chapel Hill.

5. *(Atlanta) Daily Intelligencer,* May 27, 1864, pg. 1, cols. 3–6 (entire brigade).

6. *Macon (Ga.) Daily Telegraph,* May 20, 1864, pg. 2, col. 5 (17th Ga.); *Daily Columbus (Ga.) Enquirer,* May 26, 1864, pg. 2, col. 2 (20th Ga.).

7. Lillian Henderson, ed., *Roster of the Confederate Soldiers of Georgia, 1861–1865.*

Law's Brigade

1. Returns of casualties in Confederate forces, *OR,* 27(2):339, 28:337, 30(2):291, 31(1):230, 475; Krick, *Gettysburg Death Roster,* 8.

2. Freeman, *Lee's Lieutenants,* 3:299, 303–305.

3. Rhea, *Battle of the Wilderness,* 299.

4. Ibid., 304–307; Scott, *Into the Wilderness,* 131–33.

5. Rhea, *Battle of the Wilderness,* 383–84, 399–400.

6. Rhea, *Battles for Spotsylvania,* 60–62.

7. Rhea, *To the North Anna River,* 387.

8. Ibid., 346.

9. Rhea, *Cold Harbor,* 264, 268.

10. Ibid., 348, 349, 351–57.

11. *(Montgomery) Daily Advertiser,* May 27, 1864, pg. 2[?], col. 2 (4th Ala.); and May 29, 1864, pg. 2[?], col. 3 (47th Ala.); *Richmond Daily Examiner,* May 25, 1864, pg. 2, col. 4 (15th Ala.); *(Columbus, Ga.) Daily Sun,* May 31, 1864, pg. 1, cols. 5–6 (15th Ala.); and June 19, 1864, pg. 1, col. 3 (15th Ala.); *Montgomery Daily Mail,* June 12, 1864, pg. 2, col. 2 (47th Ala.); *(Richmond) Sentinel,* June 27, 1864, pg. 2, col. 5 (4th Ala.).

12. Thomas A Nicoll, adjutant, 44th Ala. Infantry, "Letter from Virginia," *Selma Morning Reporter,* June 20, 1864.

Anderson's Brigade

1. CSRs, 59th Ga. Infantry Regiment, Records of Confederate Military Organizations, 1861–65, RG 109, NA, microfilm M266.

2. Returns of casualties in Confederate forces, *OR,* 27(2):336, 339, 399, 31(1):475; Krick, *Gettysburg Death Roster,* 8.

3. Rhea, *Battle of the Wilderness,* 299.

4. Ibid., 355, 357.

5. Ibid., 393–94.

6. *(Milledgeville, Ga.) Confederate Union,* June 7, 1864, pg. 3, col. 3.

7. Matter, *If It Takes All Summer,* 154–55.

8. Rhea, *Cold Harbor,* 264–65, 268.

9. Ibid., 346, 348, 351–52.

10. Casualty list for Field's Division, Records of the Adjutant and Inspector General's Department, RG 109, NA, microfilm M836; *Macon (Ga.) Daily Telegraph,* May 24, 1864, pg. 2, col. 3 (59th Ga.); June 4, 1864, pg. 2, cols. 4–5 (59th Ga.); May 26, 1864, pg. 2, cols. 3–4 (8th Ga.); *(Richmond) Sentinel,* May 30, 1864, pg. 2, col. 5 (brigade sharpshooter bn.); *(Atlanta) Daily Intelligencer,* June 2, 1864, pg. 3, cols. 2–3 (9th Ga.); and June 18, 1864 (Co. C, 7th Ga.).

11. Lillian Henderson, ed., *Roster of the Confederate Soldiers of Georgia, 1861–1865.*

Pickett's Division

1. Freeman, *Lee's Lieutenants,* 3:451–74; Herbert M. Schiller, *The Bermuda Hundred Campaign* (Dayton, Ohio, 1988), 17, 51–53, 55, 59, 69–74, 79, 83, 95–96, 108, 110, 115, 127, 150, 165.

2. Schiller, *Bermuda Hundred Campaign,* 229–309.

3. Miller, *North Anna Campaign,* 8, 16, 21, 24, 27.

4. Rhea, *To the North Anna River,* 324–26.

5. Rhea, *Cold Harbor,* 108, 123.

6. Ibid., 148, 157.

7. Ibid., 232; National Park Service, *Cold Harbor Battlefield Maps,* 16 maps, Drawing NBP-R1C 3014 (Washington, D.C.: National Park Service, 1960), maps 5–10.

8. Freeman, *Lee's Lieutenants,* 3:532.

Kemper's Brigade

1. Return of casualties in Confederate forces, *OR,* 27(2):339; Krick, *Gettysburg Death Roster,* 7.

2. Schiller, *Bermuda Hundred Campaign,* 222; *Richmond Daily Dispatch,* May 17, 1864, pg. 1, cols. 1–2 (1st, 11th Va.); *Daily Richmond Examiner,* May 20, 1864, pg. 1, cols. 3–4 (11th, 24th Va.); and May [?], 1864, pg. 1, col. 4 (7th Va.).

3. Miller, *North Anna Campaign,* 16–18; Rhea, *To the North Anna River,* 197–98, 225–27.

4. Rhea, *To the North Anna River,* 237–39.

5. *Lynchburg Virginian,* May 21, 1864, pg. 4, cols. 1–2 (11th Va., brigade report).

6. Lee Wallace, *1st Virginia Infantry Regiment* (Lynchburg, Va., 1985); Wallace, *3rd Virginia Infantry Regiment* (Lynchburg, Va., 1986); David F. Riggs, *7th Virginia Infantry Regiment* (Lynchburg, Va., 1982); Robert T. Bell, *11th Virginia Infantry Regiment* (Lynchburg, Va., 1985); Ralph G. White, *24th Virginia Infantry Regiment* (Lynchburg, Va., 1987).

Hunton's Brigade

1. Return of casualties in Confederate forces, *OR,* 27(2):339; Krick, *Gettysburg Death Roster,* 7.

2. John W. Busey and David G. Martin, *Regimental Strengths at Gettysburg* (Baltimore, 1982), 146.

3. Schiller, *Bermuda Hundred Campaign,* 165, 343.

4. Rhea, *To the North Anna River,* 51–53.

5. Rhea, *Cold Harbor,* 264–65.

6. Ibid., 343, 345.

7. *Richmond Whig,* May 14, 1864, pg. 2, col. 4 (19th Va.); and May 16, 1864, pg. 2, col. 7 (32nd Va.); *Daily Richmond Enquirer,* June 7, 1864, pg. 1, col. 4 (19th Va.); June 8, 1864, pg. 2, col. 4 (28th Va.); and June 14, 1864, pg. 2, col. 6 (56th Va.); *Daily Richmond Examiner,* June 10, 1864, pg. 1, col. 5 (18th Va.).

8. John E. Divine, *8th Virginia Infantry Regiment* (Lynchburg, Va., 1983); James I. Robertson, *18th Virginia Infantry Regiment* (Lynchburg, Va., 1984); E. I. Jordan and H. A. Thomas, *19th Virginia Infantry Regiment* (Lynchburg, Va., 1987); Frank E. Fields Jr., *28th Virginia Infantry Regiment* (Lynchburg, Va., 1985); and William A. Young and Patricia C. Young, *56th Virginia Infantry Regiment* (Lynchburg, Va., 1990).

Barton's Brigade

1. Return of casualties in Confederate forces, *OR,* 27(2):339; Krick, *Gettysburg Death Roster,* 7.

2. Schiller, *Bermuda Hundred Campaign,* 222.

3. Ibid., 151–54, 156–58, 222–40.

4. Return of casualties for Confederate forces, *OR,* 36(2):205.

5. *To the North Anna River,* 197, 262.

6. Return of casualties for Confederate forces, *OR,* 36(2); *Richmond Whig,* May 16, 1864, pg. 2[?], cols. 5–6 (57th Va.); *Daily Richmond Enquirer,* May 20, 1864, pg. 1, col. 5 (14th Va.); and May 24, 1864, pg. 1, col. 6 (53rd Va.); *Richmond Daily Dispatch,* May 31, 1864, pg. 1, col. 2 (38th Va.).

7. Benjamin Trask, *9th Virginia Infantry Regiment* (Lynchburg, Va., 1984); Edward R. Crews and Timothy A Parrish, *14th Virginia Infantry Regiment* (Lynchburg, Va., 1987); G. Howard Gregory, *38th Virginia Infantry Regiment* (Lynchburg, Va., 1988); and *53rd Virginia Infantry Regiment* (Lynchburg, Va., 1999); Charles W. Sublett, *57th Virginia Infantry Regiment* (Lynchburg, Va., 1985).

Corse's Brigade

1. John Perry Alderman, *29th Virginia Infantry Regiment* (Lynchburg, Va., 1989).

2. Return of casualties in Confederate forces, *OR,* 27(2):627.

3. Schiller, *Bermuda Hundred Campaign,* 222, 247–50, 263–64.

4. Miller, *North Anna Campaign,* 16–18; Rhea, *To the North Anna River,* 197–98, 225–27.

5. National Park Service, *Cold Harbor Battlefield Maps,* 16 maps, Drawing NBP-R1C 3014 (Washington, D.C.: National Park Service, 1960), maps 6–7.

6. *Richmond Daily Dispatch,* May 19, 1864, pg. 1, col. 1 (15th Va.); *(Richmond) Sentinel,* May 19, 1864, pg. 1, col. 3 (29th Va.); June 9, 1864, pg. 2, col. 6 (entire brigade); and June 23, 1864, pg. 2, col. 5 (30th Va.); *Daily Richmond Enquirer,* May 20, 1864, pg. 4, cols. 3–4 (entire brigade); and June 7, 1864, pg. 2, col. 4 (15th Va.).

7. Louis H. Manarin, *15th Virginia Infantry Regiment* (Lynchburg, Va., 1990); Lee Wallace, *17th Virginia Infantry Regiment* (Lynchburg, Va., 1990); Robert K. Krick, *30th Virginia Infantry Regiment* (Lynchburg, Va., 1985); Les Jensen, *32nd Virginia Infantry Regiment* (Lynchburg, Va., 1990).

Artillery

1. Rhea, *Battles for Spotsylvania,* 52, 56–58.

2. Ibid., 62; Matter, *If It Takes All Summer,* 94–95.

3. Rhea, *To the North Anna River,* 124; National Park Service, *Spotsylvania Court House Battle Maps,* 12 maps, Drawing NMP-F5 3026 (Washington, D.C.: National Park Service, 1950), maps 10–11.

4. Rhea, *To the North Anna River,* 298.

5. Rhea, *Cold Harbor,* 125.

6. National Park Service, *Cold Harbor Battlefield Maps,* 16 maps, Drawing NBP-R1C 3014 (Washington, D.C.: National Park Service, 1960), maps 7–8.

7. Haskell's Battalion: *(Raleigh) Daily Confederate,* May 26, 1864, pg. 2, col. 6; *Daily Richmond Enquirer,* June 8, 1864, pg. 2, cols. 3–4; *Columbia (S.C.) Guardian,* June 13, 1864, pg.

1, col. 2; *Daily Richmond Examiner,* Aug. 3, 1864, pg. 2, col. 6; Manarin and Jordan, *N.C. Troops,* vol. 1; W. C. Sherwood, *Nelson Artillery* (Lynchburg, Va., 1991). Cabell's Battalion: *Daily Richmond Enquirer,* June 2, 1864, pg. 2, col. 5; and June 29, 1864, pg. 2, col. 5; *(Raleigh) Daily Confederate,* June 10, 1864, pg. 2, col. 3; Manarin and Jordan, *N.C. Troops,* vol. 1; Lee Wallace, *Richmond Howitzers* (Lynchburg, Va., 1993).

8. *Richmond Daily Dispatch,* May 27, 1864, pg. 1, col. 2; *Charleston Mercury,* May 28, 1864, pg. 2, col. 4; Marilyn B. Kolezar, *Ashland, Bedford, and Taylor Artillery* (Lynchburg, Va., 1994); Homer D. Musselman, *Caroline, Parker, and Stafford Artillery* (Lynchburg, Va., 1992).

9. See notes 7 and 8.

5. SECOND CORPS

Johnson's/Gordon's Division

1. Rhea, *Battle of the Wilderness,* 125.
2. Ibid., 142–52.
3. Ibid., 179–82.
4. Rhea, *Battles for Spotsylvania,* 84.
5. Ibid., 87–88.
6. Ibid., 89.
7. Matter, *If It Takes All Summer,* 103.
8. Rhea, *Battles for Spotsylvania,* 167–68; Matter, *If It Takes All Summer,* 160–61.
9. Rhea, *Battles for Spotsylvania,* 169–73; Matter, *If It Takes All Summer,* 162–65.
10. Rhea, *Battles for Spotsylvania,* 219; Matter, *If It Takes All Summer,* 172.
11. Rhea, *Battles for Spotsylvania,* 233–42; Matter, *If It Takes All Summer,* 195–99.
12. *(Raleigh) Daily Confederate,* May 30, 1864, pg. 2, col. 4.
13. Rhea, *To the North Anna River,* 77.
14. Ibid., 327; Miller, *North Anna Campaign,* 108–109, 119.
15. Rhea, *Cold Harbor,* 301–303, 305.

Walker's (Stonewall) Brigade

1. Returns of casualties in Confederate forces, *OR,* 25(1):808, 27(2):335, 341, 29(1):837.
2. Freeman, *Lee's Lieutenants,* 2:703–705.
3. Rhea, *Battle of the Wilderness,* 179–81.
4. Rhea, *Battles for Spotsylvania,* 84.
5. Matter, *If It Takes All Summer,* 103.
6. Ibid., 164; Rhea, *Battles for Spotsylvania,* 172–73.
7. Matter, *If It Takes All Summer,* 198–99; Rhea, *Battles for Spotsylvania,* 240–41.
8. Rhea, *To the North Anna River,* 177, 183.
9. Rhea, *Cold Harbor,* 301–303, 305.
10. *Staunton Spectator & General Advertiser,* May 17, 1864, pg. 2, cols. 5–6 (5th Va.); and May 24, 1864, pg. 2, col. 5 (2nd, 5th Va.); *Lexington (Va.) Gazette,* May 18, 1864, pg. 2, col. 3;

and May 25, 1864, pg. 2, col. 3 (4th partial, 27th Va.); and *Wytheville (Va.) Dispatch,* May 20, 1864, pg. 2, col. 4 (Co. A, 4th Va.).

11. Elizabeth L. Sayers, *History of Smythe County, Virginia,* ed. Joan Tracy Armstrong, vol. 2, *1832–1870: Antebellum Years through the Civil War* (Marion, Va., 1986), Appendix 6, "Smythe County Muster Rolls, Roster of Company D, 4th Virginia Infantry," comp. Clara Hill Carter, 221–23; Charles W. Crush, ed., *The Montgomery County Story, 1776–1957* (n.p., 1957); Thomas D. Gold, *History of Clarke County, Virginia, & Its Connections with the War between the States* (Berryville, Va., 1962); Dennis Frye, *2nd Virginia Infantry Regiment* (Lynchburg, Va., 1984); James I. Robertson, *4th Virginia Infantry Regiment* (Lynchburg, Va., 1982); Lee Wallace, *5th Virginia Infantry Regiment* (Lynchburg, Va., 1988); Lowell Ridenbaugh, *27th Virginia Infantry Regiment* (Lynchburg, Va., 1993); Ridenbaugh, *33rd Virginia Infantry Regiment* (Lynchburg, Va., 1987).

12. James N. Bosang, *Memoirs of a Pulaski Veteran of the Stonewall Brigade, 1861–1865* (Radford, Va., 1912; reprint, Pulaski, Va.: B. D. Smythe and Brother, 1930).

13. "Diaries, Writings, and Stories of George D. Buswell," Genealogical Society, Page County Library, Luray, Va., 10, 12, 13.

Jones's Brigade

1. Returns of casualties in Confederate forces, *OR,* 25(1):809, 27(2):335, 341, 29(1):837.

2. Rhea, *Battle of the Wilderness,* 153–54; Scott, *Into the Wilderness,* 59.

3. John R. King (Co. K, 25th Va.), "My Experiences in the Confederate Army and in Northern Prisons," Library of Congress, Washington, D.C.

4. Rhea, *Battle of the Wilderness,* 182; Scott, *Into the Wilderness,* 97.

5. Rhea, *Battles for Spotsylvania,* 219; Matter, *If It Takes All Summer,* 103.

6. Matter, *If It Takes All Summer,* 164, 172.

7. Ibid., 193–94; Rhea, *Battles for Spotsylvania,* 231.

8. Matter, *If It Takes All Summer,* 192.

9. "Civil War Letters of Abram Schultz Miller, written to his wife, Julia Virginia Miller, 1861–1864," 21 (May 18, 1864), James A. Miller Collection, Handley Regional Library, Winchester, Va., 18–23; "Diaries, Writings, and Stories of George D. Buswell," 13.

10. Robert A. Withers [to editor], May 16, 1864, *Lynchburg Virginian,* May 23, 1864, pg. 1, col. 3.

11. "Why Was Artillery Not in Place on Fateful Spotsylvania Field?," *Richmond Times/Dispatch,* Oct. 4, 1914, pg. 7, sec. 4, cols. 1–2.

12. "Letters by Lieut. Overton Steger" (Co. D, 21st Va.), Book 19-36-40, Lewis Leigh Collection, Virginia Historical Society, Richmond.

13. *Lynchburg Virginian,* May 23, 1864, pg. 1, col. 3.

14. *Staunton Spectator & General Advertiser,* May 17, 1864, pg. 2, col. 5 (25th Va. partial); *(Richmond) Sentinel,* June 1, 1864, pg. 2, col. 4 (44th Va.); *Abington Virginian,* June 10, 1864, pg. 1, col. 2 (48th, 50th Va.); *Daily Richmond Examiner,* June 17, 1864, pg. 1, cols. 4–7 (21st Va.).

15. John S. Holley (48th Va.) to Mathew R. Blackwell, May 6, 1864, letter to editor, *(Abington) Journal-Virginian,* May 12, 1932; *Abington Virginian,* June 10, 1864, pg. 1, col. 2.

16. Withers [to editor], May 16, 1864, *Lynchburg Virginian,* May 23, 1864, pg. 1, col. 3; Susan A. Riggs, *21st Virginia Infantry Regiment* (Lynchburg, Va., 1991); Richard Armstrong, *25th Virginia Infantry Regiment* (Lynchburg, Va., 1990); John D. Chapla, *42nd Virginia Infantry Regiment* (Lynchburg, Va., 1983); Chapla, *48th Virginia Infantry Regiment* (Lynchburg, Va., 1989); Chapla, *50th Virginia Infantry Regiment* (Lynchburg, Va., 1997); Kevin C. Ruffner, *44th Virginia Infantry Regiment* (Lynchburg, Va., 1987).

17. "Civil War Letters of Abram Schultz Miller," 18–19; *Abington Virginian,* June 10, 1864, pg. 1, col. 2.

Steuart's Brigade

1. Returns of casualties in Confederate forces, *OR,* 25(1):809; 27(2):335, 341; 29(1):837; Krick, *Gettysburg Death Roster,* 10.

2. Rhea, *Battle of the Wilderness,* 149.

3. Scott, *Into the Wilderness,* 27.

4. Rhea, *Battle of the Wilderness,* 149–50.

5. Ibid., 179.

6. Rhea, *Battles for Spotsylvania,* 172–73; Matter, *If It Takes All Summer,* 164–65.

7. Rhea, *Battles for Spotsylvania,* 237–38; Matter, *If It Takes All Summer,* 195–97.

8. Manarin and Jordan, *N. C. Troops,* vol. 3; *(Raleigh) Daily Confederate,* May 28, 1864, pg. 2, col. 4 (3rd N.C.); *Wilmington Daily Journal,* May 30, 1864, pg. 1, cols. 2–3 (1st N.C.).

9. *(Richmond) Sentinel,* May 17, 1864, pg. 2, col. 5 (23rd Va.); *Staunton Spectator & General Advertiser,* May 17, 1864, pg. 2, col. 5 (10th Va. partial); *Daily Richmond Enquirer,* May 20, 1864, pg. 1, cols. 4–5 (10th Va.); *Abingdon Virginian,* May 27, 1864, pg. 2, col. 2 (37th Va.).

10. Terrance V. Murphy, *10th Virginia Infantry Regiment* (Lynchburg, Va., 1989); Thomas M. Rankin, *23rd Virginia Infantry Regiment* (Lynchburg, Va., 1985); Rankin, *37th Virginia Infantry Regiment* (Lynchburg, Va., 1987).

Stafford's Brigade

1. Rhea, *Battle of the Wilderness,* 179–80.

2. Returns of casualties in Confederate forces, *OR,* 25(1):809, 27(2):335, 341, 29(1):837.

3. Steven H. Newton, *Lost for the Cause: The Confederate Army in 1864* (Mason City, Iowa, 2000), 172, 186.

4. Rhea, *Battle of the Wilderness,* 152.

5. Ibid., 179–181.

6. Rhea, *Battles for Spotsylvania,* 76.

7. Matter, *If It Takes All Summer,* 103.

8. Ibid., 128; Rhea, *Battles for Spotsylvania,* 219.

9. Matter, *If It Takes All Summer,* 172; Rhea, *Battles for Spotsylvania,* 219.

10. Matter, *If It Takes All Summer,* 194–95; Rhea, *Battles for Spotsylvania,* 238–40.

11. Matter, *If It Takes All Summer,* 195.

12. Rhea, *To the North Anna River,* 177, 388–89.

13. *Richmond Whig,* June 16, 1864, pg. 2, cols. 5–6.

Early's/Ramseur's Division

1. Freeman, *Lee's Lieutenants,* 3:265–68.
2. Rhea, *Battle of the Wilderness,* 159–62, 166–67.
3. Ibid., 252–53, 322–23, 407–411.
4. Rhea, *Battles for Spotsylvania,* 171–73, 246–52.
5. Rhea, *To the North Anna River,* 145, 177–80.
6. Rhea, *Battles for Spotsylvania,* 76.
7. Rhea, *To the North Anna River,* 20.
8. Ibid., 231.
9. Rhea, *Cold Harbor,* 60.
10. Ibid., 145.
11. Ibid., 306, 368.

Hays's Brigade

1. Returns of casualties in Confederate forces, *OR,* 25(1):808; 27(2):335, 340; 29(1):836, 840–41; Krick, *Gettysburg Death Roster,* 9.
2. Freeman, *Lee's Lieutenants,* 3:265–68.
3. Return of casualties for Confederate forces, *OR,* 29(1):624, 629.
4. Rhea, *Battle of the Wilderness,* 182; Scott, *Into the Wilderness,* 97.
5. Rhea, *Battle of the Wilderness,* 247.
6. Rhea, *Battles for Spotsylvania,* 76.
7. Ibid., 219; Matter, *If It Takes All Summer,* 128.
8. Rhea, *Battles for Spotsylvania,* 220.
9. Ibid., 219; Matter, *If It Takes All Summer,* 172.
10. Rhea, *Battles for Spotsylvania,* 241; Matter, *If It Takes All Summer,* 198.
11. *(Richmond) Sentinel,* June 8, 1864, pg. 3, col. 6 (5th La.).
12. *Richmond Whig,* June 11, 1864, pg. 2, cols. 4–6 (entire brigade).

Gordon's/Evans's Brigade

1. Returns of casualties in Confederate forces, *OR,* 25(1):808, 27(2):335, 341, 29(1):836, 840–41; Krick, *Gettysburg Death Roster,* 10.
2. Rhea, *Battle of the Wilderness,* 159–60; Scott, *Into the Wilderness,* 61–62; Cannan, *Wilderness Campaign,* 109.
3. Rhea, *Battle of the Wilderness,* 166–67.
4. Ibid., 406–22; Scott, *Into the Wilderness,* 171–75.
5. Rhea, *Battles for Spotsylvania,* 76, 173.
6. Ibid., 173; Matter, *If It Takes All Summer,* 165.
7. Matter, *If It Takes All Summer,* 200.
8. Ibid., 201–203; Rhea, *Battles for Spotsylvania,* 250–51.
9. Matter, *If It Takes All Summer,* 204, 224; Rhea, *Battles for Spotsylvania,* 252.

10. Matter, *If It Takes All Summer,* 307.

11. Ibid., 322–23; Rhea, *To the North Anna River,* 177, 183.

12. Rhea, *Cold Harbor,* 257, 259, 301, 303, 305.

13. Ibid., 303.

14. *Augusta (Ga.) Daily Chronicle & Sentinel,* May 19, 1864, pg. 1, col. 1 (31st, 60th, 61st Ga., all partial); June 16, 1864, pg. 1, col. 3 (38th Ga., 12th Ga. Bn.); and June 28, 1864, pg. 3, col. 5 (12th Ga. Bn.); *(Atlanta) Daily Intelligencer,* May 27, 1864, pg. 3, cols. 2–4 (13th, 31st Ga., both partial); and June 15, 1864, pg. 1, col. 2 (13th Ga.); *Columbus (Ga.) Daily Sun,* May 31, 1864, pg. 2, col. 4 or 5 (31st Ga.); *Savannah Republican,* May 31, 1864, pg. 2, col. 2 (26th Ga.); *Macon (Ga.) Daily Telegraph,* Nov. 1, 1864, pg. 1, col. 5 (60th Ga.).

15. Lillian Henderson, ed., *Roster of the Confederate Soldiers of Georgia, 1861–1865;* Alton J. Murray, *South Georgia Rebels: The True Wartime Experiences of 26th Georgia Volunteer Infantry* (St. Mary's, Ga., 1976); G. W. Nichols, *A Soldier's Story of His Regiment (61st Georgia) and Incidentally of the Lawton-Gordon-Evans Brigade, Army of Northern Virginia* (N.p., 1898).

Pegram's Brigade

1. Returns of casualties in Confederate forces, *OR,* 25(1):808, 27(2):335, 340, 29(1):624, 836; Krick, *Gettysburg Death Roster,* 9.

2. Rhea, *Battle of the Wilderness,* 125–26, 179, 245.

3. Ibid., 247, 250; Scott, *Into the Wilderness,* 97–98.

4. Rhea, *Battle of the Wilderness,* 253, 422.

5. Ibid., 322–23.

6. Ibid., 412, 416, 418, 422–23; Cannan, *Wilderness Campaign,* 199–201.

7. Matter, *If It Takes All Summer,* 165.

8. Rhea, *Battles for Spotsylvania,* 239, 246–47, 249.

9. Ibid., 249–50; Matter, *If It Takes All Summer,* 201–202.

10. Rhea, *Battles for Spotsylvania,* 250–52; Matter, *If It Takes All Summer,* 202–204.

11. Matter, *If It Takes All Summer,* 257, 260.

12. Rhea, *To the North Anna River,* 183–84, 187.

13. Rhea, *Cold Harbor,* 144–45.

14. Ibid., 145–48.

15. Ibid., 368.

16. *(Richmond) Sentinel,* May 17, 1864, pg. 1, col. 5 (49th Va. partial); May 25, 1864, pg. 1, col. 6 (58th Va.); May 31, 1864, pg. 2, col. 5 (31st Va.); June 2, 1864, pg. 2, col. 2 (13th, 49th Va.); June 3, 1864, pg. 2, col. 5 (49th Va.); and June 6, 1864, pg. 2, col. 5 (58th Va.); *Daily Richmond Enquirer,* May 20, 1864, pg. 1, col. 5 (52nd Va.); *Staunton Spectator & General Advertiser,* May 31, 1864 (58th Va.); *Daily Richmond Examiner,* May 24, 1864, pg. 1, cols. 3–4 (13th Va.); May 31, 1864, pg. 3, col. 3 (31st Va.); and June 6, 1864, pg. 1, col. 5 (52nd Va.). For a complete listing of casualties in the 31st Virginia during 1864, see Letters Received by the Confederate Adjutant & Inspector General, 1861–65, RG 109, NA, reel 474-163, no. 897-598.

17. David F. Riggs, *13th Virginia Infantry Regiment* (Lynchburg, Va., 1988); John M. Ashcraft, *31stVirginia Infantry Regiment* (Lynchburg, Va., 1988); Richard Kleese, *49th Virginia In-*

fantry Regiment (Lynchburg, Va., 2000); Robert J. Driver, *52nd Virginia Regiment* (Lynchburg, Va., 1986); Driver, *58th Virginia Infantry Regiment* (Lynchburg, Va., 1990).

Hoke's Brigade

1. Freeman, *Lee's Lieutenants,* 3:265–68.

2. Returns of casualties in Confederate forces, *OR,* 25(1):808, 27(2):335, 304, 29(1):629, 841; Krick, *Gettysburg Death Roster,* 9.

3. Freeman, *Lee's Lieutenants,* 3:336.

4. Ibid., 486, 80n.

5. Schiller, *Bermuda Hundred Campaign,* 220, 219–31, 233, 235, 239, 245, 251.

6. Return of casualties for Confederate forces, *OR,* 36(2):205.

7. Miller, *North Anna Campaign,* 31; Rhea, *To the North Anna River,* 197.

8. National Park Service, *Cold Harbor Battlefield Maps,* 16 maps, Drawing NBP-R1C 3014 (Washington, D.C.: National Park Service, 1960), maps 6, 11–12.

9. *Petersburg Daily Express,* June 15, 1864, pg. 1, col. 3 (6th N.C.); *(Raleigh) Daily Confederate,* June 17, 1864, pg. 2, col. 3 (21st, 54th, 57th N.C.).

10. Manarin and Jordan, *N.C. Troops,* vols. 4, 6, 13, and 14.

Rodes's Division

1. Schiller, *Bermuda Hundred Campaign,* 228, 340.

2. Rhea, *Battle of the Wilderness,* 410.

3. Ibid., 82.

4. Ibid., 125.

5. Ibid., 159–62; Scott, *Into the Wilderness,* 61–62.

6. Rhea, *Battle of the Wilderness,* 275; Scott, *Into the Wilderness,* 107.

7. Rhea, *Battles for Spotsylvania,* 83–84; Matter, *If It Takes All Summer,* 91–94.

8. Rhea, *Battles for Spotsylvania,* 169–70; Matter, *If It Takes All Summer,* 162–63.

9. Matter, *If It Takes All Summer,* 307.

10. Rhea, *Battles for Spotsylvania,* 171, 176–77, 179–80; Matter, *If It Takes All Summer,* 317, 321–26.

11. Miller, *North Anna Campaign,* 114–17.

12. Rhea, *Cold Harbor,* 140–42.

13. Ibid., 257, 296–98, 300–301, 308, 371–72.

Ramseur's Brigade

1. Returns of casualties in Confederate forces, *OR,* 25(1):808, 27(2):336, 342, 29(1):412, 616, 837; Krick, *Gettysburg Death Roster,* 12.

2. Rhea, *Battle of the Wilderness,* 328–30.

3. Rhea, *Battles for Spotsylvania,* 84; Matter, *If It Takes All Summer,* 86–87, 91.

4. Rhea, *Battles for Spotsylvania,* 169–71, 173; Matter, *If It Takes All Summer,* 165, 172.

5. Rhea, *Battles for Spotsylvania,* 255–59; Matter, *If It Takes All Summer,* 205.

6. Rhea, *Battles for Spotsylvania,* 255–59; Matter, *If It Takes All Summer,* 205.

7. Rhea, *Battles for Spotsylvania,* 270–71, 274–75, 280; Matter, *If It Takes All Summer,* 211, 219.

8. Rhea, *To the North Anna River,* 171–76, 180–84; Matter, *If It Takes All Summer,* 317, 321–22.

9. Rhea, *Cold Harbor,* 257, 259, 298, 300.

10. Ibid., 60, 301.

11. *(Raleigh) Daily Confederate,* May 24, 1864, pg. 2, cols. 4–5 (2nd, 4th, 14th N.C.); May 30, 1864, pg. 2, col. 2 (14th N.C.); June 2, 1864, pg. 4, col. 3 (4th N.C.); June 7, 1864, pg. 2, col. 5 (30th N.C.); June 21, 1864, pg. 2, col. 5 (4th N.C.).

12. Manarin and Jordan, *N.C. Troops,* vols. 3, 5, 8.

Daniel's/Grimes's Brigade

1. Returns of casualties in Confederate forces, *OR,* 27(2):342, 29(1):412, 616, 837; Krick, *Gettysburg Death Roster,* 11.

2. Rhea, *Battle of the Wilderness,* 157, 164; Scott, *Into the Wilderness,* 60.

3. Rhea, *Battles for Spotsylvania,* 169–71, 173; Matter, *If It Takes All Summer,* 163, 165.

4. Rhea, *Battles for Spotsylvania,* 241, 244, 247, 249, 255–56; Matter, *If It Takes All Summer,* 199.

5. Rhea, *Battles for Spotsylvania,* 268; Rhea, *To the North Anna River,* 30.

6. Rhea, *To the North Anna River,* 176.

7. Ibid., 176, 179; Matter, *If It Takes All Summer,* 317, 322.

8. Rhea, *Cold Harbor,* 140–42.

9. *Fayetteville (N.C.) Observer,* June 2, 16,1864, pg. and col. nos. unknown (entire brigade for May 5 20 and May 21–June 2); *(Raleigh) Daily Confederate,* June 1, 1864, pg. 1, col. 1 (43rd N.C.); June 18, 1864, pg. 1, col. 2 (43rd N.C.); and June 9, 1864, pg. 2, col. 3 (45th N.C.); Manarin and Jordan, *N.C. Troops,* vols. 3, 9–11, 13.

Doles's Brigade

1. Returns of casualties in Confederate forces, *OR,* 25(1):808, 27(2):336, 342, 29(1):412, 837; Krick, *Gettysburg Death Roster,* 11.

2. Rhea, *Battle of the Wilderness,* 159–62; Scott, *Into the Wilderness,* 61–62.

3. Rhea, *Battles for Spotsylvania,* 380n2.

4. Ibid., 164, 168–73, 176–77; Matter, *If It Takes All Summer,* 162–63.

5. Trudeau, *Bloody Roads South,* 161.

6. Rhea, *Battles for Spotsylvania,* 253, 255, 401n68; Matter, *If It Takes All Summer,* 201, 204, 235, 260.

7. Rhea, *To the North Anna River,* 177; Matter, *If It Takes All Summer,* 317.

8. Rhea, *Cold Harbor,* 396.

9. *Macon (Ga.) Daily Telegraph,* June 3, 1864, pg. 2, cols. 2–4 (entire brigade).

10. *Daily Richmond Enquirer,* May 12, 1864, pg. 2, col. 2 (12th Ga.); Lillian Henderson, ed., *Roster of the Confederate Soldiers of Georgia, 1861–1865.*

Battle's Brigade

1. Returns of casualties in Confederate forces, *OR,* 25(1):807, 27(2):336, 342, 29(1):412, 837; Krick, *Gettysburg Death Roster,* 11.

2. Freeman, *Lee's Lieutenants,* 3:189–99, 325.

3. [Cullen A. Battle], "The Third Alabama Regiment," [1905?], Papers of Rev. J. H. B. Hall, Alabama Department of Archives and History, Montgomery, 98; James W. Roberts, "The Wilderness and Spotsylvania, May 4–12, 1864," *Quarterly Periodical of the Florida Historical Society* 11, no. 2 (Oct. 1932): 60–61.

4. Battle, "Third Alabama Regiment," 98; Rhea, *Battle of the Wilderness,* 154.

5. Battle, "Third Alabama Regiment," 99.

6. Rhea, *Battles for Spotsylvania,* 84; Matter, *If It Takes All Summer,* 87, 92.

7. Rhea, *Battles for Spotsylvania,* 171; Matter, *If It Takes All Summer,* 165.

8. Rhea, *Battles for Spotsylvania,* 255–56, 259, 262.

9. Rhea, *To the North Anna River,* 176; Matter, *If It Takes All Summer,* 317, 322.

10. *Richmond Whig,* May 19, 1864, pg. 1, col. 2 (6th Ala.); *(Montgomery) Daily Advertiser,* May 30, 1864, pg. 1, cols. 1–2 (6th Ala.); and July 28, 1864, pg. 2, col. 3 (3rd Ala.); *Mobile Daily Advertiser and Register,* May 26, 1864, pg. 1, col. 5 (12th Ala.); and June 15, 1864, pg. 1, cols. 6–7 (12th Ala.); *Selma Morning Reporter,* June 11, 1864, pg. and col. nos. unknown (Co. I, 5th Ala.).

11. *(Montgomery) Daily Advertiser,* May 30, 1864, pg. 1, cols. 1–2.

Johnston's Brigade

1. Freeman, *Lee's Lieutenants,* 3:86.

2. Ibid., 201.

3. Ibid., 237.

4. Returns of casualties in Confederate forces, *OR,* 25(1):808, 27(2):336, 342, 29(1):412, 838; Krick, *Gettysburg Death Roster,* 11.

5. Rhea, *Battle of the Wilderness,* 410, 422–23.

6. Rhea, *Battles for Spotsylvania,* 76.

7. Ibid., 105–106.

8. Ibid., 171–73; Matter, *If It Takes All Summer,* 165.

9. Rhea, *Battles for Spotsylvania,* 248, 250; Matter, *If It Takes All Summer,* 200.

10. Rhea, *To the North Anna River,* 186.

11. Manarin and Jordan, *N.C. Troops,* vols. 4–7.

12. *(Raleigh) Daily Confederate,* June 8, 1864, pg. 2, col. 5 (Co. E, 5th N.C.); and June 12, 1864, pg. 2, col. 4 (Co. F, 12th N.C.); *(Richmond) Sentinel,* June 13, 1864, pg. 2, col. 4 (12th N.C.); *Fayetteville (N.C.) Observer,* June 20, 1864, pg. and col. nos. unknown (20th N.C.).

Artillery

1. Matter, *If It Takes All Summer,* 137, 161.
2. Ibid., 137, 158, 162–63, 165–66; Rhea, *Battles for Spotsylvania,* 170.
3. Rhea, *Battles for Spotsylvania,* 170–71.
4. Matter, *If It Takes All Summer,* 175–79.
5. Ibid., 175, 190.
6. Ibid., 190–91.
7. Ibid., 196.
8. Ibid., 199.
9. Rhea, *To the North Anna River,* 153.
10. Nelson's Battalion: *Daily Richmond Examiner,* June 8, 1864, pg. 3, col. 6; David G. Martin, *Fluvanna Artillery* (Lynchburg, Va., 1992); W. C. Sherwood and Richard L. Nicholas, *Amherst, Albemarle, and Studivant Artillery* (Lynchburg, Va., 1996). Braxton's Battalion: *(Richmond) Sentinel,* June 16, 1864, pg. 2, col. 7; Homer D. Mussleman, *Caroline, Parker, and Stafford Artillery* (Lynchburg, Va., 1992); Keith S. Bohannon, *Giles, Alleghany, and Jackson Artillery* (Lynchburg, Va., 1990); Robert H. Moore, *Charlottesville, Lee, Lynchburg, and Bedford Artillery* (Lynchburg, Va., 1990). Page's Battalion: *Richmond Whig,* June 8, 1864, pg. 1, col. 2; *Daily Richmond Enquirer,* June 14, 1864, pg. 2, col. 6; *Daily Richmond Examiner,* June 16, 1864, pg. 1, col. 4; Gregory J. Macaluso, *Morris, Orange, and King William Artillery* (Lynchburg, Va., 1991). Cutshaw's Battalion: *Richmond Daily Dispatch,* May 31, 1864, pg. 1, col. 2; *Daily Richmond Examiner,* May 27, 1864, pg. 2, col. 4; *Daily Richmond Enquirer,* June 29, 1864, pg. 2, col. 3; Robert H. Moore, *Charlottesville, etc. Artillery* (Lynchburg, Va., 1990); Richard L. Nicholas and Joseph Servis, *Powhatan, Salem, and Henrico Light Artillery* (Lynchburg, Va., 1997); Robert J. Driver, *Staunton Artillery and McClanahan's Battery* (Lynchburg, Va., 1988). Hardaway's Battalion: *Richmond Daily Dispatch,* May 16, 1864, pg. 1, col. 3; and June 13, 1864, pg. 1, col. 2; Robert J. Driver, *1st and 2nd Rockbridge Artillery* (Lynchburg, Va., 1987); Lee Wallace, *Richmond Howitzers* (Lynchburg, Va., 1993); Richard L. Nicholas and Joseph Servis, *Powhatan, Salem, etc. Artillery* (Lynchburg, Va., 1997).

6. THIRD CORPS

Heth's Division

1. Rhea, *Battle of the Wilderness,* 126–27; Scott, *Into the Wilderness,* 39, 44–50.
2. Rhea, *Battle of the Wilderness,* 193; Scott, *Into the Wilderness,* 73.
3. Rhea, *Battle of the Wilderness,* 200–203, 228–30.
4. Ibid., 276–79; Scott, *Into the Wilderness,* 105.
5. Rhea, *Battle of the Wilderness,* 283; Scott, *Into the Wilderness,* 109–10.
6. Rhea, *Battle of the Wilderness,* 289; Scott, *Into the Wilderness,* 115.

7. Rhea, *Battle of the Wilderness,* 315.

8. Rhea, *Battles for Spotsylvania,* 112; National Park Service, *Spotsylvania Court House Battle Maps,* 12 maps, Drawing NMP-F5 3026 (Washington, D.C.: National Park Service, 1950), map 2.

9. Rhea, *Battles for Spotsylvania,* 113–14, 126–27; Matter, *If It Takes All Summer,* 134; National Park Service, *Spotsylvania Court House Battle Maps,* map 3.

10. Rhea, *Battles for Spotsylvania,* 135–36, 141; Matter, *If It Takes All Summer,* 144–48.

11. Rhea, *Battles for Spotsylvania,* 226–28; Matter, *If It Takes All Summer,* 171–72; National Park Service, *Spotsylvania Court House Battle Maps,* map 4.

12. Miller, *North Anna Campaign,* 82–84.

13. Rhea, *To the North Anna River,* 323–24.

14. Rhea, *Cold Harbor,* 296, 300–301.

15. Ibid., 369–71, 374, 379–81.

Cooke's Brigade

1. Return of casualties in Confederate forces, *OR,* 29(1):413, 443.

2. Rhea, *Battle of the Wilderness,* 127.

3. Ibid., 193; Scott, *Into the Wilderness,* 73.

4. Rhea, *Battle of the Wilderness,* 196, 203, 228; Scott, *Into the Wilderness,* 76.

5. Rhea, *Battle of the Wilderness,* 225; Scott, *Into the Wilderness,* 86.

6. Rhea, *Battle of the Wilderness,* 289; Scott, *Into the Wilderness,* 115.

7. Scott, *Into the Wilderness,* 179.

8. Rhea, *Battles for Spotsylvania,* 136, 141.

9. Matter, *If It Takes All Summer,* 243.

10. Rhea, *Cold Harbor,* 211, 301, 370, 382; National Park Service, *Cold Harbor Battlefield Maps,* 16 maps, Drawing NBP-R1C 3014 (Washington, D.C.: National Park Service, 1960), map 7.

11. *(Raleigh) Daily Confederate,* May 17, 1864, pg. 2, cols. 1–2 (brigade staff; 15th N.C.); May 23, 1864, pg. 1, cols. 1–2 (Cos. B & K, 46th N.C.); June 1, 1864, pg. 1, cols. 1–2 (27th N.C.); June 11, 1864, pg. 2, col. 3 (27th N.C.); June 26, 1864, pg. 1, col. 2 (48th N.C.); and July 19, 1864, pg. 1, col. 1 (46th N.C.); *Raleigh Semi-Weekly Standard,* May 24, 1864, pg. 2, col. 4–5 (27th N.C.); *(Charlotte) Western Democrat,* May 31, 1864, pg. 3, col.4 (48th N.C. partial); and June 14, 1864, pg. 3, col. 3 (48th N.C. partial); *Hillsborough (N.C.) Recorder,* June 29, 1864, pg. 3, cols. 1–2 (27th N.C.).

12. Manarin and Jordan, *N.C. Troops,* vols. 5, 8, and 11.

Kirkland's Brigade

1. Return of casualties in Confederate forces, *OR,* 27(2):797.

2. Returns of casualties for Confederate forces, ibid., 344, 337; Krick, *Gettysburg Death Roster,* 14; Manarin and Jordan, *N.C. Troops,* vols. 5, 7, and 10–12; compiled rosters from the CSRs, Records of Confederate Military Organizations, 1861–65, RG 109, NA, microfilm M270.

3. Return of casualties for Confederate forces, *OR,* 29(1):413, 443.

4. Rhea, *Battle for the Wilderness,* 115, 117, 127.

5. Ibid., 284

6. Ibid., 288–89; Scott, *Into the Wilderness,* 115.

7. Rhea, *Battles for Spotsylvania,* 136.

8. Rhea, *Cold Harbor,* 211, 300–301, 370–71, 382.

9. Ibid., 301.

10. Freeman, *Lee's Lieutenants,* 3:548.

11. *(Charlotte) Western Democrat,* May 24, 1864, pg. 3, col. 3 (officers, 11th N.C.); and June 14, 1864, pg. 3, col. (Co. H, 11th N.C.).

12. *Fayetteville (N.C.) Observer,* June 13, 1864, pg. and col. nos. unknown (26th N.C); May 26, 1864 (Co. G, 26th N.C.); June 9, 1864 (Co. F, 26th N.C.); and June 22, 1864 (Co. H, 26th N.C.); *(Raleigh) Daily Confederate,* June 3, 1865, pg. 1, col. 4 (Co. D, 26th N.C.); *Wadesboro (N.C.) Argus,* June 6, 1864, pg. and col. nos. unknown (Co. K, 26th N.C.); *(Charlotte) Western Democrat,* May 31, 1864, pg. 3, col. 4 (Co. B, 26th N.C.); and Oct. 23, 1864, pg. 2, col. 2 (Co. B, 26th N.C.).

13. *Daily Richmond Enquirer,* June 22, 1864, pg. 1, col. 5 (44th N.C.); *Fayetteville (N.C.) Observer,* June 6, 1864, pg. and col. nos. unknown (Co. F, 44th N.C.); *Hillsborough (N.C.) Recorder,* June 15, 1864, pg. 2, col. 3 (Co. G, 44th N.C.).

14. *(Raleigh) Daily Confederate,* June 3, 1864, pg. 3, cols. 4–5 (47th N.C.); and June 10, 1864, pg. 2, col. 3 (47th N.C.).

Davis's Brigade

1. Freeman, *Lee's Lieutenants,* 2:710–11.

2. Rhea, *Battle of the Wilderness,* 193.

3. Returns of casualties in Confederate forces, *OR,* 27(2):344, 29(1):413, 443; Krick, *Gettysburg Death Roster,* 14; compiled rosters from the CSRs, Records of Confederate Military Organizations, 1861–65, RG 109, NA microfilm M269 (Miss.) and M270 (N.C.).

4. Rhea, *Battle of the Wilderness,* 193, 201–202, 233; Scott, *Into the Wilderness,* 73, 78.

5. Rhea, *Battle of the Wilderness,* 233; Scott, *Into the Wilderness,* 87.

6. Rhea, *Battle of the Wilderness,* 302–302.

7. Ibid., 356; Scott, *Into the Wilderness,* 146, 165.

8. Rhea, *Battle of the Wilderness,* 400.

9. Rhea, *Battles for Spotsylvania,* 136, 138.

10. Rhea, *Cold Harbor,* 300–301, 370–71, 382.

11. *Richmond Enquirer,* June 7, 1864, pg. 2, cols. 3–4 (1st Conf. Bn., 2nd, 11th, 26th, 42nd Miss.); June 14, 2864, pg. 2, cols. 3–4 (26th, 42nd Miss.); June 17, 1864, pg. 2, col. 4 (26th Miss.).

12. *Mobile Daily Advertiser and Register,* June 17, 1864, pg. 1, col. 3 (1st Conf. Bn.).

13. *(Raleigh) Daily Confederate,* June 3, 1864, pg. and col. nos. unknown (55th N.C.); *Daily Richmond Enquirer,* June 4, 1864, pg. 2, col. 4 (55th N.C.); Manarin and Jordan, *N.C. Troops,* vol. 13.

14. Dunbar Rowland, *Military History of Mississippi, 1803–1898* (Spartanburg, S.C., 1908).

Walker's/Fry's Brigade

1. Returns of casualties in Confederate forces, *OR,* 25(1):807, 27(2):334, 29(1):413, 443; Krick, *Gettysburg Death Roster,* 14. Figures for casualties in Archer's Brigade at Gettysburg compiled by Marc and Beth Storch, copy in author's possession.

2. Freeman, *Lee's Lieutenants,* 3:160, 185–86.

3. Return of casualties for Confederate forces, *OR,* 25(1):807, 27(2):334, 337, 29(1):413 443; Krick, *Gettysburg Death Roster,* 14; compiled rosters from CSRs, Records of Confederate Military Organizations, 1861–65, RG 109, NA, microfilm M311 (Ala.), M268 (Tenn.), and M324 (Va.).

4. Rhea, *Battle of the Wilderness,* 196, 199, 225, 228, 233.

5. Ibid., 287.

6. Scott, *Into the Wilderness,* 179.

7. Rhea, *Battles for Spotsylvania,* 136, 141.

8. Ibid., 295; Matter, *If It Takes All Summer,* 172.

9. Rhea, *Battles for Spotsylvania,* 299–300; Matter, *If It Takes All Summer,* 238, 241.

10. Rhea, *To the North Anna River,* 315; Miller, *North Anna Campaign,* 82.

11. Rhea, *Cold Harbor,* 414.

12. Schiller, *Bermuda Hundred Campaign,* 158.

13. Rhea, *Cold Harbor,* 381.

14. *Richmond Enquirer,* June 4, 1864, pg. 3, cols. 4–5 (13th Ala., 1st, 7th, 14th Tenn.).

15. *Richmond Daily Examiner,* May 20, 1864, pg. 1, col. 4 (Co. B, 22nd Va. Bn.); *Daily Richmond Dispatch,* May 26, 1864, pg. 1, col. 7 (22nd Va. Bn.); *(Richmond) Sentinel,* May 30, 1864, pg. 1, col. 5 (47th Va.); and June 21, 1864, pg. 2, col. 5 (40th Va.); *Richmond Daily Enquirer,* May 31, 1864, pg. 4, cols. 5–6 (55th Va.); June 14, 1864, pg. 2, col. 5 (47th Va.); and July 2, 1864, pg. 2, col. 5 (55th Va.).

16. Thomas M. Rankin, *22nd Virginia Infantry Battalion* (Lynchburg, Va., 2000); Robert E. L. Krick, *40th Virginia Infantry Regiment* (Lynchburg, Va., 1985); Homer D. Musselman, *47th Virginia Regiment* (Lynchburg, Va., 1991); Richard O'Sullivan, *55th Virginia Infantry Regiment* (Lynchburg, Va., 1989).

Wilcox's Division

1. Rhea, *Battle of the Wilderness,* 194, 223; Scott, *Into the Wilderness,* 75.

2. Rhea, *Battle of the Wilderness,* 225, 233; Scott, *Into the Wilderness,* 86–87.

3. Rhea, *Battle of the Wilderness,* 285–88, 293; Scott, *Into the Wilderness,* 112–13, 117.

4. Rhea, *Battle of the Wilderness,* 315.

5. Rhea, *Battles for Spotsylvania,* 112, 181; Matter, *If It Takes All Summer,* 129.

6. Rhea, *Battles for Spotsylvania,* 183–84; Matter, *If It Takes All Summer,* 169, 172.

7. Rhea, *To the North Anna River,* 244–45; Matter, *If It Takes All Summer,* 240–41.

8. Rhea, *To the North Anna River,* 307–316; Miller, *North Anna Campaign,* 69, 72–85.

9. Rhea, *To the North Anna River,* 323–24.

10. Rhea, *Cold Harbor,* 169.

11. Ibid., 293.

Lane's Brigade

1. Returns of casualties in Confederate forces, *OR,* 25(1):807, 27(2):344; Krick, *Gettysburg Death Roster,* 15; Manarin and Jordan, *N.C. Troops,* vols. 4, 6, 8–9; compiled rosters from CSRs, Records of Confederate Military Organizations, 1861–65, RG 109, NA, microfilm M270.

2. Rhea, *Battle of the Wilderness,* 233–34; Scott, *Into the Wilderness,* 87.

3. Rhea, *Battle of the Wilderness,* 234–36; Scott, *Into the Wilderness,* 88–89.

4. Rhea, *Battle of the Wilderness,* 286–87.

5. Ibid., 315; Scott, *Into the Wilderness,* 186.

6. Rhea, *Battles for Spotsylvania,* 219.

7. Ibid., 245–46.

8. Ibid., 252–55; Matter, *If It Takes All Summer,* 197.

9. Rhea, *Battles for Spotsylvania,* 295; Matter, *If It Takes All Summer,* 238.

10. Rhea, *Battles for Spotsylvania,* 276–301; Matter, *If It Takes All Summer,* 239–43.

11. Rhea, *To the North Anna River,* 244–45; Matter, *If It Takes All Summer,* 340–41.

12. Rhea, *To the North Anna River,* 304, 307–308, 311, 314; Miller, *North Anna Campaign,* 73–74, 82–83.

13. James H. Lane, "History of Lane's North Carolina Brigade," *Southern Historical Society Papers* 10 (1882): 243–44.

14. Rhea, *Cold Harbor,* 293; National Park Service, *Cold Harbor Battlefield Maps,* 16 maps, Drawing NBP-R1C 3014 (Washington, D.C.: National Park Service, 1960), maps 6–8.

15. *Daily Richmond Enquirer,* May 20, 1864, pg. 3, col. 3 (7th, 18th N.C.); and June 2, 1864, pg. 2, cols. 3–5 (28th, 33rd, 37th N.C.); *(Charlotte) Western Democrat,* May 24, 1864, pg. 3, col. 3 (7th N.C. partial); *Raleigh North Carolina Standard,* May 31, 1864, pg. 2, cols. 3–4 (18th N.C.); *(Raleigh) Daily Confederate,* May 24, 1864, pg. 2, col. [?] (28th N.C.); May 31, 1864, pg. 1, col. 3 (33rd N.C.); and June 20, 1864, pg. 1, col. 2 (28th N.C.).

16. Lane, "Lane's North Carolina Brigade," 124–29, 146–53, 154, 242–43, 244.

McGowan's Brigade

1. Returns of casualties in Confederate forces, *OR,* 25(1):807, 27(2):345; Krick, *Gettysburg Death Roster,* 15.

2. Rhea, *Battle of the Wilderness,* 225–28, 234–36; Scott, *Into the Wilderness,* 86–88.

3. Rhea, *Battle of the Wilderness,* 287–88.

4. Ibid., 293; Scott, *Into the Wilderness,* 113.

5. Matter, *If It Takes All Summer,* 169, 213.

6. Ibid., 214–15; Rhea, *Battles for Spotsylvania,* 273–74.

7. Matter, *If It Takes All Summer,* 218, 244–45, 254–56; Rhea, *Battles for Spotsylvania,* 275–76, 303–306.

8. Rhea, *Battles for Spotsylvania,* 274, 306.

9. Matter, *If It Takes All Summer,* 326.

10. Rhea, *To the North Anna River,* 291–93, 303–304, 308, 311–12, 314; Miller, *North Anna Campaign,* 61, 69–70, 73–74, 77–78, 81–83.

11. Rhea, *To the North Anna River,* 439n103.

12. Rhea, *Cold Harbor,* 293.

13. Freeman, *Lee's Lieutenants,* 3:512.

14. Report of General McGown for the Wilderness, *OR,* 36(1):1094.

15. *(Columbia) Daily South Carolinian,* May 22, 1864, pg. 4, cols. 1–2 (1st S.C. Rifles; Co. F, 12th S.C.); May 25, 1864, pg. 2, col. 5 (Co. H, 12th S.C.; Co. L, 1st S.C.); May 28, 1864, pg. 2, col. 3 (14th S.C.); May 29, 1864, pg. 2, col. 3 (Co. D, 13th S.C.); June 1, 1864, pg. 2, col. 3 (12th S.C.); and June 14, 1864, pg. 3, col. 1 (13th S.C.); *Charleston Mercury,* May 28, 1864, pg. 1, cols. 1–2 (14th S.C.); and July 19, 1864, pg. 1, cols. 4–5 (1st S.C.); *(Spartanburg, S.C.) Carolina Spartan,* June 2, 1864, pg. 2, col. 2 (Co. I, 13th S.C.); and June 9, 1864, pg. 2, col. 2 (six cos., 13th S.C.).

16. J. F. J. Caldwell, *The History of a Brigade of South Carolinians, First Known as Gregg's, and Subsequently as McGowan's Brigade* (Philadelphia, 1866).

Scales's Brigade

1. Freeman, *Lee's Lieutenants,* 3:196.

2. Returns of casualties in Confederate forces, *OR,* 25(1):807, 27(2):334, 337; Krick, *Gettysburg Death Roster,* 15; Manarin and Jordan, *N.C. Troops,* vols. 5–7, 9–10; compiled rosters from CSRs, Records of Confederate Military Organizations, 1861–65, RG 109, NA, microfilm M270.

3. Freeman, *Lee's Lieutenants,* 3:217–18.

4. J. B. Smith, "The Charge of Pickett, Pettigrew and Trimble," *Battles and Leaders,* 3:355.

5. Rhea, *Battle of the Wilderness,* 225, 233–35; Scott, *Into the Wilderness,* 86–88, 90; Cannan, *Wilderness Campaign,* 132–34.

6. Rhea, *Battle of the Wilderness,* 285–87.

7. Rhea, *Battles for Spotsylvania,* 253–55; Matter, *If It Takes All Summer,* 235.

8. Rhea, *To the North Anna River,* 244–45; Matter, *If It Takes All Summer,* 340–41.

9. Rhea, *To the North Anna River,* 304.

10. Miller, *North Anna Campaign,* 72–73, 77–78, 81.

11. Rhea, *Cold Harbor,* 293.

12. *(Charlotte) Western Democrat,* May 17, 1864, pg. 3, col. 3 (Co. E, 34th N.C.); May 24, 1864, pg. 3, col. 3 (Co. G, 34th N.C.); and June 21, 1864, pg. 1, col. 6 (16th N.C.); *Daily Richmond Enquirer,* June 4, 1864, pg. 2, col. 4 (13th N.C,); *Greensboro (Weekly) Patriot,* June 2, 1864, pg. 2, col. 2 (22nd N.C.); and June 23, 1864, pg. 2, col. 6 (Cos. I & L, 22nd N.C.); *Fayetteville (N.C.) Observer,* June 13, 1864, pg. [?], cols. 4–5 (38th N.C.); *(Raleigh) Daily Confederate,* June 17, 1864, pg. 1, col. 2 (13th N.C.).

Thomas's Brigade

1. Returns of casualties in Confederate forces, *OR,* 25(1):807, 27(2):334; Krick, *Gettysburg Death Roster,* 15.

2. Rhea, *Battle of the Wilderness,* 233; Scott, *Into the Wilderness,* 87–88.

3. Rhea, *Battle of the Wilderness,* 237; Scott, *Into the Wilderness,* 91.

4. Rhea, *Battle of the Wilderness,* 287.

5. Ibid., 287; Scott, *Into the Wilderness,* 112.

6. Rhea, *Battles for Spotsylvania,* 253–54.

7. Ibid., 254.

8. Rhea, *To the North Anna River,* 304, 308–311, 314–15; Miller, *North Anna Campaign,* 72–73, 77–78, 81–82, 85.

9. Miller, *North Anna Campaign,* 71.

10. *Augusta (Ga.) Daily Chronicle & Sentinel,* May 19, 1864, pg. 4, cols. 1–2 (45th, 49th Ga.); *(Augusta, Ga.) Daily Constitutionalist,* May 28, 1864, pg. 1, cols. 3–4 (49th Ga.); *Macon (Ga.) Daily Telegraph,* May 19, 1864, pg. 2, col. 3 (45th Ga.); June 6, 1864, pg. 1, col. 2 (Co. F, 45th Ga.); and June 10, 1864, pg. 2, col. 4 (45th Ga.).

11. W. T. Irvine, "Old 35th Georgia," *(Atlanta, Ga.) Sunny South,* May 7, 1891.

12. Lillian Henderson, ed., *Roster of the Confederate Soldiers of Georgia, 1861–1865.*

Anderson's/Mahone's Division

1. Rhea, *Battle of the Wilderness,* 82; Scott, *Into the Wilderness,* 27.

2. Rhea, *Battle of the Wilderness,* 313.

3. Ibid., 374; Scott, *Into the Wilderness,* 160.

4. Rhea, *Battles for Spotsylvania,* 78–80; Matter, *If It Takes All Summer,* 82.

5. Rhea, *Battles for Spotsylvania,* 113; Matter, *If It Takes All Summer,* 129.

6. Rhea, *Battles for Spotsylvania,* 322; Matter, *If It Takes All Summer,* 206, 223.

7. Rhea, *To the North Anna River,* 80–81, 84–86; Matter, *If It Takes All Summer,* 285.

8. Rhea, *To the North Anna River,* 338, 340 (map).

9. Ibid., 339, 341–42; Miller, *North Anna Campaign,* 103, 105–106.

10. Rhea, *Cold Harbor,* 293–94.

11. Ibid., 307–308, 321 (map).

12. Ibid., 325–26, 329.

13. National Park Service, *Cold Harbor Battlefield Maps,* 16 maps, Drawing NBP-R1C 3014 (Washington, D.C.: National Park Service, 1960), maps 13–16.

Perrin's/Sanders's Brigade

1. Returns of casualties in Confederate forces, *OR,* 25(1):806, 27(2):343, 29(1):412; Krick, *Gettysburg Death Roster,* 13.

2. Rhea, *Battle of the Wilderness,* 313.

3. Ibid., 364–65; Scott, *Into the Wilderness,* 133, 136.

4. Rhea, *Battle of the Wilderness,* 400; Scott, *Into the Wilderness,* 163.

5. Rhea, *Battles for Spotsylvania,* 268–69; Matter, *If It Takes All Summer,* 206–207.

6. Freeman, *Lee's Lieutenants,* 3:548.

7. Rhea, *Battles for Spotsylvania,* 339, 341–42; Miller, *North Anna Campaign,* 103, 105–106.

8. National Park Service, *Cold Harbor Battlefield Maps,* 16 maps, Drawing NBP-R1C 3014 (Washington, D.C.: National Park Service, 1960), maps 13–16.

9. *(Montgomery) Daily Advertiser,* May 30, 1864, pg. [?], cols. 4–5 (10th Ala.); June 15, 1864, pg. [?], cols. 4–5 (8th Ala.); June 19, 1864, pg. and col. nos. unknown (9th, 11th, 14th Ala.); July 16, 1864, pg. and col. nos. unknown (brigade staff, 8th Ala.); and July 22, 1864, pg. 2, cols. 2–3 (9th, 10th, 14th Ala.); *Daily Richmond Enquirer,* July 28, 1864, pg. 1, cols. 5–6 (8th, 9th, 10th, 14th Ala.); H. H. Cruikshank (10th Ala.) letter, June 1, 1864, *Selma Morning Reporter,* June 9, 1864; R. L. McGinnis (11th Ala.) letter, May 31, a864, ibid.

Mahone's Brigade

1. Returns of casualties in Confederate forces, *OR,* 25(1):806, 27(2):343, 29(1):412.
2. Rhea, *Battle of the Wilderness,* 355, 357; Scott, *Into the Wilderness,* 145–46.
3. Rhea, *Battle of the Wilderness,* 370; Scott, *Into the Wilderness,* 158.
4. Rhea, *Battles for Spotsylvania,* 345.
5. Scott, *Into the Wilderness,* 168 (map).
6. Rhea, *Battles for Spotsylvania,* 78, 80.
7. Ibid., 140, 133 (map).
8. Ibid., 296–301; Matter, *If It Takes All Summer,* 239.
9. Matter, *If It Takes All Summer,* 243; Lane, "Lane's North Carolina Brigade," 146–53.
10. Rhea, *Battles for Spotsylvania,* 302.
11. Miller, *North Anna Campaign,* 103–104.
12. *Petersburg Daily Express,* May 13, 1864, pg. 2, cols. 6–7 (12th, 41st Va.); *Richmond Whig,* May 16, 1864, pg. 2, col. 5 (12th Va.); *Daily Richmond Examiner,* May 24, 1864, pg. 1, col. 4 (6th Va.); May 30, 1864, pg. 1, col. 5 (16th Va.); May 28, 1864, pg. 1, col. 4 (61st Va.); and June 16, 1864; pg. 1, col. 4 (61st Va.); *Daily Richmond Enquirer,* May 17, 1864, pg. 3, col. 3 (12th Va.); July 2, 1864, pg. 2, col. 5 (6th Va.); and July 22, 1864, pg. 1, col. 4 (61st Va.).
13. M. A. Cavanaugh, *6th Virginia Infantry Regiment* (Lynchburg, Va., 1988); William D. Henderson, *12th Virginia Infantry Regiment* (Lynchburg, Va., 1984); Henderson, *41st Virginia Infantry Regiment* (Lynchburg, Va., 1986); Benjamin H. Trask, *16th Virginia Infantry Regiment* (Lynchburg, Va., 1986); Trask, *61st Virginia Infantry Regiment* (Lynchburg, Va., 1988).
14. Report of William Mahone for the Wilderness, *OR,* 36(1):1091.

Harris's Brigade

1. Returns of casualties in Confederate forces, *OR,* 25(1):806, 27(2):343, 29(1):412.
2. Rhea, *Battle of the Wilderness,* 400.
3. Rhea, *Battles for Spotsylvania,* 125, 140.
4. Ibid., 267–77; Matter, *If It Takes All Summer,* 211–13, 244–45, 254–55, 260.
5. Rhea, *To the North Anna River,* 82, 86; Matter, *If It Takes All Summer,* 285.
6. Rhea, *To the North Anna River,* 338–39; Miller, *North Anna Campaign,* 102, 105–106.
7. National Park Service, *Cold Harbor Battlefield Maps,* 16 maps, Drawing NBP-R1C 3014 (Washington, D.C.: National Park Service, 1960), maps 13–16.

8. *Daily Richmond Examiner,* May 31, 1864, pg. 2, cols. 3–5 (entire brigade).

9. *Daily Richmond Enquirer,* July 22, 1864, pg. 1, col. 4 (48th Miss.)

10. Rowland, *Military History of Mississippi.*

Wright's Brigade

1. Returns of casualties in Confederate forces, *OR,* 25(1):806, 27(2):343, 627, 29(1):412; Krick, *Gettysburg Death Roster,* 13.

2. Scott, *Into the Wilderness,* 168 (map).

3. Rhea, *Battles for Spotsylvania,* 111, 113, 127, 140, 322; Matter, *If It Takes All Summer,* 240; National Park Service, *Spotsylvania Court House Battle Maps,* 12 maps, Drawing NMP-F5 3026 (Washington, D.C.: National Park Service, 1950), maps 6–8.

4. Rhea, *To the North Anna River,* 81, 83, 85; Matter, *If It Takes All Summer,* 285.

5. Rhea, *To the North Anna River,* 238.

6. Freeman, *Lee's Lieutenants,* 3:547–48, 633.

7. *Macon (Ga.) Daily Telegraph,* May 31, 1864, pg. 2, col. 3 (10th Ga. Bn.); July 7, 1864, pg. 2, cols. 3–4 (10th Ga. Bn.).

8. *Augusta (Ga.) Daily Chronicle & Sentinel,* June 23, 1864, pg. and col. nos. unknown (entire brigade).

9. *(Augusta, Ga.) Daily Constitutionalist,* July 13, 1864, pg. 2, col. 2 (22nd Ga.).

10. Lillian Henderson, ed., *Roster of the Confederate Soldiers of Georgia, 1861–1865.*

Perry's/Finegan's Brigade

1. Return of casualties in Confederate forces, *OR,* 25(1):806, 27(2):343, 29(1):412; Krick, *Gettysburg Death Roster,* 13.

2. Rhea, *Battle of the Wilderness,* 384–85, 400; Scott, *Into the Wilderness,* 133, 136, 162–63.

3. Freeman, *Lee's Lieutenants,* 3:513; *Savannah Republican,* June 2, 1864, pg. 2, col. 2.

4. Rhea, *To the North Anna River,* 338.

5. Zack C. Waters, "Tell Them I Died like a Confederate Soldier: Finegan's Brigade at Cold Harbor," *Florida Historical Quarterly* 69 (Oct. 1990): 156–75.

6. Rhea, *Cold Harbor,* 293–94.

7. Ibid., 325–26.

8. Ibid., 367–68, 377, 382–84.

9. *Savannah Republican,* June 2, 1864, pg. 2, cols. 2–3 (entire brigade).

10. Rhea, *Cold Harbor,* 383.

11. Waters, "Tell Them I Died like a Confederate Soldier," 176; W. A. Hunter (Co. I, 6th Fla. Bn.) to wife, June 5, 1864, in Gary Loderhose, "History of the 9th Florida Regiment" (master's thesis, Univ. of Richmond, 1988); Archibald F. Gould (Co. F, 2nd Fla. Bn.) to Friend Rogero, June 7, 1864, University of Florida Archives, Gainesville; Henry W. Long (Ind. Co., later Co. K, 9th Fla.), "Reminiscence of the Battle of Cold Harbor," n.d., UDC Scrapbooks, Florida State University Library, Tallahassee.

Artillery

1. Rhea, *Battle of the Wilderness,* 127, 281, 294–95, 302.

2. Matter, *If It Takes All Summer,* 238; National Park Service, *Spotsylvania Court House Battle Maps,* 12 maps, Drawing NMP-F5 3026 (Washington, D.C.: National Park Service, 1950), maps 4–12.

3. Rhea, *To the North Anna River,* 139–40.

4. Rhea, *Battles for Spotsylvania,* 125, 135, 137, 140; Matter, *If It Takes All Summer,* 131.

5. Rhea, *To the North Anna River,* 293, 304, 306–307, 315; Miller, *North Anna Campaign,* 69–70, 76, 82–83.

6. Rhea, *To the North Anna River,* 326, 338.

7. Rhea, *Cold Harbor,* 328; National Park Service, *Cold Harbor Battlefield Maps,* 16 maps, Drawing NBP-R1C 3014 (Washington, D.C.: National Park Service, 1960), map 7.

8. National Park Service, *Cold Harbor Battlefield Maps,* maps 8–9.

9. Rhea, *Cold Harbor,* 370–71.

10. Poague's Battalion: *(Richmond) Sentinel,* June 6, 1864, pg. 2, col. 4; *Daily Richmond Enquirer,* June 8, 1864, pg. 2, cols. 3–4; *(Charlotte) Western Democrat,* May 31, 1864, pg. 3, col. 4; Manarin and Jordan, *N.C. Troops,* vol. 1; W. C. Sherwood and Richard L. Nicholas, *Amherst, Albemarle, and Studivant's Artillery* (Lynchburg, Va., 1996); Michael J. Andrus, *Brooke, Fauquier, Loudoun, and Alexandria Artillery* (Lynchburg, Va., 1990). Cutts's Battalion: *Augusta (Ga.) Daily Chronicle & Sentinel,* Aug. 3, 1864, pg. 3, col. 5. McIntosh's Battalion: *Richmond Daily Dispatch,* May 21, 1864, pg. 1, col. 2; *Daily Richmond Enquirer,* June 21, 1864, pg. 2, col. 7; and July 22, 1864, pg. 1, col. 4; Robert J. Driver, *1st & 2nd Rockbridge Artillery* (Lynchburg, Va., 1987); Robert H. Moore, *Danville, 8th Star, Dixie Artillery* (Lynchburg, Va., 1989). Richardson's Battalion: *Richmond Daily Dispatch,* May 21, 1864, pg. 1, col. 2; *Daily Richmond Enquirer,* June 30, 1864, pg. 1, col. 6; R. Thomas Crews Jr. and Benjamin H. Trask, *Grimes's, Grandy's, and Huger's Batteries* (Lynchburg, Va., 1994); George L. Sherwood, *Mathews Light and Pittsylvania Artillery* (Lynchburg, Va., 1999). Pegram's Battalion: *Charleston Mercury,* June 1, 1864, pg. 2, col. 1; Peter S. Carmichael, *Purcell, Crenshaw, and Letcher Artillery* (Lynchburg, Va., 1990); Robert K. Krick, *Fredericksburg Artillery* (Lynchburg, Va., 1986).

7. CAVALRY CORPS

Fitzhugh Lee's Division

1. Rhea, *Battle of the Wilderness,* 22, 24, 80; Scott, *Into the Wilderness,* 33.

2. Rhea, *Battle of the Wilderness,* 259–60.

3. Rhea, *Battles for Spotsylvania,* 30, 33–35; Matter, *If It Takes All Summer,* 37, 40–41.

4. Rhea, *Battles for Spotsylvania,* 36.

5. Ibid., 42, 47–49; Matter, *If It Takes All Summer,* 55–57.

6. Rhea, *Battles for Spotsylvania,* 49–50, 52; Matter, *If It Takes All Summer,* 59.

7. Rhea, *Battles for Spotsylvania,* 103, 114; Matter, *If It Takes All Summer,* 100.

8. Rhea, *Battles for Spotsylvania,* 114–15, 120; Matter, *If It Takes All Summer,* 129.

9. Rhea, *Battles for Spotsylvania,* 115–17.

10. Ibid., 191–93.

11. Ibid., 196–97.

12. Ibid., 201, 202 (map), 203.

13. Ibid., 203–209.

14. Ibid., 209–211.

15. Rhea, *To the North Anna River,* 38, 44.

16. Ibid., 49–51, 55–57.

17. Ibid., 195–97.

18. Ibid., 363–66.

19. Ibid., 363–67.

20. Rhea, *Cold Harbor,* 30.

21. Ibid., 70–79.

22. Ibid., 163.

23. Ibid., 184–86.

24. Ibid., 203, 226, 230, 232–33, 288.

25. M. C. Butler, "The Cavalry Fight at Trevilian Station," *Battles and Leaders,* 4:237–39.

26. *Lynchburg Virginian,* May 16, 1864, pg. 2, col. 2 (2nd Va.); May 25, 1864, pg. 1, col. 3 (2nd Va.); and June 9, 1864, pg. 2, cols. 1–2 (2nd Va.); *Richmond Whig,* May 20, 1864, pg. 2, cols. 5–6 (Wickham's Brigade); *(Richmond) Sentinel,* June 17, 1864, pg. 2, col. 6 (Wickham's Brigade); and July 2, 1864, pg. 2, col. 4 (Wickham's Brigade).

27. *Richmond Whig,* May 20, 1864, pg. 2, cols. 4–5 (Lomax's Brigade).

28. Rhea, *Cold Harbor,* 185.

29. Robert J. Driver, *1st Virginia Cavalry Regiment* (Lynchburg, Va., 1991); Driver, *5th Virginia Cavalry Regiment* (Lynchburg, Va., 1997); Robert J. Driver and H. E. Howard, *2nd Virginia Cavalry Regiment* (Lynchburg, Va., 1995); Thomas P. Nanzig, *3rd Virginia Cavalry Regiment* (Lynchburg, Va., 1989); Kenneth L. Stiles, *4th Virginia Cavalry Regiment* (Lynchburg, Va., 1985); Michael Musick, *6th Virginia Cavalry Regiment* (Lynchburg, Va., 1990); John Fortier, *15th Virginia Cavalry Regiment* (Lynchburg, Va., 1993).

Hampton's/Butler's Division

1. Freeman, *Lee's Lieutenants,* 1:li; Rhea, *To the North Anna River,* 62; Rhea, *Cold Harbor,* 64, 66.

2. Rhea, *To the North Anna River,* 62; Freeman, *Lee's Lieutenants,* 3:436.

3. Rhea, *Cold Harbor,* 66, 216.

4. Freeman, *Lee's Lieutenants,* 3:517–22.

5. Ibid., 551.

Young's Brigade

1. Rhea, *Battles for Spotsylvania,* 33, 80; Matter, *If It Takes All Summer,* 37, 41–42.

2. Rhea, *Battles for Spotsylvania,* 373n6; Matter, *If It Takes All Summer,* 125.

3. Rhea, *To the North Anna River,* 231, 238–39.

4. Ibid., 282–83, 288, 289; Miller, *North Anna Campaign,* 50–51, 54–55.

5. Rhea, *To the North Anna River,* 360; Miller, *North Anna Campaign,* 128.

6. Rhea, *Cold Harbor,* 66.

7. Ibid., 97–98, 174–77.

8. Ibid., 214, 218, 222.

9. Ibid., 67.

10. Ibid., 79, 84, 87.

11. Ibid., 138–39.

12. "The Opposing Forces at the Beginning of Grant's Campaign against Richmond," *Battles and Leaders,* 4:183.

13. Butler, "Cavalry Fight at Trevilian Station," 237–39.

14. "Special Correspondence to the *Constitutionalist,*" July 20, 1864, *Atlanta Daily Constitutionalist,* n.d., n.p. (Co. I, Cobb's Legion); *Savannah Republican,* June 16, 1864, pg. 2 col. 2 (20th Ga. Bn.); *Augusta (Ga.) Daily Chronicle & Sentinel,* June 28, 1864, pg. 1, col. 2 (field & staff; Co. A, 7th Ga.); Oct. 6, 1864, pg. 3, col. 3 (Phillips's Legion); and Nov. 11, 1864, pg. 1, col. 5 (20th Ga. Bn.).

Rosser's Brigade

1. Thomas L. Rosser, *Riding with Rosser,* ed. S. Roger Keller (Shippensburg, Pa., 1997), 19.

2. Rhea, *Battles of the Wilderness,* 113–17.

3. Ibid., 256–57.

4. Ibid., 341, 343, 345–48.

5. Rhea, *Battles for Spotsylvania,* 88–89; National Park Service, *Spotsylvania Court House Battle Maps,* 12 maps, Drawing NMP-F5 3026 (Washington, D.C.: National Park Service, 1950), map 8.

6. Rhea, *Battles for Spotsylvania,* 101–107.

7. Rhea, *To the North Anna River,* 184.

8. Rhea, *Cold Harbor,* 70–72, 81, 83.

9. Ibid., 216–18, 220.

10. Butler, "Cavalry Fight at Trevilian Station," 237–39.

11. *(Richmond) Sentinel,* June 7, 1864, pg. 1, col.4 (11th Va.).

12. Inspection Report, Sept. 1, 1864, 35th Va. Bn. CSRs, Records of Confederate Military Organizations, 1861–65, RG 109, NA; Franklin M. Myers, *The Comanches* (Baltimore, Md., 1871), 395–99.

13. George Baylor, *Bull Run to Bull Run or Four Years in the Army of Northern Virginia: The Baylor Light Horse, Company B, Twelfth Virginia Cavalry, C.S.A.* (Richmond, Va., 1900), 203; Diary of Pvt. James F. Wood (Co. F, 7th Va. Cav.), May 5, 1864, no. 25506, Selected Civil War Resources, Personal Papers and Military Collections, Library of Virginia, Richmond.

14. Diary of W. H. Arehart (Co. H, 12th Va. Cav.), *Rockingham Recorder* 2, no. 3 (Oct. 1959): 151.

15. Wood Diary, May 6, 1864.

16. Richard L. Armstrong, *7th Virginia Cavalry Regiment* (Lynchburg, Va., 1992); Armstrong, *11th Virginia Cavalry Regiment* (Lynchburg, Va., 1989); Dennis E. Frye, *12th Virginia Cavalry Regiment* (Lynchburg, Va., 1989); John E. Divine, *35th Virginia Cavalry Battalion* (Lynchburg, Va., 1985).

17. Patrick A. Bowmaster, ed., "A Confederate Cavalryman at War: The Diary of Sergeant Jasper Hawes of the 14th Regiment Virginia Militia, 17th Virginia Cavalry Battalion, and the 11th Virginia Cavalry" (independent study, Virginia Polytechnical Institute and State University, Dec. 1994), Eleanor S. Brockenbrough Library, Museum of the Confederacy, Richmond, Va.; Letters of John Wise (Co. F, 11th Va. Cav.), Wise Family Papers, 1846–91, no. 13688, Albert and Shirley Small Special Collections Library, University of Virginia, Charlottesville.

18. John Warwick (Co. G, 11th Va. Cav.) to sister, May 21, 1864, A. C. L. Gatewood Papers, H. L. Sheets Collection, Marlinton, W.V.

Butler's Brigade

1. Col. M. B. Stokes, "A Long March to Battle," *Cavalry Journal* 40, no. 165 (May–June 1931): 38–39, 64.

2. Rhea, *Cold Harbor,* 66.

3. Ibid., 77–78.

4. Ibid., 134–39.

5. Butler, "Cavalry Fight at Trevilian Station," 237–39.

6. *Charleston Mercury,* May 27, 1864, pg. 1, col. 4 (5th S.C.); June 6, 1864, pg. 2, col. 2 (4th, 7th S.C.); and June 23, 1864, pg. 1, col. 1 (6th S.C.); *Charleston Daily Courier,* June 3, 1864, pg. 1, col. 4 (5th S.C.); June 9, 1864, pg. 1, col. 1 (5th S.C.); and July 13, 1864, pg. 2, col. 1 (4th, 5th S.C.); *(Columbia) Daily South Carolinian,* June 5, 1864, pg. 2, col. 3 (4th S.C.); and Aug. 3, 1964, pg. 1, cols. 1–3 (entire brigade).

W. H. F. Lee's Division

1. Freeman, *Lee's Lieutenants,* 3:16, 411.

2. Rhea, *To the North Anna River,* 303–304; Miller, *North Anna Campaign,* 69.

Chambliss's Brigade

1. Inspection Report, 9th Va. Cav. CSRs, Records of Confederate Military Organizations, 1861–65, RG 109, NA.

2. Rhea, *Battles for Spotsylvania,* 23, 27.

3. Ibid., 373n6.

4. Rhea, *To the North Anna River,* 22; Matter, *If It Takes All Summer,* 80.

5. Rhea, *To the North Anna River,* 79, 81–82, 85–87; Matter, *If It Takes All Summer,* 83, 85.

6. Rhea, *To the North Anna River,* 107, 109.

7. Ibid., 124–25, 219.

8. Ibid., 214–16, 242, 257, 272–80; Miller, *North Anna Campaign,* 44–45.

9. Rhea, *Cold Harbor,* 66, 81, 83.

10. Ibid., 87.

11. Ibid., 177–78.

12. Ibid., 180, 217–18, 220.

13. *(Richmond) Sentinel,* Sept. 6, 1864, pg. 1, col. 2 (9th Va.).

14. *Daily Richmond Enquirer,* June 21, 1864, pg. 3, col. 6 (10th Va.); Oct. 18, 1864, pg. 3, col. 6 (10th Va.).

15. Robert K. Krick, *9th Virginia Cavalry Regiment* (Lynchburg, Va., 1982); Robert J. Driver, *10th Virginia Cavalry Regiment* (Lynchburg, Va., 1992); Daniel T. Balfour, *13th Virginia Cavalry Regiment* (Lynchburg, Va., 1986).

16. Rhea, *Cold Harbor,* 222.

Gordon's Brigade

1. Freeman, *Lee's Lieutenants,* 3:209–210, 215.

2. Rhea, *Battle of the Wilderness,* 80.

3. Rhea, *Battles for Spotsylvania,* 33; Matter, *If It Takes All Summer,* 37, 41.

4. Rhea, *Battles for Spotsylvania,* 120.

5. Ibid., 191–92.

6. Ibid., 198–99.

7. Rhea, *To the North Anna River,* 48–49, 51–54.

8. Ibid., 62.

9. Ibid., 53.

10. Ibid., 363–66.

11. Rhea, *Cold Harbor,* 50; 3rd N.C. Cavalry CSRs, Records of Confederate Military Organizations, 1861–65, RG 109, NA.

12. Rhea, *Cold Harbor,* 51–52, 55.

13. Ibid., 66.

14. Ibid., 177.

15. Ibid., 177–78, 180.

16. Ibid., 217–18.

17. Ibid., 222.

18. Ibid., 379–80.

19. Ibid., 393.

20. *(Richmond) Sentinel,* May 31, 1864, pg. 2, col. 7 (entire brigade); *Raleigh North Carolina Standard,* June 7, 1864, pg. 2, col. 5 (entire brigade).

21. *Daily Richmond Enquirer,* June 17, 1864, pg. 2, cols. 3–4 (entire brigade).

22. Manarin and Jordan, *N.C. Troops,* vol. 2.

Horse Artillery (Breathed's Battalion)

1. Rhea, *Battle of the Wilderness,* 113–14.
2. Ibid., 348.
3. Rhea, *Battles for Spotsylvania,* 48–49.
4. Ibid., 197.
5. Ibid., 110–11; Matter, *If It Takes All Summer,* 125, 321, 327.
6. Rhea, *To the North Anna River,* 244, 249, 272–72; Matter, *If It Takes All Summer,* 283, 285.
7. Rhea, *Battles for Spotsylvania,* 197, 204, 206–208.
8. Rhea, *Cold Harbor,* 70, 81.
9. Ibid., 175–76.
10. Ibid., 163, 288.
11. Ibid., 218.
12. Butler, "Cavalry Fight at Trevilian Station," 239.
13. *(Richmond) Sentinel,* May 20, 1864, pg. and col. nos. unknown (Shoemaker's Battery); *Charleston Daily Courier,* July 13, 1864, pg. 2, col. 1 (Hart's Battery).
14. Diary of Pvt. William J. Black (Shoemaker's Battery), 1864, Preston Library, Virginia Military Institute, Lexington; Diary of Pvt. Charles McVicar (Thompson's Battery), printed in *Richmond Dispatch,* June 7, 1896.
15. Robert H, Moore, *Chew's Ashby, Shoemaker's Lynchburg, and Newtown Artillery* (Lynchburg, Va., 1995); Moore, *1st and 2nd Stuart Horse Artillery* (Lynchburg, Va., 1998).

8. SEPARATE COMMANDS

Hoke's Division

1. *OR,* 33(1):1056–57.
2. Freeman, *Lee's Lieutenants,* 3:99.
3. Ibid., 335–36.
4. Rhea, *Cold Harbor,* 159–60.
5. Ibid., 162–63.
6. Ibid., 182–85.
7. Ibid., 175–96, 202.
8. Ibid., 232.
9. Ibid., 235–47.
10. Ibid., 308.
11. Ibid., 332–43, 362–63, 383–84.

Clingman's Brigade

1. "The Opposing Land Forces at Charleston, S.C.," *Battles and Leaders,* 4:74–75.

2. "The Opposing Forces at Roanoke Island and New Berne, N.C.," *Battles and Leaders,* 1:670.

3. Rhea, *Cold Harbor,* 184–85.

4. Ibid., 244.

5. Ibid., 245–47.

6. Ibid., 363.

7. *(Raleigh) Daily Confederate,* June 18, 1864, pg. 1, col. 2 (31st N.C.).

8. Manarin and Jordan, *N.C. Troops,* vols. 4, 8, 12, 14.

Hagood's Brigade

1. Schiller, *Bermuda Hundred Campaign,* 86, 89–93, 95–96.

2. Ibid., 125–27, 129–30, 132.

3. Ibid., 243–35, 247, 250–53.

4. Rhea, *Cold Harbor,* 342–43, 345.

5. *Charleston Mercury,* June 15, 1864, pg. 2, col. 1 (entire brigade); and June 20, 1864, pg. 1, col. 2 (entire brigade); *(Columbia) Daily South Carolinian,* June 18, 1864, pg. 2, col. 3 (7th S.C. Bn., 11th, 21st, 27th S.C.).

Colquitt's Brigade

1. Freeman, *Lee's Lieutenants,* 2:664.

2. Ibid., 710.

3. Samuel Jones, "The Battle of Olustee or Ocean Pond, Florida," *Battles and Leaders,* 4:76–79.

4. Schiller, *Bermuda Hundred Campaign,* 222, 239–40, 296–97, 306.

5. Rhea, *Cold Harbor,* 253–54.

6. Ibid., 332–35, 339.

7. *(Augusta, Ga.) Daily Constitutionalist,* June 16, 1864, pg. 2, col. 1 (28th Ga.); *Macon (Ga.) Daily Telegraph,* June 25, 1864, pg. 2, col. 4 (6th Ga.); *Athens (Ga.) Southern Watchman,* June 29, 1864, pg. 2, col. 3 (23rd Ga.); *(Atlanta) Daily Intelligencer,* June 28, 1864, pg. 2, col. 5 (27th Ga.).

Martin's Brigade

1. "The Opposing Forces at Roanoke Island and New Berne, N.C.," *Battles and Leaders,* 1:670.

2. Schiller, *Bermuda Hundred Campaign,* 273, 275, 277–78.

3. Ibid., 305.

4. Rhea, *Cold Harbor,* 235–36, 253, 322, 331, 335–38, 340–41.

5. *(Salisbury, N.C.) Carolina Watchman,* June 27, 1864, pg. 3, col. 3 (available online at North Carolina State Archives, North Carolina Newspaper Digitization Project, http://ncecho.cdmhost.com/cdm/compoundobject/collection/p15016coll1/id/4901/rec/1, accessed Oct. 24, 2012).

Read's Artillery Battalion

1. Schiller, *Bermuda Hundred Campaign,* 326n45.

2. Rhea, *Cold Harbor,* 228; National Park Service, *Cold Harbor Battlefield Maps,* 16 maps, Drawing NBP-R1C 3014 (Washington, D.C.: National Park Service, 1960), maps 4–8.

3. Robert H. Moore, *Richmond Fayette, Hampden, Thomas, and Blount's Lynchburg Artillery* (Lynchburg, Va., 1991); *Daily Richmond Enquirer,* June 22, 1864, pg.1, col. 5.

Breckinridge's Division

1. John D. Imboden, "The Battle of New Market, Virginia, May 15, 1864," *Battles and Leaders,* 4:480–86, 491.

2. Rhea, *To the North Anna River,* 124, 161; Miller, *North Anna Campaign,* 8.

3. Rhea, *To the North Anna River,* 194, 229; Miller, *North Anna Campaign,* 24, 27.

4. Rhea, *To the North Anna River,* 287, 324–25; Miller, *North Anna Campaign,* 92, 119.

5. Rhea, *Cold Harbor,* 45.

6. Ibid., 86, 97.

7. Ibid., 99, 115–17, 125–27, 151, 166–68.

8. Ibid., 285, 287, 291–92.

9. Ibid., 292, 321 (map).

10. Ibid., 293, 308, 311.

11. Ibid., 320, 322–25.

12. Ibid., 325–29.

13. Ibid., 320, 322–25.

14. Jubal Early, "Early's March to Washington in 1864," *Battles and Leaders,* 4:493.

15. *Richmond Daily Examiner,* June 9, 1864, pg. 3, cols. 5–6 (26th Va. Bn.).

16. *(Richmond) Sentinel,* June 9, 1864, pg. 2, col. 5 (Wharton's Brigade).

17. Terry Lowry, *22nd Virginia Infantry Regiment* (Lynchburg, Va., 1984); Lowry, *26th Virginia Infantry Battalion* (Lynchburg, Va., 1991); James A. Davis, *51st Virginia Infantry Regiment* (Lynchburg, Va., 1984); R. U. Delauter, *62nd Virginia Mounted Infantry Regiment* (Lynchburg, Va., 1988); J. L. Scott, *23rd Virginia Infantry Battalion* (Lynchburg, Va., 1991); P. Michael West, *30th Virginia Infantry Battalion* (Lynchburg, Va., 1995).

McLaughlin's Artillery Battalion

1. *(Richmond) Sentinel,* June 3, 1864, pg. 2, col. 5; *Daily Richmond Examiner,* June 4, 1864, pg. 4, col. 5.

Maryland Line

1. "The Opposing Forces at the Beginning of Grant's Campaign against Richmond," *Battles and Leaders,* 4:184.

2. Rhea, *Battles for Spotsylvania,* 118–19, 195.

3. Rhea, *To the North Anna River,* 360.

4. Rhea, *Cold Harbor,* 51–53.

5. Ibid., 214–15.

6. Rhea, *Battles for Spotsylvania,* 197, 204, 206–208.

7. Rhea, *Cold Harbor,* 32.

8. Rhea, *To the North Anna River,* 197.

9. Rhea, *Cold Harbor,* 292.

10. Ibid., 325–26.

11. *Richmond Enquirer,* May 20, 1864, pg. 3, col. 3 (1st Md. Cav. Bn.); June 4, 1864, pg. 1, col. 4 (1st Md. Cav. Bn.); and June 7, 1864, pg. 2, col. 4 (2nd Md. Battery); *(Richmond) Sentinel,* June 8, 1864, pg. 1, col. 5 (2nd Md. Inf. Bn.); *Daily Richmond Enquirer,* June 22, 1864, pg. 1, col. 4 (2nd Md. Inf. Bn.).

12. W. W. Goldsborough, *The Maryland Line in the Confederate Army, 1861–1865* (Baltimore, Md., 1900).

Miscellaneous Units

Richmond Garrison

1. "The Opposing Forces at the Beginning of Grant's Campaign against Richmond," *Battles and Leaders,* 4:184.

2. Rhea, *To the North Anna River,* 52–53; *Daily Richmond Examiner,* May 14, 1864, pg. 1, col. 3 (Caroline Battery; Co. C, 20th Va. Hvy. Art. Bn.); *Richmond Daily Dispatch,* May 14, 1864, pg. 1, col. 4 (25th Va. Bn.).

3. *Richmond Daily Examiner,* June 16, 1864, pg. 1, col. 4 (42nd Va. Cav. Bn.).

4. Rhea, *Cold Harbor,* 138–39.

Gracie's Brigade

1. Schiller, *Bermuda Hundred Campaign,* 222.

2. Rhea, *To the North Anna River,* 54.

3. Ibid., 54–55.

4. *(Montgomery) Daily Advertiser,* May 30, 1864, pg. 1, cols. 2–4 (entire brigade).

SUMMARY AND CONCLUSIONS

1. *OR,* 33:1036, 1045, 36(3):665–66.

2. Alexander S. Webb, "Through the Wilderness," *Battles and Leaders,* 4:152n.

Index

www.ingramcontent.com/pod-product-compliance
Lightning Source LLC
LaVergne TN
LVHW041056080826
845145LV00007B/1595

* 9 7 8 0 8 0 7 1 8 8 7 5 0 *